How To D(
with Shak(

How To Do Things with Shakespeare

New Approaches, New Essays

Edited by

Laurie Maguire

Blackwell
Publishing

BLACKWELL PUBLISHING
350 Main Street, Malden, MA 02148–5020, USA
9600 Garsington Road, Oxford OX4 2DQ, UK
550 Swanston Street, Carlton, Victoria 3053, Australia

First published 2008 by Blackwell Publishing Ltd

1   2008

Library of Congress Cataloging-in-Publication Data

How to do things with Shakespeare: / new approaches, new essays / edited by Laurie
Maguire.
     p. cm.
   Includes bibliographical references and index.
   ISBN 978-1-4051-3526-9 (hardcover : alk. paper)—ISBN 978-1-4051-3527-6
(pbk. : alk. paper)   1. Shakespeare, William, 1564–1616—Criticism and
interpretation.   2. Shakespeare, William, 1564–1616—Examinations—Study
guides.   3. Criticism—Authorship.   4. Report writing.   I. Maguire, Laurie E.

   PR2976.H69 2007
   822.3′3—dc22

                                                                2007003778

A catalogue record for this title is available from the British Library.

Set in 10.5 on 13 pt Galliard
by SNP Best-set Typesetter Ltd., Hong Kong
Printed and bound in Singapore
by C.O.S Printers Pte Ltd

The publisher's policy is to use permanent paper from mills that operate a sustainable
forestry policy, and which has been manufactured from pulp processed using acid-free
and elementary chlorine-free practices. Furthermore, the publisher ensures that the text
paper and cover board used have met acceptable environmental accreditation standards.

For further information on
Blackwell Publishing, visit our website at
www.blackwellpublishing.com

Contents

Notes on Contributors   vii

Introduction   1
Laurie Maguire

Part I   How To Do Things with Sources   5
Editor's Introduction   7
  1   French Connections: The *Je-Ne-Sais-Quoi* in Montaigne
      and Shakespeare   11
      Richard Scholar

  2   Romancing the Greeks: *Cymbeline*'s Genres and Models   34
      Tanya Pollard

  3   How the Renaissance (Mis)Used Sources: The Art
      of Misquotation   54
      Julie Maxwell

Part II   How To Do Things with History   77
Editor's Introduction   79
  4   *Henry VIII*, or *All is True*: Shakespeare's "Favorite" Play   82
      Chris R. Kyle

  5   Catholicism and Conversion in *Love's Labour's Lost*   101
      Gillian Woods

Part III   How To Do Things with Texts   131

Editor's Introduction   133

  6   Watching as Reading: The Audience and Written Text
      in Shakespeare's Playhouse   136
      Tiffany Stern

  7   What Do Editors Do and Why Does It Matter?   160
      Anthony B. Dawson

Part IV   How To Do Things with Animals   181

Editor's Introduction   183

  8   "The dog is himself": Humans, Animals, and
      Self-Control in *The Two Gentlemen of Verona*   185
      Erica Fudge

  9   Sheepishness in *The Winter's Tale*   210
      Paul Yachnin

Part V   How To Do Things with Posterity   231

Editor's Introduction   233

  10 Time and the Nature of Sequence in Shakespeare's
      Sonnets: "In sequent toil all forwards do contend"   236
      Georgia Brown

  11 Canons and Cultures: Is Shakespeare Universal?   255
      A. E. B. Coldiron

  12 "Freezing the Snowman": (How) Can We Do
      Performance Criticism?   280
      Emma Smith

Index   298

Notes on Contributors

Georgia Brown works on sixteenth- and seventeenth-century English literature. She is the author of *Redefining Elizabethan Literature* (2005) and has published numerous articles on Marlowe, Queen Elizabeth I, Renaissance translation, *Antony and Cleopatra*, Spenser, attitudes to war in ancient Greek literature, teaching Renaissance poetry, disgust in Marston's drama, and Ottoman representations of Constantinople. An essay on the monstrous in *Othello* and *Macbeth* is forthcoming at the end of 2007 and she is currently revising a book on Renaissance embroidery.

A. E. B. Coldiron, Associate Professor of English, Florida State University, specializes in late medieval and Renaissance literature, with publications on such authors as Chaucer, Christine de Pizan, Spenser, Du Bellay, Sidney, Donne, and Milton. In *Canon, Period, and the Poetry of Charles of Orleans: Found in Translation* (2000), she examines a fifteenth-century poet's trilingual oeuvre as a strong challenge to traditional literary periodization. In *Gender, Translation, and Print Poetics 1476–1558* (forthcoming), she studies early Tudor printers' and translators' complex, resistant appropriations of French discourses on gender. Her current inquiries are about how the cross-cultural traffic in early printed poetry affected the long-term development of English literary aesthetics.

Anthony B. Dawson is Professor of English (emeritus) at the University of British Columbia. He is the author of several books, including *Watching Shakespeare* (1988), *Hamlet* (in the *Shakespeare in*

Performance series), and *The Culture of Playgoing in Shakespeare's England* (co-written with Paul Yachnin). The author of many articles on Elizabethan drama and on textual and performance theory and practice, he has as well edited Marlowe's *Tamburlaine* for the New Mermaids and *Troilus and Cressida* for the New Cambridge Shakespeare series. He is currently editing, with Gretchen Minton, *Timon of Athens* for Arden Shakespeare.

Erica Fudge is Reader in Literary and Cultural Studies at Middlesex University. She is the author of *Perceiving Animals: Humans and Beasts in Early Modern English Culture* (2000), *Animal* (2002), and *Brutal Reasoning: Animals, Rationality and Humanity in Early Modern England* (2006), editor of *Renaissance Beasts: Of Animals, Humans and Other Wonderful Creatures* (2004), co-editor with Ruth Gilbert and Susan Wiseman of *At the Borders of the Human: Beasts, Bodies and Natural Philosophy in the Early Modern Period* (1999), and co-founder of the Animal Studies Group whose book, *Killing Animals*, was published in 2005. She has written for *The Times Higher Education Supplement* and *History Today*, and is Associate Editor for the Humanities of the journal *Society and Animals* and director of *The British Animal Studies Network*.

Chris R. Kyle is Associate Professor of History and the Humanities at Syracuse University, New York. He has edited *Parliament, Politics and Elections 1604–1648* (2001) and co-edited with Jason Peacey *Parliament at Work* (2002). The author of numerous articles on seventeenth-century political culture, he is currently finishing a monograph, *Theatre of State: Parliament and Political Culture in Early Modern England*. He is also co-directing an exhibition at the Folger Shakespeare Library on "Renaissance Journalism: The Invention of the English Newspaper," due to open in December 2008.

Laurie Maguire is a Fellow of Magdalen College and Reader in English at Oxford University. Her books include *Shakespearean Suspect Texts* (1996), *Studying Shakespeare* (2004), *Where There's a Will There's a Way* (2006), and *Shakespeare's Names* (2007). She has published widely on Renaissance drama, textual problems, performance, and women's studies.

Julie Maxwell is Fellow and Lecturer in English at Lucy Cavendish College, University of Cambridge. Her first book, *You Can Live*

Forever (2007), is a novel and is published by Jonathan Cape. She has written pieces for *Renaissance Quarterly*, *The Ben Jonson Journal*, *Notes and Queries*, *Areté*, and the forthcoming *Blackwell Companion to the Bible in English Literature*. She is currently working on a book about religion in the life and works of Ben Jonson.

Tanya Pollard is Associate Professor at Brooklyn College, City University of New York. Her publications include *Drugs and Theater in Early Modern England* (2005), *Shakespeare's Theater: A Sourcebook* (2003), and essays on early modern theater in *Shakespeare Studies*, *Renaissance Drama*, and various edited volumes. She is currently writing a book on the emergence of new literary genres in early modern England and their debts to the ancient world.

Richard Scholar is University Lecturer in French and a Fellow of Oriel College, Oxford. His research focuses on the connections between early modern European literature and thought. He is the author of *The Je-Ne-Sais-Quoi in Early Modern Europe: Encounters with a Certain Something* (2005) and co-editor of *Thinking with Shakespeare: Comparative and Interdisciplinary Essays* (2007). He is currently writing a book on Montaigne and the art of free thinking.

Emma Smith is Fellow and Tutor in English at Hertford College, Oxford. She is the author of *The Cambridge Introduction to Shakespeare* (2007), *Shakespeare in Production: King Henry V* (2002) and *Othello* (2005), as well as articles on Shakespeare and early modern theater. She is working on ideas of authorship and anonymity on the early modern stage, and on the intersections between film theory and Renaissance drama.

Tiffany Stern is the Beaverbrook and Bouverie Fellow and Tutor in English Literature at University College, Oxford. Her monographs are *Rehearsal from Shakespeare to Sheridan* (2000) and *Making Shakespeare* (2004); with Simon Palfrey she co-authored *Shakespeare in Parts* (2007). She has edited the anonymous *King Leir* (2002) and Sheridan's *The Rivals* (2004), and is editing George Farquhar's *Recruiting Officer*, Brome's *Jovial Crew*, and Shakespeare's *Merry Wives*. She is a general editor of the New Mermaids play series, and is on the editorial board of the journals *Shakespeare*, *Shakespeare Bulletin*, *Shakespeare Yearbook*, and *Review of English Studies*. Her current project is to complete a monograph, *The Fragmented Playtext in Shakespearean England*.

Gillian Woods is a Junior Research Fellow at Wadham College, Oxford. She teaches literature of the sixteenth, seventeenth, and eighteenth centuries. She is currently working on a book-length study of Catholic semiotics in Shakespearean drama.

Paul Yachnin is Tomlinson Professor of Shakespeare Studies and Chair of the English Department at McGill University. He is co-director of the Shakespeare and Performance Research Team and director of the Making Publics project. Among his publications are *Stage-Wrights: Shakespeare, Jonson, Middleton, and the Making of Theatrical Value* and (with Anthony Dawson) *The Culture of Playgoing in Shakespeare's England*. He is an editor of the forthcoming Oxford *Works of Thomas Middleton*. Works-in-progress include editions of *Richard II* and *The Tempest*, and a book-length study, *Shakespeare and the Social Thing: Making Publics in the Renaissance Theatre*.

Introduction

Laurie Maguire

One of the first reactions to the exciting new field of feminist criticism was to point out that there are many kinds of feminism(s). Gilbert and Gubar's influential discussion of *Jane Eyre* (1979) didn't necessarily work for writing by women, for black women, for lesbians, for dramatic works, for language theorists, for French feminists, and so on. The field became subdivided and its various allegiances specifically nominated – French feminism, Anglo-American feminism etc.

The sheer vastness of Shakespeare studies in recent decades has meant that critical subdivision is essential (consequently one aligns oneself with an approach – textual, new historicist – rather than with the period or subject: Renaissance/Shakespeare). But sometimes the newly emergent *Companion* literature, in seeking to summarize each of these subdivisions, runs the risk of flattening critical diversity into a series of cultural positions which have been inadvertently reduced to a template.

In many ways this is inevitable: in seeking to grasp a new territory, students need an overview. In overviews it is not always possible to explore why textual specialists do not all agree that Shakespeare revised his plays, or prepared them for publication (for example); it is not possible to consider what is the next step for those who do, nor to chronicle how new orthodoxies come to prevail or what was wrong with the old. *How To Do Things with Shakespeare* stems from my sense that the publishing market is good at helping students identify and understand the current positions, but not so helpful in showing them how to think ahead – or indeed, to think back to the questions, problems, omissions, and dissatisfactions which led us to our current critical positions.

All literary research (like research in general) is a reaction to something. This is as true of large critical movements (feminism as a desire from female academics to see their experiences reflected in the critical literature) as it is of individual articles which respond to a sense of unease (something is omitted in current literature, misrepresented, simplified), a discovery or a reposing of an old question (what is the evidence for the received wisdom that Shakespeare wasn't interested in publishing his plays? Didn't know Greek drama?), a disagreement with an opinion currently in print, a meandering reflection: What if I inverted the question? We see this most clearly in medicine where breakthroughs are made when researchers approach things from a different angle (not: "why do some people get cancer?" but "why doesn't everyone get cancer?"). Literary research is no different, although its preliminary questions may not be posed as starkly.

Our research questions tend to be implicit in the methodology of our subsequent published research. What I asked contributors to do in this volume was to foreground not their methodology but the questions that led them to their topic or essay in the first place. Essays on (for example) animals or Catholicism or the culture of quotation do not simply emerge like Minerva, fully formed. What led up to the essay? What caught the writer's attention which meant that s/he had to write this essay? What questions preceded the essay?

For each of the essays that follow I offer a short introduction explaining the critical needs that I had or perceived which led me to commission the topic of the essay and why I chose that particular contributor. The contributor then offers a short autobiographical introduction which sets the essay in the context of his or her interrogative thoughts, needs, and practices. Readers will judge for themselves how well or how differently the essays follow on from the questions which prompted them; often, research moves in an unanticipated direction. There are many ways to do things with Shakespeare. But when these contributors show us how to do things with the topics and questions with which they set out, they show us not what to think but how we might begin to think.

The idea is that we can then go on and do things like that (or not like that) ourselves.

Work Cited

Gilbert, Sandra and Gubar, Susan 1979: *The Madwoman in the Attic*. New Haven: Yale University Press.

Part I

How To Do Things
with Sources

Editor's Introduction

Just thirty years ago Philip Brockbank viewed source-study as one of the highest forms of Shakespeare scholarship; by the end of the twentieth century the esteem in which this activity was held had fallen irrecoverably and Stephen Greenblatt could declare that source-hunting is "the elephant's graveyard of literary history." Greenblatt's metaphor continues to encapsulate the dominant attitude. His image is regularly quoted approvingly (see Goldberg 1987: 243) and developed sympathetically; thus Jonathan Gil Harris (1994: 408) talks of "that tired terrain" of source-study; and in a recent online article Peter Bilton (2000: §1) extends Greenblatt's image: "The paths once worn by Shakespeare source-hunters are becoming faint and overgrown. They lead through footnote graveyards with dismissive headstones. Modern warning signs tell angels where not to tread." When scholars do investigate sources they now feel the need to position themselves carefully or defensively in relation to Greenblatt's metaphor. For example, in her survey of the field of romance as Shakespeare inherited it, Darlene Greenhalgh (2004) concludes with a defense of source studies as a form of what we now call intertextuality.

There was, certainly, something mechanical, linear, and often unimaginative about the methodology of the New Critics who collated Shakespeare texts with their sources. There was also something distorting: Boswell-Stone's edition of Shakespeare's Holinshed, for example, focuses on what Shakespeare used, not on the vast chunks he didn't. And there was textual prejudice, with the ideological traffic tending to move only one way: Shakespeare rewrites/adapts/improves his sources, but when others use Shakespeare as a source, their product is inferior or derivative. In one of the most interesting essays of recent years – Stephen Miller's comparison of *The Taming of the Shrew* with its related version, *The Taming of a Shrew* (Q 1594) – Miller shows what we miss by concentrating only on what is most similar in the two texts (i.e., the areas where *A Shrew* runs closest to Shakespeare) and not on the areas of greatest divergence. His focus on the latter makes it clear that the writer of *A Shrew* had a coherent agenda in adapting Shakespeare's unconventional comedy and that his adaptation of his Shakespearean source makes him, in effect, a literary critic, the first Shakespeare critic. Miller's argument is a wonderful example of How To Do Things with Sources.

So, too, are the three essays which follow, all of which offer new and flexible ways of thinking about questions of influence. Richard Scholar is a comparative literature specialist (French/English), and his work is rooted in philosophy as much as it is in literature. Consequently, he was well positioned to realize that a verbal tic in Shakespeare – "I know not what" – was part of a continental philosophical current, the struggle to put indefinable emotional affinity (or antipathy) into words. His study of Shakespeare's most important humanist contemporary, the French essayist Michel de Montaigne (1533–92), looks at the way both writers respond to this intellectual Zeitgeist without one writer being demonstrably influenced by the other. Instead, he shows the influence this contemporary issue has on the language and ideas of *Merchant of Venice*, *Midsummer Night's Dream*, and *Much Ado About Nothing*. Scholar's essay chronicles not the specific influence of one author on another, but the air that both breathed. (This is source-study as literal inspiration, from the Latin *inspirare*, to breathe in.) Because his essay is such a bracing example of comparative criticism, and because it shows us how to shed our preconceived approaches, it provides a critically supple starting point for both this volume and this section.

Tanya Pollard has degrees in both Classics and English, so she is doubly qualified to write about the twin subjects of classical influence and generic inheritance in Shakespeare. Genre is usually a problem for readers and critics alike. It is the first subject we encounter when we read a Shakespeare play: individual quarto volumes – and plays in performance – tell readers and audiences what genre of drama they are about to see or read. The Folio collection of Shakespeare's plays, prepared by his contemporaries and published in 1623, divides the canon into three generic categories (indeed, the volume is titled *Mr William*

Shakespeare's Comedies, Histories, Tragedies). Modern editors add a fourth genre – romance – and all criticism acknowledges that Shakespeare, particularly the Jacobean Shakespeare, liked to mix genres. But criticism rarely moves beyond listing comic moments in tragic plays and vice versa. Surely there must be more to the subject than that?

When did genre first become a problem? Genre was presumably unproblematic in Greek festival drama where the nature of the festival told the audience what kind of play they were going to see. And because festivals were competitions for dramatists, the dramatist must have had a rough idea of the generic rules by which he was playing. How did we get from the Greeks to the Renaissance? This was the question which prompted me to seek out Tanya Pollard, as it seemed to me that they could best be addressed by an expert in both Classics and English. In "Romancing the Greeks" Pollard turns her critical acumen on Shakespeare's most generically mixed play, *Cymbeline*, and uses her classical knowledge to place it in context. Her essay not only offers new information about *Cymbeline* in relation to Greek romance, but redefines what used to be called source-study.

Redefinition is also Julie Maxwell's project in "The Art of Misquotation." In this essay she shows us not just How To Do Things with Biblical Quotations but, more important, How the *Renaissance* Did Things with Biblical Quotations. Maxwell's work in this area first came to my attention in her (forthcoming) book on Ben Jonson. Here, she inverts our paradigmatic assumption that an author is paying most attention to his source – in this case, the Bible – when he is reproducing it most accurately. This twenty-first-century attitude, with its high valuation of textual fidelity, views early modern authors as occupying a position somewhere between a photocopier (the original must be faithfully reproduced) and a modern academic (accurate reproduction of sources is essential). But our modern attitudes, Maxwell demonstrates, are the opposite of the Renaissance approach in which considerable artistic energy is expended on alteration – alteration which can look to us like misquotation. Maxwell's careful analysis of biblical sources and their Shakespearean variants uses conventional source-study identification and linguistic tallying for completely different artistic ends. Her essay has given me a new perspective on Renaissance authors because it shows me how they, in turn, approached the texts they read.

In fact Maxwell's essay, like those of Richard Scholar and Tanya Pollard, has much in common with recent studies in the new territory of Renaissance reading: one thinks of the work of William Sherman, Heidi Hackel, and Lisa Jardine and Anthony Grafton. In these studies critics look at how Renaissance readers read. And Shakespeare was a reader before he was a writer. What the three essays below investigate is not so much what Shakespeare read, but *how* he did things with what he read.

Works Cited

Bilton, Peter 2000: "Another Island, Another Story: A Source for Shakespeare's *The Tempest.*" *Renaissance Forum* 5/1. www.hull.ac.uk/renforum/v5no1/bilton.htm.

Goldberg, Jonathan 1987: "Speculations: Macbeth and Source." In *Shakespeare Reproduced: The Text in History and Ideology.* Ed. Jean E. Howard and Marion F. O'Connor. New York: Methuen, 242–64.

Greenblatt, Stephen 1985: "Shakespeare and the Exorcists." In Patricia Parker and Geoffrey Hartman (eds.) *Shakespeare and the Question of Theory.* New York: Methuen, 163–87.

Greenhalgh, Darlene C. 2004: "Shakespeare and Romance." *Literature Compass* 1/1. www.blackwell-synergy.com/doi.

Harris, Jonathan Gil 1994: "'Narcissus in thy Face': Roman Desire and the Difference it Fakes in *Antony and Cleopatra.*" *Shakespeare Quarterly* 45, 408–25.

Miller, Stephen 1998: "The Taming of a Shrew and the Theories: Or, 'though this be badness, yet there is method in't'." In Laurie E. Maguire and Thomas L. Berger (eds.) *Textual Formations and Reformations.* Newark: University of Delaware Press, 251–63.

Chapter 1

French Connections: The *Je-Ne-Sais-Quoi* in Montaigne and Shakespeare

Richard Scholar

Rationale

I first became interested in the connections between the French literary tradition and the English as an undergraduate at Oxford in the 1990s. My undergraduate degree in English and French offered the chance to study the two subjects in parallel, but not to compare them, and I've been exploring how one might do so meaningfully ever since. This essay is one such exploration. It prolongs a long-running conversation with my English tutor at that time, Tony Nuttall, to whom it is dedicated. Nuttall, the most philosophically minded of literary critics, taught his students to take Shakespeare seriously as a thinker. For Nuttall, this chiefly meant reading Shakespeare alongside Greek and Latin authors, and I remember him telling me early on that I had chosen the wrong combination: I should be reading Classics with English, not French. I felt inspired to disagree, not only by my contrarian nature, but also because I was at that time discovering Montaigne. Here too was a writer who, when read closely, turned out to be a thinker. I quickly learnt, as all students of the question do, that *The Tempest* contains a demonstrable textual reminiscence of the essay "Des cannibales." This intrigued me but hardly satisfied me:

the connection between Montaigne and Shakespeare seemed at once harder to pin down and more important than that.

As a research student, I moved away from the business of literary comparison, and became interested in the words and phrases that early modern authors use to explore the limits of what can be known and explained. I chose as my case study the phrase "je ne sais quoi," which I had encountered in various writers of the period, including Montaigne and Pascal. I came to see the *je-ne-sais-quoi* not only as a phrase with a rich early modern history but as more besides: a means of tracing, in the texts, first-person encounters with a certain something – whether love or hatred, sympathy or antipathy – that is as difficult to explain as its effects are intense. Such encounters recur in Montaigne's essays and in Shakespeare's plays, of course, and they seem to provoke in both texts a parallel process of mental and literary experimentation. I was ready to return to the old question of what connects Montaigne and Shakespeare from a new angle of approach.

Why, four centuries on, do we go on wanting to do things with Shakespeare? The most powerful reason, I suggest, is that his work stages with a haunting intelligence questions that still concern us. We watch, read, teach, study, and perform Shakespeare today because he moves us and, at the same time, makes us think with him. The questions that his work raises have to do, among other things, with the nature of being, the fabric of the world, human identity and motivation, the actions of individuals and groups, and the status of the artistic imagination. Those questions may appear, when extracted from their dramatic contexts in this way, to belong to the realms of metaphysics, physics, psychology, ethics, politics, history, and aesthetics. However, they should only ever be temporarily extracted from their dramatic contexts, for it is there alone that Shakespeare encounters them and invites us to do the same. Twentieth-century criticism was marked by T. S. Eliot's assertion that, where Dante was a great poet and philosopher, Shakespeare was merely a great poet (Eliot 1934). Eliot rightly saw that underlying the work of Shakespeare there is no stable intellectual system comparable to the medieval Christian Aristotelianism of the *Divine Comedy*. He did a disservice to the thoughtfulness of Shakespeare's work, however, in implying that it might be measured against some such external system. Thinking with Shakespeare must involve both thinking about the questions that his work explores and thinking through the poetic, dramatic, and rhetorical – in short, the literary – modes of their exploration.

Critical interest in Shakespeare as a literary thinker has started to revive from Eliot's famous assertion only in recent years (see Nuttall 2007; Poole and Scholar 2007). This revival might be aligned with certain tendencies in both Shakespearean studies and in early modern studies at large. Work on the history of the book has countered the established view of Shakespeare in his own lifetime as a writer of ephemeral texts for stage performance alone and portrayed him instead as a "literary dramatist," in Lukas Erne's phrase, who also produced texts for a new kind of reader (Erne 2003). The growing body of interdisciplinary and comparative work in early modern studies, meanwhile, has reinforced the idea of a thinking dramatist as well as a literary one. It has tended to emphasize that, however difficult it may be to determine with precision the nature and extent of his learning, Shakespeare belongs to an age that tested the limits of what could be thought and said, whether by prizing rhetorical exercises such as disputation *in utramque partem* (presenting arguments on either side of an established topic), or by recreating literary genres such as the learned paradox (opposing received wisdom in a given discipline) which remind their users of the provisionality and fragility of apparently stable systems of thought (see Maclean 1998; McDonald 2001).[1] Shakespeare's work can be seen as an expression of the same experimental intellectual culture: it draws upon ideas, themes, and propositions from the philosophies of the ancient world and from various strands of medieval and Renaissance thought, not to demonstrate its allegiance to them, but to put them to the test.

Seen in this light, the work of Shakespeare appears to have little in common with that of Dante, but much more with that of Montaigne. Readers have long been fascinated by the encounter, real or imagined, of these two near contemporaries. As early as 1780, Edward Capell pointed out that Gonzalo's description of an ideal commonwealth in *The Tempest* (act 2, scene 2) is based upon Montaigne's chapter "Of the Caniballes" (book I, chapter 31), and John Sterling went on to establish in 1838 that Shakespeare's source for the passage was not Montaigne's first book of *Essais* (first published in 1580) but John Florio's 1603 English translation. This intertext still provides the single piece of indisputable evidence of a connection between the two authors. Subsequent efforts to strengthen or supplement that connection, most of them designed to define and measure Montaigne's "influence" upon Shakespeare, have been concentrated in two main areas of enquiry.

The first is the external context: this includes, among other things, the reception of Montaigne in early modern England and the question of Shakespeare's place in that reception history. J. M. Robertson's 1909 study portrays a self-taught Shakespeare whose mind reaches its philosophical maturity only after reading Florio's Montaigne. In recent years, Warren Boutcher has countered this view, arguing that Montaigne's book was read in England from the 1590s to the 1620s principally as a means of promoting the secular household education of the social élite rather than as a repository of philosophical wisdom (Boutcher 2003). He then examines Shakespeare's dramatic use of the *Essais* from that perspective.

The second area of enquiry is what might be called the internal context: this includes, among other things, the lexical, conceptual, and literary parallels between the two writers. Lexical studies inevitably focus on the role that Montaigne's translator John Florio, a teacher of modern languages to the English nobility wishing to demonstrate the richness of his linguistic resources, plays as a mediator in the process of transmission. George Coffin Taylor's 1925 study lists over 750 words coined by Florio in his English Montaigne and picked up by Shakespeare in plays written in the years following the translation's first appearance in print (1603). Taylor concludes from his study that, in thought as well as in word, "Shakespeare was, beyond any doubt, profoundly and extensively influenced by Montaigne" (Taylor 1925: 5). Philippe Desan has revised Taylor's findings, suggesting that extracts of Florio's translation may have circulated in manuscript among the London literati as early as 1597–8, while arguing that Shakespeare seems to have been more interested in Florio's coinages than in Montaigne's ideas (Desan 2003). Desan is not alone in wishing to reduce the number and size of Shakespeare's conceptual "debts" to Montaigne as chalked up by Taylor and his more enthusiastic successors. Many critics have objected that the ideas Shakespeare seems to have borrowed from Montaigne may often come from elsewhere since they are commonplaces of the intellectual and rhetorical culture shared by the two authors. With these strictures in mind, Robert Ellrodt's 1975 article suspends the question of Montaigne's conceptual influence over Shakespeare, preferring instead to place the development of a new kind of self-consciousness in Montaigne and the post-1603 Shakespeare within the broader context of the European history of ideas. This approach runs the risk, although it is one that Ellrodt generally avoids, of transforming the two authors into conventional thinkers whose work can be easily identified with some external intellectual system or tradition: in other words, philosophers of the kind that Eliot saw in Dante. A transformation of this kind takes place each time, to take one frequent example, that Montaigne is characterized in the secondary literature as a straightforward "skeptic." Montaigne, like Shakespeare, does of course borrow material – ideas, topics, and commonplaces – from various philosophical traditions, including skepticism, but one needs also to understand how both writers operate upon this material with the structures, devices, and strategies – the literary resources – at their disposal.

The idea that these resources might in turn become the object of a comparison has been put forward recently by Terence Cave (2007). Returning from a different perspective to the topic explored by Ellrodt – the marked self-consciousness of Montaigne and Shakespeare – Cave argues that this serves both authors as an instrument of experimental thought. He groups moments of theatrical self-dramatization in Shakespeare (including the mechanicals' play at the end of *A Midsummer Night's Dream*, statements such as "All the world's a stage" in *As You Like It*, and the Mousetrap in *Hamlet*) together with quasi-theatrical situations (the bed-trick in *All's Well that Ends Well*, the Duke's experiment in *Measure for Measure*, and the trials and false trials of plays like *The Merchant of Venice*, *Macbeth*, and *King Lear*). These examples, Cave says, are not to be understood as the dramatist's self-congratulatory asides, but as his experiments, second-level strategies by means of which the characters are induced to think about their situations and we with them. In this, they resemble key passages in the work of Montaigne, who consistently foregrounds the unfolding process of reflection over the matter ostensibly in hand. The term that Montaigne uses for this process is *essai*, meaning literally a "trial," and referring here not to a literary genre – this is a later development – but to a mental and writerly experiment. This etymology allows Cave to encapsulate his literary parallel thus: "Shakespeare's trials, and the other procedures that operate in the same way, are his *essais*" (Cave 2007: 117).

Note that the comparative approach here is no longer the one taken by Robertson, Taylor, and others of an earlier generation. It is no longer designed to establish "influence" or even necessarily historical connection: some of the plays mentioned, such as *A Midsummer Night's Dream* (ca. 1595), precede the earliest conjectured date upon which Shakespeare is thought to have read Florio's Montaigne. The encounter between the two writers is not located in history so much as in a quasi-allegorical critical fiction. The comparison is designed to do other work: it sets out, as A. D. Nuttall (2004) does in his work on Shakespeare and the ancient Greek playwrights, to account for a case of apparent literary "action at a distance"; it discovers in Montaigne and Shakespeare two near-contemporary literary masterminds, connected by a common European cultural tradition and by certain shared preoccupations, and producing works that, when read side by side, illuminate one another.

What follows is a comparative reading of Montaigne and Shakespeare that reveals their differences, as much as their similarities, by means of what might be called a fluid analogy. This reading combines two of the approaches outlined above in so far as it examines a preoccupation that Montaigne and Shakespeare inherit from their shared intellectual culture and, at the same time, the literary resources with which they handle that preoccupation. It should quickly become apparent, however, that this combined approach is the effect of no distant methodological calculation: it is dictated by the topic in question itself. The *je-ne-sais-quoi*, by its very nature, threatens established norms of reflection and control and so compels Montaigne and Shakespeare to put it, and their own resources for dealing with it, on trial.

Early Modern Encounters with a Certain Something

What, then, is the *je-ne-sais-quoi*? Dropping the phrase into conversation today inevitably raises an eyebrow. In the early modern period, however, the term posed a problem. It happens sometimes, in our encounters with others, that we are moved by a certain something for which we struggle to find an explanation or a name even as its effects transform us. What is that something? And how – if at all – can it be put into words? Such questions fascinated early modern Europeans and are to be found at work in a wide range of their literary and philosophical texts, some of them well known today, others all but forgotten. These texts show the *je-ne-sais-quoi*, a term with precursors in Latin and the Romance languages, emerging in early seventeenth-century France as a keyword in the debate. The term spreads to other vernacular languages of early modern Europe, particularly English, in the following decades. By the middle of the seventeenth century, the earlier questions are ready to be rephrased: what is the *je-ne-sais-quoi*? And how – if at all – can it be put into words?

The emergence of the *je-ne-sais-quoi* as a keyword serves to crystallize a set of hitherto unrelated preoccupations already present in the intellectual culture of early modern Europe. Natural philosophers of the period commonly point out that humans encounter effects whose physical causes are imperceptible to them: we observe that a piece of iron moves towards a nearby magnet, for example, but experience can determine neither what is responsible for this attraction nor how it takes place. Other paradigm cases include the fall of heavy bodies, the vacuum, and the ebb and flow of the tides. Strange cases of attraction and repulsion do not just occur between inanimate substances. The couple "sympathy" and "antipathy" designates a powerful relation between people, as well as things, by virtue of which they are affected by the same influence, one which draws them together in the case of "sympathy," and which mutually repulses them in the case of "antipathy." Such relations are observed throughout nature: between inanimate substances and animate beings (e.g., in the effects upon animals and humans of drugs and poisons); between different animals (e.g., in the fascination of cats for birds and the antipathy between wolves and lambs); between animals and humans (e.g., in phobias such as the fear of spiders); and between humans (e.g., in affection and loathing, love and hatred, at first sight). These cases are legion. Montaigne, surveying the infirmities of human perception and knowledge in the chapter entitled "An Apologie of Raymond Sebond," asks: "how many hidden properties and quintessences doe we daily discover?" (Florio 1965: II. 12, 232; Montaigne 1992: II. 12, 526). His interrogative syntax leaves room for occult qualities and quintessences, sympathies and antipathies, to multiply infinitely. Unresolved phenomena are thought also to baffle human understanding in the realm of culture: it is commonly said that the qualities required for artistic and social distinction are as elusive as any found in the realms of nature and the human passions. Such commonplaces should not be assumed to be inert formulations of general consensus, however, for their truth, application, and explanation are hotly disputed: in this domain as in so many others, the commonplace is best understood as a stretch of disputed territory between conflicting discourses, a borderland open for further exploration.

Montaigne and Shakespeare put commonplace instances of sympathy and antipathy to different uses in their work. Here Montaigne is describing phobias he has seen develop in people who, as children, were not taught to control them:

> I have seene some to startle at the smell of an apple, more than at the shot of a peece [firearm]; some to be frighted with a mouse, some readie to cast their gorge [vomit] at the sight of a messe [dish] of creame, and others to be scared with seeing a fetherbed shaken: as *Germanicus*, who could not abide to see a cocke, or heare his crowing. (Florio 1965: I. 25, 176; Montaigne 1992: I. 26, 166; note that the chapter numberings in book 1 of Florio's translation are slightly different from those in modern editions of Montaigne)

Here he is listing tricks that the senses play upon the judgement:

> I have seene some, who without infringing their patience, could not well heare a bone gnawne under their table: and we see few men, but are much troubled at that sharp, harsh, and teeth-edging noise that Smiths make in filing of brasse, or scraping of iron and steele together: others will be offended, if they but heare one chew his meat somwhat aloude; nay, some will be angrie with, or hate a man, that either speaks in the nose, or rattles in the throat. (Florio 1965: II. 12, 316; Montaigne 1992: II. 12, 595)

Here is Shakespeare, or rather Shylock in the trial scene of *The Merchant of Venice*, on being pressed to explain why he prefers to claim his pound of flesh from Antonio than to receive the 3,000 ducats owed to him:

> I'll not answer that –
> But say it is my humour: is it answered?
> What if my house be troubled with a rat,
> And I be pleased to give ten thousand ducats
> To have it baned? What, are you answered yet?
> Some men there are love not a gaping pig;
> Some that are mad if they behold a cat;
> And others when the bagpipe sings i'the nose
> Cannot contain their urine: for affection
> Masters oft passion, sways it to the mood
> Of what it likes or loathes. Now for your answer:

As there is no firm reason to be rendered
Why he cannot abide a gaping pig,
Why he a harmless necessary cat,
Why he a woolen bagpipe, but of force
Must yield to such inevitable shame
As to offend, himself being offended:
So can I give no reason, nor will I not,
More than a lodged hate and a certain loathing
I bear Antonio, that I follow thus
A losing suit against him. Are you answered? (4.1.42–62)

These three passages, the last of which I shall return to later in this essay, differ above all in their contexts. They are similar, however, not just in their taste for the weird and whimsical but also in their content and phrasing. The most striking parallels between them – their listing of powerful antipathies towards harmless animals, their anaphoric sequences starting "some . . ." and finishing "and others . . . ," and their use of phrases such as "in the nose" and "cannot abide" – lead George Coffin Taylor to conclude that, "except for the early date of *The Merchant of Venice*, one would naturally con-clude the Shakespeare passage had been influenced by the Montaigne passage" (Taylor 1925: 7). Since Taylor considers influence in this case to be impossible, the passages appear as a dead-end in his study, a wrong turning narrowly avoided. Despite recent conjectures about the earlier circulation of Florio's manuscript, influence still seems highly unlikely here, and it may be fruitless to search for a source shared by both writers given how often commonplaces about sympathies and antipathies are repeated in a variety of late sixteenth-century European texts.[2] Influences are not the only fruits of critical enquiry, however, and these passages may also be investigated, using the comparative approach outlined above, as examples of Montaigne and Shakespeare's different encounters with the *je-ne-sais-quoi*.

Neither writer, of course, would have described these encounters in this way. In the passages quoted above, Montaigne talks of "hidden properties" and Shakespeare of "affection," and elsewhere both writers refer to "sympathy" and "antipathy." The rise to prominence of the *je-ne-sais-quoi* postdates the work of Montaigne and Shakespeare by several decades. Yet, when the phrase does emerge as a keyword, early modern Europeans consider that they are using it to talk about the

very things that their predecessors called by other names: the Jesuit
author Dominique Bouhours, in a polite philosophical conversation
of 1671 on the topic, has one of his interlocutors claim that the *je-
ne-sais-quoi* is "the foundation of what people call 'sympathy' and
'antipathy'" (Bouhours 1962: 146). The new term visibly supplants
its more established neighbors in the same semantic field and, as a
result, passages such as those in Montaigne and Shakespeare quoted
above appear to us to take their place in the genealogy of the *je-ne-
sais-quoi*. This impression is reinforced by the fact that at various
moments, as we shall see, Montaigne and Shakespeare call upon various
non-substantival forms of the French phrase and its English cognates
("I know not what" and "I wot not what") to describe encounters
with a certain something – as though, with hindsight, one could see
in their work the emergence of the *je-ne-sais-quoi* as a keyword for
such encounters waiting to happen.

Such an impression would prove misleading if it were allowed to
impose a reductive coherence on the variety of terms and phrases used
by both writers. The *je-ne-sais-quoi* offers no more than a synthesis,
after the fact, of various encounters. If handled with caution, however,
hindsight may prove of benefit here. The *je-ne-sais-quoi* articulates
with greater clarity than its precursors a number of early modern preoccupations about the role of powerful sympathies and antipathies in
human relations. These relations presuppose the presence of three
things: the two parties mutually affected by the relation, and the relation itself, that subtle *tertium quid* which links their fortunes. The *je-
ne-sais-quoi*, thanks to its constituent elements and to the different
grammatical forms the phrase can take, may designate each of these
three things. It adds above all to the notions of "sympathy" and
"antipathy" its inbuilt subjective perspective and its pithy assertion that
the subject's experience cannot be explained. Encountered by a subject
(the *je*) otherwise capable of knowledge (*savoir*), the *je-ne-sais-quoi*
frustrates all positive attempts to explain or express what it is, and
forces the subject to say "I know not what." In the process, it raises
questions about the subject of experience (what does it do to one to
encounter a certain something?), about its object (what is that "something"?), about the limits of knowledge (is it truly inexplicable?), and
about the resources of expression (how – if at all – can it be put into
words?). These, as we shall see, are some of the questions that
Montaigne and Shakespeare explore as they put the *je-ne-sais-quoi*
through its different literary trials.

Montaigne

Montaigne puts the *je-ne-sais-quoi* to its most extreme test when writing about his friendship with Étienne de La Boétie. He carries out other tests in the fields of nature, the passions, and social interaction. The *je-ne-sais-quoi* unites these within a single succinct formulation, but this formulation must always remain provisional, since each test requires the telling of a different story and each story needs to be read in its context. The two passages quoted in the previous section, relating to natural antipathies in certain individuals, have the status of examples supporting a broader argument. Other encounters with a certain something, however, form the object of the discourse as it moves restlessly between the experience and its possible explanations. The encounters described by Montaigne vary, too, in the intensity of their effects. Puzzling and disruptive though they may be, the antipathies discussed in the previous section are the individual signatures of the people who suffer them, the features by means of which they can be recognized for who they are. The *je-ne-sais-quoi*, in such cases, provides a confirmation of personal identity. But perfect friendship, as Montaigne describes it, is an altogether more intense experience; it is the thing that changed his life; all the rest, he says in "Of friendship," is mere smoke compared to the four years that he and La Boétie, a legal colleague and humanist writer who died seventeen years before Montaigne first published the chapter in 1580, spent together. Their friendship appears as an objective correlative for the *je-ne-sais-quoi* at its most transformative, a certain something that not only eludes Montaigne's every attempt to pin it down in an explanation, but also leaves him unable to say "I."

"Of Friendship" describes how, on first meeting, Montaigne and La Boétie were each overtaken by a vital movement of sympathy towards the other, one whose sudden and transformative effects were instantly felt, but whose causes remain forever inexplicable. In reflecting on this experience, Montaigne uses non-substantival forms of the *je-ne-sais-quoi* with a unique insistence, and Florio replicates this in his translation as follows:

> If a man urge me to tell wherefore I loved him [La Boétie], I feele it cannot be expressed, but by answering; Because it was he, because it was my selfe. There is beyond all my discourse, and besides what I can particularly report of it, I know not what inexplicable and fatall power, a meane and Mediatrix of this indissoluble union. Wee sought one

another, before we had seen one another, and by the reports we heard one of another; which wrought a greater violence in us, than the reason of reports may well beare: I thinke by some secret ordinance of the heavens, we embraced one another by our names. And at our first meeting, which was by chance at a great feast, and solemne meeting of a whole towneship, we found ourselves so surprised, so knowne, so acquainted, and so combinedly bound together, that from thence forward, nothing was so neere unto us, as one unto another. He writ an excellent Latyne Satyre; since published; by which he excuseth and expoundeth the precipitation of our acquaintance, so suddenly come to her perfection; Sithence it must continue so short a time, and begun so late (for we were both growne men, and he some yeares older than my selfe) there was no time to be lost. And it was not to be modelled or directed by the paterne of regular and remisse friendship, wherein so many precautions of a long and preallable conversation are required. This hath no other *Idea* than of itself, and can have no reference but to it selfe. It is not one especiall consideration, nor two, nor three, nor foure, nor a thousand: It is I wot not what kinde of quintessence, of all this commixture, which having seized all my will, induced the same to plunge and lose it selfe in his, which likewise having seized all his will, brought it to lose and plunge it selfe in mine, with a mutuall greedi-nesse, and with a semblable concurrance. (Florio 1965: I. 27, 201–2; Montaigne 1992: I. 28, 188–9)

The second sentence of this passage reads thus in Montaigne's French: "Il y a, au delà de tout mon discours, et de ce que j'en puis dire particulièrement, ne sais quelle force inexplicable et fatale, média-trice de cette union." His final sentence starts: "Ce n'est pas une spe-ciale considération, ni deux, ni trois, ni quatre, ni mille: c'est je ne sais quelle quintessence de tout ce mélange." Montaigne uses "force" and "quintessence," stable enough terms in the early modern discourse of natural philosophy, before revealing them to be wholly insufficient explanations of this unique and perfect friendship. In both cases, the adjectival form of the *je-ne-sais-quoi* is the agent of this revelation, stripping the nouns it describes of their explanatory pretensions and transforming them into acausal names for something, I know not what, which cannot be explained. Montaigne strengthens the effect of his sentences by placing "inexplicable" after "force" and by preparing the unsettling of "quintessence" through an anaphora of negation: "it is not one especiall consideration, nor two, nor three, nor foure, nor a thousand." It is none of those things: it is, in Florio's words, "I wot not what kinde of quintessence, of all this commixture."

This fusion has obvious consequences for the *je-ne-sais-quoi*, a phrase which requires its subject to say "I." A textual alteration to the first instance of the adjective *je ne sais quel* in the passage, not recorded in Florio's translation, offers a striking image of the relinquishment of the power to say "I" in friendship. The first printed edition of the *Essais* (1580) refers to "je ne sçay quelle force" (I know not what power), but from the 1582 edition onwards, the *je* disappears. The construction "ne sçay quel," close in form to the Latin *nescio quid*, is current in other sixteenth-century French authors. Montaigne, however, always includes *je* when using the phrase elsewhere in the *Essais*. It may be that he makes the change simply for reasons of rhythm. In this singular context, however, a more tempting speculation is at hand: namely, that the relinquishment of the *je* in the phrase replicates the alteration of the self in perfect friendship. The *je-ne-sais-quoi* starts to dissolve under the shock of experience as Montaigne, through the successive revisions of his text, writes his way ever closer to that certain something which brought friendship into being.

The movement of the writing in this passage is typically indirect, unsettled, errant. Montaigne, far from simply accepting the inexplicability of his friendship with La Boétie, renews his search for explanations of his experience. This search can be traced through the manuscript changes that Montaigne made to his book between its first publication in 1580 and his death in 1592. The two instances of the adjectival *je-ne-sais-quoi* fell in successive sentences of the early editions. After 1588, Montaigne inserts several sentences after the first instance and completes the sentence in which the second instance falls, as if he were trying to write his way closer to the encounter itself. This restless attempt, to capture the stuff of experience by putting different ways of understanding that experience to the test, encapsulates the process of trial-thinking known as the *essai*. The phrase "I know not what inexplicable and fatall power" appears to provoke a reaction of unease in the writing: "am I sure that no one could explain this force?" The search for causes flickers back into life as Montaigne wonders whether the friendship was not, after all, influenced by some ordinance from heaven. The act of revisiting their first meeting, however, serves only to convince Montaigne of its absolute singularity and intensity. All he can say ultimately about friendship with La Boétie is that some inexplicable force drew them together. Where the *je-ne-sais-quoi* elsewhere in Montaigne provides a confirmation of personal identity, it acts here with unsettling power upon two equal partners, divesting them of their identities and making them one. The question of whether Montaigne is describing his absorption *by* his friend in the last sentence of the passage, or his absorption *of* his friend, is beside the point. Both alternatives adopt the perspective of a self that simply no longer exists. There is no more "he and I"; or, when these words cannot be avoided, "and" marks the seal of an absolute fusion. This fusion is captured in the final sentence through a chiasmus of mutual loss of will ("my will . . . in his" / "his will . . . in mine"). But "loss" is hardly the right word: the loss of individual will, of a sense of self, is simply the most striking effect of the fusion of two-in-one called friendship.

Shakespeare

A study of the *je-ne-sais-quoi* could be entirely devoted to the plays of Shakespeare. They dramatize its themes, whether the stroke of passion, the ghostly apparition of a powerful force whose nature is not known, or the super-subtle artifice of signs of quality; and they show the characters involved in such situations – think (say) of Beatrice, Hamlet, and Iago – attempting, with extraordinary mental and linguistic sophistication, to come to terms with them. Shakespeare stands apart from the later history of the *je-ne-sais-quoi*, a stranger on its threshold, while effortlessly revealing his mastery of its terms and themes. As is the case with so many of the problems and approaches that literary critics and philosophers bring to his plays, so it is with the *je-ne-sais-quoi* that, although we may start out wanting to "do" things with Shakespeare, we soon find that he has already done them to us – and more besides. To illustrate the point, I propose to examine the two plays in which Shakespeare may be said to put the *je-ne-sais-quoi* most visibly on trial, *A Midsummer Night's Dream* (ca. 1595) and *The Merchant of Venice* (ca. 1597). The term "trial" is to be understood here in the complex sense defined earlier: it refers in the first instance to scenes involving legal or quasi-legal proceedings; it considers such scenes, together with related moments of theatrical self-reference, to be instruments of dramatic experimentation through which the characters are induced to reflect on their situations and we with them. Both plays use trial-thinking of this kind to test how individual characters react to encounters with a certain something – whether love or hatred, sympathy or antipathy – that challenge their capacities for understanding and endurance. Those encounters pose an equal threat, at the same time, to the established order of things in the societies depicted – hence the need for legal proceedings – and this means that, as much as the individuals concerned, it is the societies themselves, their capacities for equity and justice, that Shakespeare puts on trial.

The certain something at work in *A Midsummer Night's Dream*, as in Montaigne's "Of Friendship," is a powerful force of sympathy that inexplicably draws individuals together. Shakespeare's characters discuss the nature of this force, as Montaigne does, with an interest bordering on the obsessional: some characters attempt to dispel, subdue, and explain it away; others sense that it is something really inexplicable and inexplicably real and, in saying so, grasp at forms of the phrase "I know not what." Compared to its fusional counterpart in Montaigne's chapter, however, the force portrayed in Shakespeare's play is at once less intense, more diffuse, and more potentially subversive. The threat it poses to social order provides, indeed, the play with its opening. Hermia's father appears before Theseus to threaten his daughter with the full rigor of Athenian law if she fails to approve his choice of son-in-law (Demetrius) over her own (Lysander). Hermia, pressed by Theseus to submit, offers a defiant reply:

> I do entreat your Grace to pardon me.
> I know not by what power I am made bold,
> Nor how it may concern my modesty
> In such a presence here to plead my thoughts,
> But I beseech your Grace that I may know
> The worst that may befall me in this case
> If I refuse to wed Demetrius. (1.1.58–64)

Hermia invokes, through a syntactic string of the adjectival "I know not what," the power of her love for Lysander in opposing the will of her father and the Duke. In reply, Theseus threatens her with death or a nunnery, and Hermia flees the city with Lysander. The *je-ne-sais-quoi* is the prime force behind the plot of *A Midsummer Night's Dream* from its opening scene.

The four young Athenian lovers continue to suffer the ebb and flow of this force in the dark wood outside the city into which they stray. The night they spend there is full of strange happenings, with the women suffering a breach in their friendship, and the men falling in and out of love with the women. Titania suffers a sudden magical stroke of passion for Bottom, the mechanical who has been "translated" into an ass. Disaster awaits lovers at every turn in the wood. The night's events are a living illustration of Lysander's claim that "the course of true love never did run smooth," for even "if there were a sympathy in choice," he explains, "war, death, or sickness did lay siege to it," and in this way, "quick bright things come to confusion" (1.1.132–49). The earlier theme of love as socially subversive gradually retreats from view as the lovers are put through individual trials. The women prove altogether more constant than the men. Throughout, Hermia loves Lysander, and Helena, Demetrius; both men, however, are drawn irresistibly first to Hermia and then, under the effect of the love-juice that Puck puts on their eyes, to Helena. Puck eventually brings Lysander and Hermia back together while leaving Demetrius magically smitten with Helena – "I wot not by what power," Demetrius stammers, "But by some power it is" (4.1.163–4) – and in this way, with all the skill of a dramatist, he turns the confusions of a darkened pastoral towards the brightness of a comic resolution. When the Duke eventually comes across the lovers in the wood and summarily reverses his earlier ruling against Hermia (4.1.178), poetic justice is satisfied, and the way is smoothed for the celebrations of act five.

But the force that brought the lovers into confusion remains to be explained. What happened to them in the wood? Theseus and Hippolyta, at the beginning of the final act, provide a retrospective and conflicting commentary on events that raises one critical question about the *je-ne-sais-quoi* – can it really not be explained? – to the level of conscious reflection in the play. Theseus confidently dismisses the entire phenomenon. Its cause is to be found merely in the power of the imagination, he says, which is all too strong in lunatics, lovers, and poets: it "gives to airy nothing / A local habitation and a name" (5.1.16–17). Hippolyta disagrees:

> But all the story of the night told over,
> And all their minds transfigur'd so together,
> More witnesseth than fancy's images,
> And grows to something of great constancy;
> But howsoever, strange and admirable. (5.1.23–7)

She reverses the ontological value that Theseus gave to the events described by the lovers. The fact that they all told the same story, and the manner in which they did so, she insists, suggest that the story contains more than an intersubjective mental illusion. The event to which they all refer is not merely real *qua* dream but, more than that, it "grows to something of great constancy." It is real *qua* "something" that pertains in the world. What this "something" may be, Hippolyta cannot say, other than that it is "strange and admirable."

Shakespeare invites us to recognize as much of his play when, in the Epilogue, Puck advises any dissatisfied spectators to think of the play, Theseus-style, as "No more yielding than a dream." Those who enjoyed it, he implies, will understand that the play is something other than that. The playwright invites, in this way, our assent to the thought expressed by Hippolyta. The play itself, we feel, is no mere fiction: it is itself "something of great constancy / But howsoever, strange and admirable," a *je-ne-sais-quoi* encountered in the course of a midsummer adventure.

The tone darkens in *The Merchant of Venice*. To call it Shakespeare's play about antipathy, and *A Midsummer Night's Dream* his play about sympathy, would make for a tempting headline distinction. It is only a partial truth: in the darkened wood, Demetrius and Lysander both find that loving Hermia means hating Helena with an equal force, and vice versa (e.g., see 3.2.189–90 and 280–1); and when Portia tells Bassanio in sunlit Belmont, "There's something tells me, but it is not love, / I would not lose you" (3.2.4–5), she sounds for all the world like Hermia. The two plays certainly share more than at first meets the eye. As W. H. Auden points out in a famous essay on *The Merchant of Venice*, one has simply to omit Antonio and Shylock, "and the play becomes a romantic fairy tale like *A Midsummer Night's Dream*" (Auden 1962: 221). That omission is so difficult to imagine, of course, because the two characters bring to the play a violent, defining antipathy that overshadows all else.

How is this antipathy to be understood? What are its causes? Can, and if so, how should it be controlled? As he does in *A Midsummer Night's Dream*, Shakespeare has his characters face such questions time and again before he raises them to the level of conscious reflection in the play. He does so by means of a dramatic device, that of the trial in act four. Both Antonio and Shylock give plenty of reasons for hating one another with such intensity. Their first encounter in the play takes place when Bassanio, a particularly spendthrift member of Venice's gilded youth who needs to finance the wooing of Portia in Belmont, seeks a loan from the Jewish money-lender and offers him his friend, the Christian merchant, as its guarantor. At that moment in the negotiation, Bassanio introduces Antonio to Shylock, who comments in an aside:

> How like a fawning publican he looks!
> I hate him for he is a Christian;
> But more, for that in low simplicity
> He lends out money gratis, and brings down
> The rate of usance here with us in Venice.
> If I can catch him once upon the hip,
> I will feed fat the ancient grudge I bear him.
> He hates our sacred nation, and he rails
> Even there where merchants most do congregate
> On me, my bargains, and my well-worn thrift
> Which he calls interest. Cursed be my tribe
> If I forgive him! (1.3.33–44)

It is hard to imagine a speech that could more thoroughly satisfy the cause-hunters. Shylock describes, at some length, a public mutual hatred based on age-old religious and racial grounds and sharpened by a bitter professional rivalry that sees the two men not only compete for business but also disagree fundamentally about how that business should be conducted. He goes on talking to himself for so long that he entirely fails to acknowledge Antonio's presence – and continues to do so for some time after Bassanio's prompt: "Shylock, do you hear?" Shylock's delay in greeting Antonio is clearly not the effect of self-absorption but of a fear and loathing that expresses itself in a physical urge to avoid the company, the gaze even, of the other. Antonio clearly feels the same: he directs his first question for Shylock at Bassanio. Later in the same scene, Shylock complains how Antonio has often spat upon him in the Rialto and called him a dog, and Antonio gives the chilling reply: "I am as like to call thee so again, / To spit on thee again, to spurn thee too" (1.3.122–3). Their instinctive mutual repulsion is of the kind that the intellectual culture of Montaigne and Shakespeare's age calls "antipathy" and which it finds typified, as I mentioned earlier, in wolves and lambs, cockerels and lions, and other strange cases.

Antipathy, as much as sympathy, is a relation, a secret bond, that for better or worse makes people act in the same way. This is one of the hypotheses that *The Merchant of Venice* puts to the test. No two characters in the play are more similar than Shylock and Antonio.

Enemies understand one another. A complicity in their mutual hatred, from which the uneasy onlooker Bassanio is excluded, appears in act one as they concoct the terms of the loan. Antonio invites Shylock to lend the money neither to a friend nor even to a rival in business, but "rather to thine enemy, / Who if he break, thou mayst with better face / Exact the penalty" (1.3.127–9). Shylock responds with an offer that is wholly irresponsible in that it is based on personal inclination alone and goes against his usual business practice (of taking interest). He is murderous in his intent as well as irresponsible in his actions, of course, and, as we shall see, he pays dearly for this. Antonio is full of hatred alone rather than murderous intent as well, but he abandons all sense of responsibility in precisely the same way as Shylock, and enters freely into an agreement born of mutual antipathy.

Shylock and Antonio themselves acknowledge their antipathy in the course of the trial scene. Antonio, by then resigned to Shylock's claim on a pound of his flesh, now casts himself in the role of the lamb and his enemy as the wolf: "You may as well question with the wolf / Why he hath made the ewe bleat for the lamb" (4.1.73–4; see also 130–8). This complements the more whimsical instances involving gaping pigs, harmless cats, and woolen bagpipes that Shylock uses, in the long speech quoted earlier in this chapter (4.1.42–62), to justify his claim. The two men, for all their differences, share an understanding of, and a vocabulary for, the antipathy that unites them. They say what Montaigne says about his friendship with La Boétie: that there is between them, and beyond all that the cause-hunters could find to explain it, a certain something that they are powerless to resist. In their case, of course, that certain something is, in Shylock's words, "a certain loathing." Stephen Greenblatt has described this speech as the moment at which Shakespeare "compels" his audience's assent to "a reassuring perception of [Shylock's] difference." The examples chosen, he says, are anything but whimsical in their context: "they bespeak impulses utterly inaccessible to reason and persuasion; they embody what the rational mind, intent upon establishing an absolute category of difference, terms *madness*" (Greenblatt 1990: 43–4). I agree that there is something one might call madness in these lines, but I suggest that it is a madness the two men share, and that Shakespeare challenges his audience to perceive this by having Shylock and Antonio speak the same language of antipathy here and elsewhere in the play. Anything but the principle of difference separating the Jew from the Christian, the madness of antipathy is another effect of their sameness, a sameness which, as Greenblatt himself says, "runs like a dark current through the play, intimating secret bonds that no one, not even the audience, can fully acknowledge" (Greenblatt 1990: 43). Shylock says as much in his famous tirade: "Hath not a Jew eyes? Hath not a Jew hands, organs, dimensions, senses, affections, passions?" (3.1.46–7). It is striking that the last two words in his list are drawn from the vocabulary of sympathy and antipathy.

What is a society to do with those of its members in whom "affection masters oft passion," as Shylock puts it, to such a degree that they threaten the social fabric? Venice is presented in this play, and in the early modern period more generally, as the multinational city par excellence, a place where the state needs to maintain justice for all, since, as Antonio puts it, "the trade and profit of the city / Consisteth of all nations" (3.3.30–1). This idea is also put on trial in *The Merchant of Venice*. That Portia finds a way of overturning Shylock's claim in Antonio's favor comes as a relief to audiences and readers. They are often left uneasy, however, by her final revelation that Venetian law reserves the harshest punishment "if it be proved against an alien / That by direct or indirect attempts / He seek the life of any citizen" (4.1.345–7). Their discomfort tends to increase as they see Shylock, the alien, forced to hand over half his wealth to Antonio and to convert to Christianity – at Antonio's suggestion (4.1.376–86). W. H. Auden is perhaps right when he suggests that Shakespeare introduces this draconian law so as to work a particular effect on the audience: "at the last moment when, through his conduct, Shylock has destroyed any sympathy we may have felt for him earlier, we are reminded that, irrespective of his personal character, his status is one of inferiority" (Auden 1962: 229). Even the law, by which Shylock and Antonio both set such store, does not regard a Jew as an equal member of Venetian society.

Shylock submits to the judgement and makes to shuffle off. Before he leaves, Gratiano, the most virulent of the Christians, aims a parting shot at him:

> In christening shalt thou have two godfathers:
> Had I been judge, thou shouldst have had ten more,
> To bring thee to the gallows, not to the font. (4.1.394–6)

Gratiano's reference to trial by jury suddenly draws the attention of audiences and readers to the dramatic illusion that has been so powerfully sustained throughout the scene. This shift of attention is not best understood as an act of self-congratulation on the part of the dramatist, but as another of his experiments, performed this time on his audiences and readers. What do you think of Gratiano's joke? How would Shylock be treated in (say) an English court? What would you do if you were his judge? We need to keep thinking with Shakespeare today because he continues to put, along with those of his characters, the most intimate sympathies and antipathies of his audiences and readers on trial.

Notes

I thank Tim Chesters, Ita Mac Carthy, and Will Poole for their help with this essay. It is dedicated to A. D. Nuttall.

1   For further examples of literary and rhetorical exercises, see Julie Maxwell's essay, chapter 3.
2   The Italian natural philosopher Girolamo Cardano discusses sympathy and antipathy in bk. 18 of his treatise *De subtilitate* (On Subtlety) (1550); his near contemporary Giovanni Battista Della Porta returns to the same topic in his *Magia naturalis* (On Natural Magic) (1558). Both treatises appeared in vernacular translations as well as multiple Latin editions (see Daston and Park 1998: 170–1). Discussion of sympathy and antipathy is by no means confined to the learned sphere of natural philosophy; it appears, for example, in popular vernacular works investigating demonic and ghostly apparitions. In his skeptical demonological study *The Discovery of Witchcraft* (1584), a work with a long-established connection to *A Midsummer Night's Dream* since it surveys beliefs concerning a sprite by the name of Robin Goodfellow, Reginald Scot starts a chapter on sympathy and antipathy in the following terms (1584: bk. 13, ch. 8, p. 301): "If I should write of the strange effects of Sympathia and Antipathia, I should take great pains to make you wonder, and yet you would scarce beleeve me . . . A man would hardlie beleeve, that a cocks combe or his crowing should abash a puissant lion: but the experience herof hath satisfied the whole world. Who would thinke that a serpent should abandon the shadow of an ash, etc: But it seemeth not strange, bicause it is common, that some man otherwise hardie and stout enough, should not dare to abide or endure the sight of a cat." Zachary Jones adds to his English translation of Pierre Le Loyer's 1586 French study of ghosts, *A Treatise of Spectres*

(1605), the case of a gentleman living near Exeter who "could not endure the playing on a bagpipe" (quoted in a note on Shylock's speech in Mahood's edition of *The Merchant of Venice*).

Works Cited

Auden, W. H. 1962: "Brothers and Others." In *The Dyer's Hand and Other Essays*. London: Faber and Faber, 218–38.

Bouhours, Dominique 1962: *Les Entretiens d'Ariste et d'Eugène*. Ed. F. Brunot. Paris: Armand Colin.

Boutcher, Warren 2003: "Marginal Commentaries: The Cultural Transmission of Montaigne's *Essais* in Shakespeare's England." In Kapitaniak and Maguin 2003, 13–29.

Cave, Terence 2007: "When Shakespeare met Montaigne." In Poole and Scholar 2007, 115–19.

Daston, L. and Park, K. 1998: *Wonders and the Order of Nature, 1150–1750*. New York: Zone Books.

Desan, Philippe 2003: "'Translata proficit': John Florio, sa réécriture des *Essais* et l'influence de la langue de Montaigne-Florio sur Shakespeare." In Kapitaniak and Maguin 2003, 79–95.

Eliot, T. S. 1934: "Dante." In *Selected Essays*. London: Faber and Faber, 237–81.

Ellrodt, Robert 1975: "Self-consciousness in Montaigne and Shakespeare." *Shakespeare Survey* 28, 37–50.

Erne, Lukas 2003: *Shakespeare as Literary Dramatist*. Cambridge: Cambridge University Press.

Florio, Jean (trans.) 1965: *Montaigne's Essays*. 3 vols. New York: Dent and Dutton.

Greenblatt, Stephen J. 1990: "Marlowe, Marx, and Anti-Semitism." In *Learning to Curse: Essays in Early Modern Culture*. New York: Routledge, 40–59.

Kapitaniak, P. and Maguin, J.-M. (eds.) 2003: *Shakespeare et Montaigne: vers un nouvel humanisme*. Paris: Société Française Shakespeare.

McDonald, Russ 2001: *Shakespeare and the Arts of Language*. Oxford: Oxford University Press.

Maclean, Ian 1998: "Foucault's Renaissance Episteme Reassessed: An Aristotelian Counterblast." *Journal of the History of Ideas* 59, 149–66.

Montaigne, M. de. 1992: *Les Essais*. 3 vols. (paginated as one). Ed. P. Villey and V.-L. Saulnier. Paris: Presses Universitaires de France.

Nuttall, A. D. 2004: "Action at a Distance: Shakespeare and the Greeks." In C. Martindale and A. B. Taylor (eds.) *Shakespeare and the Classics*. Cambridge: Cambridge University Press, 209–22.

Nuttall, A. D. 2007: *Shakespeare the Thinker*. New Haven: Yale University Press.

Poole, William and Scholar, Richard (eds.) 2007: *Thinking with Shakespeare: Comparative and Interdisciplinary Essays*. London: Legenda.

Robertson, J. M. 1909: *Shakespeare and Montaigne, and Other Essays on Cognate Questions*. London: Adam and Charles Black.

Scholar, Richard 2005: *The Je-Ne-Sais-Quoi in Early Modern Europe: Encounters with a Certain Something*. Oxford: Oxford University Press.

Scot, Reginald 1584: *The Discovery of Witchcraft*. London.

Shakespeare, William 1979: *A Midsummer Night's Dream*. Ed. H. F. Brooks. New York: Methuen.

Shakespeare, William 2003: *The Merchant of Venice*. Ed. M. M. Mahood. Cambridge: Cambridge University Press.

Taylor, George Coffin 1925: *Shakspere's Debt to Montaigne*. Cambridge, MA: Harvard University Press.

Chapter 2

Romancing the Greeks:
Cymbeline's Genres and Models

Tanya Pollard

Rationale

Why write about *Cymbeline*'s relationship to Greek romance, and why now? Although the topic might strike some as a retreat to old-fashioned source study, I wanted to explore this material precisely to show that there are new and provocative possibilities to this often-overlooked critical approach, especially when examined through the lens of genre. In the wake of the New Historicism, early modern scholarship has become so focused on juxtaposing texts with contemporary historical and political events that critics have tended to move away from the more traditionally literary topics of form and literary genealogy. Although the insights of historicism are often exciting and fruitful, literary texts respond to past literary texts as well as to contemporary non-literary texts and events, and focusing on one of these contexts at the expense of another can lead us to miss important areas of meaning. Traditional source study, identifying a text's influences based on borrowed content, similarly often misses crucial forms of inspiration and dialogue. The concept of genre – etymologically linked to family origins (genealogy), inheritance (genetics), and birth (generation) – usefully points us towards the powerful, if often invisible, structural and stylistic ties that bind literary works to authors and texts that have preceded and inspired them. I had long been intrigued by *Cymbeline*'s outrageous leaps from genre to genre, but it wasn't until I looked at it in the context of Greek romance

– and especially the *Aethiopica* of Heliodorus – that I realized that this particular juxtaposition of genres was inspired by a specific generic model, rather than just arbitrary playfulness. This observation, in turn, sparked further insights about the intended effects of both that original model and Shakespeare's motivations for imitating it, allowing me to understand and explain the purposes of the play's tongue-in-cheek parody more clearly.

The particular identity of *Cymbeline*'s most important model suggested the second primary point I wanted to make. Despite plenty of evidence to the contrary, critics insist that Shakespeare was unaware of, and uninfluenced by, any literary works from the ancient Greek world. This claim is based on the arguments that Shakespeare did not read Greek – which is probably incorrect but, more importantly, I argue, irrelevant – and that Greek literature was not available in England at this time, which is patently wrong. In fact, as this essay discusses, not only were the Greek romances frequently translated into English during the sixteenth century, but their profound influence on contemporary readers and writers was widely noted. Other Greek texts were similarly more available and influential than has been acknowledged, but the conspicuous popularity of the romances makes them a particularly useful case study. I wanted to write this essay, then, both to challenge scholarly dismissal of Greek literary influence and to show how linking genre analysis with source study can open up new lines of inquiry and insight.

What was Shakespeare thinking when he wrote *Cymbeline* (ca. 1610)? Throughout its history, the play has vexed and confounded critics, who have found it clumsy, incoherent, and generally troublesome. Samuel Johnson famously complained about its "unresisting imbecility," finding its "faults too evident for detection, and too gross for aggravation" (Johnson 1925: 183). From the perspective of genre, the play presents a particular problem. While all of Shakespeare's plays question and toy with their generic boundaries, *Cymbeline* does so with an exaggerated intensity that verges on parody. The sprawling plot juxtaposes a conventional love story with a pastoral fairy tale about lost children and a historical saga about war and national origins; characters slide into caricature, and tone veers incongruously from pathos to farce. Editors and critics have been consistently unable to agree on its generic type, categorizing it variously as tragedy, history, comedy, Roman play, pastoral, tragicomedy, and romance. Clearly, the play's competing generic affiliations go further than the overlapping elements typically seen in Shakespeare's plays; *Cymbeline* carries Shakespeare's characteristic generic playfulness to an almost anarchic extreme. But what if we were to look at these eccentricities as deliberate and artful rather than as errors? What can the play tell us about Shakespeare as an observer and manipulator of literary tradition?

Although *Cymbeline*'s disorderliness often alienates its readers and audiences, it has an underlying logic that offers insights into the kinds of things Shakespeare did with generic conventions and literary sources. Despite its apparent generic promiscuity, the play in fact draws on a fairly specific model. Many modern editions describe the play as a romance, but scholars rarely pursue seriously the play's debts to the Greek romances that are the earliest examples of the genre. Based loosely on the model of Homer's *Odyssey*, the Greek romances are works of prose fiction featuring romantic love, travel, separations, deaths and apparent deaths, recognitions, and reunions. As a handful of critics have pointed out, the disparate elements of *Cymbeline*'s plot are explicitly indebted to Greek romance: the lovers' separation, suspicions, apparent deaths, and eventual reconciliation; Cymbeline's loss of, and reunion with, his sons; and the war between Britain and Rome (Wells 1966; Gesner 1970; Reynolds 2004). The *Aethiopica* (Ethiopian Story) of the Greek writer Heliodorus in particular offers a model for each of these threads.

Taking these observations as a starting point, this essay asks why Shakespeare turned to the model of Greek romance in *Cymbeline*. What did this genre offer him, and what made it such an attractive resource at this point in his career? In particular, why did he choose to transform romance, a prose genre, into a theatrical form, and what is the significance of his turning to an ancient Greek model rather than his more typical English, Italian, French, or Latin sources? Although attention to this literary debt has been recently growing, why have scholars been slow to identify and analyze this significant generic influence? What does blindness to Shakespeare's Hellenism reveal about our own critical prejudices, and what can we learn from reexamining it?

Romancing the Renaissance

Although we may never have definitive proof that Shakespeare read Heliodorus' *Aethiopica*, or that he had it deliberately in mind when he was composing his late plays, he was clearly familiar with both the story and its sensational impact on his contemporaries. After the manuscript was rescued during the sack of Buda (modern Budapest) in 1526, it took Europe by storm. The Greek text was published in 1534, and a series of translations quickly followed: into French in 1547, Latin in 1552, Spanish in 1554, Italian in 1556, and German in 1559. Coinciding with the rediscovery of Aristotle's *Poetics* and the renaissance of literary criticism that it sparked, the text was quickly seized upon by critics as an example of the ideal literary structure, inducing wonder and delight without sacrificing moral instructiveness. In his *Poetices Libri Septem*, for instance, the Renaissance literary critic Julius Caesar Scaliger (1484–1558) described the *Aethiopica* as the best possible model for epic, which he considered the highest literary form (Scaliger 1561: 144; Forcione 1970: 66).

Its reception in England came somewhat later than in continental Europe, but the *Aethiopica* made a dramatic impression when it arrived. James Sanford translated parts of the romance into English in 1567, and Thomas Underdowne's 1569 full translation was so popular that it was reprinted in 1577, 1587, 1605, 1606, 1622, and 1627. By 1620, its popularity was so pervasive that the satirist Joseph Hall wondered, "What Schole-boy, what apprentice knows not Heliodorus?" (Bush 1945: 53). Although the *Aethiopica* was by far the most popular of the Greek romances, many others were also available and popular in Shakespeare's England: Longus' *Daphnis & Chloe* was translated in 1587, and Achilles Tatius' *Clitophon & Leucippe* in 1597. *Apollonius of Tyre*, which had already been translated in Gower's *Confessio Amantis* (1390), reappeared in new editions of Gower in 1483, 1532, and 1554, and in a new version by Laurence Twine in 1576, which was reprinted at least twice in the following decades.

The emergence and popularity of these texts in sixteenth-century England had significant consequences for Elizabethan literature. Steven Mentz argues persuasively that the *Aethiopica* "was a – perhaps *the* – key structural model for Elizabethan prose fiction. . . . Heliodorus showed Elizabethan writers how to flesh out the bare dicta of Aristotelian theory with a complex, suspenseful narrative game of economy and amplitude" (Mentz 2006: 14). Pastoral romances such as Philip Sidney's *Arcadia* and Robert Greene's *Pandosto* imitated the *Aethiopica* conspicuously and self-consciously, inspiring further indirect copying as well. While the emerging genre of prose romance shows the most obvious literary impact, the influence of Greek romances on the popular theater was also considerable. The antitheatrical critic Stephen Gosson claimed in 1582 that "*the Palace of pleasure, the Golden Asse, the Aethiopian historie . . .* have beene throughly ransackt, to furnish the playe houses in London" (Gosson 1582: D5v).

With such a pervasive following at the time, the Greek romances hardly needed Shakespeare's direct attention in order to affect his work: their shaping power over his contemporaries, many of whom served as important sources for him, would have been enough to exert a significant influence. Shakespeare's plays, however, point to his specific knowledge of these texts. Most notably, another late play, *Pericles* (1607–8), written in collaboration with George Wilkins, is based explicitly on the narrative of *Apollonius of Tyre* via Gower and Twine, with considerable debts also to Sidney's *Arcadia*. (Underscoring the permeability of dramatic and non-dramatic romance, Wilkins published his own prose version of *Pericles* in 1608, fusing material from the play with material from Twine.) Although the play, in this case, was based on Gower's version of the romance, and even features Gower as its chorus, Shakespeare's use of the story shows his familiarity with, and interest in, the romance tradition. Similarly, Shakespeare demonstrates his awareness of the *Aethiopica* itself in an off-hand reference by Orsino in *Twelfth Night*: "Why should not I (had I the heart to do it), / Like th'Egyptian thief at point of death, / Kill what I love?" (5.1.117–19). Orsino, characteristically, gets it wrong – in the *Aethiopica*, the Egyptian thief Thyamis tries to kill the woman he loves, but in fact gets the wrong person – but the casual aside indicates both Shakespeare's knowledge of the romance and his assumption of his audience's familiarity with it as well.

Cymbeline, then, was hardly the only play of Shakespeare's that was influenced by Greek romance. As the example of *Pericles* shows, it wasn't even necessarily the play most indebted to the genre. As the most generically unstable of his plays, however, and the source of considerable critical vexation, *Cymbeline* is the one whose debt to Greek romance may be the most illuminating. By the same token, the *Aethiopica* was not the only Greek romance that was influential in the period, and certainly not the only one that Shakespeare drew upon in his writing. It was, however, the most popular and visible example of the genre. As the most rhetorically and stylistically complex of the Greek romances, moreover, it offered the most fertile resource for Shakespeare's dramatic imagination.

Shakespeare's Heliodoran Romance

Although Shakespeare was clearly familiar with Heliodorus, tracing the ways the romance influenced his work is complex. The *Aethiopica* is not a source for *Cymbeline* in the conventional sense of the word: the play, very loosely based on Holinshed's account of the reign of King Cunobelinus, does not explicitly borrow the romance's characters or plot. The most obvious debts, as noted earlier, appear at the level of themes and structure. Both texts juxtapose three parallel, if somewhat thematically incongruous, narratives: the trials of lovers, followed by their eventual reconciliations; the separation of parents and children, followed by their eventual reunion; and war between nations, followed by eventual peace. Beyond this particular combination of narratives (which doesn't recur anywhere else in Shakespeare), specific episodes in the plot – such as a false death and a failed recognition scene – suggest the romance's influence. The texts have far more in common, moreover, than their narrative structures. The plots' forceful yoking together of public and private, fracture and unity, mourning and rejoicing is matched by an acute doubleness of tone in both works: each counterbalances emotional intensity with a wry, ironic detachment. Like the *Aethiopica*, *Cymbeline* simultaneously exploits and mocks the turbulent upheavals and recoveries of romance, allowing sophisticated audiences to have their generic cake and eat it too.

The false death offers a useful example for examining how Shakespeare recreates these Heliodoran effects. Following the impact of the *Aethiopica*, this plot device quickly became popular in the Elizabethan prose romances influenced by Heliodorus, such as Sidney's *Arcadia*, and in numerous Renaissance plays. Shakespeare employs it almost obsessively, both in poems, such as *Venus and Adonis*, and in plays, including *Romeo and Juliet*, *Much Ado About Nothing*, *Measure for Measure*, *All's Well That Ends Well*, *Antony and Cleopatra*, *Pericles*, and *The Winter's Tale*. However, *Cymbeline* stands out for both the number and prominence of its false deaths. These disconcerting scenes, which lie at the heart of the play's incongruity, suggest echoes of the *Aethiopica* and hint at the significance of its influence. In presenting Shakespeare's strangest versions of this device, *Cymbeline* casts light on his motivations for mining this literary resource.

The details of the main false death in the *Aethiopica* differ from those in *Cymbeline*, but the effects are similar. Early in the romance, the male protagonist Theagenes sinks into mourning upon seeing flames coming from the cabins where his beloved Chariclea had last been housed. Although he assumes her dead, he is reassured by his friend Cnemon that Chariclea had earlier been taken to a safe cavern. When the two of them reach the cavern in search of her, however, they are horrified to come upon a female corpse, which they take to be Chariclea's. In a darkly comic twist, Theagenes' violent lamentation over the corpse (whose face he has not seen) is interrupted by Chariclea's voice calling out his name, which he interprets as meaning that she is already "above the earth" (Underdowne 1924: 44). He refuses to accept Cnemon's insistence that Chariclea must be alive, until they turn the corpse upward and see that it is not Chariclea:

> Therewithal Theagenes came somewhat to him selfe, and began to conceive some better hope in his minde . . . and desired [Cnemon] in all hast to carrie him to Cariclia. . . . Cnemon was contente, and so taking the letter in his hand and the swoord also went in to Cariclia, who creeping both on handes and feete to the light, ranne to Theagenes, and hanged about his necke. Nowe Theagenes thou art restored to me againe, saide she. Thou livest, mine owne Cariclia, quoth he oftentimes. At length they fell soudenly to the grounde, holding either other in their armes, without uttering any woord, except a little murmuring, and it lacked but a little, that they were not both dead. (Underdowne 1924: 45)

The zig-zagging scheme of assumptions and expectations in this scene offers a concise microcosm for the *Aethiopica*'s broader literary strategies. The scene shamelessly exploits its emotional drama of terror and euphoria for melodramatic effect, but there is also a certain wry absurdity to it. The speed of Theagenes' emotional switchbacks is slightly ludicrous: he believes Chariclea dead, then alive, then dead again, then alive again, all within a tightly compressed time and space. His outpouring of grief, moreover, is naive to the point of silliness: why didn't he look at the corpse's face to identify it in the first place? And how could he continue to believe Chariclea dead after hearing her call his name? By juxtaposing this emotional whirlwind with an implicitly tongue-in-cheek mockery of it, Heliodorus invites several potential reactions from readers. We can surrender ourselves to the soap-opera-like emotional drama; we can laugh at Theagenes and congratulate ourselves on the sophisticated detachment which distinguishes us from him; or (most plausibly) we can simultaneously enjoy the cathartic pleasures of the former and the knowing satisfaction of the latter.

Shakespeare's treatment of false deaths in *Cymbeline* imitates and escalates this juxtaposition of irony and emotional intensity. Not only does he portray a heroine falsely believed to be dead, but he does so on two separate occasions and for two separate reasons, and then constructs a false death for the hero as well. When Imogen's servant Pisanio reveals that her husband has commanded him to kill her on the grounds of suspected infidelity, Imogen is so distraught that she welcomes the thought of death, but Pisanio advises its appearance instead, sending a bloody token as proof of her murder. This pretense of death is quickly followed by its own unintended imitation when Imogen falls into a stupor after drinking an apparent cordial. Like the false death scene from the *Aethiopica*, this episode combines pathos with dark comedy and fairy-tale reprieve. The potion, from Imogen's evil stepmother, the Queen, is intended to be fatal, but the Queen's attempt at murder has been foiled by her doctor, who deceives her by providing a sleeping potion instead of the poison she requested. While the audience knows that Imogen is only in a drugged sleep, her brothers Arviragus and Guiderius – who know her as the boy Fidele – mourn her apparent death with funeral rites that are as strangely moving as they are conspicuously mistaken. The failed poisoning, then, proves both a farcical caricature of incompetent malice, and a cause of real distress. As in the *Aethiopica*, the play simultaneously generates grief and mocks it, offering the audience a range of possible responses: humor towards the Queen's shameless and unsuccessful attempt to do away with her stepdaughter, sympathy for mourning that is genuinely felt (if artificially constructed), and relief at knowing that all will ultimately turn out well.

The ironies and contradictions surrounding Imogen's apparent deaths are multiplied in the case of Posthumus. Although Imogen, as a beautiful, desirable, and chaste ingenue, is the play's parallel to Chariclea, Chariclea's false death in the *Aethiopica* bears a closer likeness to Posthumus's apparent death than to Imogen's. While Imogen's body only seems to be dead, the body taken for Posthumus genuinely *is* dead: it just isn't Posthumus. Yet while Theagenes corrects his mistake by looking more carefully at the corpse, Imogen's close study of the body ironically confirms her conviction that it is her husband. Upon waking from her drugged sleep and seeing Cloten's headless body, she cries out:

> A headless man? The garments of Posthumus?
> I know the shape of 's leg; this is his hand,

His foot Mercurial, his Martiall thigh,
The brawns of Hercules; but his Jovial face –
Murder in heaven! How? (4.2.308–12)

As critics have noted, this scene combines the pathos of genuine grief with both the grotesque and the comic. Imogen claims to know her husband's various body parts intimately, but in practice she cannot distinguish them from those of the lout Cloten, whom she has earlier described as his polar opposite. Imogen's analogies heighten this disorienting discrepancy: the man she identifies with heroic gods is in fact a graceless would-be murderer and rapist, who has been foiled by his own incompetence and weakness. By implicitly conflating the two figures, moreover, she calls attention to one of the play's darker ironies: while Cloten plotted to murder Posthumus and rape Imogen, Posthumus himself directly commissioned the murder of his own wife, suggesting that the contrast between the two men may be both more tenuous, and less advantageous to Posthumus, than Imogen believes.

Although Imogen's grief is authentic and the stolen clothing makes her initial error somewhat understandable, the outlandishness of her inability to distinguish her husband from a man she hates undermines both her credibility and the scene's seriousness. Much of the scene's effect depends on how it is staged, but there is no erasing either the intensity or the ludicrousness of Imogen's grief. Spectators committed to the emotional intensity of romance can surrender themselves to the former; those attuned to the play's mocking parody of the genre can enjoy the latter; and the many who, appropriately, sense both effects will feel divided – whether uncomfortably or pleasurably or both – between the two. Although critics have routinely derided this moment as clumsy and worse, its stark juxtaposition of melodrama and deflation epitomizes the play's deliberately ironic literary strategy.

If *Cymbeline*'s false deaths echo that of the *Aethiopica*, highlighting its divided effect on audiences, the play's closing reunion evokes another, related, feature of its generic model. In the play's final act, Imogen (now disguised as Fidele) hears Posthumus lamenting his wife's death and approaches him, only to be struck:

Imogen	Peace, my Lord. Hear, hear.
Posthumus	Shall's have a play of this? Thou scornful page,
	There lie thy part. *He strikes her down*
Pisanio	(*coming forward*) O gentlemen, help

> Mine and your mistress! O my lord Posthumus,
> You ne'er killed Imogen till now. Help, help!
> (5.5.227–31)

In the rapid disentangling that follows, all is revealed; Imogen is reunited with both her husband and her father, and her brothers are brought back into the family fold. After the unsettling, albeit ironic, turbulence of the false death episodes, this hasty round-up brings us firmly back into the realm of comedy. Intriguingly, though, this happy scene is inaugurated not only with violence and a momentary flash of anxiety – *has* Posthumus now actually killed Imogen? – but also with an apparently gratuitous metatheatrical reference. Posthumus's account of this moment as a scene from a play, in which the page has a particular role to play, calls attention to the artificial nature of the scene's revelations, reconciliations, and reunions. What, after all, are the odds that Iachimo should spontaneously choose to unburden himself of his crime at just the moment when all the relevant characters happen to be standing around in the same place, much less that the evil Queen should expire at precisely that same moment, freeing her doctor to explain her role in the plot? Clearly, Shakespeare could have unraveled the play's threads more gradually and naturalistically had he wanted to. As with his self-conscious use of the *deus ex machina* of Jupiter's prophecy to straighten out Posthumus, he revels here in an extravagantly overstated theatricality, serving – like the play's ironic melodrama – both to invite audiences into the unfettered realm of art, and to alienate them from easy belief in this fictive world.

This artificial and self-conscious theatricality is significant not only in highlighting *Cymbeline*'s echoes of the *Aethiopica*, but in demonstrating the way both works explicitly tinker with generic paradigms, shedding light on some of the specific reasons why Heliodorus offered an attractive model for Shakespeare. The metadramatic overtones of Imogen's reunion with her husband and father are even more pronounced in the two scenes towards the end of the *Aethiopica* that depict the equivalent reunions. When Chariclea is reunited with her adoptive father, Calasiris, the narrator refers explicitly to the episode as a scene from a comedy:

> you might have heard often these wordes, O my father, O my daughter Cariclia in deede, and not Cnemons Thisbe. Nausicles, for wondering,

had almost forgotten himselfe, and was astonied when he sawe Calasiris imbrace Cariclia, and not refraine from teares, and knew not what that sudden acquaintaunce, as if it had beene in a Comedie, ment, until Calasiris had kissed him, and said thus: The Gods geve you (good man) so much as may content your desire and will, who have saved my daughter which I never looked for, and caused me to beholde the dearest thing that I might possibly see. (Underdowne 1924: 126–7)

Despite the text's prose format, Heliodorus not only addresses readers in the direct second person, but invites us into this scene as a live audience, with a privileged vantage point for both seeing and hearing the events described. This vividness, along with the theatrical analogy ("as if it had beene in a Comedie"), is directly identified with the emotional effects of the scene's recognition and reunion. Like Nausicles, the scene's internal audience, we are caught up in "wondering," and find ourselves "astonied" by the events; at the same time, we are left outside of them, forcefully reminded of their fictional status.

The romance's other central reunion, between Chariclea and Theagenes, continues in this vein, though curiously, it expands its generic frame of reference. Heliodorus introduces the scene with the phrase "An other Acte was interlaced in the tragedie." After describing the lovers' moving recognition and reunion – in which Theagenes strikes the disguised Chariclea before she conveys who she is by a shared sign, and the two embrace – he continues:

To bee shorte, al that part . . . was full of such wonderfull affections, as is commonly represented in Comedies. The wicked battell betweene the two brothers was ended, and that which men thought should be finished with bloud, had of a Tragicall beginning, a Comicall ending. (Underdowne 1924: 174)

This scene has a clear parallel with *Cymbeline*'s final reunion: in both, a blow is the turning point leading to the couple's recognition and reconciliation. The scene is also striking, however, for its self-consciously theatrical vocabulary, which anticipates Posthumus's similar language. Theagenes' blow to Chariclea is an "Acte interlaced in the tragedie," and the reunion that follows carries emotion "as is commonly represented in Comedies." Running in parallel, the battle that has been taking place between the brothers Thyamis and Petosiris similarly comes to a happy end, developing "of a Tragicall beginning, a Comicall ending." And although readers might suspect Underdowne's Elizabethan translation of anachronistically imposing this specific theatrical and genre-laden language, it in fact exists in Heliodorus' Greek, albeit with minor changes. The phrases "an Acte interlaced in the tragedie" and "as is commonly represented in Comedies" give more generic specificity than the Greek, which simply refers to scenes from drama, but the subsequent reference to a comic ending developing from a tragic beginning is true to the original Greek text. Despite its prose format, then, the *Aethiopica* explicitly identifies itself as not only theatrical, but simultaneously tragic and comic. Although neither the term nor the genre existed when Heliodorus was writing, the text offers a non-dramatic prototype for tragicomedy, the popular and controversial genre rapidly taking over the Renaissance stage.

Shakespeare's Greek Tragicomedy

Cymbeline's relationship to the *Aethiopica*'s tragicomic rhetoric offers important insights into Shakespeare's debts to both the text and its genre. Heliodorus is unusually self-conscious about his generic mixing, but the Greek romances and their Elizabethan imitations are all similarly hybrid, typically combining love and war, death and rescue, separation and reconciliation. The influence of Greek romance on Elizabethan England, however, has not traditionally been linked with the later rise of tragicomedy, which responded to a number of factors. Italian Renaissance literary criticism, with its significant debt to Aristotle's *Poetics* and corresponding interest in the emotional effects of literary genres, prized tragicomedy as an especially valuable and sophisticated form (Henke 1997: 120–40). Giambattista Guarini's *Compendio della Poesia Tragicomica* (1601) described it as capable of tempering the undesirable extremes of violent terror, on the one hand, and coarse laughter, on the other, into more subtle and complex responses, appropriate for more sophisticated audiences. Italian Renaissance critics, including Guarini, influenced English writers, and Guarini's own tragicomedy, *Il Pastor Fido* (1590), quickly spawned many translations and imitations in English (Hunter 1973).

As a complex, experimental, and innovative form, tragicomedy flourished in the urbane milieu of the indoor, "private" theaters. Individual playwrights – such as John Fletcher, who based his tragicomic play *The Faithful Shepherdess* (1609/10) loosely on *Il Pastor Fido*, and drew heavily on Guarini's *Compendio* in a preface defining tragicomedy – have been identified with the genre's rise, but its development is especially indebted to the collaborative practices of theatrical playing companies, especially the intellectually avant-garde Children of the Queen's Revels, for whom Fletcher and his frequent collaborator, Beaumont, wrote (Munro 2005: 96–133). Critics widely regarded the new genre as monstrous; famously, Philip Sidney had much earlier complained in his *Defense of Poesy* that the emerging "mongrel tragicomedy" lacked the virtues of either individual genre (Sidney 1966: 67). Mingling higher and lower classes of people as well as higher and lower genres, the form evoked complex social and political debates as well as literary upheaval (McMullan and Hope 1992; Lesser 2002). Yet despite widespread complaints about its impropriety, generic and otherwise, the genre leapt into prominence early in the seventeenth century, and stayed that way for many decades to come.

Although Shakespeare's experimentation with tragicomedy has at times been identified with "problem plays" such as *Measure for Measure* and *All's Well that Ends Well*, his later plays, such as *Pericles*, *Cymbeline*, and *The Winter's Tale*, show the most marked debts to the genre. Beyond the genre's rising popularity by this point in his career, this development could be attributed especially to the influence of the Children of the Queen's Revels, and of Fletcher in particular. Beaumont and Fletcher came to write tragicomedies for Shakespeare's playing company, the King's Men – *Philaster* (ca. 1610) and *A King and No King* (ca. 1611) – and Fletcher clearly caught Shakespeare's attention and interest: the two went on to co-write *Two Noble Kinsmen* and *Henry VIII*, and Fletcher ultimately succeeded Shakespeare as the chief playwright of the King's Men. Also around this time, the King's Men's takeover of the lease on the indoor Blackfriars theater (former home to the Children of the Queen's Revels) may have encouraged theatrical innovation for the Blackfriars' more sophisticated audience (Bentley 1948). The evidence for when the King's Men began performing in Blackfriars is uncertain: the company certainly continued performing at the Globe as well, and some of the late plays, such as *Pericles*, were too early to have been performed at Blackfriars in any case (Barroll 2005). Still, the decision suggests at the very least the company's attentiveness to the theater's reputation and trademark style.

With its mingling of serious and ridiculous, danger and pleasure, fear and relief, *Cymbeline* has often been identified with tragicomedy.

Not all critics find the term an exact fit: the play differs in many ways from other contemporary plays of the genre, and its tragicomic false deaths are juxtaposed with notoriously real ones, such as those of Cloten, the evil Queen, and the many soldiers killed in the war between Britain and Rome. Nonetheless, the play's generic fracturing and divided tone suggest at least an affinity with the hybrid genre, and some critics feel that tragicomedy is a better term than romance for it and Shakespeare's other late plays, especially given that romance is historically a prose genre (Henke 1997: 31). Why, then, in constructing the play's tragicomic effects, did Shakespeare turn to plot devices and structures from Greek romance? Why is Heliodorus the source that Shakespeare imitates in responding to Jacobean tragicomedy?

As suggested earlier, the romance genre is already intrinsically generically mixed. Tragicomedy and romance are, in fact, intimate, if strange, bedfellows. If Fletcher's tragicomedies, along with the Black-friars theater more broadly, influenced Shakespeare, and were in turn influenced by Guarini and Italian tragicomedies, both writers were also very likely influenced by the success of *Mucedorus*, an Elizabethan romance based on *The Arcadia* which the King's Men seem to have revived twice, around 1605 and 1609–10 (Thornberry 1977; Bliss 1986). The play's popularity, and its impact on other theatrical developments, points to the close relationship between tragicomedy and romance. Genealogically, the two genres might at first glance seem to have different literary roots, the one stemming especially from Guarini and Italian Renaissance theory and the other from prose fiction imitating Greek romances. In fact, however, the rush of interest in Aristotle that nurtured Italian criticism was closely linked with the rush of interest in Heliodorus arising at the same time: as mentioned earlier, the latter was routinely taken as a prized example of the former's theory in action.

Though there is kinship between these two genres, however, they are hardly identical. By turning to romance in *Cymbeline* and other late plays, and in particular to an ironic, self-conscious, Heliodoran model of romance, Shakespeare simultaneously acknowledged the significance of the new theatrical developments coming from the Children of the Queen's Revels, and announced his own distinctive response to them. The popular appeal and emotional intensity of romance would have been a useful selling point for his general Globe audiences, while the wry self-parody of the Heliodoran template would appeal to his more sophisticated clientele and especially to any possible

Blackfriars performances. And although romance's typically non-dramatic status has troubled some critics, this aspect of the genre offers distinct advantages as well. Conventionally, dramatic genres such as tragedy and comedy have a limited narrative and temporal scope. As its genealogical ties to the *Odyssey* suggest, however, and as Scaliger's earlier-mentioned description of the *Aethiopica* as the ideal model for epic confirms, a sprawling prose genre such as romance mimics the expansive space of epic, opening up new dimensions for the stage. Shakespeare experimented with translating epic into drama at least as early as *Henry V* (1598–9) and *Troilus and Cressida* (1602), but *Cymbeline*, with its foreign travel, battles, allusions to Troy, and fascination with national sovereignty, is especially insistent about its relationship to epic and imperial history (James 1997). Like the Greek romances, the play fuses the political and geographical scope of epic with the erotic and domestic emphasis of comedy to create a hybrid structure self-consciously bridging high and low, serious and ridiculous.

Other aspects of the *Aethiopica* offer insights into Shakespeare's decision to turn to an ancient Greek literary model rather than his more typical English, French, Italian, or Latin sources. If the text's structure, tone, and genealogical history modeled new dramatic possibilities, its historical setting suggests political significance as well. As a Greek living in Roman North Africa, Heliodorus offered provocative material for a play on Roman Britain explicitly examining the nature of colonial and imperial power. The self-conscious literary artifice of Heliodorus and other Greek writers from the first centuries of the common era (known as the Second Sophistic) is now widely viewed as a direct response to, in part, the constraints imposed by Roman rule on elite Greek culture (Whitmarsh 2005). The wry mockery of conventional form could be understood similarly as a model for questioning governing structures while living within them. It is difficult, if not impossible, to work out exactly what Shakespeare knew or thought about Heliodorus, but his keen interest in Plutarch (another Second Sophistic Greek living in a Roman-occupied world) suggests that he was alert to the period's political and intellectual complexities. Moreover, his extensive literary attention to the imaginative powers and rebellious schemes of another Greek intellectual living in Roman North Africa – Cleopatra – suggests both fascination and sympathy with this position.

More concretely, Shakespeare would certainly have been aware of the conventional Renaissance truism, echoing Virgil, that the Greeks were men of letters, while the Romans were men of statecraft and war.

As the dedicatory letter in Underdowne's popular translation of the *Aethiopica* put it, "The Greekes in all manner of knowledge and learning, did farre surmount the Romanes, but the Romanes in administring their state, in warlike factes, and in common sense were much their superiours" (Underdowne 1924: 3). To a man of letters who explored the nature of Roman power throughout much of his work, this characterization can hardly have been insignificant. Regardless of the extent of his direct knowledge about Heliodorus, or of Greek literature more broadly, Shakespeare's decision to write a play about Roman-occupied Britain imitating both the genre and the tongue-in-cheek literary artifice of a Roman-occupied Greek suggests not only attentiveness to the reputation of the Greek literary tradition, but an implicit identification with it.

Greek romance, then, provided a template for extending and intensifying the generic mixing that had been a trademark of Shakespeare's drama from the beginning of his literary career, and for defying audiences' expectations in order to intensify their emotional responses. Heliodorus' literary self-consciousness and wry distance from the narrative's conventional turbulence, moreover, offered a model for juxtaposing melodramatic intensity with witty detachment, allowing *Cymbeline* to mock the romance genre even while serving up its characteristic pleasures. The timing of Shakespeare's explicit turn towards Greek romances, moreover, suggests further, and more specific, attractions. By revisiting a pastoral romance mode popular in England several decades earlier, Shakespeare tapped into Jacobean nostalgia for the Elizabethan period: a nostalgia evident in the popularity of *Mucedorus* and the pastoral tragicomedies that flourished in its wake. At the same time, imitating Heliodorus' narrative strategies enabled him to construct his own response to tragicomedy just as the genre was gaining popular currency. As we have seen, a rival playing company, as well as individual rival playwrights, achieved significant popular success with their experiments in a dark, satiric, Italian-influenced tragicomedy. Not to be left behind, Shakespeare came up with an alternative – a different hybrid tragicomic genre, simultaneously offering the crowd-pleasing melodrama of romance for his popular audiences and a tongue-in-cheek mockery of it for his more sophisticated viewers – bringing an alternative literary and generic tradition, Greek romance, to the model of Italianate tragicomedy. In the ongoing competition between playwrights, and between playing companies, Shakespeare's turn towards Heliodorus gave him a specific

strategy for appealing simultaneously to multiple audiences with widely
ranging tastes and desires.

Shakespeare's Greece

As this essay has shown, Shakespeare's debt to Heliodorus was both
substantial and specifically motivated. Given the striking parallels
between the *Aethiopica* and *Cymbeline*, the conspicuous literary
impact of Heliodorus at the time, and Shakespeare's self-conscious
references in his plays to both the *Aethiopica* and other Greek
romances, it is worth asking why this important model has been so
often ignored. *Cymbeline*'s genre is not, in fact, so perplexing when
examined in its genealogical context, and the play's plot and tone,
similarly, are neither outlandish nor unsatisfying relative to their
generic conventions and history. Yet attention to the influence of
Greek romances in the Renaissance is, although notably growing, still
very slight. Why?

Beyond the fact that Heliodorus no longer carries the same recognition and popularity today as he did in Shakespeare's time, the most
obvious reason is the widely accepted critical truism that Shakespeare
was not aware of, or influenced by, Greek literature. Following on
Ben Jonson's famous claim that Shakespeare had "small Latin and less
Greek," scholarly attention to Shakespeare's sources has focused on
English, Italian, French, and Latin literature, giving short shrift to
possible Greek influences. In 1709, Nicholas Rowe wrote, "It is
without controversy, that in his works we scarce find any traces of any
thing that looks like an imitation of the ancients" (Rowe 1848: 3).
More recently, Robert Miola has argued that "Though Elizabethan
schools emphasized the study of Greek, no Greek text has appeared
behind Shakespeare's works," and Charles and Michelle Martindale
voice common scholarly beliefs in stating that "If he had any
Greek, it was quite insufficient to read the great works of archaic and
classical Greece, even had he wanted to do so – but there is no reason
to think that he did" (Miola 2000: 166; Martindale and Martindale
1990: 11). More broadly, the Martindales argue that if Shakespeare
had read Greek texts, even in translation, "he gained little from
the experience" (Martindale and Martindale 1990: 41). Even those
few critics who suggest an affinity between Shakespeare and ancient
Greek works typically claim, with bemusement, that there is no line

of reception between the two, and that any commonality of structure and tone must therefore be coincidental (Nuttall 2004: 211; Silk 2004: 241).

As the example of *Cymbeline* shows, these pervasive claims for the irrelevance of Greek literature to Shakespeare are not only wrong, but a serious impediment to our understanding of his literary strategies. The moment is long overdue to rewrite the scholarly consensus on the place of Greece in Shakespeare's imagination, as well as that of the Renaissance more broadly. Recent research has made clear that Shakespeare's knowledge of the classics was actually considerably more substantial than generally believed, as was English consumption of Greek texts more broadly in the period. Shakespeare probably did read at least some Greek, but the precise level of his knowledge may not even matter. As we have seen, even if Shakespeare had little or no direct exposure to literary works in Greek, it is clear that he had access to Greek works such as the *Aethiopica* in translation, as well as to plentiful imitations of those works; it is equally clear that they played a significant role in his literary thought. Even beyond the romances, with their conspicuous visibility, Greek drama was widely available in early modern England, especially (though not exclusively) in Latin translations, and much remains to be said about its reception and impact (Smith 1988; Schleiner 1990). Ongoing critical blindness to this literary presence and its influence has closed off important lines of research and questioning in Shakespeare studies. By tracing the echoes of Heliodoran romance in *Cymbeline* and demonstrating their significance to our understanding of the play, and to Shakespeare's late work more generally, this essay offers a challenge to this critical blindness, and an invitation to further work in this area.

Works Cited

Barroll, Leeds 2005: "Shakespeare and the Second Blackfriars Theater." *Shakespeare Studies* 33, 156–70.
Bentley, G. E. 1948: "Shakespeare and the Blackfriars Theatre." *Shakespeare Survey* 1, 38–50.
Bliss, Lee 1986: "Tragicomic Romance for the King's Men, 1609–1611: Shakespeare, Beaumont and Fletcher." In A. R. Braunmuller and J. C. Bulman (eds.) *Comedy From Shakespeare to Sheridan: Continuity and Change in the English and European Dramatic Tradition*. Newark: University of Delaware Press, 148–64.

Bush, Douglas 1945: *English Literature in the Earlier Seventeenth Century*. Oxford: Oxford University Press.

Forcione, Alban K. 1970: *Cervantes, Aristotle, and the Persiles*. Princeton: Princeton University Press.

Gesner, Carol 1970: *Shakespeare and the Greek Romance: A Study of Origins*. Lexington: University Press of Kentucky.

Gosson, Stephen 1582: *Playes Confuted in Five Actions*. London.

Henke, Robert 1997: *Pastoral Transformations: Italian Tragicomedy and Shakespeare's Late Plays*. Newark: University of Delaware Press.

Hunter, G. K. 1973: "Italian Tragicomedy on the English Stage." *Renaissance Drama* n.s. 6, 123–48.

James, Heather 1997: *Shakespeare's Troy: Drama, Politics, and the Translation of Empire*. Cambridge: Cambridge University Press.

Johnson, Samuel 1925: *Johnson on Shakespeare*. Ed. Walter Raleigh. Oxford: Oxford University Press.

Lesser, Zachary 2002: "Mixed Government and Mixed Marriage in *A King and No King*: Sir Henry Neville Reads Beaumont and Fletcher." *English Literary History* 69, 947–77.

McMullan, Gordon and Hope, Jonathan (eds.) 1992: *The Politics of Tragicomedy: Shakespeare and After*. New York: Routledge.

Martindale, Charles and Martindale, Michelle 1990: *Shakespeare and the Uses of Antiquity*. London: Routledge.

Mentz, Steven 2006: *Romance for Sale in Early Modern England: The Rise of Prose Fiction*. Aldershot: Ashgate.

Miola, Robert S. 2000: *Shakespeare's Reading*. Oxford: Oxford University Press.

Munro, Lucy 2005: *Children of the Queen's Revels: A Jacobean Theatre Repertory*. Cambridge: Cambridge University Press.

Nuttall, A. D. 2004: "Action at a Distance: Shakespeare and the Greeks." In C. Martindale and A. B. Taylor (eds.) *Shakespeare and the Classics*. Cambridge: Cambridge University Press, 209–22.

Reynolds, Simon 2004: "*Cymbeline* and Heliodorus' *Aithiopika*: The Loss and Recovery of Form." *Translation and Literature* 13, 24–48.

Rowe, Nicholas 1848: *Life of William Shakspeare, with remarks on his genius and writings*. In Nicholas Rowe (ed.) *The Dramatic Works of William Shakspeare*. London: Routledge.

Scaliger, J. C. 1561: *Poetices libri septem*.

Schleiner, Louise 1990: "Latinized Greek Drama in Shakespeare's Writing of *Hamlet*." *Shakespeare Quarterly* 41, 29–48.

Sidney, Philip 1966: *A Defence of Poetry*. Ed. J. A. Van Dorsten. Oxford: Oxford University Press.

Silk, Michael 2004: "Shakespeare and Greek Tragedy: A 'Strange Relationship'." In C. Martindale and A. B. Taylor (eds.) *Shakespeare and the Classics*. Cambridge: Cambridge University Press, 241–57.

Smith, Bruce 1988: *Ancient Scripts and Modern Experience on the English Stage, 1500–1700*. Princeton: Princeton University Press.

Thornberry, Richard T. 1977: "A Seventeenth-Century Revival of *Mucedorus* Before 1610." *Shakespeare Quarterly* 28, 362–4.

Underdowne, Thomas 1587/1924: *An Aethiopian History of Heliodorus*. London: Abbey Classics, Chapman and Dodd.

Wells, Stanley 1966: "Shakespeare and Romance." In John Russell Brown and Bernard Harris (eds.) *Later Shakespeare*. London: Edward Arnold, 49–79.

Whitmarsh, Tim 2005: *The Second Sophistic*. Oxford: Oxford University Press.

Chapter 3

How the Renaissance (Mis)Used Sources: The Art of Misquotation

Julie Maxwell

Rationale

We all know what a quotation is, or a misquotation. Or do we?

This essay arose because I found peculiarities in the way Renaissance writers use quotations that were not explained in the available criticism. Isn't it rather odd, I thought, that there is so much concern in sixteenth-century England about establishing reliable texts and translations of the Bible, and yet there are so many misquotations of scripture? The standard comment about Renaissance misquotation was that writers were sloppy about quoting in the same way that they were unstandardized in their spelling. Also, the English Bible existed in different translations. This explained some cases – but not the creatively inventive misquotations I had found. So why, I wondered, wasn't this intriguing paradox tackled in current scholarship?

The underlying principle of my enquiry was cultural-historical: conventions of quotation were different in the Renaissance than they are now. Sometimes scholarship has a blind spot because it imagines that writers are like scholars. The modern scholarly expectation is that a quotation will be verbally exact, properly attributed, and taken from the best available edition. Quotation studies regard this as the norm from which to track deviations. But what if it was not the norm in the Renaissance? What if misquotation, not accurate quotation, was prized? Might Renaissance quotation be a *faux ami*, like a word in Shakespeare that we recognize ("quick") but which now means something different ("speedy" instead of "living")?

So I tried to discover what Renaissance writers thought about quotation. I asked myself how their thinking would have been shaped, and what surviving evidence I could draw on to find the answers. For example, how might their early training as readers and writers at school have influenced their attitudes? (This would involve looking at educational treatises, commonplace books, etc.) Could it be demonstrated that there was a connection between educational precepts and literary results? (This would involve comparing educational theories to specific examples in Shakespeare and others.)

Writers themselves have known for a long time that quotation practices require careful recovery, that a history of quotation habits needs writing. They may express this comically, as George Eliot does in *Adam Bede* (1859), when Mr Joshua Rann suddenly booms, " 'Sehon, King of the Amorites: for His mercy endureth for ever; and Og the King of Basan: for His mercy endureth for ever,' – a quotation which may seem to have slight bearing on the present occasion, but, as with every other anomaly, adequate knowledge will show it to be a natural consequence" (Eliot 1992: 18). Eliot offers "adequate knowledge" in the form of an explanation of Joshua Rann's ecclesiastical attitudes. I tried to find adequate knowledge, to explain the seeming anomalies of Renaissance misquotation, in Renaissance educational theory, literary culture, and censorship practices.

Beyond that, I tried to imagine what it was like to be a Renaissance writer. Literary criticism can easily become dominated by history or politics. Shakespeare's genius was for words. My other underlying principle, then, was transhistorical, but indisputable: great writers are creative people. They invent. They experiment. They alter.

They don't merely copy – or quote.

In scholarship, misquotation is vexing. In literature, it is an art.

This explains a seeming paradox in Shakespeare's world: a scholar like Erasmus, concerned to establish reliable biblical texts, careful to check the variants in patristic quotations of the Bible, could be deliberately capricious when it came to quoting scripture himself, in *The Praise of Folly* (1511). That is because the biblical scholar was also a writer of genius. Exact quotation demands no inventive talent. John Donne, not lacking in invention certainly, rebuked spiritual pedants by reminding them that the Bible itself contained inaccurate quotations. "Neither Christ in his preaching nor the Holy Ghost in penning the Scriptures of the New Testament were so curious as our times . . . in citing the very, very words of the places" (Donne 1953–62: 44). Discrepancies sometimes arise when New Testament writers quote, not the Hebrew Bible directly, but its translation into Greek in the second century bce, the Septuagint. Donne thought the Bible was a great work of literature. "Curious" carries his writerly contempt for the nit-pickers.

Of course, unreliable quotation is not necessarily proof of genius. In *Love's Labour's Lost*, the curate and pedant Nathaniel makes proverbial pronouncements, claiming they are patristic quotations. The results are decidedly lackluster, as Holofernes' reluctance to hear further examples illustrates:

> *Nathaniel*   . . . and as a certain father saith–
> *Holofernes* Sir, tell me not of the father (4.2.148–9)

In the mock-preface to *Don Quixote* (1615), Cervantes pretends that he needs to show off, in a similar fashion, some scholarship in the margins of his book. The procedure is simple: "Go to the Holy Scripture," his friend directs, "if you have never so little curiosity, and set down God's own words" (Cervantes 1999: 20). If you can't think of anything better, quote a bit of the Bible – which the friend then proceeds to do with appropriate precision. But Cervantes' ripe invention requires no shrivelled garnish of this kind.

Nor does Shakespeare's. The quotations (mostly misquotations) from the Bible in the plays are not his own literary embellishments. They are partly a replication of other people's quoting habits, partly an alteration of familiar words to achieve specific effects. In other words, he is a dramatist and a poet.

The imprecision of Shakespeare's biblical quotations has been noticed before – but either as a mundane impediment to scholars trying to determine which translations he used (Shaheen 1999: 38–48), or else as a sign, not of art, but of creative hindrance. According to George Steiner:

> To this ubiquity of biblical presence in English literature, there is a paramount and challenging exception. Secondary studies tell of a goodly number of allusions to biblical material in Shakespeare. Quotations, mostly muted or indirect, have been identified. There is, however, no central encounter, no engagement of any scope (as there is, in contrast, with Homer or Plutarch). It is as if Shakespeare had deliberately evaded not only the narrative storehouse of the Old and the New Testaments, but the flowering of this great resource as it shaped the language from Wycliffe and Tyndale to his own immediate contemporaries. I would conjecture that some wary instinct of sovereign autonomy inhibited Shakespeare from too close a contact with the only texts, with the only discourse in action, which might dim his own powers. (Steiner 1996: xliii)

This Shakespeare is afraid of the Bible. He is the exception to the literary rule observed by Steiner: he avoids clear direct quotation and muffles it instead. But before accepting Steiner's view, we need to know what rules and expectations governed literary uses of the Bible in Shakespeare's world – just as Kate Rumbold asks, what rules governed the quotation *of* Shakespeare in the eighteenth century? (Rumbold 2007). Only then can we ask, do the conditions for quotation in Shakespeare differ significantly from those of other writers, and if so, what are the results? Otherwise, we rest at Steiner's "conjecture" and cannot discover any more. For instance, is it purely arbitrary that quotations are sometimes precise, sometimes fudged? If all quoting is inevitably (as the paradoxical phrase has it) "out of context," when is it acceptable, and when is it not? And most important, is the act of quotation, or (more often) misquotation, really such an impoverished anxiety of influence as Steiner would have us believe? These are the sorts of questions which this essay sets out to answer, in order to understand what it meant to misquote scripture in Shakespeare's world, and how that world is recreated in his drama.

Renaissance Education: Sentences, Synonyms, and Morals

Misquotation occurs in two distinct ways: the first is verbal inexactness, the loose recollection or startling adaptation of the exact words of the original text. The second is quoting out of context, in ways that are recognizably transgressive: irreverent, self-serving, devious, and so on. "The devil can cite scripture for his purpose," Antonio observes disgustedly in *The Merchant of Venice* (1.3.98). Frequently, the two forms of misquotation coincide.

In Renaissance England there are clear and easily discoverable reasons for the first kind of misquotation, verbal imprecision. There are the usual suspects – faulty memory, simple ignorance, cavalier disregard. A culture that did not stabilize spelling did not fuss over getting its quotations right either (Norton 2000: 106). And accidents happen: the lawyer-scholar John Selden reported a case of a thousand Bibles printed in England with "the Text thus (Thou shalt committ adultery) The word (not) left out" (Selden 1927: 12). More fundamentally, however, when we are dealing with trained Renaissance readers and writers, verbal misquotation has to do with inculcated conventions of quotation. As we will see, they were taught to misquote creatively.

Renaissance England was a quoting culture. The first book printed in England, by William Caxton in 1477, was *The Dictes or Sayengis of the Philosophres*. Ben Jonson's measure of a great work of literature was its quotability. A reader of Virgil, for instance, "might repeat part of his workes, / As fit for any conference, he can use" in *Poetaster* (5.1.124–5). The Reformation period as well as the Renaissance directed attention to quotation. The cry of *sola scriptura* necessitated an organized use of biblical quotation, which was catered for in the creation of personal theological commonplace books, as well as published ones like Philip Melanchthon's *Loci Communes Rerum Theologicarum* (1512).

In the sixteenth-century grammar school, the humanist curriculum privileged grammar and rhetoric. Education was literary and heavily influenced by the pedagogical principles of Erasmus. Two projects stand out in particular. The first directed the way reading was to be done: with the use of a commonplace book. The second directed the way writing was to be done: in imitation of the best classical authors. Both impacted significantly on Renaissance habits of quotation.

The systematic recording of quotations in a commonplace book was a practice that many took with them into adult life. When a Renaissance pupil read a book, it was with a view to copying interesting excerpts from it, placing these quotations under relevant headings of subject (like "ambition") or of style (like "periphrasis") and then reusing the material that had been arranged in these "common places" for composition (Moss 1996). Shakespeare finds the perfect Renaissance metaphor for mental disarray when Hamlet describes his brain as a commonplace book that has lost this whole function. From now on, it will contain only one quotation: "Adieu adieu remember me," the ghost's injunction (1.5.111; cf. 1.5.91). There is no common heading under which Hamlet's discovery can be tidily placed, because it is utterly unlike anything that has happened before in his life. As we will see, it is typical of Shakepeare's characters to refer to a familiar practice, only to implode it. In contrast to Hamlet's single quotation, "Renaissance literature of the imagination is at its most typical when accumulating variations round a commonplace theme and playing textual allusions against each other" (Moss 1993: 19). Literature is a Chinese dinner table, rotating with dishes that can all be seen and sampled together.

If reading sought out the best expressed sentiments of classical authors, writing was meant to imitate them. First, though, languages had to be learned. Schoolboys construed phrases or short passages from English to Latin. Sometimes the English text was a schoolmaster's translation from a Latin source, sometimes it was scripture. The authorized St Paul's School grammar suggested the Psalter, Solomon's Proverbs, or Ecclesiastes as possibilities (Baldwin 1944: 143). Parts of the Bible that fell readily into small pieces were preferred for pedagogic as well as morally improving reasons. They stuck in the memory. There was also an inseparable aesthetic element to this. Witty *sententiae* (sentences) were thought to capture the imagination, and thereby the moral soul, of the young. It was not only a few pious extremists who thought Solomon could be used better for this purpose than Cicero.

Francis Meres, who recognized a Shakespeare when he saw one, wrote in *Palladis Tamia* (1598): "I judge him of a happie Wit, who is profound and substantiall in Sentences; eloquent and ingenious in Similitudes; rich and copious in Examples" (A3v). *Pace* Steiner, quoting "sentences" was considered the height of literary eloquence and Shakespeare benefited from these educational expectations – but then created characters who subverted their purposes.

Consider Falstaff and Prince Hal. The first time Hal quotes scripture, in *1 Henry IV* (see below), Falstaff has just praised the insulting originality of his similes. Their huge verbal abilities rival each other affectionately, Falstaff encouraging Hal to play the brilliant schoolboy. Falstaff says he is as melancholy as a gib cat [tomcat], a lugged bear [led by a chain], the drone of a Lincolnshire bagpipe. Hal adds an old lion, a lover's lute, a hare, Moor-ditch (1.2.74–8). "Ingenious in Similitudes," there is no doubt. Or, as Falstaff tells Hal, "Thou hast the most unsavoury [similes]" (1.2.79). Will they be equally "profound and substantiall in Sentences" from scripture? Falstaff starts to tell a story about his recent clash with authority. He uses words that tickle Hal – and the audience – into a shared recollection of one of Solomon's sentences:

> *Falstaff* An old lord of the Council rated me the other day about you, sir, but I marked him not, and yet he talked very wisely, but I regarded him not, and yet he talked wisely, and in the street too.
>
> *Prince* Thou didst well, for wisdom cries out in the streets and no man regards it. (1.2.83–9)

Wisdom crieth without; she uttereth her voice in the streets: . . . and no man regarded. (Proverbs 1:20, 24)[1]

There is a schoolboy giggle here about an abstract noun crying in a concrete street. Falstaff gifts the punch line to Hal, whose rejoinder chimes like a rhyme. The quote has to be close to the original. The pleasure it gives is proportional to the precision, which is more easily achieved here because they speak prose. First there is the pleasure of recognition. Then there is the pleasure of a close verbal quotation that is nonetheless a misquotation, a misuse, so far as context goes. The standard Renaissance justification for contextual misquotation was that the misquoter might make "better use," morally, of the author's "sentences (such as poynt towards any good matter) then they could themselves" (Baldwin 1944: 707). This was particularly the case with classical authors.

Zestily, Falstaff reverses this familiar logic. From Christian texts he teaches the ethics of robbery: "'Tis no sin for a man to labour in his vocation" (1.2.104–5) ("Let every man abide in the same calling" ["vocation," GB], 1 Corinthians 7:20). That is, there's nothing wrong with thieving so long as it's your job. Later, Falstaff imagines King Henry IV quoting the Bible in his (Falstaff's) favor too: "If then the tree may be known by the fruit, as the fruit by the tree, then peremptorily I speak it, there is virtue in that Falstaff" (2.4.428–30) ("The tree is known by *his* fruit," Matthew 12:33). Interpreting "fruit" as a man's physical looks rather than (as in the Bible) his words and deeds, Falstaff puts a naive argument in the king's mouth: appearances are not deceptive. Falstaff "must" be virtuous.

Falstaff is Chaucerian in his use of the Bible. In *The Canterbury Tales*, scripture is encountered, again in characters' oral pronouncements, as a set of wise saws. They can be quoted lightly and then lightly disregarded. "*If* then the tree" is provisional – Falstaff is trying out a conceit. Biblical proverbs may be worldly-wise, but so are people. This is *folk* wisdom. Many of the biblical phrases or images used by Shakespeare had already become proverbial, prompting editors to point out that the source cannot be determined. The exclamation of the imaginary Chaucer in the prologue to Shakespeare and Fletcher's *The Two Noble Kinsmen* is a case in point: "O fan / From me the witless chaff of such a writer . . . !" (Prol. 18–19). Possibly an adaptation of Matthew 3:12, fanning the chaff away from the wheat was also a commonplace image. This "Chaucer" puts the familiar conceit in a new verbal form to describe, appropriately enough, inadequate writers.

What happens when Shakespeare's characters are not misquoting biblical proverbs – whose exact words might be easier to recall than other parts of scripture, and which it was clever and amusing to repeat with some precision? Again, educational factors offer suggestions. This time the subject we turn to is synonyms, not sentences.

According to Renaissance educators, "right choyce of words" was "indeed the foundation of all eloquence" (Baldwin 1944: 686). Pupils learned imitation of classical authors by finding synonymous Latin phrases for ones given to them in English or Latin itself. This was "a translating of the same speach into another like sentence, but altered with many varieties at once, and chiefly with the last[,] varietie of the words" (Baldwin 1944: 444). In *The Schoolmaster* (1570), the royal tutor Roger Ascham directed pupils to examine closely passages in which Virgil had adapted Homer or Cicero had adapted Demosthenes. Then they would learn how borrowed "matter," "sentences," and "words" could be altered "wittelie" for present purposes (47–8). The pupil was to observe such eloquence in classical authors, in order to replicate it. Again, the ultimate aims were didactic and social: to educate new generations of able speakers and writers, who would direct their skills of rhetorical persuasion to moral ends.

Imitation exercises affected the practice of quotation. Imitation was the larger project, but its principles and methods applied to quotation.

Borrowing was fluidly creative, and resulted in the creation of conventions of quotation quite unlike those of modern scholarship. Quotations did not need to be precise – not (or not necessarily) because writers could not be bothered to refer back to the original text, but because the Renaissance pupil had been taught to omit and to add words deliberately. In other words, to misquote. In particular, he was to alter the original vocabulary. This triumph of freely creative misquotation over slavish repetition is Erasmian: "the reader does not recognize an insertion taken from Cicero, but a child born from one's brain" (Pigman 1980: 9). Even when "quotations" are attributed – and recognition seems called for – they may be creative paraphrases.

Inert reproduction quotations were mocked by writers. Philip Sidney scorned "diligent imitators" of Cicero and Demosthenes who "keep Nizolian paper-books of their figures and phrases" – reference books for would-be quoters (Vickers 1999: 386). He wishes these imitators would instead "by attentive translation (as it were) devour them whole, and make them wholly theirs" (ibid.). What does Sidney's wavering parenthetical comment mean? Not that it is enough to have read the whole of these authors, because "translation" refers to writing. Nor that would-be imitators of the classics must translate the whole of Homer first. The difference between slavish quotation – or a parade of classical knowledge in schoolboy tags – and a more ideal, imitative kind is not size. The point is that a quotation superficially faithful to its source may be casually, lazily, uncomprehendingly, reproduced. It has undergone no attempt at creative transformation. Conversely, the quotation that appears loosest may actually have been most closely worked over. The writer has digested his authority and imitated it, not with easy diligence, but with true invention. Misquotation makes one's source one's own.

And, like many of the rhetorical skills learned at school, this habit was transferable from Latin to vernacular composition. While Latin language quotations, from the Bible as well as the classics, are likely to be preserved intact in vernacular writings, vernacular misquotation of the Bible in vernacular texts is frequent. The Latin Vulgate had once been regarded as *the* Bible and there was an attachment to its exact words. No English translation attained such status during this period (Norton 2000). Instead, the words of the Bible were available in differing English renderings. And writers invented their own versions.

The influence of imitation exercises on quoting practices has implications for how we identify and understand quotations in Renaissance texts. Even the most apparently sensible premises are challenged. Modern quotation studies regard verbal fidelity as the norm from which to track deviations. They list quotations and allusions, prioritizing those wordings that are closest to the original texts. Yet put up against the deliberate Renaissance attempt to make verbal alterations, especially to vocabulary, the hierarchies of such studies start to look upside-down.

For example: "The scripture says, Adam digg'd" (*Hamlet* 5.1.36–7). Well, no. In Renaissance Bibles, the scripture says Adam dressed, kept, and tilled the garden of Eden – all more decorous terms, and sometimes used by Shakespeare (Genesis 2:15). In *The Comedy of Errors*, the jailer Adam is not the Adam "who kept the paradise" (4.3.17–18). Shakespeare retains the familiar biblical verb here, because the point is for the jailer, not the line, to diverge from the scriptural precedent. In *Richard II* likewise, a gardener, "old Adam's likeness," is "set to dress this garden" (3.4.73). The preserved biblical synonym suits the ancient resemblance. "Digged," by contrast, is the gravedigger's unsubtle misquote. He wants to make his occupationally motivated point. It has to be an invented synonym because there is no translation of the Bible from which it could have been taken. Like Hal and Falstaff, he is playing with an established misquoting convention.

Probably unschooled, the gravedigger must have been listening hard in church. His prefatory questions – "What, art a heathen? How dost thou understand the Scripture?" (5.1.35–6) – imitate the way Jesus introduces scripture to support his rhetorical authority in the gospels. Are they ignoramuses? Jesus asks the Pharisees. "Have ye not read what David did. . . . Or have ye not read in the law . . . ?" (Matthew 12:3, 5). The New Testament is full of quotations from the Old, used mainly to justify arguments. So to quote or misquote the Bible, argumentatively, is to imitate its strategies. (Mis)quoting the Bible is not necessarily, *pace* Steiner again, a poor substitute for a more satisfying encounter with it. It is literary imitation.

What about cases when Shakespeare's wording appears to follow a particular translation? For instance, he is closest to the Bishops' Bible, the official translation of the Church of England that was read out in services, when misquoting Revelation 3:5 in *Richard II*. "My name be blotted from the book of life," Mowbray offers boldly, "if ever I were traitor" (1.3.201–2). Only the Bishops' Bible has "blot out," while all other Renaissance translations prior to the King James have "put out" (Shaheen 1999: 367). But is Shakespeare copying, or is it simply that, like the Bishops' translator, he is continuing the bibliographical metaphor more explicitly – blotting a line from a book? When there is a translation Shakespeare could have followed, generally there is unwillingness to allow him any verbal enterprise. This is an extraordinary assumption to apply to a creative genius. Only Shakespeare's inventiveness can explain other cases when his vocabulary anticipates the King James, not published until 1611.

For example: "We'll set thee to school to an ant" (i.e., we'll make you learn from the wise ant), the Fool says in *King Lear* (2.4.66). The Bible advises the same schoolmaster – "Go to the ant" in the King James (Proverbs 6:6), but "Go to the pismire" or "Go to the emmet" in earlier Renaissance translations (pismire and emmet are both synonyms for ant). In *Coriolanus*, "We call a nettle but a nettle, and / The faults of fools but folly" (2.1.190–1). Not until the King James Version, we don't. There "the foolishness of fools *is* folly" (Proverbs 14:24). The Geneva Bible, a popular reading version which some consider to have been "Shakespeare's" Bible, calls "the folie of fooles . . . foolishness" instead. Shakespeare substitutes "faults" for "folie" and uses "folly" for "foolishness." He creates, as educators directed, "another like sentence" but varied with "right choyce of words" (Baldwin 1944: 444, 686).

Flagrant examples of Shakespeare's alteration of vocabulary, while retaining the original form of the sentence, occur in his use of the biblical construction "O death, where *is* thy sting? O grave, where *is* thy victory?" (1 Corinthians 15:55). In *Hamlet*, "O shame, where is thy blush?" (3.4.81). In *Troilus and Cressida*, "O beauty, where is thy faith?" (5.2.67). Shakespeare's disillusioned sons and lovers fill in the desired blanks. Compare Falstaff's touchingly rewritten beatitude in *2 Henry IV*: "Blessed are they that have been my friends" (5.5.137–8), "friends" substituting for the merciful, the pure in heart, the peacemakers (Matthew 5:3–11). Obviously, Shakespeare follows no translation here.

Arguments for the use of a particular translation are more persuasive when (as occasionally happens) Shakespeare uses two or more terms peculiar to it. Othello, for instance, paraphrases Proverbs 5:15–18, which urges marital fidelity and compares it to drinking from your own water source. Othello's vocabulary choices ("fountain" and "cistern," 4.2.59, 61) seem owed to the Geneva Bible. All other translations have "wells" (Shaheen 1999: 593–4). And yet the idea that Shakespeare was short on synonyms is risible; indeed, the water source metaphor itself is continued quite independently of the Bible. The Bible's cisterns are now inhabited, in Othello's hideous imaginings, by foul toads.

What about the reverse case – when two words of a scriptural passage appear to have been taken from two different translations? In *The Comedy of Errors* (2.2.86–7) and again in *The Winter's Tale* (4.4.721–2), Shakespeare contrasts wittily two words that describe Rachel's twins in Genesis 25:25, 27. Esau is a "hairy" man, while Jacob is a "plain" one – but not in the same Renaissance translation (again, not until we get to the King James). Did someone of Shakespeare's verbal powers really need to consult two Bibles to come up with the words "plain" and "hairy"? Since the success of these jokes depends partly on recognition of the biblical narrative encoded in the adjectives, Shakespeare has evidently chosen the terms mostly commonly associated with Jacob and Esau.

Quite often his characters hit the proper biblical words, not to be exact but, like Falstaff and Hal, because it is the way to be perverse. In *Troilus and Cressida*, the servant takes the terms "Lord" and "praise," referring to his master Paris, in deliberately the wrong sense. "The Lord be praised!" he exclaims mock-piously (3.1.8), borrowing the frequent biblical command from the Psalms. The words are all right, the context all wrong.

What is happening is clearest in examples when someone misquotes overtly, like *Hamlet*'s gravedigger. Then it is unmistakable that Shakespeare and many of his characters are inventive misquoters. Some, like Justice Shallow in *2 Henry IV*, are nowhere close to the text: "Death, as the Psalmist saith, is certain to all, all shall die" (3.2.37–8). The psalmist saith nothing like that. The closest verbal parallel that Naseeb Shaheen can find is Psalm 89:47 (89:48, GB), "What man is he that liveth, and shal not see death?" (Shaheen 1999: 441).

Bottom in *A Midsummer Night's Dream* is more charmingly unable to misquote effectively. Would-be actor, he promises to "roar . . . as gently as any sucking dove" (1.2.82–3), instead of sucking lamb or harmless dove. These are biblical pairings (1 Samuel 7:9, Matthew 10:16) which previously occur together in *2 Henry VI* (Shaheen 1999: 146). Unlike the pleasant chime of Hal's correctly chosen quotation about Wisdom (above), this is a clanger. Bottom's senses are, as usual, misaligned. The blunder may have been funnier to a Renaissance audience than to us on account of the educational practice it parodies.

In the best-loved example, a baffled Bottom swaps around the verbs of 1 Corinthians 2:9. He makes an awestruck attempt to describe his experience with Titania, queen of the fairies:

> The eye of man hath not heard, the ear of man hath not seen, man's hand is not able to taste, his tongue to conceive, nor his heart to report, what my dream was. (4.1.211–13)

Bottom confuses the existing senses in the biblical text ("Eye hath not seen, nor ear heard" ["the eie hath not seen, and the eare hath not heard," BB], 1 Corinthians 2:9) and compounds this with the introduction of two new innovations, a tasting hand and a thinking tongue. Just possibly this was prompted by the Geneva Bible's marginal note on the verse: "Man can not so much as thinke of them, much lesse conceive them with his senses." This comment puts the experience beyond all of the senses. Perhaps Shakespeare's eye saw, and the pen in his hand reported. For the Bible's "entered into the heart" we have instead a heart attempting to report – just as Bottom's is. It is a perfect confusion, the perfection Shakespeare's and the confusion all Bottom's. Unlike the groomed Erasmian misquotation, Bottom's erring is delightfully unintentional. He knows it is time to call in the professional: "I shall get Peter Quince to write a ballet of this dream" (4.1.214–25).

Erasmus, when misquoting in *The Praise of Folly*, points it out. He invents synthetic, imitative biblical idioms like "the foolishness of the cross" – a conflation of biblical phrases rather than the exact wording of any one of them (Erasmus 1998: 85). He is wittily self-deprecating about this verbal play. Having exposed the literal-minded idiocy of pedant theologians who discovered "meaning" in tiny pieces of the Vulgate text, Erasmus suggests: "since things like that are permitted to theological masters, it is but fair to allow the same indulgence also to me (who am obviously but a pinchbeck divine), if I shall not make every quotation and citation with absolute exactness" (Erasmus 1998: 83). Erasmus loosely quotes Paul, who was, after all, a loose quoter himself. Erasmus confesses to cavalier erring. The scholar in him tells us that the mistakes are not bungles, like Bottom's. This is not licensing a mindlessly casual quotation. Rather, the educator and the writer in Erasmus are demonstrating the art of misquotation.

An Erasmian education taught copiousness – to say the same thing a thousand ways. Beatrice in *Much Ado About Nothing* offers copious synonymous phrases for the biblical text "And the Lord God formed man *of* the dust of the ground" (Genesis 2:7). This is because she is ranting – in her protesting alternatives, "Would it not grieve a woman to be overmaster'd with a piece of valiant dust? to make an account of her life to a clod of wayward marl?" (2.1.60–3). The familiar biblical text becomes humorous when defamiliarized with inventive synonyms – "marl" avoids the stale religious connotations of "clay" – and unpredictable adjectives. Whereas Bottom's dove (to borrow American slang) sucks, the valor of dust and the waywardness of marl are deliberately and brilliantly inapposite. Dust is easily blown away. Clay is stiff.

Shakespeare's misquotations often economize, however. It's *Measure for Measure* – not, "with what measure ye mete, it shall be measured to you again" (Matthew 7:2). In this case, the abbreviation was already proverbial. In *The Merchant of Venice*, Launcelot Gobbo says he'll take his leave of the Jew "in the twinkling" (2.2.167–8). This clips the rest of the biblical quotation, "of an eye" (1 Corinthians 15:52). The quotation twinkles Launcelot past the Jew even more quickly. Similarly, in *The Comedy of Errors*, Egeon "coasting homeward, came to Ephesus" (1.1.134). The first verb does, singly and speedily, the work of the Bible's clause, "having passed through the upper coasts came to Ephesus" (Acts 19:1). In *The Two Noble Kinsmen*, the Bible's "fulness of bread, and abundance of idleness" (Ezekiel 16:49) contracts to "full of bread and sloth" (1.1.158–9). Shakespeare's version of the sentence doesn't hang about, even if its subjects do. The wronged queen who quotes it is urging immediate action.

Compare the deposed king's biblical misquotations in *Richard II*. The passage is particularly important for the present discussion because Richard is consciously pondering the act of quoting biblical texts. This helps to confirm some of the quoting practices that I have been inferring so far. The scene opens with Richard trying to find a way of using a common Renaissance simile. How is his prison like the world? The simile doesn't appear to be working because "the world is populous" and Richard is alone (5.5.3). He solves the problem by breeding thoughts to inhabit his world:

> In humours like the people of this world:
> For no thought is contented. The better sort,

> As thoughts of things divine, are intermix'd
> With scruples and do set the word itself
> Against the word,
> As thus: "Come, little ones," and then again,
> "It is as hard to come as for a camel
> To thread the postern of a small needle's eye." (5.5.10–17)

"Thought" is restless. There is no rest for the wicked, as the Bible also says (Isaiah 57:21), or even for the righteous in this case. Unsure if they are saved, they quote apparently contradictory texts on the subject. One thinks of John Bunyan – alternately consoled and terrorized by biblical sentences in his spiritual autobiography *Grace Abounding* (1666). As we might by now expect, when Richard imagines people quoting the Bible, they are not rigidly strict about it. "Come, little ones" abbreviates "Suffer the little children to come unto me" (Mark 10:14). The pathway to heaven is quicker that way. It is also an invitation to the persons coming to heaven, rather than (as in the Bible) a rebuke to the persons trying to obstruct them. Conversely, the second misquotation complicates the biblical analogy "It is easier for a camel to go through the eye of a needle, than for a rich man to enter into the kingdom of God" (Mark 10:25). Shakespeare's misquotation finds room for three possible interpretations of Jesus' words. Some thought Jesus meant literally what he said – a camel going through the eye of a needle. However, "threading the postern," or gate, allows for two other possibilities. One is that by "camel" he means a "cable-rope" trying to get through a needle's eye. Or that by "small needle's eye" he means "postern," a small pedestrian gate through which the camel must try to go (Shakespeare 1956: 170). All this slows the getting to heaven.

In such cases, the misquotations *do* what they *say* (speed us up, slow us down). They practise what they preach. They behave in a Ricksian manner (Ricks 2002).

Time generates misquotation for another reason in *Timon of Athens*. Biblical precepts can seem out of date to Shakespeare's characters. "How rarely," the faithful servant Flavius laments when he sees the state of Timon, "does it meet with this time's guise / When man was wish'd to love his enemies!" (4.3.465–6). Man was so instructed by Jesus: "But I say unto you, Love your enemies" (Matthew 5:44). If only it were that simple. "Wish'd" is appositely wishful. Who are a man's enemies? Seeming friends are worse than open enemies, so Flavius amends accordingly: "Grant I may ever love, and rather woo

/ Those that would mischief me than those that do [me mischief while pretending to love me]!" (4.3.467–8). Jesus' command is in urgent need of modernization – that is, misquotation.

In *1 Henry IV*, Hotspur modernizes biblical proverbs, rather differently, with contemporary detail. Impatient of Glendower, whom he finds "tedious . . . as a railing wife" (3.1.157–8), Hotspur conflates the sayings "*It is* better to dwell in the corner of the housetop, than with a brawling woman and in a wide house," "Better *is* a dinner of herbs where love is, than a stalled ox and hatred therewith," and "Better *is* a dry morsel, and quietness therewith, than an house full of sacrifices *with* strife" (Proverbs 25:24, 15:17, 17:1). What he says is this:

> . . . I had rather live
> With cheese and garlic in a windmill, far,
> Than feed on cates and have him talk to me
> In any summer house in Christendom. (3.1.159–62)

The misquotation orders off the menu of Hotspur's preferences. The variety is deliberate: it is the spice of the quotation's life.

Hotspur imagines what might be better. Behind him is Shakespeare, imagining how the texts of the English Bible might be bettered for his purposes too. In Rudyard Kipling's story "Proofs of Holy Writ," an imaginary Shakespeare goes one step further (Pasternak Slater 1972: 125). He is requested to submit an English translation of Isaiah 60:1–3, 19–20 to one of the translators working on the King James Bible. Shakespeare's fellow dramatist Jonson is with him for the afternoon. First, Jonson reads out the Latin Vulgate version – "Ben rolled forth, richly" – and then enquires doubtfully, "Er-hum? Think you to better that?" (Kipling 1937–9: 346). This is exactly what Shakespeare does. Ben reads Coverdale's, the Bishops', and the Geneva versions too, and Shakespeare creates a rendering better than any of them. He is minutely concerned with each possible aesthetic improvement:

> "Darkness covers" – no – "clokes" (short always). "*Darkness clokes the earth, and gross – gross darkness the people!*" (But Isaiah's prophesying, with the storm behind him. Can ye not *feel* it, Ben? It must be "shall") – "*Shall cloke the earth.*" (Kipling 1937–9: 348)

A fanciful story, biographically, but not critically. Shakespeare is improving on the English Bible when Richard III advises one of the young princes he will soon murder:

> Nor more can you distinguish of a man
> Than of his outward show, which, God he knows,
> Seldom or never jumpeth with the heart. (3.1.9–11)

Critics cite 1 Samuel 16:7: "Man looketh on the outward appearance, but the LORD looketh on the heart." The important verbal innovation here is "jumpeth." God sees the movement of the heart on which he "looketh" in the Bible. Shaheen suggests this is perhaps an analogy rather than a reference (Shaheen 1999: 351). But again, this is to grant Shakespeare (and Richard) no verbal initiative, surely not a quality lacked by either of them. "Jumpeth" works well because it is what hearts do, especially in emotionally pressured situations. Speakers of English have agreed ever since: "my heart jumped, his heart leapt." Richard may be edgy, but he is giving nothing away outwardly. "Can ye not *feel* it, Ben?"

Receptions: Renaissance, Augustan, and Present-Day

Not everyone was thrilled by the methods of Renaissance educators. There were people who subscribed to St. Augustine's view: words would not be learned out of morally degenerate literature (classical literature was pagan literature) so fast as moral degeneration would be learned out of words. Theoretically, the Bible should have been safer than classical authors. However, the Bible is full of immoral behavior, as those who criticized the stage recognized anxiously. Shortly after the theatrical entrepreneur Philip Henslowe had commissioned a number of biblical plays (on the subjects of Jepthah, Joshua, and Samson), one Henry Crosse snapped: "Is it fit that the infirmities of holy men should be acted on a Stage, whereby others may be inharted [put into heart, i.e., emboldened] to rush carelessly forward into unbrideled libertie?" (Chambers 1923: 247).

Furthermore, the quoter may be, like Richard III, deliberately perverse. Hal and Falstaff look like innocents after this would-be king, who confesses, gleefully, to making morally depraved exploitation of scripture. These quotations are mostly variants on one biblical conceit:

> . . . I sigh, and, with a piece of scripture,
> Tell them that God bids us do good for evil:

And thus I clothe my naked villainy
With odd old ends stol'n forth of holy writ,
And seem a saint, when most I play the devil. (1.3.333–7)

Whenever Richard wishes to persuade people to clemency for his own purposes, he tries to sound biblical. "Sweet saint, for charity, be not so curst," he urges Anne (1.2.48). Or, "Lady, you know no rules of charity, / Which renders good for bad, blessings for curses" (68–9). In this respect Richard is like George Eliot's (virtuous) Caleb Garth, who, whenever he wished to express awe, "was haunted by a sense of Biblical phraseology, though he could hardly have given a strict quotation" (Eliot 1985: 447).

Misquotation need not be evil, however, nor even facetious. In the possibly Shakespearean scenes of *Edward III*, for instance, a morally improper misquoter (King Edward) is reformed by a morally conscientious misquoter (the Countess of Salisbury). Rather than merely quoting or referring to biblical material, the Countess's misquotations imitate – like Shakespeare's gravedigger – the *manner* of Jesus's powerful replies to the Pharisees. On one occasion, Jesus was asked the trick question, "Is it lawful for us to give tribute unto Caesar, or no?" Instead of giving a yes/no answer, either of which would have landed him in trouble, he gave a brilliantly Socratic reply: "Render ["give," BB] therefore unto Caesar the things which be Caesar's, and unto God the things which be God's." His critics "marvelled at his answer, and held their peace" (Luke 20:22–6). The Countess, tricked by Edward into swearing a morally improper vow to commit adultery with him, replies:

That love you offer me, you cannot give,
For Caesar owes that tribute to his queen.
The love you beg of me I cannot give,
For Sarah owes that duty to her lord. (2.1.251–4)

The Countess evokes, but significantly alters, Jesus's reponse and thus staggers Edward with its unanswerability anew. There is an additional reference to 1 Peter 3:6: "Sara obeyed Abraham [her husband], calling him lord." Edward is left to marvel "whether is her beauty by her words divine / Or are her words sweet chaplains to her beauty?" (278–9). Which is ornamenting which?

The Countess' father speaks of sin "apparell'd . . . in virtuous sentences" (2.1.410). Misquoting is an art – an attractive appareling – that may be abused. In *The Merchant of Venice* Antonio says "what a goodly outside falsehood hath" in response to Shylock's scripture-twisting (1.3.102). Bassanio echoes:

> What damnèd error but some sober brow
> Will bless it and approve it with a text,
> Hiding the grossness with fair ornament? (3.2.77–80)

With such concern about misuse of the Bible's beauties, what did Shakespeare's contemporaries make of writers using biblical misquotation, in plays, for artistic purposes?

The surviving pieces of evidence suggest anxiety. The antiquarian John Aubrey reported that Jonson, late on in life, regretted misusing the Bible (Aubrey 2000: 174). This story was repeated by the anti-theater clergyman Jeremy Collier: "When *Ben Johnson* was in his last Sickness, 'he was often heard to repent of his profaning the Scripture in his Plays, and that with Horrour'" (Jonson 1925–53: 554). There is the nervousness here of someone hoping to make it to heaven. After all, Falstaff calls Hal's misquotations "damnable iteration." It is certainly iteration, or repetition, creating verbal repartee. Is it damnable? In the play the judgement is funny because it is so draconian. And yet, in Shakespeare's world, the hot puritan types whom Falstaff parodies would have found evidence of reprobation. So might anyone of a serious religious inclination. When the play was printed in the First Folio (1623), the most closely quoted biblical words, "wisdom cries out in the streets, and" were omitted by a sensitive editor or compositor (Shaheen 1999: 409–10). A biblical misquotation in *2 Henry IV* was also omitted from the Folio text: "God knows whether those that bawl out the ruins of thy linen shall inherit his kingdom" (2.2.23–4) ("Neither fornicators, nor idolaters, nor adulterers . . . shall inherit the kingdom of God. And such were some of you," 1 Corinthians 6:9–11). Richard II's counterbalancing of scriptural texts was also described differently in the Folio where the 1608 quarto text's "set the word itself / Against the word" became "set the Faith it selfe / Against the Faith" (TLN 2680–1). Possibly this was to suggest that religions are mutually contradictory, but not the texts of the Bible ("the word") itself.

This brings us to censorship. As far as political censorship of the drama went, being *un*blasphemously serious could be more offensive than being blasphemously silly. Hartley Coleridge said of Massinger, one of Shakespeare's successors in writing plays for the Globe, who avoided scriptural profanity:

> But I doubt whether the simple perversion of words found in the Bible to a ludicrous sense, however offensive to taste and decorum, would so much shock a modern hearer, as solemn appeals to Heaven, and discourses on the most awful mysteries, uttered by a painted player, or a boy in petticoats, upon a stage but just vacated by a buffoon or a ribald rake . . . Some people complain of the want of religion in plays; I complain of its superabundance. (Garrett 1991: 166–7)

Censors of the Shakespearean stage agreed. Whereas witty use of biblical sentences was generally licensed, sustained preaching on stage was not. Use of the names God, Jesus Christ, the Holy Ghost, and the Trinity was also forbidden by the Jacobean Act for the Restraint of Abuses in 1606 (Chambers 1923: 338–9). The profane or jesting use of these words was particularly offensive. Otherwise, biblical material in plays raised concern only if it had topical applicability to contemporary politics. This explains the censor's deletion of lines involving a long biblical paraphrase in *2 Henry IV* (Shaheen 1999: 432). History could be flammable.

So could comedy. Jonson's *The Magnetic Lady* offended sufficiently with its "prophane speaches in abuse of Scripture and wholly thinges" to draw the attention of Archbishop Laud and the High Commission (Feil 1958: 109). Here the scriptural misquotations were considered unacceptable because, while obviously humorous, they were used to touch on matters of contemporary religious controversy (Maxwell 2003).

Censors were the first critics of Shakespeare's use of the Bible. They were followed – although not until the eighteenth century – by scholars. It was then that interest in Shakespeare's use of the Bible resurfaced. And the contrary impulses that were mentioned in the introduction to this essay – to correctness and to creativity – were alive and well. This time, however, they did not coexist in the same person. Instead, they provoked a quarrel between a scholar and a poet.

The parties in this paper duel were Alexander Pope and Lewis Theobald. They both produced editions of Shakespeare. Theobald thought Pope had done a bad job. In an appendix to his *Shakespeare Restored* (1726), Theobald listed several places "in which our Poet has an Eye to *Scripture-History*" (144). He wanted to show that

Shakespeare must have had in mind Matthew 5:22 ("whosoever shall say, Thou fool, shall be in danger of hell fire") when writing the first scene of *The Merchant of Venice*. Here Gratiano is referring to people who get a reputation for wisdom and gravity by saying nothing, but "who I'm very sure if they should speak, would almost DAMN those Ears, / Which, hearing them, would call their Brothers Fools" (ibid., 143–4). The presence of the biblical reference mattered. It meant that Pope's edition had neither the best text nor the right gloss when it printed "DAMM" and explained it as "daunt" (ibid.). The scholarly Theobald was aware that Shakespeare's glancing reference to Matthew was nothing like an exact quotation. An allusion at most. But he bolstered his claim by stating, correctly, that there were other places where Shakespeare quoted scriptural texts more closely.

Pope mocked the efforts of "piddling *Tibalds*," as he calls him in the "Epistle to Dr Arbuthnot" (164). Pope's Augustan mock-epic *The Dunciad* (1728, Variorum edition 1729) is at once fascinated and repelled by the bibliographical apparatus of the scholarly edition. Theobald becomes one of the subjects of Pope's own biblical misquotation, the enjoyer of

> Calm Temperance, whose blessings those partake
> Who hunger, and who thirst for scribling sake. (49–50)

A footnote feigns to explain the significance of this misquotation of Matthew 5:6 ("Blessed *are* they which do hunger and thirst after righteousness.") Pope parrots Theobald's argument about Shakespeare's use of the Bible:

> This is an infamous Burlesque on a Text in "Scripture, which shews the Author's delight in Prophaneness," (said *Curl* upon this place.) But 'tis very familiar with *Shakespeare* to allude to Passages of Scripture. Out of a great number I'll select a few, in which he both alludes to, and quotes the very Texts from holy writ. (Pope 1943: 65–6)

Theobald's scholarly justification for his editorial decision is now Pope's spoof absolution of his own profane verse.

Pope's misquotation perhaps comes via Jonson. In *The Staple of News* Jonson reproved those who "hunger and thirst after published pamphlets of news," more printed ephemera unworthy of attention ("To the Readers," 11–12). Jonson's play is, like Pope's poem, a satire on the age of print. But the good writer and his audience are also always hungering and thirsting after more, ideally something rewardingly imaginative. Jonson and his co-authors, Chapman and Marston, had in fact employed the same phrase as a witty refrain in *Eastward Ho!* (2.2.150–5, 3.2.223–5, 3.3.72–6). In the 2003 RSC production of this play in the Swan Theatre, Stratford-upon-Avon, the humorous verbal repetitions (including Touchstone's non-biblical "*Worke upon that now*," 1.1.17) were unmissable. Punctuating the unfolding of the plot, they offered ticklish pleasure at each perceived repetition – although the modern audience probably did not, for the most part, recognize whether they were biblical or not.

   And so the thoroughly unscholarly, thoroughly enjoyable, art of misquotation continues.

Note

1   Unless otherwise indicated, all quotations of the Bible are from the King James Version (1997). Significant variants from earlier Renaissance translations are placed in square brackets and indicated as BB (the Bishops' Bible) and GB (the Geneva Bible).

Works Cited

Aubrey, J. 2000: *Brief Lives*. Ed. J. Buchanan-Brown. London: Penguin.

Baldwin, T. W. 1944: *William Shakspere's Small Latine & Lesse Greeke*, vol. 1. Urbana: University of Illinois Press.

Bible. 1996: *The English Bible on CD-Rom*. Cambridge: Chadwyck-Healey.

Bible. 1997: *The Bible. Authorised King James Version with Apocrypha*. Ed. R. Carroll and S. Prickett. Oxford: Oxford University Press.

Bunyan, J. 1998: *Grace Abounding with other Spiritual Autobiographies*. Ed. John Stachniewski with Anita Pacheco. Oxford: Oxford University Press.

Cervantes, M. 1999: *Don Quixote de la Mancha*. Trans. C. Jarvis. Oxford: Oxford University Press.

Chambers, E. K. 1923: *The Elizabethan Stage*, vol. 4. Oxford: Clarendon Press.

Donne, J. 1953–62: *The Sermons of John Donne*, vol. 4. Ed. G. R. Potter and E. M. Simpson. Berkeley: University of California Press.

Eliot, G. 1985: *Middlemarch*. Ed. W. J. Harvey. London: Penguin.

Eliot, G. 1992: *Adam Bede*. London: David Campbell.

Erasmus, D. 1998: *The Praise of Folly*. Trans. H. H. Hudson. Ware: Wordsworth Editions.

Feil, J. P. 1958: "Dramatic References from the Scudamore Papers." *Shakespeare Survey* 11, 107–16.

Garrett, M. (ed.) 1991: *Massinger: The Critical Heritage*. London: Routledge.

Jonson, B. 1925–53: *The Works of Ben Jonson*, vol. 11. Ed. C. H. Herford and P. and E. Simpson. Oxford: Clarendon Press.

Kipling, R. 1937–9: *The Sussex Edition of the Complete Works in Prose and Verse of Rudyard Kipling*, vol. 30. London: Macmillan.

Maxwell, J. 2003: "Ben Jonson Among the Vicars: Cliché, Ecclesiastical Politics and the Invention of Parish Comedy." *Ben Jonson Journal* 9, 37–68.

Moss, A. 1993: "Commonplace Books." Unpublished conference paper.

Moss, A. 1996: *Printed Commonplace-Books and the Structuring of Renaissance Thought*. Oxford: Clarendon Press.

Norton, D. 2000: *A History of the English Bible as Literature*. Cambridge: Cambridge University Press.

Pasternak Slater, A. 1972: "Variations Within a Source: From Isaiah XXIX to *The Tempest*." *Shakespeare Survey* 25, 125–35.

Pigman, G. W. 1980: "Versions of Imitation in the Renaissance." *Renaissance Quarterly* 33, 1–32.

Pope, A. 1939: *Imitations of Horace*. Ed. John Butt. London: Methuen.

Pope, A. 1943: *The Dunciad*. Ed. James Sutherland. London: Methuen.

Ricks. C. 2002: *Allusion to the Poets*. Oxford: Oxford University Press.

Rumbold, K. 2007: "'All The Men and Women Merely Players': Quoting Shakespeare in the Mid-Eighteenth-Century Novel." Oxford: DPhil thesis.

Selden, J. 1927: *The Table Talk of John Selden*. Ed. Frederick Pollock. London: Quaritch.

Shaheen, N. 1999: *Biblical References in Shakespeare's Plays*. Newark: University of Delaware Press.

Shakespeare, W. 1956: *King Richard II*. Ed. Peter Ure. London: Methuen.

Shakespeare, W. 1968: *The First Folio of Shakespeare*. Prepared by Charlton Hinman. New York: Hamlyn.

Shakespeare, W. 1997: *The Riverside Shakspeare*. Ed. G. B. Evans et al. Boston: Houghton Mifflin.

Steiner, G. 1996: *The Old Testament*. London: Everyman Publishers.

Vickers, B. 1999: *English Renaissance Literary Criticism*. Oxford: Clarendon Press.

Part II

How To Do Things
with History

Editor's Introduction

The New Criticism which dominated literary criticism in the early- to mid-twentieth century kept the literature student within her/his comfort level: the words on the page were approached systematically and linguistically in what T. S. Eliot dubbed the "lemon-squeezer" school of criticism; extra-textual considerations were not essential. But historical issues have always pressed in, and even during the reign of the New Criticism monographs and anthologies of historical material (albeit historical material from literary texts) acknowledged, if only implicitly by their very existence, that texts do not exist in a vacuum and that the dramatic material that we call "literature" was to the Renaissance what we call journalism. I do not invoke this noun pejoratively: by journalism I mean material of daily, contemporary relevance, and often of contemporary urgency, contributing political and social opinions about everything from monarchy, succession, civil war, and republicanism to issues like wards of court, arranged marriages, and the education of women.

Joel Hurstfield's work on the Queen's wards in 1958 and J. W. Lever's monograph on Jacobean drama in 1971 (to take but two examples) paved the way for the investigation of power which was to be the backbone of the new historicism in the 1980s. New historicism thus has some roots in the old. Under both critical systems, students of literature are encouraged to move beyond the self-contained territory of the well-wrought urn and to read texts historically; the differences between old and new are seen in the emphasis accorded the historical reading – whether as background or foreground (new historicism favors the latter) – and the particular historical voices listened to (new historicism ventriloquises the minority voice, the disempowered who cannot speak for themselves). But the continuum or disjunction between old and new is not my focus here. Reading historically is. What does this mean? How does one read a text historically? And do historians – trained to read "historically" – approach this activity differently from literary critics?

There has been something of a turf war in recent years between historians and literary critics. Historians have turned their attention to literary texts (one thinks of the work of Blair Worden, for instance, on Sidney's *Arcadia* or Jonson's tragedies) and literary critics are chronicling historical movements (see David Norbrook (1999) on Milton and republicanism or Diane Purkiss (2006) on the civil war). Historians are finding employment in departments of English literature (but not, I think, vice versa). Are historians implicitly sending literary critics, or at least those who want to work historically, a signal that they are redundant? That, if literary works are redefined as historical texts, the historians, professional readers of history, can do the literature specialist's job so much better?

Perhaps we can all have our historical/literary cake and eat it too. To belong to an academic discipline means to ask certain kinds of questions. Just as textual specialists will ask different questions from feminist critics and the theater historian will ask different questions from the theater director, so historians will ask different kinds of questions from literary critics. And one of the intellectual pleasures of reading literature is probing how many different ways one text can have meaning(s). How many different interrogative approaches are there to this work? Do they yield different answers? Do their answers overlap? Contradict? Complement?

So I asked two critics, a historian and a literature specialist, to confront historical issues. The introductions to their essays show the issues which first caught their attention, the questions they phrased for themselves, and the paths they followed towards solutions. Chris Kyle, a historian, wondered why Shakespeare wrote *Henry VIII*, and why he wrote it in 1611; these questions led him to the world of the Jacobean court favorite. Gillian Woods wondered why Shakespeare used topical political names in *Love's Labour's Lost* and appeared to do nothing with them. Her answers are aesthetic, and reveal as much about the problems of genre as they do about sectarian politics in the 1590s.

Works Cited

Hurstfield, Joel 1958: *The Queen's Wards: Wardship and Marriage under Elizabeth I*. London: Longmans, Green.

Lever, J. W. 1971: *The Tragedy of State*. London: Methuen.

Norbrook, David 1999: *Writing the English Republic: Poetry, Rhetoric and Politics 1627–1660*. Cambridge: Cambridge University Press.

Purkiss, Diane 2006: *The English Civil War: A People's History*. London: Harperpress.

Worden, Blair 1999: "Politics in *Catiline*: Jonson and His Sources." In Martin Butler (ed.) *Re-Presenting Ben Jonson: Text, History, Performance*. Basingstoke: Macmillan, 152–73.

Worden, Blair 2004: "Shakespeare and Politics." In Catherine M. S. Alexander (ed.) *Shakespeare and Politics*. Cambridge: Cambridge University Press, 22–43.

Worden, Blair 2005: "Historians and Poets." *Huntington Library Quarterly* 68, 71–93.

Chapter 4

Henry VIII, or *All is True*: Shakespeare's "Favorite" Play

Chris R. Kyle

Rationale

In recent years, as literary critics have increasingly turned to history to "answer" their questions, so too, albeit more slowly and reluctantly, historians have turned their attentions to literature as a site of cultural reflection and explanation and have begun to regard literature as a species of historical evidence. What can writers of imaginative literature (prose, drama, and poetry) tell us about the era in which they wrote? And what can works of specifically historical fiction tell us about how they and their society viewed their collective past? While literature will never replace eyewitness testimony or "factual" documents as historical sources, it can proffer valuable illumination about both the impetus towards the cultural representation of documentable historical events and about the highly mediated relationships between imaginative and perhaps ideologically motivated reconstruction and "real" events, as well as between fact and fiction, past and present.

Bearing in mind the methodological conundrum that literature poses for the historian, my goal in the essay that follows was not how to provide some controversial or scintillating critical reading of the play, but the historically necessary task of ascertaining precisely where and how *Henry VIII* is rooted in histories. I use the plural because the play is anchored in the constraints and possibilities of the period in which it was written as much as it is in the events of Henry's reign. It is, of course, the history play closest in time to which Shakespeare actually wrote. For all that, critics and historians have (up until the present volume at least) largely avoided it because it neither easily provokes reflections on literary complexity nor provides an accurate account of the actual events of Henry's reign. The play is structured around two dominant themes in early modern England, which although they were, as my essay will demonstrate, of prime importance in early modern England, have excited little interest in the wake of postmodern theories of decentralized and diffuse power relations. These are the role of the monarch as a leader – a figure of power – and the relationship between a monarch and his closest advisors, or favorites.

In writing a play about Henry VIII, Shakespeare chose a monarch whose larger than life persona has been instantly recognizable from 1509 to the present day. Henry may, like his Holbein portrait, bestride the map of English history, but he is curiously understudied: we still lack a satisfactory scholarly biography and Shakespeare's Jacobean play about Henry is one of the least discussed in the canon. The following essay is written from the point of view of a historian seeking to illuminate how Shakespeare and his contemporaries viewed history, and also to how drama as a popular, and arguably privileged, cultural form processed historical events.

Shakespeare started his life as a historian. *Henry VI part 2* (ca. 1590) was probably his first play and this was closely followed by *Henry VI part 3* (1590–1) and *Henry VI part 1* (1590–1) and *Richard III* (1592–3).[1] Well-versed in the historical classics of the day, Raphael Holinshed's *Chronicles*, Edward Hall's *Union of Two Noble . . . Families*, John Foxe's *Acts and Monuments* and quite possibly, John Speed's *The Theatre of the Empire of Great Britain* (1611), of the thirty-nine plays (including *Sir Thomas More*) that Shakespeare wrote or co-authored, twelve were history plays ranging chronologically from his exploration of the Roman Empire in *Julius Caesar* to his last play, *Henry VIII, or All is True*.[2] Engagement with history was one of the hallmarks of Shakespeare's writings; nowhere is this clearer than in his exploration of the events surrounding the Henrician Reformation and the rise and fall of the figure of a favorite.

Let us begin by summarizing the events as Shakespeare represents them. The central themes of the play are the struggle for power among favorites, their relationship to the King, and the emergence of Henry as an assertive, wily king. The theme of the favorite is foregrounded from the very beginning of the play, which opens with Cardinal Wolsey, the King's principal advisor and a man who has risen far above his humble birth status, being subject to excoriating criticism by a member of the old nobility, the Duke of Buckingham. Jealous of Wolsey's influence, the Duke rails against the Machiavellian motivations of the Cardinal. His tirade is ended, however, by his own arrest on charges of treason. All is not well though with the "rule of Wolsey." The people are up in arms at his policy of high taxation, and Henry's wife, Catherine of Aragon, intervenes with the King to explain why the people have revolted. Realizing the damage that this has caused to the image of his sovereignty, Henry pardons those who rebelled and cancels the unjust taxation. Wolsey then lets it be known that it was he who convinced the King to pardon the rebels and also presents an ex-servant of Buckingham to testify that the Duke planned to overthrow the King. Wolsey's next ploy to enhance his standing at Court is to throw a lavish masqued ball for the King and nobles. The visored King dances with Anne Boleyn but is recognized and unmasked by Wolsey. Henry expresses his admiration for the beauty of Anne and the ball proceeds with much gaiety. Wolsey has by now ingratiated himself with the monarch so far that the next section of the play sees Buckingham convicted of treason and executed amidst considerable grieving for his loss by the common people. Furthermore, there is also much concern among the commoners about the rumor that Henry and Queen Catherine will soon be divorced – a situation they believe was engineered by Wolsey because the Spanish emperor, Catherine's nephew, refused to give him the Archbishopric of Coledo. The papal legate, Cardinal Campeius, has arrived in England to present Rome's position in the proceedings. Learned men from all over the Continent arrive to debate the King's divorce in Blackfriars. Henry continues to woo Anne, giving her a title (Marchioness of Pembroke) and a pension (£1,000 per annum). Catherine in the meantime forces a halt to the divorce through her refusal to participate in the debate and appeals for help from the Pope.

Wolsey though, is increasingly under threat from those jealous of his position as the King's favorite and Henry discovers papers which show the immense wealth that Wolsey has accumulated from his position and a letter Wolsey wrote to the Pope asking him to halt the divorce. The tide finally turns and Wolsey is banished to Asher House, forced to surrender his riches and the Great Seal. The King's marriage to Anne is announced to great celebration among the common people, who have now come to accept her position. Catherine is made Princess Dowager and her demotion leads to illness and subsequently death, although not before she has forgiven Wolsey for his role in her downfall. Anne meanwhile has gone into labor and the King's recently returned friend, Archbishop Cranmer, is the subject of a plot against him by the Lords in the Privy Council. Cranmer succeeds in convincing the King that he is his true and loyal servant and Henry gives him a ring to show he has the King's support. The kingdom then has the chance to celebrate the birth of Henry and Anne's as yet unnamed child, a daughter.

When the Privy Council examines Cranmer, Henry secretly watches the proceedings and intervenes to scold the Lords after Cranmer has shown the ring to illustrate he has the King's trust. Cranmer's forgiveness of those who sought to bring him down turns into a day of celebration as he baptizes Henry and Anne's child as Elizabeth and effusively praises her future success as a ruler as well as the greatness of her successors. The future of England rests safe in her hands and that of her successor. The play ends with the epilogue coming onto the stage to urge the audience to cheer.

Before we examine further the details of *Henry VIII*, it is important to contextualize briefly the idea of "history" in Shakespeare. Given this engagement in the field of English history it is a little disconcerting to realize that Shakespeare often wrote history plays which seem to miss the most salient or dramatic episodes of a reign. For example, to the modern eye it seems absurd that William Shakespeare wrote a play about King John without ever mentioning the defining moment of his reign, Magna Carta (1215). But when Shakespeare wrote in ca. 1596–7, Magna Carta was a marginalized document, if not forgotten then certainly buried under a mountain of subsequent legislation in the Jewel Tower. It seems even more amazing that the sheer drama of Runneymede and the clash between the barons and the monarch did not make the stage. But of course, this is to ahistoricize. Magna Carta resurfaces as an important constitutional document only in the seventeenth century when debates between Crown and Parliament brought to the fore constitutional clashes between monarchs and the governing class (Butterfield 1969) – for Barons read MPs and for John read Charles.

We may say that Shakespeare wrote for all time and view him as "always modern" or "speaking through the ages," but we must also attempt to construct meaning and authorial content in the context of Elizabethan and Jacobean England. What can we gain by this historical approach in recovering why Shakespeare wrote *Henry VIII* and what "historical fiction" allows us to say about Henry VIII and early modern England? Of course, we should not discuss the play as if it were meant to be an accurate reflection of history. Dramatic license by its very nature is meant to present the illusion of reality rather than reality itself. Anyone who has endured tedious committee meetings or even perused the *Acts of the Privy Council* will find little to recognize in Shakespeare's lively descriptions of the Henrician Privy Council. However, the dramatic representation of history gives us a starting point to understand how contemporaries viewed the reign of Henry VIII and the contrasts between James I and Henry VIII – the reign in which it was staged and the reign it represents. Shakespeare and Fletcher's *All is True* is both a vision of the future of England post-Henry VIII and the courtio-political state of England at the start of the 1610s. What is at stake here is the precise relationship between two historical moments, not just one.

It was the great whig historian and bardolator, A. F. Pollard, who stated that historically everything was right about the trial of the Duke of Buckingham in *Henry VIII* except the dates (Pollard 1905: 182)! Historians may never tire of telling their students that history is not really about dates, rather themes and concepts, but dates underpin our understanding of those ideas, give them validity, and provide part of the apparatus upon which we hang our explanations. Of course, Pollard as a great admirer of Henry VIII would have found Shakespeare's sympathetic portrayal of the King sufficiently "accurate" to overlook the chronological problems, of which there are many. Buckingham's trial in 1521 is linked with Henry's first meeting with Anne Boleyn which took place in 1527, while Wolsey fell from power in the play after Henry's marriage to Anne when in fact Wolsey was disgraced in 1529 and the marriage took place in 1533. Catherine also is made to miss the birth of Elizabeth in 1533 when she actually died three years later. R. A. Foakes has argued that "the play seems designed to challenge the idea that historical truth can be known" (Foakes 2002: 225). This, however, provides an overly literal reading of the text and perhaps overemphasizes the meaning of the original title, *All is True*. Questions remain as to whether the title simply reflects a juxtaposition with Samuel Rowley's *When You See Me, You Know Me* (1605, 1613) rather than any meaningful statement of historical methodology or intent (see below).

In many ways the content of *Henry VIII* has been subsumed under its fame as "the play" which burnt down the Globe. For it was during one of the first performances of *Henry VIII* that the explosive stage-effects set fire to the theater, resulting in its destruction, but remarkably, no loss of life:

> Now, to let matters of state sleep, I will entertain you at the present with what hath happened this week at the Bank's side. The King's players had a new play, called *All is True*, representing some principal pieces of the reign of Henry VIII, which was set forth with many extraordinary circumstances of Pomp and Majesty, even to the matting of the stage; the Knights of the Order, with their Georges and garters, the Guards with their embroidered coats, and the like: sufficient in truth within a while to make greatness very familiar, if not ridiculous. Now, King Henry making a masque at the Cardinal Wolsey's house, and certain chambers being shot off at his entry, some of the paper, or other stuff, wherewith one of them was stopped, did light the thatch, where being thought at first but an idle smoke, and their eyes more attentive to the show, it kindled inwardly, and ran around like a train, consuming within less than an hour the whole house to the grounds. This was the fatal period of that virtuous fabric; wherein nothing did perish but wood and straw, and a few forsaken cloaks; only one man had his breeches set on fire, that would perhaps of broiled him, if he had not by the benefit of a provident wit put it out by bottle ale. (Smith 1907: 32–3)

That the play was new can also be adduced from the comments of Henry Bluett in early July 1613:

> On Tuesday last [June 29, 1613] there was acted at the Globe a new play called *All is Triewe*, which had been acted not passing 2 or 3 times before. There came many people to see it insomuch that the house was very full, and as the play was almost ended the house was fired with shooting off a chamber which was topped with towe which was blown

up into the thatch of the house and so burned to the ground . . . (Cole 1981: 352)

It is from here that we also get the contention over the title. Both sources refer to it as *All is True*, a title changed by Heminges and Condell in the first folio to *The Famous History of the Life of King Henry the Eight*. This too was the title of the play's subsequent revival in 1628, or at least as it was referred to in its abbreviated form, *King Henry VIII* (British Library, Harleian MS 383: f. 65). Although some modern scholars continue to refer to it as *All is True*, generally it is known by the substitute title given it by Heminges and Condell (Wells 1994: 374–5).

Whatever title we may refer to it by, there is no doubt that it has always been a play which has suffered from critical neglect and occasionally outright hostility. For many Victorian bardolators it was scarcely believable that such a "bad play" could have been written by Shakespeare. "Blame" for the play was placed firmly in the hands of John Fletcher, with whom Shakespeare collaborated in a number of plays (McMullan 2000: 3–8). It was not until Foakes's Arden edition of 1957 that more serious attention was devoted to the play and with Lee Bliss's seminal article in 1975 the revision was well under way. However, despite the fact that recent editors have stressed the unity of the play and argued for its rightful place in the Shakespearean canon, it still remains marginalized among the histories. But if we move the focus of the play to the political system of early modern England then much of the criticism that *Henry VIII* is disjointed and episodic, or as G. K. Hunter put it, "a series of brilliant rhetorical moments linked together without being attached to an overriding purpose," simply falls away (Hunter 1997: 268).

Henry VIII was Shakespeare's only Stuart history play and perhaps more importantly, the closest in time to when he wrote it. It also fitted into a genre of plays at the time which focused on the reign of Henry and the principal characters of the Henrician era. *Thomas Lord Cromwell* (1602, 1613), *Cardinal Wolsey* (1601), *The First Part of Cardinal Wolsey*, and *Sir Thomas More* (both ca. 1590s) were all recent productions or texts. It clearly took a cue from a play we will take up later in this essay, Samuel Rowley's *When You See Me, You Know Me* (1605, 1613).

In *Henry VIII* Shakespeare returned to his earlier focus on the nature of history through the elaboration of a system of politics, a system dominated by the rise and fall of favorites and the exploitation of power and influence.[3] Shakespeare certainly exploited this infatuation with favorites in *Richard II*, *Henry IV*, and *Julius Caesar*. We witness the rise to power of Brutus and Cassius in *Julius Caesar* while, in *Richard II*, the King's decline is accompanied by the increasing dominance of Bolingbroke. In the *Henry IV* plays Falstaff's intimacy with Hal is eroded as the Prince ascends in political power. In Henry VIII though, Shakespeare moves the ascent and/or decline of the favorite to center stage, echoing the exposition of a centralized political system exploited so effectively by Christopher Marlowe in *Edward II* (1591), the anonymous authors of *Thomas of Woodstock* (ca. 1592), and by Ben Jonson in *Sejanus His Fall* (1603) (Worden 1994).[4] In *Henry VIII* the attention of the play shifts through (and revolves around) four figures, Buckingham, Catherine, Wolsey, and Cranmer, charting their trials and respective falls from grace or rise to power. This has led many critics to view the play in the medieval tradition of *de casibus*[5] tragedies and see in it a close relation to Chaucer's Monk's Tale and *A Mirror for Magistrates* (Kermode 1948; Frye 1962; Felperin 1966). However, the *de casibus* tradition cannot account for the fact that Cranmer is not sacrificed on the altar of fortune but ultimately saved by Henry, or for the different causes in the falls of the other three central characters (Halio 1999: 25–6).

As the European early modern state became more complex, powerful intermediaries between the monarch and governing elite(s) came more to the fore, culminating in the careers of George Villiers, Duke of Buckingham in England, Cardinal Richelieu in France, and Count-Duke Olivares in Spain (Bérenger 1974; Elliott and Brockliss 1999). This combined with the new-found interest in Tacitus and his portrayal of Sejanus perhaps led Shakespeare in the direction of thematically centralizing the favorite. This is also evident from both the political situation at the time the play was written in 1612–13 and its subsequent revival in 1628 under the patronage of Buckingham.

Henry VIII appeared on the stage around the time of the death of King James's principal advisor, Robert Cecil, Earl of Salisbury (1612). And after the death of his favorite, James created a political situation dominated by courtly-faction politics between the crypto-Catholic Howards and an increasingly anti-Catholic, anti-Spanish grouping led by the Earls of Pembroke and Southampton, Lord Zouch and George Abbot, Archbishop of Canterbury. As Peter Lake has persuasively argued, there is a clear parallel between the events in the play (the loss of a favorite minister, and factional politics played out around political and religious turmoil) and Jacobean England, ca. 1613 (Lake: forthcoming). Lake also situates the topicality of the play within the context of Court politics about to be dominated by the outcome of a divorce and marriage – the divorce of Frances Howard from the Earl of Essex and her subsequent nuptials with the King's personal favorite, Robert Carr, Earl of Somerset. Giving even greater credence to the contemporaneity of *Henry VIII* is the emergence of the King from under the influence of a dominant political favorite to become more assertive and confident and to take a more hands-on approach to governing the kingdom. This is the characterization that Shakespeare gave Henry and certainly James also appeared to be acting in this fashion. No political favorite had emerged to replace Cecil, the treasury was in commission, and the realm lacked a secretary of state – the King appeared to be taking a more active, assertive role in governing the nation.

The prologue highlights the role of the favorite and exhibits a concentration on the shifting sands of Court power:

> Think ye see
> The very persons of our noble story
> As they were living; think you see them great,
> And followed with the general throng and sweat
> Of thousand friends; then, in a moment, see
> How soon this mightiness meets misery. (1.1.25–30)

Immediately we are thrown into a world in which the "thousand friends" of the favorite slip away, leaving the previously dominant minister (Wolsey as we will see later) in "misery." Buckingham, in the next scene, continues this theme of political power and rails against one of the dominant tropes of a favorite, the patronage and influence wielded by them:

> No man's pie is freed
> From his ambitious finger. (1.1.52–3)

For Buckingham, a member of the old nobility, it is galling to see a humble-born "upstart" influencing all the affairs of the kingdom. Later in act 2, the character of the first gentleman also talks about Wolsey's influence, commenting on how he has organized

Buckingham's son-in-law, the Earl of Surrey, to be in Ireland so that he cannot support Buckingham (2.1.43–4). We see also how Wolsey can force aside those who also strove to have the King's ear:

> And generally, whoever the king favours,
> The cardinal instantly will find employment,
> And far enough from court too. (2.1.47–9)

The idea of a favorite using his influence to remove someone from the Court certainly had contemporary relevance in the early seventeenth century and was one of the charges leveled against Sir Robert Cecil, Earl of Salisbury, by a member of Essex's faction.

> The Earles ambition now beinge discovered, eager of forraigne Employment, and the contrarie faction being now growne strong by the advauncement of Sir Robert Cecill [as secretary of state in July 1596], and the accesse of the Lord Admirall, and his partie; It was by them thought best to make use of his humor, and to sett him forth againe, that in his absence, they might effect those dissigns which in his presence they could not compasse. And knowing Sir Francis Vere was in ward with him, they first wrought him to bee sure unto them selves, yett continuing his outward shew of affection and obligacion to the Earle: then they made him an Instrument with others to perswade and animate the Earle for another forraigne Employment . . .[6]

Furthermore, while Buckingham is executed for his supposed designs on the throne we can also see Shakespeare playing with the idea that Wolsey is usurping the King's position. The opening discussion on the events of the Field of the Cloth of Gold is shown to be all the doing of Wolsey, while Norfolk cynically refers to him as the "king-cardinal." The examination of Wolsey by the Council is worth quoting at length as an example of a favorite overstepping the boundaries of power:

> *Surrey*   First, that without the king's assent or knowledge
> You wrought to be a legate, by which power
> You maimed the jurisdiction of all bishops.
> *Norfolk*   Then that in all you writ to Rome, or else
> To foreign princes, "*Ego et Rex meus*"[7]
> Was still inscribed – in which you brought the king
> To be your servant.

> Suffolk Then, that without the knowledge
>   Either of king or council, when you went
>   Ambassador to the emperor, you made bold
>   To carry into Flanders the Great Seal.
> Surrey   Item, you sent a large commission
>   To Gregory de Cassando to conclude,
>   Without the king's will or the state's allowance,
>   A league between his highness and Ferrara.
> Suffolk That out of mere ambition you have caused
>   Your holy hat to be stamped on the king's coin.
>   (3.2.311–26)

Being a favorite, as Wolsey in the play and Buckingham in the 1620s were to discover, was a dangerous occupation and one which aroused bitter jealousy. Access to the monarch and monopoly of offices were two of the most commented upon attributes of the favorite and we can see how, in act 5, Shakespeare portrays both Cromwell and Cranmer in this fashion:

> Lovell Now, sir, you speak of two
>   The most remarked i'th'kingdom. As for Cromwell,
>   Beside that of the jewel house, is made master
>   O'th'rolls, and the king's secretary; further, sir,
>   Stands in the gap and trade or moe preferments
>   With which the time will load him. Th'archbishop
>   Is the king's hand and tongue, and who dare speak
>   One syllable against him? (5.1.32–9)

And again during the Council proceedings against Cranmer, after the Archbishop has shown he is in the King's favor by revealing he possesses the King's ring, Norfolk cries out:

> Do you think, my lords,
> The king will suffer but the little finger
> Of this man to be vexed? (5.2.139–41)

And Henry himself shows his reliance on Cranmer:

> Well, well, my lords, respect him,
> Take him and use him well; he's worthy of it.

> I will say thus much for him, if a prince
> May be beholding to a subject, I
> Am for his love and service, so to him. (5.2.187–91)

Even greater credence can be given to the idea of *Henry VIII* as a play about favorites when we examine the 1628 revival sponsored by George Villiers, the Duke of Buckingham. As Tom Cogswell and Peter Lake have noted, it was only a fortnight before his assassination on August 23 at Portsmouth (by a naval officer who held a personal grudge against him) that Buckingham attended the performance at the Globe, sitting in the most prominent seat above the stage, and dramatically leaving after act 2, scene 1, when the Henrician Buckingham protests his innocence and how he has been evilly betrayed by his servants (Cogswell and Lake: forthcoming). Buckingham was, in Cogswell and Lake's words, playing the game of the "politics of popularity" in presenting himself to the London audience as a wrongly maligned favorite, innocent of the recent charges (see below) which had been leveled against him.

Buckingham had long been the favorite of Charles I and his father, James I, before him. However, his position as the King's chief minister had been increasingly under attack for his incompetence in managing the war with Spain and France (1625–8), engrossment of offices, and a host of other real or alleged offenses against the nation. That Villiers should so publicly stage and "act" in *Henry VIII* certainly must have required him to weigh carefully the benefits of portraying himself as the successor to the Duke. After all, in the play, Buckingham, despite his protestations of innocence, was executed for treason. Furthermore, some of the allegations made about the corrupt counsel of Wolsey (at this point in the play, still the King's favorite) could easily have been seen by contemporaries as equally applicable to Buckingham:

> If you cannot Bar this access to th' King, never attempt
> Anything on him. For he hath a witchcraft
> Over the King in's tongue. (3.2.16–19)

Given that the criticism of Villiers included his monopolization of patronage and restricting access to the King, his strategy was fraught with danger. This too was the point made by Robert Gell, who reported the incident:

On teusday his Grace was present at [the] acting of K[ing] Hen[ry] 8 at [the] Globe, a play bespoken of purpose by himself; whereat he stayd till [the] Duke of Buckingham was beheaded, [and] then departed. Some say, he should rather have seen [the] fall of Cardinall Woolsey, who was a more lively type of himself, having governed this kingdom 18 yeares, as he hath done 14. (British Library, Harleian MS 383: f. 65)

There seems little doubt that Shakespeare took an important cue from Samuel Rowley's light-hearted piece on Henry VIII, *When You See Me, You Know Me* (1605, reprinted in 1613) (Wilson 1952). Indeed, it has often been speculated that the prologue in *Henry VIII* specifically references Rowley:

> Only they
> That come to hear a merry, bawdy play,
> A noise of targets, or to see a fellow
> In a long motley coat, guarded with yellow,
> Will be deceiv'd: for gentle hearers know
> To rank our chosen truth with such a show
> As fool and fight is . . .

Rowley's "romp" through the reign of Henry VIII focuses on Henry's son, Edward (VI), and the role he played in the development of Protestant England. Spanning the years 1514–44, Rowley's play is certainly wider in chronological scope than Shakespeare's and seems designed more as a pure spectacle of entertainment than any attempt at thematic or historical verisimilitude. Large sections of the play are devoted to the antics of the fools Will Summers and Patch. Even more striking is the scene in which Henry VIII wanders the streets of London in disguise, gets into a fight with Black Will, a robber, and ends up in the Counter gaol.[8] Like Shakespeare's *Henry VIII*, Rowley's can be situated in the political, historical circumstances of its dating – probably first performed in 1604 before its publication the following year. James's recent accession to the throne, bringing with him two sons (Henry and Charles), makes it feasible that Rowley's concentration on Edward as the son of Henry was designed to embody the idea of a male, Protestant heir. We can also see this in the scene in which Archbishop Cranmer, as Edward's tutor, frets about the time the Prince spends playing tennis instead of learning his lessons and the references to his lessons on music and the relationship between animals and humans (Bullough 1962: 440–1). However, we need to be wary in ascribing too much deliberate common ground between the plays. The similarities in language (and character) have been well-described by Karl Elze in the nineteenth century and more recently by other literary scholars (Candido 1983), but as Geoffrey Bullough notes, "many of them were unavoidable in plays drawing upon the same source material" (Bullough 1962: 441).

Where we can see a clear link between the two plays is in the portrayal of Henry in the first half of the play. Here Shakespeare drew upon the "Bluff King Harry" tradition which formed the basis of Rowley's work. The King is a larger than life figure, frivolous, lecherous, and occasionally out of touch with the political world he inhabits. "Ha," Henry is want to opine in both Rowley (1.2.232, 361, for example) and Shakespeare (2.2.62, 65, 71, for example). But Shakespeare's view of Henry VIII is much more subtlely developed, and the King emerges later in the play from under this persona gradually to take the reins of power as a true Renaissance monarch.

Having established then the "ideological purpose" of *Henry VIII*, its textual contextualization so to speak, we must ask: why produce a play so heavily reliant on spectacle and pageantry? The most obvious answer is that the play was designed to capitalize on the celebrations surrounding the recent wedding of Princess Elizabeth to Frederick, Elector Palatine (Foakes 1964: xxx–xxxiv). Despite the fact that this play was not performed during the celebrations (six of Shakespeare's plays were in fact put on by the King's Men; Chambers1930: II, 343), it is possible that it was written with the wedding in mind but perhaps for production on the public stage rather than the royal one. The wedding was the cause of great pageantry and celebration and coming as it did, shortly after the death of the great Protestant hope of England's future, Prince Henry, it assumed even greater significance as Elizabeth was betrothed to one of the Protestant champions of Europe. It is also possible that the emphasis on spectacle reflects not only the marriage of Elizabeth and the funeral of Henry, but the political use of great pomp and ceremony so recently seen in the 1610 investiture of Henry as Prince of Wales (Croft 1992).

Although the connection with Elizabeth's wedding and other royal ceremonies is circumstantial, the spectacle and pageantry embodied in the play fit neatly into the idea of the Renaissance Court. John Margeson has noted how "there are no armed insurrections, no rival armies, no ultimate decisions by means of murder or battle. *Henry VIII* is remarkable for being a history play without corpses" (Margeson 1990: 33). Or at least visible corpses. Gone are the violent political games which characterized the medieval period, replaced by courtly intrigue and faction politics – a violence of rhetoric rather than the sword. The dominant trope here is of a King who is himself secure on the throne but needs to beget a male heir in order to safeguard his dynasty.

The idea of the Renaissance monarch can be seen in the opening scenes when the most lavish and spectacular courtly event of the sixteenth century, the meeting of Francis I and Henry on the Field of the Cloth of Gold, is examined in retrospect. Here and in the later scenes of the banquet and masque at Wolsey's residence, York House, Anne's coronation, and the procession for Elizabeth's christening, the whole ceremonial splendor of the Renaissance Court is presented. This is also apparent from the detailed stage directions which accompany many of these scenes. The coronation in particular is remarkable for its attention to detail and emphasis on stately procession and the rich trappings of the Court. The Lord Chancellor carries both the Great Seal and mace of office; the Lord Mayor of London his mace; the Garter King of Arms, a gilt copper crown and his coat of arms; the Marquis of Dorset, a scepter of gold "and wearing on his head a demi-coronal of gold, and about his neck, a collar of esses" (S-shaped links). Following Dorset, the Dukes of Suffolk and Norfolk sport coronets and collars of esses. Anne herself enters under a canopy wearing pearls and a crown and is followed by the Duchess of Norfolk in a coronal of gold and ladies of the Court, also adorned with gold circlets (4.1.36.5–36.34). This was a procession bedecked in valuable metals. Although the prologue may decry the idea that *Henry VIII* was a "show," it clearly was designed and performed as a spectacle. Not a spectacle of fools as Rowley presented, but a spectacle of Renaissance monarchy.

For the historian, Shakespeare's *Henry VIII* offers a commentary on contemporary politics and the role of faction and courtly intrigue in kingly, conciliar government. It is a view of history through the rise and fall of favorites – a play about a system of politics which uses recent history to explore the spectacle and infighting of Henrician *and* Jacobean political life. Although in many ways, as we have seen above, it is an ahistorical and episodic rendering of Henry's reign replete with untimely deaths and misdating (all is certainly not true), the play captures the essence of Henry's emergence as a dominant Renaissance monarch and the religious transition of the Reformation. Shakespeare did indeed end his life as a historian.

Notes

1 Dating (and all citations in my text) are taken from Greenblatt et al. (1997).
2 It is generally accepted that the play was co-authored by Shakespeare and John Fletcher. However, for convenience I will refer to it throughout as Shakespeare's *Henry VIII*. See Vickers (2002: 333–402).
3 Blair Worden has noted "if there is a single register of the extent and persistence of the early-modern preoccupation with the power of royal favourites it is in the theatre" (Worden 1999: 159). Worden, however, has overstated the case. There are very powerful strands concerning the dominance of the favorite in Parliament and in the burgeoning libel and satire market. See, for example, Cogswell (1990, 2002), Croft (1991), and www.earlystuartlibels. net/htdocs/index.html.
4 On *Sejanus* see Worden (1994).
5 The genre is named after Boccaccio's *De Casibus Virorum Illustrium* (*Examples of Famous Men*), which charted the decline of those who fell from the heights of happiness.
6 Anon. British Library, Egerton MS 2026, f. 32. The belief that the Cecils were deliberately encouraging Essex's absence from the Court for their own purposes was also current at the time these events occurred. The duc de Bouillon said as much to Essex when they met at Dover in April 1596, while Essex himself wrote to Antonio Perez in September 1596 that he was now convinced his enemies were trying to pull precisely this sort of trick (Hammer 1999: 365–6, 370–1). I am very grateful to Paul Hammer for these references.
7 The implication in this phrase is that Wolsey has placed himself before the King.
8 Although there are conscious echoes of Shakespeare's *Henry V* here, the difference in location (the capital city of Henry VIII's

kingdom and his royal residences versus a battlefield encampment)
are too strikingly different to invite close comparison.

Works Cited

Anon., early seventeenth century: "Observacions in the Earle of Essexs
Example. That it is exceeding dangerous to a Favorite to bee long absent
from his Prince." British Library. Egerton MS 2026, f. 32.
Bérenger, Jean 1974: "Pour une enquête européenne: le problème du minis-
tériat au XVIIe siècle." *Annales* 29, 166–92.
Bliss, Lee 1975: "The Wheel of Fortune and the Maiden Phoenix in
Shakespeare's *King Henry the Eighth*." *English Literary History* 42,
1–25.
Boccaccio, Giovanni 1494: *De Casibus Virorum Illustrium*. London.
Budra, Paul 2000: *A Mirror for Magistrates and the De Casibus Tradition*.
Toronto: University of Toronto Press.
Bullough, Geoffrey 1962: *Narrative and Dramatic Sources of Shakespeare*,
vol. 4. London: Routledge and Kegan Paul.
Butterfield, Herbert 1969: *Magna Carta in the Historiography of the Sixteenth
and Seventeenth Centuries*. Reading: University of Reading Press.
Candido, Joseph 1983: "Fashioning Henry VIII: What Shakespeare
Saw in *When You See Me, You Know Me*." *Cahiers Elisabéthains* 23,
47–59.
Chambers, E. K. 1930: *William Shakespeare: A Study of Facts and Problems*,
2 vols. Oxford: Clarendon Press.
Cogswell, Tom 1990: "The Politics of Propaganda: Charles I and the People
in the 1620s." *Journal of British Studies* 29, 187–215.
Cogswell, Tom 2002: "The People's Love: The Duke of Buckingham and
Popularity." In Tom Cogswell, Richard Cust, and Peter Lake (eds.) *Politics,
Religion and Popularity in Early Stuart Britain*. Cambridge: Cambridge
University Press, 211–34.
Cogswell, Tom and Lake, Peter (forthcoming): " 'Full of State and Woe':
Shakespeare, the Duke of Buckingham and the 'Politics of Popularity' in
the 1620s."
Cole, Maija Jansson 1981: "A New Account of the Burning of the Globe."
Shakespeare Quarterly 32, 352.
Croft, Pauline 1991: "The Reputation of Robert Cecil: Libels, Popular
Opinion and Popular Awareness in the Early Seventeenth Century."
Transactions of the Royal Historical Society 6th ser. 1, 43–69.
Croft, Pauline 1992: "The Parliamentary Installation of Henry, Prince of
Wales." *Historical Research* 65, 177–93.

Early Stuart Libels: www.earlystuartlibels.net/htdocs/index.html.

Elliott, J. H. and Brockliss, L. W. B. (eds.) 1999: *The World of the Favourite*. New Haven: Yale University Press.

Felperin, Howard 1966: "Shakespeare's *Henry VIII* as Myth." *Studies in English Literature* 6, 225–76.

Foakes, R. A. (ed.) 1964: *King Henry VIII*. London: Methuen.

Foakes, R. A. 2002: "Shakespeare's Other Historical Plays." In Michael Hattaway (ed.) *The Cambridge Companion to Shakespeare's History Plays*. Cambridge: Cambridge University Press, 214–28.

Foxe, John 1563: *Acts and Monuments*. London.

Frye, Northrop 1962: "The Tragedies of Nature and Fortune." In B. W. Jackson (ed.) *Stratford Papers on Shakespeare 1961*. Toronto: University of Toronto Press, 38–55.

Greenblatt, Stephen, Cohen, Walter, Howard, Jean E., and Maus, Katherine Eisaman (eds.) 1997: *The Norton Shakespeare*. New York: Norton.

Halio, John (ed.) 1999: *King Henry VIII*. In *The Oxford Shakespeare*. Oxford: Oxford University Press.

Hall, Edward 1548: *The Union of Two Noble and Illustre Families of Lancaster and York . . .* London.

Hammer, Paul E. J. 1999: *The Polarisation of Elizabethan Politics: The Political Career of Robert Devereux, 2nd Earl of Essex, 1585–1597*. Cambridge: Cambridge University Press.

Holinshed, Raphael 1587: *The Third Volume of Chronicles . . .* London.

Hunter, G. K. 1997: *English Drama 1586–1642: The Age of Shakespeare*. Oxford: Clarendon Press.

Kermode, Frank 1948: "What is Shakespeare's *Henry VIII* About?" *Durham University Journal* new ser. 9, 48–55.

Lake, Peter (forthcoming): *Shakespeare's Elizabeth*.

McMullan, Gordon (ed.) 2000: *King Henry VIII*. London: Thomas Nelson.

Margeson, John (ed.) 1990: *King Henry VIII*. Cambridge: Cambridge University Press.

Pollard, A. F. 1905: *Henry VIII*. London: Longmans.

Smith, Logan Pearsall (ed.) 1907: *The Life and Letters of Sir Henry Wootton*, 2 vols. Oxford: Clarendon Press.

Speed, John 1611: *The Theatre of the Empire of Great Britain*, 2 vols. London.

Vickers, Brian 2002: *Shakespeare, Co-Author*. Oxford: Oxford University Press.

Wells, Stanley 1994: *Shakespeare: A Dramatic Life*. London: Sinclair-Stevenson.

Wilson, F. P. (ed.) 1952: Samuel Rowley, *When You See Me, You Know Me*. Oxford: Oxford University Press.

Worden, Blair 1994: "Ben Jonson among the Historians." In Peter Lake and Kevin Sharpe (eds.) *Culture and Politics in Early Stuart England*. Basingstoke: Macmillan, 67–89.

Worden, Blair 1999: "Favourites on the English Stage." In J. H. Elliott and L. W. B. Brockliss (eds.) *The World of the Favourite*. New Haven: Yale University Press, 159–83.

Chapter 5

Catholicism and Conversion in *Love's Labour's Lost*

Gillian Woods

Rationale

Very little labour has been lost on (or rather applied to) the question of the literary and dramatic significance of the topical names in *Love's Labour's Lost*. Information about the French contemporary counterparts to the male dramatis personae is the kind of dry historical detail it is tempting to skim over when we come across it in introductions to the play. But, as Paul Voss has shown, for Elizabethan audiences these onomastic allusions to the French wars of religion were alive with controversies about England's spiritual and political security. In particular, the "real-life" Navarre (Henri IV of France, King of Navarre) was both inescapably famous and troublingly shifty since this once-celebrated Protestant war hero had converted to Catholicism. Modern viewers, readers, and critics overlook a question that Elizabethan audiences could not have failed to wonder at: what are these names doing in a comedy? And more specifically, what are they doing in *this* comedy?

In order to think about this question we need to explore not just historical context but also literary content, thinking broadly about the various different themes and aspects of the drama. Like most literary texts, *Love's Labour's Lost* makes idiosyncratic use of conventions. In other early comedies we might be suspicious of the sincerity of a character's "development" or the long-term prospects for a romantic union; *Love's Labour's Lost* makes a plot feature of such tensions and advertises its generic awkwardness in its title. It is also intensely linguistically self-conscious. I address the fact that the meaning of the oddly topical names takes shape in the interactions between all these dramaturgical quirks, and is not a separate or dominating message.

My study is underpinned by another question about a broader literary oddity: what is the function of Catholicism in post-Reformation texts? In recent years critics have become increasingly sensitive to the importance of theology (or theologies). We have learnt about the heterogeneity of the Elizabethan Settlement, of the fluidity of confessional categories, and of the paradoxically nostalgic/antipathetic attitudes to the old faith. Yet in looking at names I am aware that when scholars "name" Catholic or Protestant features within a text, description can (implicitly or explicitly) translate as a declaration of a text's final meaning, as if denominational detail "answers" or explains a play. This is not how we experience drama. Thus I reverse the emphasis of much theologically inflected criticism by focusing not on the religious motivations behind literary texts, but on the literary motivations for the use of a religious semiotic. This is not to invalidate other methodologies, but to contribute to discussion by taking a new angle that helps us to see what has fallen into shadow. All criticism is inevitably partial (i.e., both non-comprehensive and personally biased), but in asking questions that highlight the limitations of our current paradigm we make gains with our losses. In the case of *Love's Labour's Lost* I think that in retrieving the resonance that is lost to us as twenty-first-century audiences we can better understand the loss that structures the play.

Navarre of *Love's Labour's Lost* shares his name with a man who for a short period prior to 1593 was "the most famous and beloved non-English person of the time" (Voss 2001: 103). Henri IV of France, King of Navarre had been fighting the Protestant cause in the French religious wars, to great acclaim in England. However, in July 1593 the name "Navarre" gained new Catholic significance when Henri abjured Protestantism and converted to Catholicism in a move which if not spiritually insincere was certainly politically expedient. Catholic signifiers elsewhere in Shakespeare's plays are imbued not just with the anti-Catholic associations of the Elizabethan present, but also the Catholic meaning accrued over many centuries prior to Reformation (Woods 2006). The "Navarre" of *Love's Labour's Lost* (Ferdinand rather than Henri) alludes to a Catholic signifier that has, peculiarly, a Protestant history. Furthermore, Shakespeare's Navarre is a representation that apparently does little to represent its topical referent.

For the English populace throughout the 1590s, anxiety about Protestant Navarre's martial success and Catholic Navarre's spiritual health was felt in a range of different ways. Morning and evening prayers featured petitions to God for the success of the Protestant King in winning his country from the Catholic League (Clay 1847: 647–51), the English Government sent money to assist this operation, and families sent loved ones as soldiers to protect the Protestant faith generally and England specifically.[1] The proximity of France rendered it a potential station for Catholic invasion should the Catholic League defeat Navarre. Furthermore, English Protestants could respond emotionally and spiritually to a martial hero whose endeavors looked set to confirm their view that the rest of the world would join England in a providential and reformed future. In order to secure victory in Paris, the man who was once famed for his Protestantism converted to the infamous Roman Catholic religion. Gabriel Harvey (1593: D3r) cited "Navarre *wooes* Roome" as an example of how 1593 was a "wonderfull" (i.e., astonishing) year.

In the past, the (few) critics who have demonstrated the topical nature of certain names in *Love's Labour's Lost* have not considered Henri of Navarre's conversion as central to the contemporary connotations (see Richmond 1978–9; Tricomi 1979; Lamb 1985; Voss 2001; Asquith 2003). Even Paul Voss, whose fascinating and detailed analysis provides the foundation for this essay, speculates that the "newly corrected and augmented" extant text has been supplemented by an oath-breaking story missing from an original play written prior to Henri of Navarre's 1593 denominational change.[2] It seems incredible to Voss that Shakespeare, writing before 1593, could coincidentally anticipate an act of oath-breaking; but he thinks it equally unlikely that the playwright would choose to write a play with a central character called Navarre after the topical counterpart's maligned conversion (Voss 2001: 138). Given the centrality of the theatrical Navarre's oath-breaking to an otherwise plotless play, I am unconvinced by this argument. It is my proposal that the topical constellation of names is introduced precisely *because* of the anxiety generated by the conversion and the violent struggles to succeed to the French throne. Voss's argument is influenced by his awareness of the disappearance of one kind of textual representation of Navarre: the news pamphlets celebrating the soldier king cease to be published at the same time that Navarre ceases to be a Protestant, even though the wars were to rage on until 1598. But *Love's Labour's Lost* is not a eulogistic piece of journalism and so we should not think it subject to the same imperatives as the popular Protestant press. Instead, it is important to situate Shakespeare's Navarre in this newly created representational void. The absence of the previously ubiquitous Navarre-focused news quartos indicates how this particular conversion confounded the familiar strategies of representing the French king. Recent criticism has shown how Spenser uses the Burbon episode in *The Faerie Queene* to foreground the moral difficulties attendant on Elizabeth's continued support of the apostate king (Gallagher 1991; Gregory 2000; Prescott 2001), and so it is not implausible that Shakespeare should introduce onomastic tension into his text by writing about a "Navarre" after Henri of Navarre's conversion. This essay will consider the ways in which Shakespeare associates these denominationally difficult onomastics with linguistic slippage, and how the French civil war context influences the structure and generic rupture of *Love's Labour's Lost*.

Ironic Onomastics

The names of the main male characters in *Love's Labour's Lost* are insistently topical. Not only does this comedy feature a king called Navarre, but that contemporary frame of reference is highlighted and widened by the presence of Berowne (alluding to Armand de Gontant, Marshall Biron, a loyal adherent of Navarre), Longaville (Henry of Orleans, the Duke of Longueville, a loyalist Catholic who came to fight against the League with Navarre) (Voss 2001: 135), Dumaine (Charles of Lorraine, the Duke of Mayenne, a well-known Catholic opponent until 1595),[3] and Boyet (Boyset, leader of the Huguenot forces). Even Moth and Marcade have their topical counterparts (la Mothe, the French governor of Gravelines, and the Catholic Duke of Mercouer, respectively) (Woudhuysen 1998: 67–8, 344–5; Voss 2001:

125). Armado may also allude to the Spanish support of the Catholic League in France. Numerous news quartos celebrating Navarre's martial and spiritual heroism kept the Elizabethan public aware of this context. Voss points out that given the accessibility and proliferation of information on current events in France, audiences in the 1590s were more likely to be familiar with the topicality of the reference in *Love's Labour's Lost* and its deviations from news stories, than they would have been with classical or chronicle sources to other plays (Voss 2001: 129–30; see also Woudhuysen 1998: 67–8, 344–5).

The representation of characters who share names with famous living people in *Love's Labour's Lost* is unique in the Shakespeare canon and unusual in other Renaissance drama. Of course, sixteenth-century productions, like twenty-first-century drama, often carried contemporary allusions. Plays might hide contemporary references beneath a character name, but they simultaneously lampooned real people with devastatingly accurate representations. (Middleton famously got into trouble with the Privy Council for the similarity between the former Spanish Ambassador, Gondomar, and the character of the Black Knight in *A Game at Chess*.) *Love's Labour's Lost* inverts this analogical process. The names of the chief male protagonists are glaringly topical to a 1590s audience and yet their contemporary associations with sectarian warfare and conversion are transmuted into romantic comedy's battle of the sexes and the failure to keep an over-the-top oath of scholarly asceticism. Shakespeare uses specifically famous names only to avoid historical detail. Instead of engaging in character assassinations, he represents his four lords as markedly similar, though their real-life counterparts differed in age, religion, and political opinion (Voss 2001: 135). For all that an Elizabethan audience might have found it satisfying to see the great soldier king and notorious womaniser reduced to a foolish lover who is repeatedly humiliated, the play invites the audience to delight in his mistakes.[4] Albert H. Tricomi describes Shakespeare's representation of the lords as an "idealization" that "charmingly refuses to acknowledge [contemporary sectarian issues] in any but a metaphoric way" (Tricomi 1979: 31). Certainly, this was a period of Reformation, of re-forming old signs in a way that purged them of their Catholic meaning. (For example, papist holy water stoups were translated into secular wash troughs, and sanctus and sacring bells were hung on sheep and cows; see Duffy 1992: 586.) But to see Shakespeare as another reformer, stripping Navarre of Catholic meaning and representing him as a neutrally comic figure is to elide the more problematic aspects of the play: its strange ending, the perpetual linguistic slippage, and most importantly, the fact that irony and idealization make poor bedfellows.

Kenneth Burke (1969: 503) tells us that another word for irony is dialectic. The ironic naming system in *Love's Labour's Lost* means that the play does not simply move away from the disturbingly topical, but rather ensures that the audience's understanding oscillates between the contemporary and the comic. To understand the play only in terms of escapism is to deny the way irony continually returns the audience to that from which they are trying to escape. For instance, the audience's attitude to the theatrical Navarre's oath-breaking is the inverse of what we would expect to be the popular Protestant attitude to the real Navarre's conversion. The dramatized oath has undertones of ascetic Catholicism (pithily summed up by Berowne as "Not to see ladies, study, fast, not sleep"; 1.1.48) and dramatic expectation means the audience *wants* Navarre to break it. Prior to his conversion not only was Henri reputed to be "a true fulfiller of his word and promise" in general terms (Anon. 1590c: B1v), but his reformed faith was also figured in terms of an "oath" and a "promise." The Huguenot Du Bartas (1590: B2v) celebrated Henri's Protestant allegiance thus:

> [The world d]id never' see a prince religiouslie more loath
> To shake in any sort his honnor-binding oath.
> Offer unto my Lord the crowne of *Germanie*
> The diadem of *Spaine*, the Turks *Grand-Signorie*:
> Yea make him *Monarch* of the world (by guile)
> Hee'l spurne al scepters, fore his faith defile.

Even some French Catholics, who prayed for a heartfelt conversion on the part of their king, understood his Protestantism as "the expresse commandement that his mother the Q. of Navarre at her decease gave and lefte unto him, as it were a testamentarie legacie" and cautioned against a conversion based on expediency using language which related religion to promises: "Banish the ceremonies of our vows in matters of greatest co[n]science, as religion, and ye shall ere ye be aware banish a great part of all religions" (Anon. 1591a: B3r, B3v). Thus the dramatized Navarre's promise also alludes to a spiritually and politically important oath that Protestant Elizabethans did not want or expect the real Navarre to break. Frightening sectarian instability is transformed into a genre intended to delight. The fact that poems from the play appeared in Elizabethan anthologies simply as love poems indicates how beguiling this aspect of the drama is (see Anon. 1599, *The Passionate Pilgrim*; Anon. 1600a, *Belvedere*; Anon. 1600b, *England's Helicon*; Anon. 1600c, *England's Parnassus*). Nevertheless, the topical is not so easily transmuted, especially since Shakespeare lays bare the problems of representation, signification, and escapism. Notably, the lords twice fail to live out their escapist fantasies: sexual desire disrupts their chaste scholarly program, and death and female skepticism delay their attempt to validate that desire as a romantic happy ending.[5]

While France's ongoing wars of religion receive no mention in the play, martial imagery is used to describe the lords' attempts at scholarly exclusion and romance, and the ladies' defense against courtship:

> Therefore, brave conquerors – for so you are,
> That war against your own affections
> And the huge army of the world's desires –
> Our late edict shall strongly stand in force. (1.1.8–11)

King ... And, soldiers, to the field!
Berowne Advance your standards and upon them, lords!
Pell-mell, down with them! But be first advised
In conflict that you get the sun of them. (4.3.340–3)

> Prepare, madam, prepare!
> Arm, wenches, arm! Encounters mounted are
> Against your peace. Love doth approach disguised,
> Armed in arguments: you'll be surprised.
> Muster your wits, stand in your own defence,
> Or hide your heads like cowards and fly hence. (5.2.81–6)[6]

The military theme from the news quartos which stop being printed with Henri's conversion gets displaced into the alternative textual space of a play; it is further distanced by its metaphoric status in the drama. Combined with the topical names in the play the military metaphors serve to remind the audience of what is *not* being represented. If the comic comments on the topical names as an idealistic expression of how life can be, then the topical puts pressure on the comic, making clear its inadequacy to report on all aspects of life.

Theological Mutability and Linguistic Slippage

If this revision of the convert King into a comic oath-breaker is deliberately unsettling, then it is an appropriate response to the nature of
conversion. Conversion destabilizes meaning. While it may have been
something of a fiction, Elizabethans were taught that Roman Catholicism and Protestantism were distinct and oppositional confessional
categories. Michael Questier tells us:

> When an individual converted to Rome, he demonstrated the existence
> of a hidden fund of latent popery about which Protestants had every
> reason to be anxious. Paradoxically, most conversions from Rome also
> emphasized the instability of the religious settlement since they dressed
> up the providential Protestant home-coming in the language of escape
> from almost certain spiritual death and the alluring attractiveness to the
> majority of idolatry and superstition. Virtually all conversions, therefore,
> were a visible index of man's general tendency to stagger in religion.
> (Questier 1996: 8)

The conversion of Henri Navarre enacted a particularly disruptive
change in meaning. Elizabethans primarily knew him as a Protestant,
one whose confessional allegiance had been defined by his martial
opposition to Catholicism. One news pamphlet declared:

> The Lord . . . hath preserved this most worthy Prince, for the better
> enlarging of his Gospell, to be a worthy follower of our most famous
> King, King Henry the eight, in [the] pulling down of Papistry, and all
> their divelish devises. (Anon. 1590b: B2v)

This pamphlet's representation of the "worthy Prince" elides national
and temporal boundaries: at one with the past anti-Catholic victories
of "our . . . King Henry the eight," Navarre's current martial struggles
work to bring about the reformed future ordained by "The Lord."
The epistemological glue that seals this typological image is Navarre's
active Protestantism. Reformed Elizabethans had equated Navarre's
religion with fidelity itself. In 1590, a pamphlet containing *The oration
and declaration of the French king* celebrated Navarre's fidelity to his
faith in the face of temptations to recant and keep the support of the
Catholic nobles.[7] His constancy and his Protestantism are shown to
be symbiotic. He asserted that "neyther this Crowne, nor the Empire

of all the whole earth were able to make me chaunge the Religion wherein I have bene brought uppe" and that "I am resolved . . . not to varie nor chaunge in any wise my religion" (Anon. 1590d: AIIIr and AIIv). But change and vary he does, and it is in these terms that he comes to be understood. Navarre's conversion marks the climactic conclusion of a work that sets out to illustrate what a "slipperie and uncertaine estate" the realm of France is:

> Thus this noble and renowned Monarke, the hope (as it were) of al that favored Gods truth, whom God had beautified with so many excellent graces and notable vertues, as courage, wisedom, zeale, and constancy in so many apparant dangers . . . and to the admiration and wonderment of all men continually protected him in despight of all those who sought his ruine and overthrow, is another argument of the mutabilitie and interchangeable estate of all things in the world. (Anon. 1597: unsigned address "To the Reader," N3v)

"Navarre" represented a person who had changed and a person who was change itself. His conversion to Catholicism denied stability of representation and identification.

In the modern world a famous figure's divergence from their celebrated representational persona is exposed and analyzed in graphic detail in the media. By these standards Elizabethan reactions to Henri's conversion seem curiously muted. Modern newspapers detail every aspect of the ideological hypocrisy displayed by politicians. After 1593, however, Elizabethan news pamphlets simply stop being printed about Navarre. While a work detailing the fraught history of France might utilize Navarre's conversion to make a broader point about mutability, there are apparently no works that focus on Navarre's conversion to a religion that in orthodox terms has to be regarded as "false and superstitious" (Anon. 1597: N3v). This does not suggest that the conversion was unremarkable in the sense of being unworthy of mention, but rather that it was difficult for the English news pamphlet writers to pass remark on such an event because it caused representational crisis. While it would of course have been politically dangerous to criticize a king who continued to receive military aid from Elizabeth, the fact that we do not find post-1593 pamphlets that celebrate Navarre's wartime exploits, but which simply avoid religious themes, indicates how important sectarianism was to representation and identification.

I think it is significant, then, that Shakespeare should put his fractured and ironic representation of the unrepresented convert in a play where language and signs constantly mislead. We can understand *Love's Labour's Lost* as being influenced by sectarian reversal and semiotic difficulty. As the play opens the audience are pointedly made aware of the lords' topical names: the scene centers on their subscribing their names to an oath already "passed" (1.1.19, 49). As Katherine Maus points out, this focus on oaths and contracts means that the play opens with "performative" language: "This kind of language is not referential; it performs actions rather than describe or point to an extralinguistic reality. As such, performative utterances seem to close the gap between signifier and signified, *verba* and *res*, word and world" (Maus 1991: 209). Navarre looks on his and his lords' names as epistemological anchors:

> Your oaths are passed, and now subscribe your names,
> That his own hand may strike his honour down
> That violates the smallest branch herein. (1.1.19–21)

That Navarre should view names as a guarantor of an oath would have been ironic to an Elizabethan audience, since the news pamphlets' representations of the king as resolute in character and an exemplar of "constancie" were now notable by their absence (Anon. 1590d: AIIv; Anon. 1591b: A4v). Navarre's own name, rather than sealing the deal, breaks it, and supplements the comic expectation that the oath will be broken.

Words relating to oath-breaking saturate the play: forms of the verb *forswear* appear twenty times and forms of *perjury* appear thirteen times. Yet such words are in concert with the antithetical word *faith* which (with its cognates) appears seventeen times in the text. "Faith" is popular as an exclamation in *Love's Labour's Lost* (4.3.8; 4.3.22; 5.2.280; 5.2.577; 5.2.671); its meaning is poised liminally between interjection (an almost meaningless verbal tic) and asseveration (an emphatically meaningful assertion). "Faith" is repeatedly used to describe the lords' original oath of scholarly asceticism:

> If I break faith, this word shall speak for me:
> I am forsworn "on mere necessity." (1.1.151–2)

> Ah, never faith could hold, if not to beauty vowed.
> Though to myself forsworn, to thee I'll faithful prove. (4.2.106–7)

You would for paradise break faith and troth;
And Jove for your love would infringe an oath.

What will Berowne say when that he shall hear
Faith infringed which such zeal did swear? (4.3.140–3)

. . . good Berowne, now prove
Our loving lawful and our faith not torn. (4.3.280–1)

In each instance faith is thought of as either broken or potentially broken. As well as referring to a linguistic act (a promise), "faith" also has obvious religious connotations so that the historical Navarre's switching (and breaking) of his celebrated Protestant faith is kept in the audience's minds. Prior to his conversion Henri's faith (in both senses) was celebrated as absolute: "For what Prince was there ever more carefull of his faith then the King?" (Anon. 1591b: B3v). Even Catholics who hoped for the day when their king would share their faith were concerned that a sudden conversion would be "very unseemely" to Navarre's reputation of "inviolable faith . . . to his constancie" (Anon. 1591b: A4v). Given that these fears were expressed prior to Navarre's convenient conversion it seems likely that they were *felt* after it. Gabriel Harvey annotated his copy of Du Bartas's *A Canticle of Victorie* (cited earlier) which acclaims Henri's heroism and steadfast Protestant allegiance:

An vnquam fides Heroica frigeat? Quicquid non est ex fide, est peccatum. Nisi quatenus Sol interdum latet; aut etiam patitur Eclypsin. (Cited in Relle 1972: 414)

What if heroic virtue cools? Whatever is not of faith is a sin, lest the sun hide or even suffer eclipse. (Translated by Prescott 2001: 206)

Shakespeare's repeated references to broken faith would seem to support an understanding of the play as influenced by topical conversion. In particular it relates religion to semiotics, a sectarian shift to an individual's fractured word, and a more general sense of ruptured linguistics. The theatrical Navarre's "torn faith" is multiplied throughout the linguistics of the play. Much of the dialogue of the play is concerned with semantic slippage: the many puns split signifiers into different signifieds and its synonyms split signifieds into multiple signifiers. It is not just the initial performative language that is subject to fracture.

Contemporary English "hard word" dictionaries defined the word "apostate" as "a backslider" (Coote 1596: L2r; Cawdry 1604: B5r). No longer following Henry VIII, Navarre was now celebrating a religion prior to that king's reforms. Shakespeare chooses to use the name of this famous backslider in a play that, as Patricia Parker tells us, puts "relentless emphasis on the inversion of order and sequence, on the reversal of beginning and end, front and back, prior and 'posterior'" (Parker 1993: 443–4). There are even toponymous hints about the issue of rebounding apostasy. Berowne asks Rosaline, "Did not I dance with you in Brabant once?" (2.1.114), but the reference is doubled back as Rosaline simply repeats it word for word. Brabant was a core province in the Low Countries that, although officially converted to the Dutch Reformed Church, in large part apostasized to Catholicism in the 1580s and 1590s. Onomastic allusions to contemporary theological (backwards) slippage form another important strand in this play's interrogation of signs. At one point the Princess punningly relates aesthetic, semantic, and theological value. When the tongue-tied Forester unintentionally denies the Princess's beauty she gives him money:

> *Princess*   Fair payment for foul words is more than due.
> *Forester*   Nothing but fair is that which you inherit.
> *Princess*   See, see, my beauty will be saved by merit!
>   O heresy in fair, fit for these days! (4.1.19–22)

Being "saved by merit" alludes to the Catholic doctrine of saving one's soul by good works (or by literal or metaphorical monetary purchase, as the reformers understood this dogma). In pointing out that this is "heresy in fair, fit for these days" the Princess also underlines the change in value of theological signs. The detail of "these days" paradoxically could be specific (for example, referencing the newly Catholic Court of Navarre) or entirely general (heresy can exist wherever there is orthodoxy), but in either case the audience is reminded of a relativity of value that extends beyond the theatrically pleasing pun to the nature of divine truth.[8]

Shakespeare's linking of linguistic slippage with a character called Navarre stands in contrast to the way Spenser writes about Navarre in *The Faerie Queene*. Spenser allegorizes the French king as a character called Burbon. It seems that Protestants (and some Catholics, including the Pope) were suspicious of the integrity of Navarre's newfound

Catholic faith. The writer of *The Mutable and wavering estate of France* describes "continual *practising* to draw the king to the liking of Poperie: wherein there was such paines taken, and so farre humane *pollicie* prevailed," resulting in "*apparant* inclination to Poperie" (Anon. 1597: N3r–N3v; my emphasis). Elizabeth herself implies to Navarre that he has done "ill that good may come of it" (Harrison 1968: 225). Spenser seems to reflect such opinions when he describes Burbon's forsaking of his shield (read "conversion") as merely an act of temporizing. Spenser's focus is on the ethical tension this causes. Artegall calls temporizing "forgerie" and declares it wrong "Under one hood to shadow faces twaine. / Knights ought be true, and truth is one in all" (*FQ* 5.11.55, 56.7–8). However, just as Elizabeth continued to send Navarre martial support after what she calls an "iniquitous" act (Harrison 1968: 225),[9] so too does Artegall aid Burbon. It is character motivation and morals that are primarily called into question.

By contrast, Shakespeare registers these problems in linguistic terms. Rather than present us with one character who is shifty and untrustworthy, he places that character in a semantic context that is full of slippage. Whereas Burbon's crime is his alone, Shakespeare quadruples Navarre's perjury, making the three other lords simultaneously break their oaths with him.

The lords are casual about their perjury, betraying an attitude to language that prioritizes the surface meaning of words at the expense of their referents. Berowne believes he can satisfy the lords' request to "cheat" perjury by a process of deferral along a chain of signifiers (4.3.284). He simply reclassifies women's eyes as "the books, the arts, the academes" (4.3.326) and thus relies on signifiers that seem convenient rather than have any actual fidelity to meaning. Berowne claims "It is religion to be thus forsworn" (4.3.337). The juxtaposition of the contrary words "religion" and "forsworn" evidences Berowne's rhetorical skill while simultaneously referring to Henri of Navarre's religious forswearing. Berowne predicts perjury in the first scene: "Necessity will make us all forsworn" (1.1.147). Spenser's Burbon justifies his infidelity in the same terms:

> To temporize is not from truth to swerve,
> Ne for advantage terme to entertaine,
> When as necessitie doth it constraine. (*FQ* 5.11.56.3–5)

This might reflect English Protestants' best hope, that Henri Navarre's apostasy was an act of temporizing, a hiding behind the signifier of Catholic conversion while biding time until he could display his true, Protestant faith. However, Shakespeare shows this attitude to language to be flawed. While the play celebrates the transformative power of language, allowing its audience to revel in comic puns, the ladies put pressure on the lords' reliance on signifiers. They switch love tokens and wear masks, deceiving the men with external signs and causing them to swear love to the wrong partner. This game exposes the problems of semantic temporizing, making the lords look foolish and indicating how they have "wooed but the sign of she" (5.2.469).

Furthermore, the ironically topical naming of the lords comments on their attitude to language. Berowne's casual (if virtuoso) rhetoric is introduced by his disregard for the significance of naming:

> These earthly godfathers of heaven's lights,
> That give a name to every fixed star,
> Have no more profit of their shining nights
> Than those that walk and wot not what they are.
> Too much to know is to know naught but fame,
> And every godfather can give a name. (1.1.88–93)

Astronomers are "earthly godfathers" because they name stars, an act that does not impress Berowne. In describing knowledge as "fame" Berowne does not simply reject scholarship as vanity, but also suggests that knowledge is merely the knowledge of the names things have been given rather than of the things themselves. It is this belief in the unsurpassable distance between *verbum* and *res* which allows Berowne casually to reclassify women's eyes as books. To him there are no true correspondences between the signifier and the signified and so there is no need to be limited by traditional semantic relationships. However, while words may not be the things themselves, *Love's Labour's Lost* reveals the importance of the kind of meaning that is located in words and names, the "fame" of the communal understanding of a thing. Ironically, these male characters go about their theatrical existence and "wot not what they are," blissfully unaware of the topical suggestiveness of their names. Words are not the things themselves, the actors are not French lords, and these characters are not French military leaders, but nevertheless the play does not release the characters from their onomastic associations (embedded as they are in a whole network of onomastic contemporary allusions, military metaphors, and in a plot that constantly refers back to oath-breaking). The characters are not determined by their names in any Cratylic sense whereby etymology would predetermine their actions; instead, it is contemporary "fame" that matters to their representation and which has real significance. When the lords cruelly mock Holofernes for attempting to represent Judas Maccabeus even though there is another (in)famous Judas who haunts that name, the audience watches characters similarly onomastically afflicted.

Navarre in Different Genres

Topical fame presents literature with problems. Modern critics have often castigated Spenser for his inclusion of the Burbon episode in *The Faerie Queene*, considering the allegory to be too thin at this point due to the familiarity of the contemporary reference. More recently, some have seen Spenser's representation in terms of anxiety over Elizabethan foreign policy that in turn complicates and comments on the mechanics of the allegory. When Artegall reluctantly assists Burbon, he is aiding a character who is aligned with Grantorto and other markedly "bad" characters, and thus the poem would seem to question both polarity in allegorical presentation and pragmatic politics in the real world (see, for example, Gregory 2000).

Marlowe's apparently vitriolic propaganda piece, *The Massacre at Paris*, deals more directly with French politics than either *The Faerie Queene* or *Love's Labour's Lost*, representing Navarre and his contemporaries as themselves. *The Massacre* ends before Navarre's apostasy, with the newly acceded French king swearing vengeance on Catholics for the "fatal death" of Henri III (*Massacre* xxv.112). Like Spenser's and Shakespeare's representations of Navarre, this recreation of contemporary events seems to end mid-action, with the phrase "fatal death" on the one hand tautologically emphasizing the finality of death in conjunction with the end of the play, and on the other pointing to future action where Henri III's death proves "fatal" to Catholics. It means that Navarre, whose dialogue has previously been dominated by Christian aphorisms, is (possibly unsettlingly) subsumed into the analogical structure of a revenge tragedy, which until this

point has motivated only the play's nefarious Catholics. Even if the
Marlovian Navarre's acceptance of the revenge tragedy role is not seen
by a Protestant audience as a failure in character, the fact that the play
continued to be produced in the years after the real Navarre's apostasy
means that many audiences knew this character would ultimately fail
in his generic undertaking. It suggests that ironic representations of
Navarre were popular with early modern audiences.

The name Navarre also appears in another early modern drama, *The
Trial of Chivalry* (1605). The play is a pseudo-historical romance
which locates itself in an unspecified past where knights are prepared
to devote their lives to the memory of their friends, and hermits have
magic potions to cure faces poisoned by spurned lovers. On one hand
the names used in this play simply connote "historicity": there is a
"Lewes, *King of France*," King of "Navar" and a Duke "Burbon."
However, these onomastics intriguingly reproduce the recent (if the
play was written around its 1605 publication date) or current (if
written before 1598) French civil wars.[10] (They are also different
from the names used in the play's source, Sidney's *Arcadia*.) The play
opens with Navarre and France about to go to war, with the English
Pembrooke supporting Navarre. The temporary peace initially agreed
upon is broken down, in part because of the machinations of the topically named Burbon. Elizabethans would have known of the elderly,
Catholic Cardinal Charles de Bourbon (Henri Navarre's uncle) as
the Catholic League's preferred successor to the French throne,
prior to his death in 1590.[11] The two kings are symmetrical characters:
they each have a daughter and a son (who is in love with the other
king's daughter), a parallel situation that is underlined by the use
of repeated lines between the two factions (as in most of the first
scene, where they enter from opposite sides of the stage and then
again when war breaks out again at F1v). In this way the religious
difference that kept the actual French civil wars raging for so long is
here effaced by theatrical stylization. This Navarre is no oath-breaker,
and whether or not the play was written before the "wonderfull yeare"
1593, the way the play resolves the two kings' tendency to violence is
significant. The backdrop of a topically resonant "civill butchery" (I4r)
is pacified only once the younger generation successfully works through
a romance narrative and the daughters and sons of the two kings
are secure in their love for one another. Military strategy enables
Pembrooke to stop the fighting, but it is marriage which secures
long-term peace:

> . . . and now Navar and Fraunce,
> Here end your strife, and let all hatred fall,
> And turne this warre to Hymens festivall. (K2r)

This ending stands in telling contradistinction to that other highly patterned play featuring a king called Navarre.

"Making War Against Her Hair"

Two of the plays featuring a character called Navarre, then, look at civil war from different angles. Marlowe's *Massacre at Paris* reenacts the way in which the cross-faith marriage between the Protestant Navarre and the Catholic Margaret of Valois resulted in the devastation of the St. Bartholomew's Day Massacre, and the revenge cycle of civil wars that followed. This "funerall wedding" stayed in the public memory long after the French wars had ended (Vignolle 1637: 3), and Protestant Elizabethans had been relieved when marriage negotiations between their queen and the French Catholic François Hercule, Duc d'Alençon (suggested at 2.1.61 and 2.1.194 of *Love's Labour's Lost*) had failed in the 1580s.[12] By contrast, *The Trial of Chivalry* effaces differences and shows marriage to be a salve for violence, uniting opposing sides and solving the problem of succession ("What matter ist who weares both Diadems, / When the Succession lives in eythers heyre?"; A3r). The anxiety that a problematic succession leads to civil war is briefly alluded to in *The Comedy of Errors*. In a parodic blazon, Dromio of Syracuse relates the foreign and the female by representing Nell's body in terms of national spaces, stabilizing the threat of her sexuality by mapping her out in representable forms. This includes a reference to France, which is to be found "In her forehead, armed and reverted, making war against her hair" (3.2.126–7). The pun on *hair/heir* (orthographically present in the Folio's "heire") defines the French civil wars as Navarre's difficulty in securing his succession to the throne in the face of the Catholic League's "armed" opposition.

Indeed, the French wars were a constant reminder to the English of what could go wrong when there was no immediate heir to succeed to the throne. That there was a persistent anxiety about civil war throughout the early modern period up to the country's final descent into violence is evident from the number of literary works focusing on that theme.[13] In the 1590s this anxiety was specifically related to concern about who would succeed the aging queen, particularly since the number of candidates for the job made it seem unlikely that the matter would proceed straightforwardly. James VI of Scotland, Lady Arabella Stuart, Catherine Grey, and the Spanish Infanta, to name but a few, all had claims to the English throne (Hurstfield 1961: 373–4). Indeed, in the 1590s James was making it clear that he would not let the matter go without a very literal fight (Hurstfield 1961: 393). Wishing to preserve her own safety and that of any potential successor, Elizabeth forbade the publication of any such claims, and her need to do so suggests what an attractive topic it made. In 1593 Peter Wentworth was sent to the Tower for his *Pithie Exhortation* on the subject (Hurstfield 1961: 372).

In 1594 the Jesuit Robert Persons (under the pseudonym R. Doleman) printed his book *A Conference About the Next Succession to the Crowne of Ingland* (Antwerp) and it was smuggled into England in 1595. This lengthy debate favored (unsurprisingly, given Persons' Catholicism) the Spanish Infanta's claims as well as facetiously stirring up political trouble with a dedication to the Earl of Essex (Holmes 1980). This book made manifest in print the concerns about the uncertainty of the country's future:

> were the tymes never so quiet, and religion never so uniforme: yet are ther great doubtes in many mens heades, about the lawfulnes of divers pretentions of the famylies before named: but if you adde unto this, the said wonderfull diversity in matters of religio[n] also, which this tyme yealdeth: you shal finde the event much more doubtfull. (Doleman 1594: B3v)

A Conference prompted a number of Protestant rebukes, which, though contrary in religious bias, served to keep the debate alive and to indicate how Persons was correct in his claim that sectarian difference made the event "more doubtfull."

The years when *Love's Labour's Lost* was probably written (1594–5) were years when concerns about succession and civil war were both acute and intimately related. Thus far I have stressed the semantic shiftiness of the play and the way that it constantly replays the epistemological slippage of conversion. However, not just apostasy, but also issues of civil war and succession are notable as absent presences in this text. Since many of the male characters share their names with military leaders, the frame of reference is as much martial as it is sectarian. It is significant that these particular characters (rather than their less topical comedic companions in the canon) fail to secure marriage at the end of the play. Finally, the lovers are neatly paired, but the women refuse to marry the men until they pass a "trial" that is to last the fairytale duration of a year and a day (5.2.797–8).

What is lost with the traditional comic promise of certain marriage, such as we find at the end of most other comedies (and, indeed, *The Trial of Chivalry*)? Marriage is a procreative bond, and as the obstetric pun in the title suggests, in *Love's Labour's Lost* we lose the promise of a labour that would bring forth a child that would perpetuate inheritance cycles and lineage.[14] (Instead, Jaquenetta is pregnant with an illegitimate child and will be "cast away" if Armado refuses to accept paternity; 5.2.672.) If the onomastic allusions to wars of succession render this ending particularly troubling, then in some ways the play's onomastic structure also explains the open-ended finish. Anne Barton notes that speaking characters in Shakespeare's comedies tend not to have surnames (Barton 1990: 36). The Lords' topical names expand their nominal definition beyond a first name (Navarre is a *Ferdinand* only to a reader of the text, since this name never appears in the play's dialogue). It is as if they have stumbled into the wrong genre. They are nominally incompatible with the more comedically appropriate "Rosaline," "Maria," and "Katherine."

The lack of a promise of immediate marriage at the end of *Love's Labour's Lost* is tied up with expressions of theatrical failure:

> The *scene* begins to cloud. (5.2.716; my emphasis)

> Our wooing doth not end like an *old play*:
> Jack hath not Jill. These ladies' courtesy
> Might well have made our sport a *comedy*. (5.2.862–4; my emphasis)

> That's too long for a *play*. (5.2.866; my emphasis)

Irresolution dominates the final scene, since we do not know if the lords will finally be able to keep their promises. The topical concerns raised by many of the names make this irresolution all the more troubling; but it is precisely because historical processes do not have endings that the play cannot round things off and say what will happen tomorrow (though it can offer the realism of an individual's end, death). It is the combination of these topical onomastics and the comic mode that makes this tension acute, since we look for closure at the

end of a comedy in a way that we do not expect it in a history play.
As David Scott Kastan points out, "the open-endedness of the history
play recognizes the impossibility of isolating the action from its place
on the temporal continuum and makes no suggestion of a providential
context for this 'race of time' " (Kastan 1982: 48). However, history
plays do feature attempts at rounding off the action by recourse to a
traditional comic ending. For example, *Henry V* sees another King
Henry marrying a French princess. The French king blesses the
incipient marriage between his daughter and Henry, saying:

> Take her, fair son, and from her blood raise up
> Issue to me, that the contending kingdoms
> Of France and England, whose very shores look pale
> With envy of each other's happiness,
> May cease their hatred; and this dear conjunction
> Plant neighbourhood and Christian-like accord
> In their sweet bosoms, that never war advance
> His bleeding sword 'twixt England and fair France. (5.2.348–55)

The comic "marriage" ending is sought specifically because it is hoped
that it will solve the problems of succession, and put an end to "war";
that is, it will prevent the very problems that plagued Navarre in the
1590s and looked set to trouble England after Elizabeth's death. In
Henry V an epilogue undoes this comic closure as the "issue," "Henry
the Sixt . . . lost France, and made his England bleed; / Which oft our
stage hath shown" (Epilogue 9–13). This Epilogue locks Henry into
a temporal paradox which looks forward in chronological time while
looking backwards in theatrical and historical time, so that the cycle
of bloodshed begins again. The *Henry VI* plays and *King John* show
even more directly the way in which marriage can lead to political
disaster. In his comedy that is populated by historically named characters, Shakespeare eschews the comic ending that brings such problems to his other historical characters. Political chaos is avoided, but
this marriage-less ending nevertheless carries troubling connotations.

Maus points out that the aristocratic proper name "is normally an
inherited name; moreover, it is the name of *what* is inherited, the piece
of property that guarantees its owner income and status" (Maus 1991:
210). Thus, the proper name is also a toponym. In a manner contrary
to other comic characters in the canon, the lords' names raise the question of succession and lineage both by their topical connotations of a

war about succession, and in a more general indication of onomastic inheritance that is denied other comic characters. The female characters, as noted above, are primarily known by the first names common to comedy, but it is their inherited names that the lords are interested in:

Longaville	Pray you, sir, whose daughter?
Boyet	Her mother's, I have heard.
Longaville	God's blessing on your beard!
Boyet	Good sir, be not offended.
	She is an heir of Falconbridge.
Longaville	Nay, my choler is ended.
	She is a most sweet lady. (2.1.200–6)

Longaville departs without learning Maria's first name; he is more interested in her lineage and what kind of inheritance she could share with him.[15] The Princess is known only by a positional name which simultaneously nominates her a neutral fairytale type and marks her out in accordance to her position to her father, the French king, on whose business she comes to the Court of Navarre. At the very moment that the Princess becomes a Queen (and is accordingly addressed as "your majesty"; 5.2.720), the moment when succession is in action as royal title passes from deceased father to living daughter, she refuses a move that would secure succession for the generations after her. Like England's contemporary queen she prevaricates when it comes to the subject of marriage.[16]

Not trusting Navarre's oath, the new Queen sets him the year's task of enduring "frosts and fasts, hard lodging and thin weeds" (5.2.795) in some "forlorn and naked hermitage" (5.2.789), while she shuts herself up in a "mourning house" (5.2.802). The preposterous commencement of a romance tale where a comedy should end also looks temporally backwards, to a pre-Reformation time of hermits and mourning houses. Structurally this mirrors Henri of Navarre's "backsliding" to a world of Catholic ritual, an act that left Elizabethans uncertain about the future.

Diachronic Spaces

What are we to make of the Catholic symbolic residue embedded in *Love's Labour's Lost*'s open-ending? It is useful to compare its initiation of romance story with *The Trial of Chivalry*, which follows a romance narrative to its end. As I have noted, to contemporary audiences the depiction of warring kings called Navarre and France would have inescapably called to mind the French civil wars of the 1590s. The narrative displaces these onomastic allusions into an unspecified past. Alex Davis tells us that romance texts bear a "temporal signature" and are "pervaded by [a] spirit of 'pastness'" (Davis 2003: 3). Thus, while *The Trial of Chivalry* might have been written and performed a number of years prior to its 1605 publication date, I think it is also important to note that the text is deliberately old fashioned in style. The religious differences between France and Navarre are rewritten as a romance narrative that would seem to bear no relation to recent events.

Nevertheless, the text is full of Catholic residue. For example, Katharina, the daughter of the French king, falls in love with pictures and statues in a way that Elizabethan Protestants were taught to regard as distinctively Catholic. When Perdita gazes upon what she takes to be her mother's statue in *The Winter's Tale* she says: "And do not say 'tis superstition, that / I kneel, and then implore her blessing" (5.3.43–4). In using the word "superstition" she alludes to Catholic practice as understood in anti-Catholic discourse. While she denies the superstitious nature of her reverence to the "statue," her need to proffer this disclaimer suggests that it is likely that people would make this Catholic association; in using this word Shakespeare ensures that his audience *does* think of the scene in these terms. Not just indicative of the misplaced nature of her love for Pembroke (when the plot requires that she obeys the play's symmetry and fall in love with Navarre's son, Ferdinand), Katharina comes to recognize her love for Ferdinand after gazing on his picture when she believes him dead, fantasizing that:

> I claspe my Ferdinand betweene mine armes:
> So long as I behold this lively forme,
> So long am I refreshed by his smiles:
> So long, me thinks, I heare him speake to me. (G1r)

Katharina blurs the distinction between image and thing in a way that Reformers found idolatrous. Idolatrous or not, when she comes to speak to Ferdinand's statue as if it were Ferdinand himself, she is rewarded by the real Ferdinand – living and breathing and only pretending to be a statue. Yet the text does not wholly collude with the Catholic spirituality of such moments. Where one would expect a joyful acknowledgment of mutual love and no small expression of wonder at the apparent animation of a statue and resurrection of the dead, the moment is actually passed over in eight lines, with Pembroke swiftly wrapping matters up: "Of that no more: now let us haste from hence, / To quiet the dissension lately sprung" (H2r). His own attempts at living out a role as a romance protagonist in guarding a tomb honoring the perpetual memory of his "dead" friend are gently mocked by the fact that his first encounters are with women not knights and the fact that the memorial is but an "empty Monument" (F3r). Elizabeth Mazzola has shown that "abandoned symbols" persist in occupying space in the mental landscape of any generation (Mazzola 1998: 1). Clearly, Catholic symbols continue to exist even after the Reformation empties them of their sacred significance and categorizes them as false. Of such outmoded ideas and symbols Mazzola says:

> they fail to describe reality, while ignoring other cultural requirements for meaning, power or guidance. Rather than actively continuing to shape texts or readers, these ideas constitute a secret record of the imagination's failures or an arrangement of its lies. In the same way that Latin becomes a dead language, *these dead or dying symbols become poetry.* (Mazzola 1998: 4; my emphasis)

Catholic symbols are a fiction (a papist lie) and can be used to give a sense of the fictional (something more neutrally distant from the everyday). The Catholic residue of *The Trial of Chivalry* contributes to the fantastic nature of the romance genre, at the same time that the context of the romance genre neutralizes the Catholic elements as merely fiction. In pseudo-histories, political thought is provoked by the juxtaposition of different reality states: a non-real space is created where the contemporary problems suggested by the play's onomastics are resolved by fiction, in part, because the Catholic meaning present is *only* fiction (fantastic statues and fairytale hermits). It is not so much that the sectarian is idealized as that it is made distant, and importantly, reaches happy closure.

In Shakespeare's play, by contrast, the romance genre enters at the end, not as a strategy for resolving the play's troubles (an actual civil war in *The Trial of Chivalry* and a "civil war of wits" in *Love's Labour's Lost*; 2.1.225), but as a way of leaving them unanswered. Its ending mirrors the mid-1590s situation with Navarre being forced to undertake Catholic tasks in order to win France/the French queen. In ending on this particular contingency, in placing irresolution where an audience would look for resolution, Shakespeare makes it clear how unsettling this proposition is to an Elizabethan. But at the same time, whereas the contemporary Navarre was considered "mutable" and untrustworthy *because* of his shift to Catholicism, in the play an already untrustworthy Navarre is given a (post-play) Catholic trial to make good his flighty nature.[17] The text at once foregrounds a Navarre in need of correction at the same time as it looks hopefully to a future that does not deny his Catholicism as an act of temporizing. Catholic meaning has not only ruptured the generic closure of this play, it has opened up a comedy (one that was once thought to be at a courtly remove) to contemporary concerns about the national and international future.

Notes

I would like to thank Laurie Maguire, Henry Woudhuysen, and Richard Proudfoot for their invaluable advice on earlier drafts of this chapter. I am also grateful to the AHRC and the English Faculty of the University of Oxford whose funding made this research possible.

1 The law also forbade Elizabethan subjects to assist the French King's enemies (Hughes and Larkin 1969: 77–9).
2 The title page to the 1598 quarto of *Love's Labour's Lost* refers to an earlier edition which is no longer extant. Arthur Freeman and Paul Grinke (2002: 18) have discovered documentary evidence for an earlier quarto of *Love's Labour's Lost*: a catalogue of Viscount Conway's books lists "Loves Labours Lost by W: Sha: 1597" (an edition which would have been lost with the rest of Conway's books in a fire of 1641). Since even this earlier edition post-dates Navarre's conversion it remains unlikely that the oath-breaking story formed part of the later quarto's "augmentations."
3 Known as the "Duke de Maine" and as Navarre's enemy in a great number of texts (e.g., see anon. 1597; anon. 1590a; anon. 1590b: B2v). For an alternative reading of the contemporary literary significance of the Marcade-Mercury-Boyet nexus, see Clayton and Tudeau-Clayton (2004).
4 In using the term "Elizabethan audience" I do not mean to imply that we should understand as homogeneous a group of people who were varied in their confessional and political allegiances, but

acknowledge the way the Elizabethan public were subject to certain strategies of acculturation.

5   Some productions have highlighted the wilful insistence on this naive if delightful retreat, with the Branagh film, for example, setting the play against a backdrop of World War II.

6   Other military language is to be found at 2.1.86, 2.1.225, 3.1.61–2, and 3.1.78.

7   This pamplet was published by Shakespeare's Stratford contemporary, Richard Field, so it is possible that Shakespeare had particularly easy access to such material given that he seems to have maintained contact with the man who printed *Venus and Adonis* (1593) and *The Rape of Lucrece* (1594) and who is alluded to in *Cymbeline* as "Richard du Champ" (4.2.377).

8   Similarly, when Berowne asks "who can sever love from charity" (4.3.339) he potentially alludes to the instability of biblical linguistics, since Tyndale rejected the Vulgate's translation of the Greek *agape*, "charity," and instead substituted the word "love."

9   Her pragmatic support was premised on the idea that the dominance of a Catholic Navarre was preferable to the dominance of the Catholic League. In any case it seems that her religious indignation may have been emphasized because of her political displeasure with Navarre's organization of the war; see Sutherland (2002: 521–4).

10 The extant quarto for this play is dated 1605 (entered 1604) and claims to have "bin lately acted by the right Honourable the Earle of Darby his servants." However, the last recorded London performance for Derby's Men is in 1601, and after playing at Norwich in 1602 and Coventry in 1602 and 1603 the company disappeared for several years (Gurr 1996: 265–6). A number of critics have suggested (with varying degrees of evidence) an earlier date of composition for this play, which, with its end-stopped verse and lack of character motivation, would have seemed old fashioned in the seventeenth century (see Shelling 1908; Clark 1931; Bullen 1964; Chambers 1965). Indeed, Fleay (1891: 318–19) and Greg (1906: 187) speculate that *The Trial of Chivalry* should be identified with *Bourbon* mentioned in Henslowe's Diary (noted as an old play performed by the Admiral's and Pembroke's Men in November 1597). The logic for this thesis rests in the fact that "Burbon" is the chief villain of the play, which also features a heroic English character called "Pembrooke." Nevertheless, the fact that *The Trial of Chivalry* was printed in 1605 indicates that the play was thought to have a potential readership at that late date. It is worth contextualizing

The Trial in its year of publication. By the seventeenth century the French civil wars were over; however, French current affairs and recent history remained popular dramatic topics: Chapman's new *Byron* and *Bussy D'Ambois* plays were written and performed in this period, and Marlowe's *Massacre at Paris* continued to be staged. Indeed, the vogue for French gossip is mocked in *Northward Ho* (1605). Furthermore, the Navarres of both *Love's Labour's Lost* and *The Trial of Chivalry* reappear at the same time. In the winter of 1604–5 (i.e., when *The Trial* was entered and printed) *Love's Labour's Lost* was performed at Court (Woudhuysen 1998: 83). In this context, the seventeenth-century printing of *The Trial* seems less strange.

11   Spenser's "Burbon" obviously represents Navarre as the first Bourbon king, but perhaps there is also an onomastic underlining of the way that the apostasizing Henri becomes the very threat he had fought against.

12   See Corum (1999: 284) for the view that both *Love's Labour's Lost* and Elizabeth avoid the bloodshed of the historical and theatrical *Massacre at Paris*.

13   See, for example, Daniel (1594), Lodge (1594), Drayton (1596), and Fulbecke (1601). For a discussion of civil war images in England and France, see Parmelee (1996: 53–73).

14   Burnett (1993: 310) sees the ending of the play in terms of a gift exchange and Elizabeth's failure to offer her people the gift of an heir to the throne.

15   For further references to inheritance and "issue," see 1.1.7, 1.1.73, 2.1.5, 2.1.40–3, 2.1.194, 2.1.247–8, 4.1.20, 4.1.81–2, 4.3.342–3, 5.2.172, and 5.2.668–73.

16   The play's final song with its "cuckoo" (cuckold) call that "Mocks married men" (5.2.887–9, 896–8) also further undermines any hope of straightforward patrilineage; though romance is sustained in the owl's "Tu-whit, Tu-whoo" (5.2.906, 915).

17   Interestingly, Catholic League enemies of Henri IV pointed out the failure of the French king to perform the penitential acts which traditionally attested to a convert's sincerity; see Wolfe (1993: 161).

Works Cited

Anon. 1590a: *An excellent ditty made upon the great victory, which the French king obtayned against the Duke de Maine, and the Romish rebels in his kingdome*. London.

Anon. 1590b: *A briefe declaration of the yeelding up of Saint Denis to the French king the 29. June, 1590.* London.

Anon. 1590c: *The Coppie of a Letter sent into England by a Gentleman, from the Towne of Saint Denis in France.* London.

Anon. 1590d: *The oration and declaration of the French King, Henrie the fourth of that name and by the grace of God, King of Navarre.* London.

Anon. 1591a: *An answeare to the supplication Against him, who seeming to give the King counsel to become a Catholike, indevoureth to stirre up his good subjectes unto rebellion.* Trans. Edward Aggas. London.

Anon. 1591b: *A discourse uppon a question of the estate of this time.* Trans. Edward Aggas. London.

Anon. 1597: *The Mutable and wavering estate of France, from the yeare of our Lord 1460, until the yeare 1595.* London.

Anon. 1599: *The Passionate Pilgrim.* London.

Anon. 1600a: *Belvedere.* London.

Anon. 1600b. *England's Helicon.* London.

Anon. 1600c: *England's Parnassus.* London.

Anon. 1605: *The Historie of the Triall of Chevalry.* London. Facsimile edition 1912: London: Tudor Facsimile Texts.

Asquith, Clare 2003: "Oxford University and *Love's Labour's Lost.*" In Dennis Taylor and David Beauregard (eds.) *Shakespeare and the Culture of Christianity in Early Modern England.* New York: Fordham University Press, 80–102.

Barton, Anne 1990: *The Names of Comedy.* Oxford: Clarendon Press.

Bullen, A. H. (ed.) 1964: *A Collection of Old English Plays,* Vol. 3. New York: Benjamin Blom.

Burke, Kenneth 1969: *A Grammar of Motives.* Berkeley: University of California Press.

Burnett, Mark Thornton 1993: "Giving and Receiving: *Love's Labour's Lost* and the Politics of Exchange." *English Literature Review* 23, 287–313.

Cawdry, Robert 1604: *A Table Alphabeticall.* London.

Chambers, E. K. 1965: *The Elizabethan Stage,* Vol. 4. Oxford: Clarendon Press.

Clark, A. M. 1931: *Thomas Heywood: Playwright and Miscellanist.* Oxford: Blackwell.

Clay, W. K. (ed.) 1847: *Liturgical Services of the Reign of Queen Elizabeth.* Cambridge: Cambridge University Press.

Clayton, F. W. and Tudeau-Clayton, Margaret (2004): "Mercury, Boy Yet and the 'Harsh' Words of *Love's Labour's Lost.*" *Shakespeare Survey* 27, 209–24.

Constable, Henry 1600: *A Discoverye of a Counterfecte Conference.* Paris.

Coote, Edmund 1596: *The English schoole-maister.* London.

Corum, Richard 1999: "'The Catastrophe Is a Nuptial': *Love's Labor's Lost*, Tactics, Everyday Life." In Patricia Fumerton and Simon Hunt (eds.) *Renaissance Culture and the Everyday*. Philadelphia: University of Pennsylvania Press, 271–98.

Daniel, Samuel 1594: *The Civil Wars*. London.

Davis, Alex 2003: *Chivalry and Romance in the English Renaissance*. Suffolk: D. S. Brewer.

Doleman, R. [pseudonym for Robert Persons] 1594: *A Conference About the Next Succession to the Crowne of Ingland*. Antwerp.

Drayton, Michael 1596: *Mortimeriados*. London.

Du Bartas, Guillaume de Salluste 1590: *A canticle of the victorie obtained by the French King, Henrie the fourth. At Yvry*. Trans. Joshua Sylvester. London. For EEBO access see STC 21672, UMI collection/reel number: 469:08.

Duffy, Eamon 1992: *The Stripping of the Altars*. New Haven: Yale University Press.

Fleay, F. G. 1891: *A Biographical Chronicle of English Drama 1559–1642*, Vol. 2. London: Reeves and Turner.

Freeman, A. and Grinke, P. 2002: "Four New Shakespeare Quartos? Viscount Conway's Lost English Plays." *Times Literary Supplement* April 5, 17–18.

Fulbecke, W. 1601: *An historicall collection of the continuall factions, of the Romans and Italians*. London.

Gallagher, Lowell 1991: *Medusa's Gaze: Casuistry and Conscience in the Renaissance*. Stanford: Stanford University Press.

Greg, W. W. 1906: *Henslowe's Diary Part II: Commentary*. London: A. H. Bullen.

Gregory, T. 2000: "Shadowing Intervention: On the Politics of *The Faerie Queene* Book 5 Cantos 10–12." *English Literary History* 67, 365–97.

Gurr, Andrew 1996: *The Shakespearian Playing Companies*. Oxford: Clarendon Press.

Harrison, G. B. (ed.) 1968: *The Letters of Queen Elizabeth*. London: Cassell.

Harvey, Gabriel 1593: *A new letter of notable contents with a straunge sonet intituled Gorgon, or the wonderfull yeare*. London.

Hayward, John 1603: *An Answer to the First Part of a Certaine Conference*. London.

Holmes, P. 1980: "The Authorship and Early Reception of a Conference about the Next Succession to the Crown of England." *Historical Journal* 23, 415–29.

Hughes, Paul L. and Larkin, James F. (eds.) 1969: *Tudor Royal Proclamations*, Vol. 3: *The Later Tudors (1588–1603)*. New Haven: Yale University Press.

Hurstfield, Joel 1961: "The Succession Struggle in Late Elizabethan England." In S. T. Bindoff et al. (eds.) *Elizabethan Government and Society.* London: University of London Press, 369–96.

Kastan, David Scott 1982: *Shakespeare and the Shapes of Time.* London: Macmillan.

Lamb, Mary Ellen 1985: "The Nature of Topicality." *Shakespeare Survey* 38, 49–59.

Lodge, Thomas 1594: *The Wounds of Civil War.* London.

Marlowe, Christopher 1976: *The Complete Plays and Poems.* Ed. E. D. Pendry. London: Everyman.

Maus, Katherine Eisaman 1991: "The Transfer of Title in *Love's Labour's Lost*: Language, Individualism, Gender." In Ivo Kamps (ed.) *Shakespeare Left and Right.* New York: Routledge, 205–23.

Maxwell, Julie 2004: "The Part of Allusion." Unpublished DPhil thesis, University of Oxford.

Mazzola, Elizabeth 1998: *The Pathology of the English Renaissance: Sacred Remains and Holy Ghosts.* Leiden: Brill.

Parker, Patricia 1993: "Preposterous Reversals: *Love's Labour's Lost.*" *Modern Language Quarterly* 54, 435–82.

Parmelee, Lisa F. 1996: *Good Newes From Fraunce.* Rochester, NY: University of Rochester Press.

Prescott, Anne Lake 2001: "Foreign Policy in Fairyland: Henri IV and Spenser's Burbon." *Spenser Studies* 14, 189–214.

Questier, Michael C. 1996: *Conversion, Politics and Religion in England, 1580–1625.* Cambridge: Cambridge University Press.

Relle, Eleanor 1972: "Some New Marginalia and Poems of Gabriel Harvey." *Review of English Studies* 23, 401–16.

Richmond, Hugh M. 1978–9: "Shakespeare's Navarre." *Huntingdon Library Quarterly* 42, 193–216.

Shakespeare, William. See Woudhuysen, Henry.

Shelling, F. E. 1908: *Elizabethan Drama 1558–1642.* London: Archibald Constable.

Speed, John 1611: *The Theatre of God's Judgment.* London.

Spenser, Edmund 1978: *The Faerie Queene.* Ed. T. P. Roche, Jr. London: Penguin.

Sutherland, N. M. 2002: *Henry IV of France and the Politics of Religion 1572–1596*, 2 vols. Bristol: Elm Bank.

Tricomi, Albert H. 1979: "The Witty Idealization of the French Court in *Love's Labour's Lost.*" *Shakespeare Studies* 12, 25–33.

Vignolle 1637: *Abridgement of the life of Henry the Great, the fourth of that name, king of France and Navarre, Translated out of French.* London.

Voss, Paul, J. 2001: *Elizabethan News Pamphlets.* Pittsburgh: Duquesne University Press.

Wolfe, Michael 1993: *The Conversion of Henri IV: Politics, Power, and Religious Belief in Early Modern France*. Cambridge, MA: Harvard University Press.

Woods, Gillian 2006: "Catholic Semiotics in Shakespearean Drama." Unpublished DPhil thesis, University of Oxford.

Woudhuysen, Henry (ed.) 1998: *Love's Labour's Lost*. London: Thomson Learning.

Part III

How To Do Things with Texts

Editor's Introduction

Most *Companion* volumes for undergraduates contain an essay on Shakespeare's text. They explain the difference between the individual quarto volumes of plays published in Shakespeare's life-time (and after) and the handsome Folio volume of *Comedies, Histories, Tragedies* prepared posthumously by Shakespeare's colleagues Heminge and Condell in 1623. They outline the problem of the so-called "bad quartos" (a twentieth-century term), often equated with the "stolne and surreptitious copies" referred to by Heminge and Condell and now identified with the memorial reconstruction of playtexts by actors. They may talk about censorship, company repertoire, later adaptations; and they usually conclude with the challenges faced by editors, especially those editing after 1980 – the year which ushered in the new orthodoxy that Shakespeare revised his plays to suit the practical needs of performance. The editorial challenge has been further complicated since 2003, when Lukas Erne argued that, far from being indifferent to immortality in print (as had long been argued), Shakespeare revised his work for publication. Such essays survey bibliographical, textual, editorial, and performance history. What they do not do is show how to do things with Shakespeare's texts.

Nor can they. Pioneering textual work takes place in rare book rooms over many years; it strains the eyes, taxes one's patience, and sabotages one's social life. New textual discoveries are unlikely to take place in the one to four weeks granted undergraduates for a tutorial essay or a term paper. How, then, can a student Do Things with Shakespeare's Texts?

This was the question I asked Tiffany Stern and Anthony Dawson to address, from two different perspectives. Stern's work is innovative for a number of reasons. It is positioned at the interface of textual analysis and theater history. Consequently, she asks theatrical questions about textual problems and textual questions about theater performance. Her discoveries and insights (which are legion) come from reading plays – lots and lots of them – and observing patterns of reference: references to rehearsal, to audience reactions, to advertising practice, to cues. Many of her references come from plays written or published after Shakespeare's death (theater is in many ways a very conservative industry; artistic practices don't change in paradigm shifts even if some aspects of theatrical culture, such as the introduction of actresses after the Restoration, do). And in her extensive reading of non-theatrical texts she has collected references (often in the form of metaphors) to theatrical practice.

This kind of work simply (simply!) needs a keen eye – the kind of eye literary students have, or are being trained to have – and a relentless sense of interrogative inquiry. The talent is to know what questions to ask in the first place. This talent is illustrated in the essay that follows, in which Stern turns her attention to the question of how "material," how "textual" plays were in performance.

Like Stern, Anthony Dawson wears several critical hats. In addition to those of textual critic and theater historian he wears that of the new historicist. In his essay here he reflects in a wide-ranging way on the challenges he has faced as editor of some textually problematic Shakespeare plays – notably *Troilus and Cressida* and *Timon of Athens* – and muses on some intractable and baffling textual problems. Rooted in his own practical experience, his essay is a theoretical inquiry into what editors might or might not do. Running throughout his argument is a series of metaphors from the Shakespeare texts he has edited which can be aptly applied to the role of editor. Novice textual critics can follow his example and consider the ways in which metaphors can be (re)appropriated to help them think theoretically about textual practice.

Literary theory has, in many respects, opened up the field of textual study to those who are not trained in the technical aspects of bibliography. What I like about the work of both Stern and Dawson, particularly as exemplified in the essays here, is that it does not require technical expertise in inks or paper or compositors. Students can emulate Stern and Dawson's approaches without any specialist knowledge. Stern's work on actors' parts and cues, for example, shows how such emulation can work. Stern built on the long-known fact that actors received only a copy of their own part plus the preceding cue of a few words or a line: she actually prepared a cue text for Shylock. Her approach has since been adopted by acting companies: for example, a helpful education pack (on the website for the Watermill Theatre in Newbury, Berkshire) offers illuminating cue parts for two servants in *The Taming of the Shrew*.

Thus, rather than tell us things about Shakespeare's text, the two essays that follow show us how the essayists have done things. And the kinds of things they have done, we can do too.

Works Cited

Erne, Lukas 2003: *Shakespeare as Literary Dramatist.* Cambridge: Cambridge University Press.

Palfrey, Simon and Stern, Tiffany 2007: *Shakespeare in Parts.* Oxford: Oxford University Press.

Stern, Tiffany 2000: *Rehearsal from Shakespeare to Sheridan.* Oxford: Oxford University Press.

Stern, Tiffany 2004: *Making Shakespeare: From Stage to Page.* London: Routledge.

Watermill theatre education pack: www.watermill.org.uk/pdf/the_taming_of_the_shrew.pdf?download = true.

Chapter 6

Watching as Reading: The Audience and Written Text in Shakespeare's Playhouse

Tiffany Stern

Rationale

Lukas Erne in *Shakespeare as Literary Dramatist* maintains that Shakespeare's plays as published are not in fact transcriptions of productions mounted at the Globe and Blackfriars playhouses: what have come down to us are texts that Shakespeare reshaped and rewrote for readers. That Shakespeare had an interest in publication is consonant with everything we know about the playwright. But some critics have pushed Erne's argument further, arguing that Shakespeare was really a "poet," and that his concerns were literary rather than theatrical. It seemed to me that we were in danger of returning to the Victorian idea that Shakespeare was a noble poet writing in a garret well away from the day-to-day business of staging and performance. So I decided to examine whether the language of books was ever used to describe staging, and, conversely, whether the language of staging was ever used to describe reading. In this way I could challenge the terms in which assumptions were being made about what is "literary" and what is "theatrical": what do such words mean when looking at the work of an early modern playwright?

Introduction

Tremendous works of modern scholarship, like Erne's *Shakespeare as Literary Dramatist* and Cheney's *Shakespeare the National Poet-Playwright*, stress the difference between what a reader would read and what a spectator would see. This paper attempts to take on board the idea that many plays were published as "literature," whilst also suggesting that "watching" was a highly textual activity. Too often the belief in widespread illiteracy throughout early modern London leads to certain facts being ignored – facts about the highly literate, bookish spectators that were so often to be found in the London playhouses. This essay will suggest that the practise of reading critically in the theater was melded with the practise of watching critically: long before the advent of new historicism all performances were mounted and viewed in ways that brought out their similarities with written texts.

My argument, which will be in three parts, will always have the public theater as its focus, though it will include information from the private and court stage: the differences between types of playhouse are not as absolute as they are said to be, and single pieces of evidence can be seen to be part of a system when looked at in a wider context. First, I will address the role of printed books in the public theater, considering how they were regularly read in the playhouse and, indeed, were also sold there. Next, I will turn to literate members of the audience, asking how commonplace-books were used in the playhouse and to what extent performed text was immediately turned back into writing. Finally, I will discuss the way the theater pandered to and used that reading audience: how the stage, hung about with words written on large boards, inscribed itself, encouraging readers to view it as, always, a semi-textual space. Oddly, these boards have not been seriously thought about for the last hundred years, despite a newfound interest in material theater, the material book, and the playhouse's relationship to text.[1] A brief conclusion will bring out the similarities suggested throughout between watching and reading, and between performances and publications. Productions on stage were continually surrounded by a marginalia of written words, I will argue; Shakespeare, like other early modern playwrights, was obsessed with text, and his performances were "published" in many textual ways beyond or beside what happened in the printing houses.

Printed Books in the Playhouse

As there was no fixed seating in early modern playhouses, canny members of the audience would arrive an hour or so before the performance was due to begin and stake out a place for themselves. Knowing that they would have time to fill, they would often bring books with them to read. But reading was, at that time, a social activity, and these books were generally recited out loud; the contents of a book would thus be made available to everyone near a reader, whether literate or not. Written texts – in performance – filled the playhouse, and "literature" was regularly intruded into the theatrical space before the play began.

Book-owners would hope, by reciting and analyzing the texts in their hands, to draw attention to themselves, highlight their choice of literature and broadcast their critical talents. So Parrot in *The Mastiff* imagines someone whose recitation is undertaken specifically with a view to its effect on others. The reader, having acquired no less a book than Parrot's *Mastiff* itself, "hastes him to the Play, / Where, when he comes, and reads, Heer's stuffe doth say. / Because the lookers on may hold him wise."[2] Having exclaimed against the pamphlet, the man takes equally loud umbrage at the performance; he declares he "more dislike[s] the *Play*, then . . . the *Booke*" (Parrot 1615: I1b). Clearly, Parrot expects his pamphlet to suffer a playhouse reading – and dreads the prospect. Dekker, similarly, advises a "gull" to take *The Gull's Hornbook* to "the twelve-penny roome next the stage" when a new play is ready to start. There the spectator is to "draw forth this booke, read alowd [and] laugh alowd" until the rest of the audience shout "*Away with the fool*" (Dekker 1884: II, 203). In both instances, the reader is also a "performer," and what the body of the audience end up judging is a confusion between the man and the book he holds. And, just as "a good play sometimes is hissed off the stage, through the fault of the player, ill acting it," so, suggest the world-weary writers, a good book might be similarly condemned by a theater audience because of the irritating nature of its reciter (Meres 1598: 254a).

Both Dekker and Parrot fear the snap judgements of the spectators in the way that playwrights did (Dekker, a playwright himself, had suffered the audience's condemnation before). But the negotiation between performance on stage and in book could be viewed positively.

Middleton, for instance, hopes that the 1611 edition of his play *The Roaring Girl* "may be allowed . . . Gallery room at the play-house"; presumably he believes his playbook will complement or compare favorably with the production on stage (Middleton 1611: A3a). His approach must reflect the theater's attitude, for booksellers were never prevented from trading with the audience. Instead, pamphlets seem regularly to have been marketed and sold in the theater precincts, probably because a playbook, read in the playhouse in which it was first performed, or for which its playwright was now writing, worked well as a marketing ploy: it promoted the acting company's famous stock, reminded the audience of fine performances in the past, and/or advertised forthcoming productions.

Though licensing laws dictated where chapmen could trade – for which reason modern critics have assumed books were not sold at theaters – "hawkers" and "mercuries" (or their equivalents: the titles are hard to date) could vend their pamphlets wherever crowds gathered. Hawkers, "those people which go up and down the streets crying News-books, and selling them by retail" (so named, explains Blount in his *Glossographia*, "from their uncertain wandring, like those that with Hawks seek their Game where they can finde it") would head to promising trading-places with their female counterparts, "those women that sell . . . by whole-sale from the Press, called Mercury Women" (Blount 1656: T3a).[3] Playhouses were obvious sites for such sales-people, as Cowley's *The Guardian* (4.3) makes clear. In that play Blade threatens "*Dogrel*" with becoming the kind of man who "shall make and sell small Pamphlets i'the playhouse, or else Tobacco, or else snuffe Candles" (Cowley 1650: D3a). Blade's book-trader – who "makes" as well as sells his work – may stitch, but possibly even write, the texts he offers; he is presented as being, like a tobacco-seller, a playhouse staple.

Hardly surprisingly then, Parrot is as concerned about the play-house-purchaser as he is about the playhouse-reader. He fronts *The Mastiff* with an epigram "ad Bibliopolam" ("to the book-seller") demanding that his verse be not "at Play-houses, mongst Pippins solde" as though he fears that the proximity of book and apple will give the two the same rank in the eyes of the buyer (Parrot 1615: A4b). But the jumbled collection of goods he anticipates his verse joining is suggestive of the tray not of a book-centered hawker or mercury, but a pedlar. Autolycus in Shakespeare's *Winter's Tale* who mingles printed ballads with ribbons and gloves is a reflection of this kind of mixed-goods salesman. His "Trafficke is sheetes" (TLN 1691), but for him printed sheets and stolen bed-linen have much the same worth: it is not even entirely clear which of the two Autolycus intends "sheet" to mean.[4] This is a man, moreover, who markets false ballads that he claims to be "true" in a play all about the marketing of false tales said to be true. Autolycus is on many levels a comment both on the gullibility of buyers and on the questionable worth of printed texts; the *Winter's Tale* audience, through the peddler/thief, will have been asked to consider the "value" of the literature they had purchased both in page and stage form.

So there seem, at the playhouse, to have been both mixed-goods salesmen whose trays included books, and pamphlet-sellers who sold books exclusively. But whether there were specific salespeople "belonging" to certain playhouses – or whether each kind simply traveled from one theater to another – is unclear. Similarly unclear is what control, if any, the theater had over the contents of the merchants' tray. Did traders agree to promote useful or significant texts to the performance? Alternatively, might they acquire "relevant" texts themselves as part of good salesmanship? In other words, was there a direct relationship between performances and playhouse-books or a casual and random one?

Theater booksellers will, at least, have chosen texts likely to appeal to their potential customers: here was a body of people who, by definition, would not be puritanically opposed to light literature. Catchmey the vicar in Cartwright's *The Ordinary* (3.5) begins to describe a typical collection of "small books" that might be found in the tray of the playhouse trader:

> I shall live to see thee
> Stand in a Play-house doore with thy long box,
> Thy half-crown Library, and cry small Books.
> Buy a good godly Sermon Gentlemen –
> A judgment shewn upon a Knot of Drunkards –
> A pill to purge out Popery – The life
> And death of Katherin Stubs – (Cartwright 1651: 52)

These are pamphlets that sermonize, pass judgement, jibe at Catholicism, relish the lives of martyrs: they range, as plays do, from straightforward moralizing to humor, to gruesome tales vividly told. Other equally appropriate books would also be found at the theater: satires, which "*Brave Gallants*" might "peruse / For to save charges: ere the *Playes* begin"; and obsequious tales of royalty which may well "hap into your hands, before a play begin, with the importunate clamour, of *Buy a new Booke*" (Fitzgeffrey 1617: G6–7; Fennor 1616: π1b).

Cartwright's list is cut short by an interjection – would it have included playbooks had it gone on? Dekker's general expectation of playhouse sale for his works, combined with Middleton's specific anticipation of playhouse reading for his printed play, are both highly suggestive. And, of course, the theater audience did provide the most obvious market for playbooks. Given that published plays anticipate being read by spectators, often the very spectators that watched the piece in the first place, playhouse sale of playbooks seems highly likely. Richard Jones, the printer, introduces his edition of the two parts of *Tamburlaine* with the hope that the plays "will be now no less acceptable unto you to read . . . than they have been lately delightful for many of you to see" (Marlowe 1590: A2a); Basse, in his puff for Massinger's *The Bond-Man*, explains:

> The Author (in a Christian pitty) takes
> Care of your good, and Prints it for your sakes:
> That such as will but venter Six-pence more,
> May *Know*, what they but *Saw* and *Heard* before.
> (W[illiam] B[asse] 1624: A4a)

Combine with this the suggestion forcefully made by Blayney (1997: 386) and Erne (2003: 90–100) that players may deliberately have released scripts into the market for publicity or advertising, and the possibility is then raised that a theater audience might be partly shaped to and by printed playtexts that they bought in the theater. Moreover, if playbooks *were* sold in playhouses then the paper potential of the performed text will always have been felt by the audience. The "book" will have seemed what the play was likely to become next – while the enacted play will never have become entirely separated in kind, at least in the mind of the watchers, from a written one.

The playhouse was, either way, a place where literature was marketed and purveyed in two distinct but linked forms, performance and print. The actors on stage will have seemed a continuation of the light and disposable literature that had already enthralled or enraged the audience, and will have been instantly compared to the texts that had preceded them. This means that Shakespeare's plays on stage, like those of his contemporaries, may often have had books as their context, while, conversely, such plays of his as were in print may have flanked his own and other plays on the stage.

Manuscript Books in the Playhouse

The intimate relationship of play to book was acknowledged and furthered by the audience during performance. "Watching" in the early modern theater seems to have been a less passive event than today. Perhaps because the stage and audience were equally lit, perhaps because there were no rules of silence at the time, literate spectators "judged" plays, favorably or unfavorably, out loud and on paper; they sat in the playhouse with pens and notebooks in their hands (and, presumably, ink-horns on their belts). It was usual to attend the playhouse to ransack plays for conversationally useful "*mots*" that would then furnish repartee in law-courts, taverns, and lady's chambers. So it was said of magistrates that the very language they used was "oft times, but a few shreds and scraps dropt from some Stage-Poet, at the Globe or Cock-pit, which they have carefully bookt up, to serve them for such an occasion" (Trescot 1642: C3b). Others might "hoard up the finest play-scraps [they] can get"; in particular, they would home in on the jokes that, later, they could learn and pass off as their own: "there be . . . them that will get jestes by heart, that have gathred a Common-place booke out of Plaies, that will not let a merriment slip, but they will trusse it up for their owne provision" (Dekker 1884: II, 254; Rich 1606: B4b).[5] Nervous young men would collect lines useful for winning the hearts of ladies; afterwards they would flirt with "set speeches, pickt from Playes" (Richards 1630: G3b). Famously, the ridiculous "Luscus" of Marston's *Scourge of Villainy* spoke almost entirely out of Shakespeare's *Romeo and Juliet* having "made a common-place booke out of plaies . . . He writes, he railes, he jests, he courts, what not, / And all from out his huge long scraped stock / Of well penn'd playes" (Marston 1598: H4a).

Books published specifically for the conversationally insecure, like William Basse's *Help to Discourse*, mingled general observations, sayings, and anecdotes with passages out of dramas like Shakespeare's *Hamlet* (Basse 1623: 249–50). Parts of plays were so primary to good discourse, that is to say, that even people who had missed the actual performance might want to have them. Other compilation-texts mixed passages from famous poets with sections out of plays, like Robert Allot's *England's Parnassus* (1600), which includes quotations from Spenser, Sidney, Jonson, and Shakespeare. Hardly had words been spoken on the stage, it seems, before they were rendered back into inscripted text and given a fresh context amongst passages out of printed and manuscript literature.

Some spectators specialized in recording not the quotations they admired, but those they abhorred. They are referred to in the prologue to *The Woman Hater*, which suggests "if there bee any lurking amongst you in corners, with Table books, who have some hope to find fit matter to feede his – mallice on, let them claspe them up, and slinke away" (Beaumont 1607: A2a). Certain people were known for collecting "ill" passages with malicious intent. Jealous playwrights, in particular, would pounce on the dross from their rivals' performance: Hall writes of ranks of authors sitting in upper galleries in playhouses with charcoal pencils in hand – "Wo to the word whose margent in their scrole, / Is noted with a blacke condemning cole" he relates bleakly (Hall 1597: 8). The condemnatory written sign ("note") he refers to is a theta ("θ" for "θανατοσ," death); it is a letter regularly inscribed in margins to symbolize bad writing. Nashe, for instance, writes of marking sections of his enemies' texts "with a Nigrum theta . . . that all men may shunne [them]" (Nashe 1589: A1a). Thus offending quotations from plays were first put into writing, and then dismissed with a written sign of disapproval. Performances were judged, positively and negatively, in ways that highlighted their similarity to – or returned them to being – passages in books.

As all this makes clear, some members of the audience will have attended the playhouse armed with the weapons of the study: notebooks and scrolls, pens and charcoal. The theater itself was, visibly, a place in which written text was created as well as sold. Nor can the writing audience have been entirely a rarity, for the claim that whole plays could be copied during performance by spectators, whether or not it is true, only makes sense in a theater in which writing is too "normal" an activity to draw attention to itself. So when Heywood insisted that his play *Queen Elizabeth* had been taken down in shorthand ("stenography") at the theater itself years ago, he commented on the habits of the Red Bull audience that will have attended that production:

> . . . the cradle age,
> Did throng the Seates, the Boxes, and the Stage
> So much; that some by Stenography drew
> The plot: put it in print: (scarce one word trew:)
> (Heywood 1637: 248)

Passages, perhaps whole plays, might be "bookt" in the playhouse; afterwards sections of the performed play could be learned, mulled over, despised, published – all carried away from the theater by the means of writing. Spectators' mementos from visiting the theater might be printed texts acquired there or choice additions made to their "tables": either way, the souvenir from a trip to the playhouse might well have been a book.

Again, this was not something for the theater to worry about, for notebooks, too, could become a form of play-advertising. Extracted excerpts from performed plays might spread to other commonplace-books or be liberally scattered through conversations – either would ensure a play's popularity: written fragments were the way a play might be promulgated and "published," even if not printed, outside the playhouse. The theater had an investment in the writing audience, just as it had an investment in the reading audience.

Unsurprisingly, various commonplace-books survive crammed with passages from performed, rather than printed, Shakespeare plays: one contains passages from *Othello* before the text was published, another contains passages from *Henry IV part 1* seemingly taken from a performance before 1603; a third contains notes taken at a Caroline production of *Romeo and Juliet*.[6] Other table-books, harder to date, seem also to contain fragments from performances.[7] Shakespeare, always conscious of the people for whom he writes, may even have shaped his plays to the commonplace-book culture. Anticipating sections of his plays being excerpted, some of Shakespeare's punchier quotations – "A Horse, a Horse, my Kingdome for a Horse" (*Richard III*, TLN 3834), for instance – may have been intended to be "removable": to appeal to table-books.[8]

Title- and Scene-boards in the Playhouse

As might be expected, theaters often built on and encouraged the association between play and book. Far from trying to ensure plays appealed equally to all members of the audience, various playhouses "staged" written words for literate spectators. So in Jonson's *Cynthia's Revels* (Paul's, 1600) the third child remarks that any man who can read a book – specifically, a neck verse to save him from hanging – will know the name of the play that is about to be performed by reading it on a title-board: "the title of his play is *Cynthias Revels*, as any man (that hath hope to bee saved by his booke) can witnesse" (Jonson 1616a: 182). Of course, Jonson is playing a double game; whilst pandering to the literate, he makes sure the illiterate do not miss out: one of the reasons we know about this particular title-board at all is that Jonson has constructed a dialogue in which it is read. But by doing so he illustrates both that the audience might be "ranked" into literate and illiterate in the mind of the playwright, and that varieties of textual material might, nevertheless, be provided on stage for readers.

Often it is said that *Twelfth Night* is exceptional in that the dramatic performance starts before the words (the play's music must precede anything said on stage). In fact, though, many plays began before an actor had stepped onto the platform, a word had been spoken, or a gesture made. It seems to have been normal, at least in some theaters, for the title of a play to depend in written form from the *frons scenae*: performances, then, might well open with written text. So in *Wily Beguiled* (performed Paul's? 1602) the Prologue asks "what play shall wee have here to night?" and is told "Sir you may looke upon the Title." Here the joke is that when the Prologue looks at the board he finds inscribed there simply the name of an old stock play, "*Spectrum* once again." Into the scene then enters a Juggler bearing the correct title-board, and as the stage direction has it, "*Spectrum* is conveied away: and *Wily beguiled*, stands in the place of it" (Anon. 1606: A2a–b).[9] Another play, *The Knight of the Burning Pestle* (performed Queen's Revels? 1607), uses a variant of the same device when the Citizen's desire to reject the play he sees announced on the stage brings about the "actual" play. "You call your play, *The London Merchant*," exclaims the Citizen. "Downe with your Title[,] boy, downe with your Title" (Beaumont 1613: B1a). These tricks use the literacy of the audience against them – illustrating, as Autolycus did, that something is not necessarily "true" simply because it is written down. But the fact remains that written material is shown here as being a regular part of the play's look, part of its *milieu* – and one of its props.

Other performance devices involving title-boards include the way a play might negotiate between two alternate titles. In Jonson's *Poetaster*

(Chapel, 1601) the Prologue, Envy, sees first a title-board bearing what is now the subtitle of the play: "What's here?" he asks disgustedly, "Th'Arraignment? I: This, this is it, / That our sunke eyes have wak't for, all this while" (Jonson 1616b: 275). *The Arraignment* may, in fact, have been the original title of the play; on the other hand, Jonson may here be drawing attention to the punitive aspect of his play: in this induction the punishment to come may be more important than the man so humiliated, the "Poetaster." It may have been possible, that is to say, to vary one title and another during performance, or to "choose" one title over another at specific times. Indeed, the possibility of title variations may explain why some plays *have* two titles at all. But this, of course, raises questions. How does the precision of "*Twelfth Night*" relate to the nonchalance of "*What you Will*" – the latter barely related to the content of the actual play itself? Is one for private performance on a particular occasion, twelfth night, and the other for more general use? Or does the subtitle contain a sly reference to the author, "Will," so that performance-occasion and authorship define the play? Alternatively, might the two vary throughout any performance – one, perhaps, for Orsino's *laissez faire* court, one, concealing a sexual implication ("will"), for Olivia in her tight-lipped seclusion. Or might one give way to the other during the progress of the play? Not having the answers does not undercut the importance of the questions, for perhaps the whole business of title-boards should force us to rethink the meaning and use of titles and subtitles.

Sometimes a subtitle was shown to be just that against a main title. Shirley seems to have had two titles for his *Rosania*, one of which was visible at once, one of which was "revealed" by the Prologue to explain the first. He has the Prologue imagining on entrance "*Rosania*? Mee thinks I hear one say, / What's that? 'Tis a strange title to a Play." To provide further information the Prologue discloses – seemingly by flipping or uncovering more of the board – the clarifying second title:

> that you might know
> Something i'th Title, which you need not owe
> To another's understanding, you may see,
> In honest English there, *Love's Victory*. (Shirley 1646: 148–9)

Here the audience has been given one of the two titles in advance of performance; the result is to whet interest in the character of Rosania, and, later, to draw attention to the nature of the play – here described as "explicating" the first title: both titles perform slightly different functions that are characterized by the way they are made known to the audience. This particular use of title-boards, enumerated in a prologue written specially for a Dublin performance of *Rosania* by Ogilsby's Men's in 1638, is for an audience whose literacy is, as ever, being assumed and exploited.

Games involving the title-boards raise other important questions about the relationship of title to play more generally. Were weighted generic terms like "tragedy" also hung out on stage from the beginning of performance? Did *Othello*'s Iago, that is to say, perform his machinations in front of "tragedy," and *Cymbeline*'s Iachimo, a similar character, perform his in front of "comedy"? Did *Richard the Second* thrive under the heading "The Life and Death of . . ." (its running title in the folio) so that the demise of the king is always in front of the audience's eyes? Could titles, that is to say, become part of the way a performance was interpreted? Similar questions can, of course, be asked of the play in book-form; indeed, a title hanging on stage makes a performance look "book-like." Tellingly, the word "frontispiece" was used both for title-pages of playbooks and for the decorative *frons scenae* on which a play's title was hung: one poet refers to "The frontispeece or Title page of Playes, / Whose whole discourse is – As the Poet sayes . . ."; while in Blount's *Glossographia* the term "Salmacidan Spoiles" is explained with reference to Jonson's masque: "Salmacida Spolia was the Motto of the Scene or Frontispiece of a Mask at Whitehall at Christmas 1636, or 1637" (Anon. 1652: A5b; Blount 1656: 2L8b).

The plays quoted so far in this section have largely been for performance at Blackfriars' or Pauls' playhouses, and the few scholars who have considered title-boards at all have tended to assume that their use was confined to those theaters (Gurr 1992: 180; Rhodes 1924: 127). This is, of course, fascinating, with its implication that any Shakespeare plays written for performance (or revised for performance) after 1609 when his company started playing in Blackfriars are likely to have been so adorned. Only the opening of *The Tempest* contains a storm – but will the word "tempest" have overhung Stefano's quarrel, Prospero's rage, Miranda's and Ferdinand's love, insisting the audience see the word as a metaphor for the relationships in the play as much as a description of an event?

Further instances may suggest a more widespread use of title-boards. There is the fact that all court masques, pageants, and progresses were similarly labeled: a title was "normal" in an entertainment setting. So, for instance, London itself was labeled for progresses: in Dekker's *Magnificent Entertainment* for James a sign was hung over the gate at Soper Lane End in which "in Capitalles was inscribed this Title: *NOVA FÆLIX ARABIA*" (Dekker and Middleton 1604: D2a). University plays, too, might use a title-board, as when the Prologue "*TO THE UNIVERSITY*" for Cartwright's *Royal Slave* (Christ Church, Oxford, 1636) worries that a question for academic dispute might more fittingly hang in the title's space: "I could wish some Question hung up there, / *That we by Genuine sounds might take your eare*" (Cartwright 1639: A2b). In *The History of Sir John Oldcastle* (Admiral's, 1599 – a Rose theater play) the Prologue draws attention to "*The doubtfull Title (Gentlemen) prefixt / Upon the Argument we have in hand*"; in Brome's *City Wit* (King's Revels? 1630, rev. Queen Henrietta's, 1637–9) the Prologue, seemingly for the revival of the play, appears to carry the title onto the stage with him: "*Some in this round may have both seen't, and heard, / Ere I, that beare its title, wore a Beard*" (Munday 1600: A2a; Brome 1635: A2b). Shirley's *Rosania* in Dublin has already been mentioned – but even when that author imagines a play performed in prison he still conjectures a title-board for it. In Shirley's *Bird in a Cage* (Queen Henrietta's, 1633), Donella and her ladies are incarcerated and put on an entertainment to pass the time. Lacking title-boards and scene-boards (of which, more below) for their production, they advise one another to "whet your inventions and about it, imagine our scene exprest, and the new Prison, the title[,] advanc'd in forme" (Shirley 1633: G4b). In short there is a strong suggestion that over time and in various theaters title-boards were accepted and, perhaps, expected. Some, possibly many, plays were written in text letters on their stages: "writing" was, then, both an expected elucidation and a theatrical prop, and written words, whether or not the audience could read them, were visually part of "theater."

Additional staging information was also sometimes provided as text on a board hanging onstage. The name of the place in which the action was occurring (a scene-board) seems, too, to have been present for some academic and court performances: witness Sir Philip Sidney's disdain for plays in which "Thebes [is] written in great letters on an old Doore" (Sidney 1595: H1a).[10]

Many published plays – often, but not always, plays that have been put on in private theaters – provide a list of *dramatis personae*, and accompany that list by saying where the "scene" of the play is set:

Ford's *The Lady's Triall* has "THE SCENE, Genoa" (Beeston Boys, 1638); Shirley's *The Traitor* has "THE SCENE, Florence" (Queen Henrietta's, 1631); Davenant's *The Wits*, which appears to have been printed from the playhouse's official "book" – it includes on one of its pages the approval of the Master of the Revels – has "The Scene London" (King's Men, 1634) (Ford 1639: A2a; Davenant 1636: A2b; Shirley 1635: A2b).[11] Critics have often assumed that "place" in such instances is a bookish way of telling the reader that the whole play subscribes to the classical "unities." But it may also reflect or herald a scene-board, stuck up, like "Thebes," to bear public witness to the classical unities on the stage. It is notable that unpublished plays – some of which may be written for readers, some for performers – still find it important to convey "place," for instance: Arthur Wilson's *The Inconstant Lady Acted at Blackfriars*, a manuscript play from the 1630s, starts by stating "The Scaene Burgundie"; his *The Corporal Acted at Blackfriars*, of which just the opening survives in this particular manuscript, has "The Scaene Lorraine" (Wilson no date (a) and (b)); while *The Partial Law*, an anonymous tragicomedy from around 1625, starts "The scene, Corsica" (Anon. ca. 1625). And it is notable, too, that authors not interested in setting their play in a fixed place, will sometimes still name the "scene" where their events are happening. Goffe's *The Careless Shepherdess* has an induction where "THE SCENE" is "SALISBURY COURT" – probably the very place in which the production is taking place – and a play where, says the actor-list, "the Scene" is "ARCADIA" (university play revised in 1631 by Shirley for King's Revels?); and Nabbes's *Hannibal and Scipio* (Queen Henrietta's, 1635) has several scene changes, starting with "the Scene Capua" and going on to "The Scene, the Court of Syphax in Cyrtha" (Goffe 1656: B1a, C2b; Nabbes 1637: B1a, C4a). How will these "scene-changes" so visible in textual form be conveyed to the audience? In these instances, both the fact of a scene-board, and the change of the scene-board, may be indicated.

Hieronimo seems to exemplify use of just such a board in *The Spanish Tragedy* (Strange's [by 1592], 1587, rev. 1597? and 1601–2) when, preparing to present his play *Soliman and Perseda*, he says "Hang up the Title: our Scaene is *Rhodes*," a reference appearing to indicate two boards, title and scene, just as the scene was "exprest" in *Bird in a Cage* above (Kyd 1592: K2b). Hieronimo in this play-within-a-play is preparing a "court" performance, but the board he hangs up will be visible in the various public theaters in which *Spanish Tragedy* was mounted. Is there any reason to think that "scene-boards" might ever have adorned the common stage on other occasions?

Surviving information is minimal, but when Marius, in Thomas Lodge's *Wounds of Civil War,* is instructed to "Enter . . . solus from the Numidian mountaines" (1588; Admiral's Men at the Rose by 1594), he can hardly enter from the mountains themselves (Lodge 1594: E3a). Perhaps Lodge, while writing the text, has simply become engrossed with the fiction he is creating and has produced an "unstage-able" direction. But maybe the stage direction embodies a knowledge of the way the play will be (or was) performed. If that is the case, then "mountaines," which here are associated with a door of entrance, would need to be depicted in images or words around the door itself. Indeed, it seems that different doors of entrance were regularly associated with different places – as when Dekker jokily advises the man walking in Paul's to "observe your doores of entrance, and your Exit, not much unlike the plaiers at the Theaters, . . . if you prove to be a Northerne Gentleman, I would wish you to passe through the North doore, more often (especially) then any of the other: and . . . according to your countries, take note of your entrances"; or when Jasper Mayne writes a praising poem to the memory of Ben Jonson extolling the fact that in his plays "two entrances / Were not two parts oth' World, disjoyn'd by Seas" (Dekker 1884: II, 230–1; Mayne 1638: 30).

It is impossible to say how regularly scene-boards were used on the public stage, though their private theater use seems clear enough. What is the case is that various pictures from around Europe over this period show both title and scene-boards, often on temporary "booth" stages erected for country productions where a sophisticated, literate audience might not necessarily have been expected: these pictures represent stages in Germany, the Netherlands, Flanders, and Sweden.[12] Though few pictures of English productions survive from the period, a German painting that depicts a performance mounted by English traveling-players has been described: it is said to portray "a stage divided by a curtain into a large open front stage and a smaller rear stage, somewhat raised, and reached by two steps. Two sign-boards are shown, on one of which is an illegible inscription; on the other 'A room in the house'."[13] If this is a genuine report of a real picture, then English-language scene-boards were so elemental to some perfor-mances that they were used even when abroad.

If "place" was sometimes hung up on a board on the stage, then the simple words that Hieronimo uses, "the scene is," are extremely resonant: they seem to indicate what specific word is placed on the board. In Jonson's *Poetaster* (Chapel, 1601), Envy turns, it seems, from the title-board to the scene-board to see where the play is set: "The *Scene* is, ha! / Rome? Rome? and Rome?" (Jonson 1616b: 276; possibly the joke here is that each of the three doors of entrance are labeled with the same name – precisely because Jonson so carefully eschews designating different places to different doors). Similarly, in the pamphlet *Lord have Mercy upon us* (1648), which begins as though at the start of a play-performance – it includes the trumpet blasts that announced the beginning of a play – the place in which the scene occurs is provided as information available before any actor comes on stage: "The scene is Oxford, and now sound Trumpets, my Lord enters" (Anon. 1648: 3). As one set of aphorisms had it (muddling in their very description, a play read and a play acted), in a play: "The Prologue, Preface or preamble, prepares the matter. The Scene declares the stage where the things are acted, and the changes of it are called Scenes. The acts are the severall passages of the things done and represented to the hearers..." (Anon. 1642: 50). Here "changes of... Scenes" may both indicate changes of board and a progression from one section of the play to the next. As Dessen and Thomson (1999) point out, a "scene" sometimes seems to have meant the front of the tyring-house – and thus the back of the stage – the *frons scenae* (as in Shirley's stage-direction "the scene adorned with Pictures" or Gayton's "they put their heads through the hangings of the Scene"); and sometimes referred specifically to the space above the doors in the *frons scenae* (as in Nabbes' *Covent Garden*, where characters enter and leave through "the right Scoene" and "the left Scoene") (Shirley 1655: 37; Gayton 1654: 94; Nabbes 1633: B1a, C4b). A scene-board, then, might have been named from its position on the stage's "scene," in which case the very word "scene" becomes complex, referring both to a section of playtext and a bit of the stage. The two are, of course, interrelated: but this means that the structure of the written text is oddly visualized by the construction of the stage – and the very elements of a play that are thought to be purely "textual" are in fact the ones most easy to manifest in the theater.

Naturally, scene-boards will affect our understanding, whether they are labels on a particular door – as is perhaps suggested by the stage-direction in Shakespeare's *3 Henry VI* that asks Warwick and Oxford to "*Enter... in England*" (TLN 2186) – or single labels that hang on stage throughout performance. It would certainly be interesting if the place direction indicated after the "Names of the Actors" in *The Tempest*, "The Scene, an un-inhabited Island" (King's Men, 1611), were written on the stage together with the play's title. That would indicate to the anticipatory audience a slightly different story from the one that they actually see – a story in which shipwrecked noblemen arrive on a deserted island. The place name, then, would put the audience in an odd alliance with the strangers entering the island rather than the people who, slightly resentfully, live there. Were it to remain hanging on stage, it would look forward to the time when the island will be returned to its deserted state, containing only monsters and spirits.

As ever, use of boards allows authors to play games with the audience's expectations: in Shirley's *The Cardinal* (King's Men, 1641), the Prologue, it seems, denies the audience a scene-board so that the spectators will imagine the play to be taking place in the wrong country. "The Cardinal!" says the Prologue, " 'cause we express no scene, / We doe believe most of you Gentlemen / Are at this hour in France . . ." (Shirley 1652: A4a). It is as though the reading audience, scanning the Blackfriars stage for additional information, will not know how to handle an uninscribed, wordless space.

Other games for the literate involved conflating title- and scene-board so that the "place" becomes a feature of the name of the story. This, then, will have been a stage in which only one board was visible – as when, for Davenant's *Siege of Rhodes*, "The Ornament which encompass'd the Scene . . . bore up a large Freese . . . wherein was written RHODES" (Davenant 1656: B1a). Conflating the two, however, could affect the way the play was watched. In Percy's manuscript play *A Country Tragedy* (designed for performance at Paul's by boys or, alternatively, at an unidentified theater by adult performers) instructions are given to choose one of two titles:

> The Title aloft and about being both Title and Scene A COUNTRY TRAGOEDYE IN VACUNIUM or CUPIDS SACRIFICE one of the Two, The first in regard of propertie of Scene. (Percy no date: 92a)

Here one option is to have the full title doubling as scene-board – in which case the word "tragedy" is indeed part of the country setting, and title and scene are linked as though they are bringing one another about. It is worth considering the way other plays might, too, explore this hinterland between title and scene. "Troy" ("In Troy there lies the scene") could, with a tug of a flap or a removing of a lower portion of the scene-board, become "Troy-lus and Cressida," the tragedy and its protagonists both inevitably arising from the doomed city.

In a different manuscript play, Percy suggests that written words can substitute for almost all stage props if necessary. For *The Fairy Pastoral* (again, designed for performance at Paul's by boys or at an unidentified theater by adult performers) he suggests:

> The Properties.
> . . . on the Top of the Musick Tree the Title THE FAERY PASTO-RALL, Beneath . . . pind on Post of the Tree The Scene ELUIDA FORREST. Lowest off all over the Canopie ΝΑΠΑΙΤΒΟ ΑΙΟΝ or FAERY CHAPPELL. A kiln of Brick. A Fowen Cott. A Hollowe Oake . . . Now if so be that the Properties of any of These, that be outward, will not serve the turne by reason of concurse of the People on the Stage, Then you may omitt the sayd Properties which be outward and supplye their Places with their Nuncupations only in Text Letters. (Percy 1824: 94)[14]

For Percy, the written word can extend beyond title or scene to become a direct substitute for anything material: the stage is merely an extension of Percy's book. True, his is an extreme case – but more generally there is a suggestion that the reading audience were given bits of text to which to respond, and that their textual approach to plays may have been mirrored by, or brought about by, the theater's similar obsession with the written word. Productions on stage seem often to have been surrounded by a marginalia of written words: they were "published" in many textual ways beyond or beside what happened in the printing houses. Sometimes the watching experience, seemingly designedly, was shaped to recall the experience of looking at a playbook with title, sub-title, running-title (the continuance of the title-board on stage during performance) and stage-directions for scenes. The book-like appearance of the play will have lured the readers whilst reminding the illiterate that play-watching was still, essentially, a bookish activity.

Conclusion: Theater, Audience, and Text

A potential audience member will have been assailed visually with print as soon as he or she considered a trip to the theater. For the way to establish which plays were in performance was to read, or have read to you, the printed playbills produced by the official playbill-printer and hanging on posts around London. Every play, that is to say, was met in written form first, its print context preceding its performance one. Moreover, every play, in advertisement form, resembled a book in advertisement form, for the play's bill was remarkably similar in appearance to a book's title-page, hung on a post for better promotion. The two, indeed, often hung beside one another; play and book were linked in the mind of the audience well before any production began.[15]

This makes better sense of the fact that a play at a playhouse was continually thought of as having bookish qualities. Acting was judged by its perceived ability to be faithful to something unseen by the audience and yet present in the discourse of the theater: "the book" (the manuscript or printed play held by the prompter). So a good actor played "by the book"; if he needed no prompting that was because he knew his part "without book." Cowley, disappointed by the hastily mounted production of his *The Guardian*, recalled that "the haste was so great, that it could neither be . . . *perfected* by the *Author*, nor *learnt without-Book* by the *Actors*"; while Sir Richard Baker, writing slightly later, queried "what doth a Player else, but onely say that without book, which we may read within Book?" (Cowley 1656:1b; Baker 1670: 43). Of course, these terms do not have a unique theater referent – the same phrases might be used of any child who had learned his catechism – but that, too, is instructive. Actors were equated with anyone else who learned texts from books; the learning was praised not just in itself but also in its relationship to the absent written texts. The bookishness within the acting was one of its qualities.

So what is described as the "rude raskal rabble" in the public theater, the people who may well not have been literate, would extol performers who were acting particularly well with "excellent, excellent: the knaves have acted their parts in print" (Gainsford 1616: 118). "In print," a phrase meaning "precisely" or "perfectly," may have signified large letters – letters such as might be found on a title- or scene-board – as much as print itself. But "in print" as an analogy chosen by a rabble is instructive all ways. Inscribed letters, whether in type or simply large, were perceived as having a kind of perfection, and the audience, irrespective of ability to cope with the letters as words, emerge as being attuned to the glamor rather than the stigma of print in all its forms: here "print" is what the best theater achieves. It is worth considering once again Marston's *Romeo-and-Juliet*-obsessed

Luscus, who has "made a common-place booke out of plaies, / And speakes in print, at least what ere he sayes / Is warranted by Curtaine plaudites" (Marston 1598: H4a). Luscus talks with a print-like perfection the words he has taken from the stage of the Curtain. The playhouse, print-rich in its nature, was also an environment in which one could only hope that print-perfect events would take place. So, yes, Shakespeare's plays have a bookish quality – but might that be because the bookishness was an essential element of their performance?[16]

Notes

1 They were last seriously addressed by Lawrence (1912: 43–71); continental use of scene-boards was considered by Nagler (1954).

2 For the reader's convenience I have modernized play titles in the body of this essay. However, I have retained original spelling in all quotations from early modern printed and manuscript texts and in titles in the works cited.

3 There is a suggestion here in the phrasing – whole-sale, press – that mercury women were also prepared to trade other things. For the regard in which such people were held, see the title to an anonymous pamphlet of 1641, *The Downfall of Temporizing Poets, Unlicensed Printers, Upstart Booksellers, Trotting Mercuries and Bawling Hawkers . . . a . . . Dialogue between Light-foot the Mercury and Suck-bottle the Hawker . . .*

4 Quotations from Shakespeare are taken from Hinman's *Norton Facsimile* of the 1623 Folio, using the Through Line Numbering (TLN) of that edition.

5 See also Webster's additions to Marston's *The Malcontent* (1604: A3a): "I am one that hath seene this play often . . . I have most of the jeasts heere in my table-booke"; and the prologue to Nabbes (1637: A3b), which refers to "he . . . that from the Poets labours [will] gather notes" to be used "for th'exercise of wit / At Taverns."

6 Part of Edward Pudsey's manuscript *Commonplace-book* is in the Shakespeare Birthplace trust Record Office, Stratford-upon-Avon (ER82). It contains passages from *Othello* dating from before 1609. British Library manuscript Add MS 64078 contains lines, probably jotted down by the mathematician Thomas Herriot, from *Henry IV part 1*. They are transcribed and described in Kelliher (1989), which also refers to a commonplace-book, now in Japan, containing a passage from *Romeo and Juliet*.

7   Passages from other commonplace-books can be found in Ingleby (1932).
8   Quoted in Marston (1607 C1a–b): "A horse, a horse, my kingdom for a horse ... I speake play scrappes." Regularly quoted thereafter.
9   Dates of performance and company are from Harbage et al. (1989).
10 I am avoiding the confusing term "locality board" which hides the nature of the board and does not appear to have been the term in use at the time.
11 Over one hundred plays include a place designation.
12 Stage erected for a St. Laurentius play for school performance; reproduced in C. Niessen, *Dramatische Darstellungen in Köln von 1526 bis 1700* (Köln, 1917). Detail from a painting by David Vinckeboons, held by the Koninklijk Museum in Antwerp, reproduced by Thomson (1999: 57). A different version of the picture, depicting narrower, wavy-looking signs above the backcloth, is reproduced in Gascoigne (1968: 112). "Temperantina," a pen and ink drawing by Pierter Brueghel the Elder, is in Rotterdam, Museum Boijmans Van Beuningen, and is reproduced in Wickham (1985). For alerting me to these last three pictures, I am profoundly grateful to Christopher Matusiak. The unascribed Drottningholm painting is reproduced in Nicoll (1959: opp. p. 106).
13 Reynolds (1911) translates this description from E. Mentzel's *Geschichte der Schauspielkunst in Frankfort* (1882), pp. 38–9. He goes on to say that he has written to Mentzel but "personal inquiry has failed to elicit any further information concerning this picture."
14 It has been plausibly argued that this play was performed before James I at Syon House on June 8, 1603 – though the surviving text also seems to have been revised in the hope of subsequent performances elsewhere. See Dodds (1931).
15 For more on this see Stern (2006).
16 I am grateful to Alan Dessen and Holger Schott Syme for their thoughtful responses to this paper. For alerting me to various continental images containing scene- and title-boards, I owe a particular debt of gratitude to Christopher Matusiak.

Works Cited

Anon. 1606: *Wily Beguilde*. London.
Anon. ca. 1625: *The Partiall Law*. Folger Library MS, v.a.165.

Anon. 1641: *The Downfall of Temporizing Poets, Unlicensed Printers, Upstart Booksellers, Trotting Mercuries and Bawling Hawkers ... a ... Dialogue between Light-foot the Mercury and Suck-bottle the Hawker ...* London.

Anon. 1642: *The Aphorismes of the Kingdome [with] the Commission of Array.* London.

Anon. 1648: *Lord Have Mercy Upon Us.* London.

Anon. 1652: "Upon Mr. Randolph's Poems." In Thomas Randolph, *Poems*, 1652.

Baker, Sir Richard 1670: *Theatrum Triumphans.* London.

Basse, William 1623: *A Help to Discourse.* London.

B[asse], W[illiam] 1624: "The *Author's* Friend to the Reader." In Massinger 1624.

Beaumont, Francis 1607: *The Woman Hater.* London.

Beaumont, Francis 1613: *The Knight of the Burning Pestle.* London.

Blayney, Peter 1997: "The Publication of Playbooks." In Cox and Kastan, 383–422.

Blount, Thomas 1656: *Glossographia.* London.

Brome, Richard 1653: *The City Wit.* London.

Cartwright, William 1639: *The Royall Slave.* London.

Cartwright, William 1651: *The Ordinary.* London.

Cheyney, Patrick 2004: *Shakespeare: National Poet-Playwright.* Cambridge: Cambridge University Press.

Cowley, Abraham 1650: *The Guardian.* London.

Cowley, Abraham 1656: *Poems.* London.

Cox, John D. and Kastan, David Scott (eds.) 1997: *A New History of Early English Drama.* New York: Columbia University Press.

Davenant, William 1636: *The Wits.* London.

Davenant, William 1656: *The Siege of Rhodes.* London.

Dekker, Thomas 1884: *The Gull's Horn-book.* In Alexander B. Grosart (ed.) *The Non-Dramatic Works*, vol. 2. New York: Russell and Russell.

Dekker, Thomas and Middleton, Thomas 1604: *The Magnificent Entertainment Given to King James.* London.

Dessen, Alan and Thomson, Leslie 1999: *A Dictionary of Stage Directions in English Drama, 1580–1642.* Cambridge: Cambridge University Press.

Dodds, Madeleine Hope 1931: "William Percy and James I." *Notes and Queries* 61, 13–14.

Erne, Lukas 2003: *Shakespeare as Literary Dramatist.* Cambridge: Cambridge University Press.

Fennor, William 1616: *Fennors Descriptions.* London.

Fitzgeffrey, Henry 1617: *Satyres and Satyricall Epigrams.* London.

Ford, John 1639: *The Ladies Triall.* London.

Gainsford, Thomas 1616: *The Rich Cabinet.* London.

Gascoigne, Bamber 1968: *World Theater: An Illustrated History.* London: Ebury Press.

Gayton, Edmund 1654: *Pleasant Notes upon Don Quixote.* London.

Goffe, Thomas 1656: *The Careless Shepherdess.* London.

Gurr, Andrew 1992: *The Shakespearean Stage.* Cambridge: Cambridge University Press.

Hall, Joseph 1597: *Virgidemiarum.* London.

Harbage, Alfred, Schoenbaum, Samuel, and Wagonheim, Sylvia (eds.) 1989: *Annals of English Drama*, 3rd edn. London: Routledge.

Heywood, Thomas 1637: *Pleasant Dialogues and Dramas.* London.

Ingleby, C. M. et al. (comp. and ed.) 1932: *The Shakespeare Allusion Book.* Re-edited by John Monro, 2 vols. Oxford: Oxford University Press.

Jonson, Ben 1616a: *Cynthias Revels.* In *Works.* London.

Jonson, Ben 1616b: *Poetaster.* In *Works.* London.

Kelliher, Hilton 1989: "Contemporary Manuscript Extracts from Shakespeare's *Henry IV, part 1.*" *English Manuscript Studies 1100–1700* 1, 144–81.

Kyd, Thomas 1592: *The Spanish Tragedy.* London.

Lawrence, W. J. 1912: *The Elizabethan Playhouse and Other Studies.* Stratford-upon-Avon: Shakespeare Head Press.

Lodge, Thomas 1594: *The Wounds of Civill War.* London.

Marlowe, Christopher 1590: *Tamberlaine the Great.* London.

Marston, John 1598: *The Scourge of Villainy.* London.

Marston, John 1607: *What You Will.* London.

Massinger, Philip 1624: *The Bond-Man.* London.

Mayne, Jasper 1638: *Jonsonus Virbius.* London.

Meres, Francis 1598: *Wit's Academy.* London.

Middleton, Thomas 1611: *The Roaring Girl.* London.

Munday, Anthony 1600: *The first part of . . . the Life of Sir John Old-castle.* London.

Nabbes, Thomas 1633: *Covent Garden.* London.

Nabbes, Thomas 1637: *Hannibal and Scipio.* London.

Nagler, A. M. 1954: "Sixteenth-Century Continental Stages." *Shakespeare Quarterly* 5, 358–70.

Nashe, Thomas 1589: *The Anatomy of Absurdity.* London.

Nicoll, Allardyce (ed.) 1959: *Shakespeare Survey 12.* Cambridge: Cambridge University Press.

Parrot, Henry 1615: *The Mastive.* London.

Percy, William, no date: *A Country Tragedy.* MS, Huntington Library, HM 4.

Percy, William 1824: *The Cuck-Queanes and Cuckolds Errants*, ed. J. Haslewood. London: Roxburghe Club.

Pudsey, Edward, no date: manuscript *Commonplace-book*. Shakespeare Birthplace Trust Record Office, Stratford-upon-Avon (ER82).

Randolph, Thomas 1652: *Poems*. London.

Reynolds, G. F. 1911: "What We Know of the Elizabethan Stage." *Modern Philology* 9, 47–82.

Rhodes, R. Crompton 1924: *Studies in the First Folio*. Ed. Israel Gollancz. Oxford: Oxford University Press.

Rich, Barnaby 1606: *Faults Faults, and Nothing Else but Faults*. London.

Richards, Nathaniel 1630: *The Celestial Publican*. London.

Shakespeare, William 1623: In Charlton Hinman, *Norton Facsimile*. New York: W. W. Norton.

Shirley, James 1633: *The Bird in a Cage*. London.

Shirley, James 1635: *The Traitor*. London

Shirley, James 1646: *Poems &c*. London.

Shirley, James 1652: *The Cardinal*. London.

Shirley, James 1655: *Gentleman of Venice*. London.

Sidney, Philip 1595: *The Defence of Poesy*. London.

Stern, Tiffany 2006: "'On each Wall / And Corner Poast': Playbills, Titlepages and Advertising in Early Modern London." *English Literary Renaissance* 36, 57–85.

Thomson, Peter 1999: *Shakespeare's Professional Career*. Cambridge: Cambridge University Press.

Trescot, Thomas 1642: *The Zealous Magistrate*. London.

Wickham, Glynne 1985: *A History of the Theater*. Cambridge: Cambridge University Press.

Wilson, Arthur, no date (a): *The Inconstant Lady*, Bodleian MS, Rawlinson Poet 9.

Wilson, Arthur, no date (b): *The Corporal*, Bodleian MS, Rawlinson Poet 9.

Chapter 7

What Do Editors Do and Why Does It Matter?

Anthony B. Dawson

Rationale

In this essay I am trying to respond to some of the complexities involved with the editing of Shakespeare's texts at the present time. Editors prepare texts for publication, and in the case of Shakespeare this involves a complex process of modernization, adjudicating between alternative readings, coming to grips with long editorial and performance traditions, etc. But, as I outline at the beginning of the essay, how we think about what a text is has changed over the past twenty years or so. Textual theory now stresses uncertainty, instability, and indeterminacy when it used to stress stability and coherence. So I begin with a question about what difference this makes to the actual process of editing. I want to take another look at certain principles that have slipped out of fashion – ideas such as authorial intention and editorial judgement. One often comes across the view these days that an author's intention is both unknowable and irrelevant, and that basing a text on what one can discern about the author's intention is at best chimerical and perhaps even dishonest. While one can readily concede to the "new textualists" who propound such views that there are many uncertainties and instabilities surrounding Shakespeare's "original" texts, I argue that there are strong reasons for refining and sharpening our sense of the author behind the text rather than abandoning it altogether. Can we be more precise about what we can know, instead of giving up on historical knowledge altogether?

Another much-debated issue in Shakespeare studies at the moment is the relation between text and performance. Are the texts we have essentially scripts for the theater, or do they have a more literary provenance? Did Shakespeare care about publication? Who bought Shakespeare's plays in quarto, and why? Did printed texts appeal to an anti-performance snobbery? Too often in discussions of this sort, both sides seem to insist on a kind of wall between the literary and the performed, whereas I see them as intimately intertwined; so I wanted in the essay to stress that interconnectedness, to see the literary and the performative as mutually energizing. I thus offer what I hope is a riposte to the sort of thinking that isolates Shakespeare's texts, making them only one thing or the other instead of both.

Finally, and perhaps most usefully in a volume of this sort, I wanted simply to describe the kinds of things editors are faced with when they put together a modern Shakespearean text – what decisions do they have to make and what kinds of evidence and analysis will they need to pursue in order to make wise, well-informed decisions? To illustrate such matters, I adduce a couple of examples, the most extended on *Timon of Athens*, drawn from my own experience of editing. In the end, the work of editors has significant implications for the meaning of Shakespeare's plays, which is why it's important and why users of modernized texts need to be aware of what editors actually do and why they do it.

Editors today work in a climate of distrust, and perhaps not without reason. First of all there is a general distrust in the stability of texts; indeed, there is energetic debate about what a text actually is. Some have argued that texts are always and inevitably plural – that there is no such thing as *Hamlet* but only *Hamlet*s, whether printed texts or performances, instantiations at particular times and places of an unknowable object that we call *Hamlet* but which has no real existence. Secondly, there is distrust of the figure of the author, who has been dissolved into a network of collaboration, including, in Shakespeare's case, fellow actors, other writers, scribes, printers, and publishers. Thirdly, there is distrust of the work of the editor him- or herself; those who wish to argue for the radical instability of texts often scorn editors for being committed to an outmoded idea of authorial intention and the possibility of distinguishing between texts that may be closer or farther away from such intention. Some theorists have therefore called for an abandonment of editing in favor of facsimiles or what Leah Marcus (following Randall McLeod) called "unediting." An editor who ignores all this does so at her peril.

Nevertheless, editors, partly at the behest of publishing companies with an eye to the marketplace, keep on producing new versions; and their work involves thousands of small decisions about textual details which, unless they are to be entirely random, must inevitably be based on some principle or other. Usually the principles involved depend on an idea of authorship, however attenuated. Even to correct "obvious" errors, an editor has to rely on what she can infer about intention, and with more complex textual puzzles she often has to confront the possibility of contradictory intentions producing contradictory results. The solution requires a move to a narrative about how a particular text came to be the way it is. One of the key characters in such narratives is someone we can call Copytext. This character came into prominence during the heyday of the "New Bibliography" and was given a distinguished pedigree and a brilliant rationale by W. W. Greg. Copytext is a kind of trickster figure, seemingly innocuous and even helpful to the narrator/editor; but he lays traps, leading the narrator down culs-de-sac or suddenly displaying her irrationality. To rely on Copytext is both necessary and dangerous.

Let us look at a familiar example. Readers unfamiliar with the vagaries of Copytext might, innocently enough, pick up G. R. Hibbard's Oxford edition of *Hamlet* and fail to find certain well-known passages – most prominently perhaps the fourth act soliloquy in which Hamlet meditates on the mysterious reasons why he continues to delay his "dull revenge." In Hibbard's text, Hamlet does not appear at all in 4.4, which is reduced to an eight-line scene consisting of Fortinbras' instructions to his Captain. Gone is the self-lacerating soliloquy on the part of the anxious hero, as well as his chat with the Norwegian Captain; instead, we move quickly on to Gertrude's fears and the disturbances of Ophelia's mad scene. Readers accustomed to the "received" text might wonder what is going on, but those aware of the contexts (and contests) of modern editing will be able to nod sagely, knowing that the shape-changer, Copytext, has been up to his usual tricks.

At the same time, in this instance, the editor seems to be holding the trickster in check. Let us think for a minute about Hibbard's narrative. He omits from his edition 18 passages (a total of about 230 lines) that do not appear in the Folio (1623) text of the play, relegating them to an appendix. But those same passages do occur in the second quarto version of the play (Q2), printed in 1604–5, which itself substantially enlarges a still earlier, less reliable text (Q1, 1603). Hibbard decided to base his edition on F since he concluded, after a careful assessment of the existing evidence, that it represented a theatrical version of the play and, further, that it showed signs of Shakespeare's own hand in the abridgement. Indeed, he argues, Heminges and Condell, Shakespeare's fellow actors who were responsible for the compilation of his plays in F, must have rejected Q2 as the source for F since they were familiar with the *theatrical* version from twenty years of acting in it and, presumably, were aware of their colleague Shakespeare's role in establishing it. They therefore relied on the manuscript they had been using in the theater instead of on the printed texts (Q2 and a reprint of 1611, Q3) available to them.[1] Copytext, in this story, takes the shape of F, though in most of the narratives around *Hamlet* he has appeared as Q2 (and some have even seen him lurking in the shadows of Q1).

For Hibbard, F is closer to the final version that Shakespeare intended, in that it represents a theatrical trimming down of his initial version, one that he himself supervised. Hibbard's argument leaves room for collaboration – perhaps Richard Burbage, Shakespeare's main actor, suggested cutting the fourth act soliloquy ("Look, Will, we've already made that point more than once, can't we move the story more quickly toward the denouement?"); the world of the theater is always collaborative in that sense, and playwrights are often open to suggestions from colleagues. In Shakespeare's case, where the playwright was also an actor and knew the other members of his company intimately, such interchanges must have been frequent. The end result may be a text that is somewhat distant from what looks like the author's "original" intention (this is probably best represented by Q2); but it is also one that takes into account the inescapable element of collaboration without giving up on the idea of an originating author. That this is a narrative, one in which Copytext plays a crucial role, has to be acknowledged; it is not, that is, definitive proof. But this does not invalidate it; on the contrary, while the narrative may be hypothetical, it also opens an avenue toward truth. While, that is, the tales of Copytext are various and even potentially contradictory, they are also necessary as a paradoxical form of truth, a shape that is given, more or less plausibly, to the historical data before us. Narratives in this sense are heuristic – they make discovery possible.

In the early stages of my own editorial struggles with a stubbornly recalcitrant Shakespeare text, *Troilus and Cressida*, I proposed to the general editors that I be released from the restraints imposed by adhering to a particular copy-text (I here revert to the lower case, ordinary meaning of the term, abandoning the trickster to his designs). Since the situation with *Troilus and Cressida* is particularly vexed, the arguments for basing a modern text on either the Q and F versions more or less even, I thought it might be worthwhile to simply adjudicate each textual variant as it came up, without recourse to an argument about the underlying manuscripts for the two early texts. This idea would highlight the instability and uncertainty of textual relations and allow me as an editor plenty of interpretive latitude – a freedom one might say that was congruent with the uncertainty surrounding texts and underlined by recent critiques of editorial practice. The idea was quickly squashed. And in the end I am glad it was, partly because it's always helpful to have the trickster on your side, but even more because it forced me to look further into the question and construct my own narrative – one based as solidly as I was able on the data I had to work with, but a narrative nonetheless.[2] Copy-text, whether as a figure in a story or as a concept, is still a useful tool, since it encourages editors to think creatively and yet rigorously about the available data. And it enables us to think further about the implications of the stories we tell about early texts – for example, to raise another vexed issue in modern criticism, the relation of text to performance.

As Tiffany Stern notes in the previous chapter, some critics have recently asserted a divergence between early modern performance and printed texts, to the extent even of claiming that many Shakespearean texts are too long to be accommodated to what the prologue to *Romeo and Juliet* calls the "two hours traffic of our stage" and must therefore represent longer *literary* versions designed for reading, while in the theater shorter versions were the norm. This perhaps is to take the *Romeo and Juliet* chorus too literally ("two hours" sounds more like a general indication than a precise measure – equivalent to our "couple of hours"). Indeed, since *Romeo and Juliet* is in fact just about 3,000 lines long, those who take the prologue literally would have to conclude that the quick-tongued players on Shakespeare's stage were able to speak 1,500 lines an hour, which in turn would mean that even Shakespeare's longest play, Q2 *Hamlet*, could be polished off in less than two and a half hours! Or, if they wanted to assert that the play as printed contains nearly 1,000 lines that would not have been performed, they would have to explain why this supposedly "literary" text features a prologue specifically referring to performance. It is nevertheless true that Shakespeare's plays, especially the histories and tragedies, tend to be longer than those of most other playwrights. Were they routinely cut for performance? There is evidence that at least some were: it looks strongly like the F text of *Hamlet*, for example, is shorter because of theatrical cuts (though it is still longer than any other Shakespeare play), which is an important reason why Hibbard chose to base his modern version on it.

One point that seems to have been missed in the debate about "maximal" and "minimal" texts[3] is that theater people tend to make cuts not primarily to shorten the play as a whole, but to make particular scenes work more effectively. There is no direct evidence from the early modern period indicating that theater companies worried that length alone would prevent their plays from gaining audience acceptance. But there is plenty of evidence that plays were cut. Modern interpreters have too often assumed that the cuts were made mainly to shorten a play regarded as too long. While this may of course have been true from time to time, it is worth remembering that people in the theater business tend to worry about effects, and about the practical exigencies of making things work. A case in point is to be found in the first quarto of *Othello*. In act 4 of that play, in the F text, Desdemona sings a sad song about a forlorn girl pining away because of lost love. It is a beautiful, foreboding sequence, but it is missing from the (somewhat shorter, probably theatrical) Q1 text. Scott McMillin, in discussing its absence, points to the fact that in this play, as in *Hamlet* and *King Lear*, the omissions in the shorter versions tend to predominate in act 4.[4] This suggests that the players, if they were the ones responsible for the cuts, were worried not so much about overall length (as several critics have pointed out, the cuts don't shorten the playing time very much) as about a possible sag in the momentum of the performance at a point just before the action starts moving to its climax.[5] In *Hamlet* this apprehension may have coincided with a well justified sense that the role is a long and demanding one, and the lead actor might well need a rest before moving to the climax in act 5 (another reason, perhaps, why Burbage might have encouraged Shakespeare to make the cut in 4.4.). In *Othello* the parts of Emilia and Desdemona are the most affected. Perhaps, as McMillin suggests, the "boy actors were not at their best here"; it may even be that one of the reasons the "willow song" was cut was that the boy actor playing the part in whatever revival the script was prepared for was not able to sing it effectively. The precise nature of what happened is not my major concern here – rather it is to stress that the players, including Shakespeare when he wears his player's rather than his writer's hat, are interested in effect, in holding the attention of the audience, and will adjust the script accordingly. Sometimes the adjustments they make are preserved in printed texts produced from the theatrical manuscripts they used.

In the case of *Hamlet*, it has been argued that even the reduced F text is too long for actual performance. Lukas Erne, who is the strongest proponent of this view, has to go to extraordinary lengths to "prove" that F couldn't represent a theatrical text and so must have a different origin. On the basis of a not too convincing analogy with an existing theatrical manuscript of a play by Beaumont and Fletcher, Erne argues that F *Hamlet* is based on a "preliminary abridgement" that would have lost about 1,300 more lines before actually being presented on the stage (i.e., to reduce it to the approximate length of the extant Q1; Erne 2003: 182–3). He gives no reasons why such a preliminary abridgement might have been made and merely asserts that because the play is so long, it must have been cut down to what he argues is standard size.[6] This is a way of avoiding the much more likely possibility that F's cuts were indeed theatrical and that at some point at least there was a pro-duction of *Hamlet* that might have lasted three hours or more. If audi-ences today, in our hyper-visual age, are capable of sitting through and enjoying lightly cut versions of *Hamlet*, why should that not have been the case for Elizabethan playgoers, who were much less impatient with long speeches (they could easily endure a sermon of an hour or more) and more attuned to purely linguistic pleasures than we?

Erne adduces his arguments in order to support his view that literary versions of plays intended for publication were significantly different from theatrical versions intended for performance. He is right in reproaching those "performance critics" who too easily assume that because Shakespeare wrote for the stage he didn't think of his plays as appealing to readers. It was after all his fellow actors who gathered his texts together for publication in the folio, admonishing buyers to "read him." But Erne unfortunately adopts, though he also inverts, the views of performance critics by continuing to maintain that literary and theatrical aims were fundamentally in conflict. In her chapter in this volume, Tiffany Stern calls this idea into question on the grounds that the theater itself often gave prominence to literacy and reading. One could add that many of the plays of the period are themselves deeply literary – based, for example, on stories taken from earlier, highly respected literary texts. Shakespeare borrows freely from Virgil, Ovid, Plutarch, Homer, and Chaucer, plus a host of lesser known romance writers and historians. His plays are literary from the outset and successfully bridge the too often asserted chasm between perfor-mance and reading.

The scene in *Hamlet* where the player recites from an old play that was "caviare to the general" provides an intriguing example. The player's lines closely recall a scene in Marlowe's play *Dido Queen of Carthage*, which in turn translates several segments of Virgil's *Aeneid*. Shakespeare (while also implying his own writerly superiority) seems to be paying a belated tribute to his fellow playwright, now dead, who was himself deeply immersed in literary tradition; in doing so he alerts his listeners to a complex network of literary and theatrical connections directly relevant to what Hamlet elsewhere calls "some necessary ques-tion of the play" (3.2.42–3).[7] As if to bring the connections to our attention, Hamlet, when he asks the player to speak the lines, specifi-cally reminds the audience of their literary, indeed elite, appeal. Despite a few verbal variants, this sequence is more or less identical in Q2 and F and, even in the short and unreliable Q1 text, it has a prominent place. This last point might seem odd, especially if, as has frequently been claimed, the context in which the text of Q1 came into being is that of the rough and tumble world of provincial performance, hardly an elite environment. At the Globe as well, the context was more demotic than elite, but the expectation in whatever venue is clearly that the audience will appreciate both the literary references and the richly theatrical style in which they are delivered. We are invited to endorse Hamlet's enjoyment of the lines (it is Polonius who thinks the recitation "too long"), while recognizing the gap between their high artifice and the more limber, flexible rhetoric of *Hamlet* itself. Shakespeare is thus using one of the mainstays of the European poetic tradition, Virgil's *Aeneid*, for three related reasons: to add thematic weight to his story of revenge by linking it to motifs in one of the most famous of all works of literature; to remind his audience of his play's literary provenance; and to position his play as stylistically more up to date than earlier drama in its use of literary material. This strongly suggests that audiences understood the links between literary and performance modes.

We seem to have diverged from the subject of editing Shakespeare; but the issue of what surviving printed texts can tell us about early performance and reading practices is in fact directly relevant to editing, and to the narratives surrounding copy-text. Recall Hibbard's argument (above) about Heminges and Condell's choice to use a familiar theatrical manuscript as a source for the F version of *Hamlet* instead of Q2 or Q3. Now if Erne is right and the F manuscript of *Hamlet* is really only a "preliminary abridgement," Hibbard's argument about his choice of copy-text would no longer be tenable. Far from being the preferred theatrical version, the F manuscript would be an anomaly and it would be hard to explain why Heminges and Condell should have paid any attention to it. If they were after a "literary" version, why not use the readily available Q2 or Q3, which likely derive from Shakespeare's finished draft? (It would have been especially easy to rely on Q3, since it was published by John Smethwick, one of the stationers involved in publishing F.) Hibbard's argument accounts rather well for the various features of F that distinguish it from the quartos, and thus seems to me to call into question Erne's view of F *Hamlet*. And if *Hamlet*, the longest of the plays, was performed in something like the F version, as Hibbard's argument strongly suggests, then we have good reason to conclude, *a fortiori*, that Elizabethan plays sometimes ran longer than the traditional "two hours traffic."

For an editor, this is a valuable point to keep in mind. Today's Shakespearean editors are engaged in producing texts with a pronounced literary authority that at the same time must, in the current climate, attend closely to performance. They seek, that is, to bridge the gap invoked and simultaneously revoked by the author of the 1609 epistle to *Troilus and Cressida*, who in one breath praises that play for never having been "clapper-clawed by the palms of the vulgar" but who also singles it out, and indeed all of Shakespeare's comedies, for a wittiness best appreciated on stage (readers should "flock to them for the main grace of their gravities"). Since readers then, as now, were often also playgoers, it seems reasonable both to acknowledge the tension between these different modes of conceptualizing Shakespeare's dramatic writing and to seek to negotiate the distance between them.

What, then, is an editor to do these days? Can she make allowances for those elements that textual critics have argued produce textual instability, without abandoning the principle that an author is primarily, though not solely, responsible for the texts that bear his name? As I hope has been clear from what I have said so far, I think this is not only possible but necessary. Paradoxical as they inevitably are, narratives of Copytext and of the relation between text and performance are an inescapable part of the process. Such narratives imply that there is a "work" (to invoke the term provided by Thomas Tanselle) which underlies the various textual forms that that work takes over time. The early texts of *Hamlet* are all versions of that intentional object, some, one could claim, closer to it than others. There is a danger of circular logic here – we infer from the printed texts that they derive from subjects (author, scribe, printer) trying to give concrete form to a network of words, ideas, and images, but we can only get a full view of that "work" by looking at the material texts. Does this constitute an insurmountable problem? Are texts solely their material manifestations, with nothing at all behind them, or do extant printed (or even manuscript) versions point to something other than themselves? Adopting the first of these positions means subscribing to the view that all texts are independent, which results in a kind of textual apartheid, under which the different early versions of *Hamlet* are separate but equal; there are no available criteria for deciding whether one is "superior" to another. The only way to do that is to construct an intentional subject (or subjects) whose work produced the text in question on the basis of a complex of ideas, feelings, and decisions. That there are a number of intermediaries between the originating idea and a particular copy of, say, Q2, does not erase the fact there was such an origin; it only makes it harder to discern. Some critics have argued that because all the precise details of a given text's origin can never be identified, we should give up on the idea of origins altogether and concentrate instead on the perceived differences between surviving texts.[8] Because some things are indeed indeterminate, should we conclude that all knowledge of origins collapses into a generalized indeterminacy? We can't know all the determinants that produced World War I, but does this mean we should abandon the search for causes? I think not. When it comes to Shakespeare's texts, what is needed is a kind of two-way thinking, a loop or feedback mechanism. Looking closely at the details of material texts gives access to a conception of an originating consciousness and set of ideas, which in turn provokes further investigation of textual detail as a strategy of testing and refining hypotheses about the larger picture.

At present I am working on a new edition of *Timon of Athens*.[9] *Timon* is a play about profligacy and ingratitude, and no doubt, if one felt cantankerous, one might see it as a kind of allegory for editorial excesses (the editor as Timon) and the resulting critical withdrawal on the part of former friends. Leaving such outlandish flights of fancy aside, I will nevertheless suggest, in what follows, a couple of ways that *Timon* offers metaphors for what the editor seeks to do. Before doing so, however, we need to establish something about the data, the mixed messages from the past, that this text offers us. One thing we can say with certainty is that *Timon of Athens*, as it appears in F (the only early version and therefore, for better or for worse, the copy-text), is a very curious play. It may, indeed, never have been slated for publication in F at all; there is strong bibliographical evidence that it was not originally intended to occupy the place it does, between *Romeo and Juliet* and *Julius Caesar*. It seems to have been added to the collection as a kind of afterthought, to fill in a gap created when *Troilus and Cressida* became temporarily unavailable (thus creating an oddly coincidental relationship between the texts I have been editing).[10] Moreover, *Timon* has many loose ends, and seems unfinished: the subplot featuring Alcibiades and his banishment remains underdeveloped, and its relation to the main plot is obscure. Characters are announced and then don't appear, many of them are unnamed, others are named inconsistently. Nor is there any evidence of early performance (though this is true of several of the plays in F). It has therefore often been speculated that Shakespeare gave up on it before it was ready for the stage, perhaps on the grounds of its allegorical predictability and consequent lack of dramatic interest (though it has proved memorably stageworthy in modern times). The story is certainly schematic: Timon is rich and generous in the first half, so generous in fact that his bounty appears as almost pathological in its prodigality. His inevitable fall into debt leads him to appeal to his flattering friends for assistance, and they, predictably, turn away. His resulting misanthropy is as extreme as his earlier bounty and he retires to self-imposed exile in the woods, eloquently cursing mankind and digging for roots. Finding a heap of gold, he curses that too, though he derives some satisfaction from the fact that the news of his find brings the parasites back to grovel at his feet. After a series of mocking interactions, he slips silently into an undramatic, offstage death, leaving behind only a trio of confusing epitaphs.

One of the controversies surrounding the play has been its authorship. Did Shakespeare write it by himself, or is it the product of more than one hand? Although there are still some hold-outs, the scholarly consensus now is that the play was co-written with Thomas Middleton.[11] The intricacies of the arguments in favor of this view needn't concern us here; suffice it to say that suspicions about Shakespeare's sole authorship arose first on stylistic grounds. Charles

Knight, writing in the mid-nineteenth century, was the first editor to argue that the mixed and inconsistent style of the play was marked by clearly non-Shakespearean habits; for him, this pointed to a second author, and he added as well that there were incidents, notably the Alcibiades subplot, that were inadequately integrated into the whole. This kind of argument illustrates the procedure I recommended above. Starting with concrete details of the material text, including such matters as the spelling of proper names and the relative prevalence of rhymed couplets, and moving on to sophisticated computer analyses of grammatical and linguistic features, scholars have been able to show that the text as we have it is the result of more than one hand, and that the most likely second author is Middleton. But that is not the end of the process. Once established, the idea of collaboration entails assessing the intentions on the part of both authors concerning the overall shape of the play. We need to infer those intentions and then examine the extant text to see how fully it realizes them. This might yield a judgement that, as a collaboration, the text remains unfinished, the two authors' contributions insufficiently melded together.

We can, I believe, detect a fairly accurate sense of the overall intention to combine a biting satire of urban ingratitude and a more far-reaching tragic concern with Timon's generous folly, his consequent fall into misanthropic despair, and his eventual move into something like ironic transcendence. It is reasonable to assume that Shakespeare, who in the end seems responsible for about 60 percent of the play, initiated the project (he was by 1605, the year the play was probably composed, the leading dramatist in London and Middleton still an up and coming one, known mostly for city comedy). If then he approached Middleton with this subject, his perspective on the material must have already been at least partly satirical, and he no doubt recognized that his partner would be ideal for the scenes depicting Timon's false friends and their excuses for failing to help him. In dividing up the rest of the material, Shakespeare no doubt recognized the potential for invention that eventually came to mark the great speeches of imprecation that dominate the fourth act. He reserved tragic grandilo-quence for himself, combining it with the devastating depiction of self-serving flattery which marks the first scene, and the measured elegiac notes of the final act (in both of these latter aspects the play recalls, perhaps deliberately, *Troilus and Cressida*). The false gloss of the glitzy banquet in 1.2 and the lively satire of the middle acts went to Middleton.[12] It looks strongly like the playwrights were, from the outset of the project, intending something of a mixed genre, and hence a mixed audience response. It's hard to accept the view that two experienced playwrights, both successful, one extremely so, would not have had the foresight to realize that the scenario they sketched out for themselves would not work. It is more plausible to assume that they knew what they were doing when they began, and that a mix of tragic loss and satirical social commentary was the aim.

Once we have established something like an overall intention, we are better placed to assess whether or not the text that we have is in some way defective. How do we account for the various discrepancies and loose ends? One of the difficulties we face is in determining what stage in the collaborative process is represented by the text we have. Perhaps the manuscript that was available to the editors of F when it was needed to fill a gap represents an intermediate stage in the composing process and was, unfortunately, not the final version. Or, if it is an almost-final version, maybe its problems derive from insufficient communication between the two authors (a disadvantage that plagues many of the collaborative dramas of the period), which may in turn have led them to abandon the project. Whether it was the only version ever produced, thus indicating that the play was never completed to the satisfaction of the authors, or whether the manuscript behind the printed text in F derived from a draft made by the two playwrights preliminary to their blending them more smoothly, is not something we can know for certain. But there are hints.

In pursuing one or two of these hints, I want to focus on the last act, where the play moves uncertainly towards tragedy. Timon's tragic trajectory is set in counterpoint to the threat against Athens posed by the return of Alcibiades with his army; the precise reason for the threatened attack is left unclear, though it is presumably linked to Alcibiades' banishment earlier in the play. Beyond that it seems to be a kind of retribution for the Athenian senators' appalling treatment of Timon, though again the text as we have it obscures the connection. The senators plead to Timon to help in the impending crisis (though we have heard nothing earlier in the play about Timon's military experience or prowess) and he mocks them, stringing them along and then gleefully disappointing them. The result is comic, and demonstrates Timon's mastery, but in the midst of it a different tone intervenes:

> Why, I was writing of my epitaph;
> It will be seen tomorrow.

> My long sickness
> Of health and living now begins to mend
> And nothing brings me all things. Go, live still,
> Be Alcibiades your plague, you his,
> And last so long enough. (5.2.70–5)

The paradox of a wished-for death, a "nothing" that, as with Richard II, Macbeth, and King Lear, will bring him "all things," links him to many of Shakespeare's tragic figures, but his persistence in cursing is his alone. Later, in what is in fact his last speech in the play, there is an even stronger note of cosmic lyricism, a melding of Timon with the earth and ocean, but it remains inseparable from the curses that define his being:

> Timon hath made his everlasting mansion
> Upon the beachèd verge of the salt flood,
> Who once a day with his embossèd froth
> The turbulent surge shall cover; thither come,
> And let my gravestone be your oracle.
> Lips, let four words go by, and language end:
> What is amiss, plague and infection mend;
> Graves only be men's works and death their gain,
> Sun, hide thy beams, Timon hath done his reign.
> (5.2.100–8)

This is Timon's final speech, and he appears to be sending us a message: "Let four words go by, and language end." It is an extraordinary command for a tragic hero, and a dark one indeed for editors, dedicated as we are to linguistic proliferation! But note that Timon himself has not submitted to his own charge: this is, as I said, Timon's final speech but it is not the last time we hear his voice. That voice reappears in a series of enigmatic epitaphs that dot the last scenes of the play. In the penultimate scene an unknown soldier appears, looking (unaccountably) for Timon; the fact that he is in search of Timon makes him an apt, if unexpected, figure for the editor who must also seek this extremely verbal hero in the midst of his profound silences. Here is what the soldier says:

> By all description this should be the place.
> Who's here? Speak, ho! No answer? What is this?
> "Timon is dead, who hath outstretched his span,
> Some beast read this, there does not live a man."

> Dead, sure, and this his grave; what's on this tomb
> I cannot read. The character I'll take with wax;
> Our captain hath in every figure skill,
> An aged interpreter though young in days. (5.4.1–8)

I here quote from my own version of this passage. But this is not exactly the way it appears in F, where, among other minor differences, there are no quotation marks around lines 3 and 4. Adding them is an editorial intervention deriving from an interpretation of the stage action that is left obscure in F. The two rhymed lines, cryptic and indeterminate, have elicited many pages of puzzled critical commentary. Are they an epitaph, left there by Timon? Certainly the question "What is this?" must mean that the soldier finds or notices something; inserting the quotation marks around lines 3–4 signals that the soldier finds a written message, perhaps a tombstone, or a wooden sign, or even a bit of paper. If this is the case, why does the soldier then go on to say that he can't read what's on the tomb? Could there be two epitaphs, one in "English" easily read by the literate but undereducated soldier, the other in "Latin" or "Greek" and thus proving too much for him? This is the position that I, not without some misgivings, have adopted. In so doing, I have perforce limited the field of meaning, giving a shape to something that remains indeterminate in the text that has comes down to us. I've made it more definite and comprehensible, but also robbed it of some of its signifying potential. Like the soldier, I am faced here with a textual clue that I am unable fully to elucidate; but the soldier has the luxury of taking his find to a higher interpretive authority. The editor, typically, does not.

Let us consider a different narrative about the lines in quotation marks: perhaps they represent an original draft of the epitaph. If so, then the remaining lines would indicate a change of intention. Thus, the original idea would have been to end with Timon here and devote the final scene to Alcibiades' triumph; on this account, the lines about bringing the wax "character" to Alcibiades to read would have been added to provide a link with the final scene, where the soldier again appears (though he is now called "messenger") to announce Timon's death. Shakespeare, then, changes his mind in the course of writing but neglects to cancel the lines he has first written, which then end up being printed from what must be a somewhat messy manuscript. His purpose in doing so is to keep Timon's memory in the forefront of the audience's awareness through to the very end; it is an aesthetic

choice, designed to darken the tone and emphasize the feeling of loss.
This is the view adopted by the Oxford editors in their 1986 edition,
who therefore cut the two lines from their version; but John Jowett
in his recent Oxford single-volume edition reinstated the lines, arguing
that the multiple epitaphs "seem oddly appropriate" to the play,
though he doesn't say why.[13] As I have been suggesting, I think one
reason is that Timon's voice, fractured and dispersed as it is, keeps
reminding us of the tension between speech and silence, presence and
absence, belonging and alienation, that marks the play and its hero.

When the soldier re-enters in the final scene, he addresses
Alcibiades:

> My noble general, Timon is dead,
> Entombed upon the very hem o'th' sea,
> And on his gravestone this insculpture, which
> With wax I brought away, whose soft impression
> Interprets for my poor ignorance.

But wait a minute; in F these lines are given to a "messenger," the
soldier from the previous scene seemingly forgotten. At the same time,
what he says fits precisely with what the "soldier" has said and done
earlier. So are we not justified in assuming they are the same person
and emending the text accordingly? Virtually all editors have done so.
But if the soldier is also a messenger, perhaps he has a message for us
as well, especially for those of us who are in search of Timon and think
we've found him. Maybe Timon (both the man and the text) is more
elusive than we think – though part of him, we can assume, is engraved
on the "insculpture" that the "soldier" gives to Alcibiades, who then
reads the epitaph; or rather, epitaphs, for there are two of them. I
quote now directly from F without modernization:

> *Heere lies a wretched Coarse, of wretched Soule bereft,*
> *Seek not my name: A Plague consume you, wicked Caitifs left:*
> *Heere lye I Timon, who aliue, all liuing men did hate,*
> *Passe by, and curse thy fill, but passe and stay not here thy gate.*

What is striking here is that the two couplets contradict each other,
the second providing the name forbidden by the first; and the second
also, we may note, accords with the couplet from the previous scene,
presumably read by the soldier ("Timon is dead . . . "). If we try to

imagine the process that led to the textual situation we are now faced with, we can construct a narrative something like the following: uncertain as to which epitaph to use in the final version, Shakespeare, who was responsible for this part of the play, copied out both versions (making only minimal changes) from Plutarch's *Life of Antonius*, where both appear almost exactly as here but are clearly distinguished from each other rather than run together. He thus postponed the final decision about which one to include. With this detail, we seem to have caught Shakespeare in a moment of uncertainty. In order to deal with it from an editorial point of view, we have to invoke a larger intentional context.

First of all there is the context provided by the previous scene. There, the rhymed lines in the soldier's speech are, as I argued, best (but not definitively) interpreted as something written by Timon to announce that he "is dead." While those lines might have been a "first shot," the soldier's speech and his implied stage action make sense in the context of what later happens. The anonymous soldier is seeking Timon, and, it seems, seeking an explanation as well (this also aligns him with the spectator, the reader, and the editor). What he finds brings him part way along the route of explanation, but he needs help – and so he takes the wax character to Alcibiades. Timon has rejected mankind, but understanding him is a social matter, requiring collaboration. And what might we imagine is on that wax tablet? The first of the two formal epitaphs read by Alcibiades, which refuses to name the grave's occupant and admonishes us not even to seek out who may be buried in this marginal grave, does not fit with the clear statement from the previous scene, nor with the couplet that follows immediately. So in my edition I have cut that couplet, retaining only the second one.[14]

Invoking a still wider context, we might think more generally about the role of the anonymous soldier in these two scenes. He is "seeking" Timon, as F's stage direction stipulates, but finds only an ambiguously written message, not the living man. Like the audience, the soldier is thwarted in his quest, never allowed the intimacy with the tragic figure that he, or we, might desire. We can recognize him as that ordinary Shakespearean observer, typically a kind of surrogate for the audience, who enters the play near the end and whose sympathy adds dimension to the plight of the hero – like the Groom of the stable in *Richard II* (5.5), Kent returning in *King Lear*, or the anonymous soldiers in *Antony and Cleopatra* (4.3). But in this play he is denied direct connection, and this brings home the absolute isolation of Shakespeare's loneliest hero. How then might this affect our understanding of F's italicized double epitaph? What I see happening is a kind of softening of the sharply abrasive tone of Timon's isolation and misanthropy. The lone soldier's attempt to find Timon is a kind of bridge to sympathy, though a frustrating and unfulfilled one. The second epitaph seems to me more in keeping with that slightly softened tone. It doesn't abandon the harshness or the dark vision, but it adds to the invective a fleeting but not entirely insubstantial concern with those who remain; if we want, we are free to curse, but more compellingly, we are invited simply (like Yeats's "Horseman") to *passe by*, to forget what in fact refuses to be put to rest. The epitaph undermines itself, since in telling us to forget it inevitably reminds us of what has taken place. In doing so it speaks of Timon's own impossible project of forgetting mankind. We are left with nothing but our sense of loss – cursing is painful and useless, passing by our only alternative.

I have been pursuing a series of hints that might cast light on the problem of determining what kind of manuscript underlies the F text, and what that manuscript might tell us about the process of collaborative composition. The presence of the three epitaphs suggests that we have caught Shakespeare in the process of revising or thinking about revising, momentarily uncertain but with a relatively clear intention of following through. I would even speculate that he might well have been awaiting a suggestion or judgement from his collaborator before finishing up. Early modern theatrical collaboration tended for the most part to be a piecemeal affair, each collaborator writing his bit in relative isolation from the other collaborator(s). But in the case of Shakespeare's other successful collaborations (*Henry VIII*, *Two Noble Kinsmen*), this rough method seems to have been followed by a further stage of smoothing out, assuring a measure of coherence and polish missing from *Timon*. The evidence of the epitaphs suggests that this final stage was yet to be accomplished, though it was in process. I would thus infer that the manuscript that eventually ended up being printed in F was an intermediate one, a draft put together by the two writers (in their respective hands)[15] that would then serve as the basis for the final version. Somehow that version had gone missing, with the result that at first there seems to have been no intention to print *Timon* in F (the fact that it is collaborative might have been another factor in this decision); but, when the need to fill a gap arose, the draft that remained was pressed into service.

Such is my narrative. But there is a compelling objection to it, which I can outline here but not fold into the editorial process I am engaged in. Why, you might ask, try to solve the problem at all? Why cut the first two lines of this last epitaph, why not instead let indeterminacy thrive? As I have been implying throughout this paper, I think that explanatory narratives are valuable heuristic devices, and that editorial responsibility requires that we invent and/or invoke them. But in opting for rational explanation and consistency here at the end of this problematic play, I am playing the positivist, creating more clarity than might be warranted by the facts of the situation. Thus is the job of the editor a paradoxical one, wherein an excess of clarity can falsify but yet where too little intervention results in muddle. My inclination when faced with muddle is to try to clear it up, but I have at the same time to acknowledge that in doing so I run the risk of reducing complexity and multivalence to flat simplicity. But in the present case there is nothing flat in the result of my intervention. The epitaph, even in (especially in?) its reduced form, speaks of a complex dynamic befitting both the play and its hero: it both gives us something and takes it away. That in a nutshell might also stand for editing as a practice – a paradoxical blend of giving and taking.

Where then have we arrived after our circuitous survey of some of the dilemmas of, and metaphors, for editing Shakespeare? Editing reveals itself as a complex business, full of controversy and with significant implications for the meaning of Shakespeare's plays. There are two features of the business of editing to which I have paid particular attention here. The first is the matter of sorting out what the earliest surviving texts of the plays tell us (this is where the trickster Copytext comes into his own). The second is the tension between literariness and performance. As I have argued, these two are deeply interconnected, the issue of determining the text being often a matter of invoking both literary and performance values. In my effort to work though the puzzles connected to the epitaphs in *Timon of Athens*, I of course began with the textual data, but before long I found myself investigating aspects of performance (what does the soldier find on stage?) and broader "literary" elements (thematic consistency, patterns of loss). The textual analysis that editors must do these days has to be holistic in just this sense – involving interdependent modes of approach. An important element in all this is what we might call the "aesthetic"; that is, the act of interpreting textual data always draws on criteria and principles about what constitutes literary and performative value. Since such matters change with the times, it is perhaps most useful to think of editing, to invoke yet another generative metaphor, as a kind of performance, like acting; it tries to get as close to the text as possible, but it is in the end an act of interpretation that speaks from, and to, a particular cultural milieu.

Notes

1   They did this even though their usual practice was to use available quarto editions where feasible.
2   For the results of my explorations, see the "Textual Analysis" in Dawson (2003: 234–52).
3   The terms are those of Gurr (1999).
4   In *Othello*, the omissions in act 4 (totalling 76 lines) are almost exactly equal to the total number in the other four acts combined, while in *Hamlet* the number in act 4 is twice as high as in any other act, and in *King Lear* most of the omissions are in acts 3 and 4 (90 and 114 lines, respectively, as compared to 76 lines in the other three acts combined). See McMillin (2001: 9–10).
5   Although it has been argued that the additional passages in F *Othello* represent expansions by the playwright, McMillin (2001) makes a convincing case that most of them were theatrical cuts.
6   His assertion is based on an argument made in earlier chapters that the standard length of an Elizabethan play was less than 2,500 lines.
7   For a full analysis of this aspect of *Hamlet*, see Dawson (2006).
8   See, for example, Werstine (1988, 1990).
9   This edition, co-edited with Gretchen Minton, will appear in the Arden Third Series.
10   See Greg (1955) and Hinman (1963).
11   For the most thorough account of the gradual development of this consensus, together with the evidence to support it, see Vickers (2002).
12   This is to state the case rather generally; the exact division of labor is still under question, though it seems clear that each author also contributed some bits to those sections that were predominantly the responsibility of the other.
13   See Wells and Taylor (1986) and Jowett (2004: 377).
14   The only previous editor to do so is Sisson (1954).
15   See Jowett (2004: 120ff.) for a thorough account of this aspect of the manuscript.

Works Cited

Dawson, Anthony B. 2006: "Priamus is Dead: Memorial Repetition in Marlowe and Shakespeare." In Peter Holland (ed.) *Remembering Performance*. Cambridge: Cambridge University Press, 63–84.

Dawson, Anthony B. (ed.) 2003: *Troilus and Cressida*. Cambridge: Cambridge University Press.

Erne, Lukas 2003: *Shakespeare as Literary Dramatist*. Cambridge: Cambridge University Press.

Foakes, R. A. (ed.) 2002: *Henslowe's Diary*, 2nd edn. Cambridge: Cambridge University Press.

Greg, W. W. 1955: *The Shakespeare First Folio*. Oxford: Clarendon Press.

Gurr, Andrew 1999: "Maximal and Minimal Texts: Shakespeare v. the Globe." *Shakespeare Survey* 52, 68–87.

Hibbard, G. R. (ed.) 1987: *Hamlet*. Oxford: Oxford University Press.

Hinman, Charlton 1963: *The Printing and Publication of the First Folio*. Oxford: Clarendon Press.

Jowett, John (ed.) 2004: *Timon of Athens*. Oxford: Oxford University Press.

Marcus, Leah 1996: *Unediting the Renaissance*. London: Routledge.

McMillin, Scott (ed.): *The First Quarto of Othello*. Cambridge: Cambridge University Press.

Sisson, C. J. (ed.) 1954: *Complete Works of Shakespeare*. London: Odhams Press.

Tanselle, G. Thomas 1989: *The Rationale of Textual Criticism*. Philadelphia: University of Pennsylvania Press.

Vickers, Brian 2002: *Shakespeare Co-author: A Historical Study of Five Collaborative Plays*. Oxford: Oxford University Press.

Wells, Stanley and Taylor, Gary 1986: *William Shakespeare: A Textual Companion*. Oxford: Clarendon Press.

Wells, Stanley et al. (eds.) 1986: *The Complete Works of Shakespeare*. Oxford: Clarendon Press.

Werstine, Paul 1988: "The Textual Mystery of *Hamlet*." *Shakespeare Quarterly* 39, 1–26.

Werstine, Paul 1990: "Narratives About Printed Shakespeare Texts: 'Foul Papers' and 'Bad' Quartos." *Shakespeare Quarterly* 41, 65–86.

Part IV

How To Do Things with Animals

Editor's Introduction

A few years ago I found myself reflecting on what the next stage in "body" criticism might be. Feminism had set this particular critical ball rolling in the 1980s with a series of excellent articles on women's bodies as blank sheets awaiting (masculine) inscription. Gail Kern Paster then introduced the topic of incontinence and shame in a brilliant and influential article on the leaky women of Jacobean city comedy in which she analyzed scenes and tropes of bladder incontinence in Renaissance plays; this later became the foundation of a book she published in 1993. In 1995 Jonathan Sawday approached the body from a different angle with a pioneering book about anatomy theaters, dissection, and interiority. Specialists in poetry analyzed interiority via the 1590s vogue for lyric and its concern with heightened states of subjectivity (e.g., Schoenfeldt 1999; Fowler 2000). In 2004 Paster expanded her work on the body with a book on the physicality of emotions: the humors. So I was keen to see where critical writings on the body would go next and I assumed I would find any new developments in the field of feminist criticism.

Instead I heard Erica Fudge give a conference paper on animals. Her work took the concerns of Paster's early work on incontinence and applied the questions to animals: can animals feel shame? Can animals lose bladder control? Her questions, and her ways of thinking about how to answer them, opened up a new topic and new territory for me. At the same time I had a conversation with Paul Yachnin about sheep in *The Winter's Tale*. Yachnin had just begun teaching a course on animals in Shakespeare and I was intrigued by his focus on economics in the pastoral world. As chance would have it, three productions of Shakespeare I saw in the next year (and two of other plays) included flocks of sheep (not the live animals so beloved of Victorian extravaganzas, but actors imitating animals in ways that made me ponder the interface between the human and the animal world). And I read an article by novelist Jeanette Winterson on her relationship with her body in which she confessed: "Some days I look like a dog – but I like dogs." The movement from negative metaphor to positive canine relationship created an extraordinary visual and historical snapshot. So I asked Erica Fudge and Paul Yachnin to write on animals for this volume.

In the essays that follow, Fudge turns her attention to one of Shakespeare's earliest plays (if not *the* earliest), *The Two Gentlemen of Verona*, while Yachnin turns to one of Shakespeare's last plays, *The Winter's Tale*; both essays are "about" so much more than the dogs and sheep which are their focus. They take us into the world of minds, bodies, selves, society, and economics and show us not just how to do things with animals, but how animals can do things with us.

Works Cited

Fowler, Elizabeth 2000: "Chaucer and the Elizabethan Invention of the 'Selfe'." In Patrick Cheney and Anne Lake Prescott (eds.) *Approaches to Teaching Shorter Elizabethan Poetry*. New York: MLA Publications, 249–55.

Paster, Gail Kern 1987: "The Leaky Women of Jacobean City Comedy." *Renaissance Drama* 18: 43–65.

Paster, Gail Kern 1993: *The Body Embarrassed: Drama and the Disciplines of Shame*. Ithaca: Cornell University Press

Paster, Gail Kern 2004: *Humoring the Body: Emotions and the Shakespearean Stage*. Chicago: University of Chicago Press.

Sawday, Jonathan 1995: *The Body Emblazoned: Dissection and the Human Body in Renaissance Culture*. London: Routledge.

Schoenfeldt, Michael 1999: *Bodies and Selves in Early Modern England: Physiology and Inwardness in Spenser, Shakespeare, Herbert, and Middleton*. Cambridge: Cambridge University Press.

Winterson, Jeanette 2006: "What I See in the Mirror." *Guardian Weekend* October 28, 61.

Chapter 8

"The dog is himself": Humans, Animals, and Self-Control in *The Two Gentlemen of Verona*

Erica Fudge

Rationale

This essay thinks about how to do things with animals in Shake-speare studies, and how to do things with Shakespeare in animal studies. That is, it explores what the emerging field of animal studies in the humanities might bring to a reading of Shake-speare's plays by taking Shakespeare's first play, *The Two Gentle-men of Verona*, as its focus. The essay looks in particular at the meaning of Lance's dog, the only animal in the Shakespeare canon to appear on stage.

The challenge offered by animal studies to literary criticism is a simple one: as literary critics, of whatever persuasion – liberal humanist, poststructuralist, new historicist, etc. – our focus is on culture created by humans and, conventionally, on the representa-tions of humans within those cultural, and in particular, literary products. Recent critical foci – for instance, on gender, sexuality, race – are without doubt expanding our critical horizons but remain questions focused on humans. Animal studies proposes that important issues concerning what it means to be human, and how we humans live in our world, are missed if the focus excludes animals, if literary (and other) studies remain anthropocentric. Historical animal studies also argues that ignoring animals in our reconstructions of the past is also failing to fully represent those past worlds. Animals were important in early modern England, just as they are important in the early twenty-first century, and, I would argue, the debates surrounding them – their status, meaning, use – were, while different, just as complex then as they are now. If animals are absent from the histories we write, then those histories remain incomplete.

This essay, then, is a historicist analysis, in that it attempts to reconstruct some of the contemporary ideas that may have underpinned one Shakespeare play. But the essay's particular focus on the place of animals in debates about civility in the early modern period also challenges many of the unexplored assumptions about the separation of humans from animals – and thus the lack of importance of animals – in conventional Shakespeare criticism. The essay argues for the meaningful significance of animals and the historical constructedness of humans. That is, it argues that it is not possible to fully understand humans without also thinking about animals, and that *The Two Gentlemen of Verona*, a play in which a live dog is present on stage, offers in the most explicit – visible – way just what that inseparability of human and animal might mean.

Shakespeare's Animals

What does it mean to open *The Complete Works* of Shakespeare and think about animals? Is this a digression from the true focus of the plays and poems or is it paying attention to an important aspect of them that has been previously ignored? Is reading for animals in the writings of William Shakespeare reading anachronistically? In this essay I will attempt to address these questions and show how a concern about animals in an analysis of early modern writing is not simply exercising a modern preoccupation that sits happily alongside the development of welfare organizations such as the RSPCA and PETA but that fails to reflect sixteenth- and seventeenth-century ideas. Rather, I want to argue that concern about the representation and meaning of animals should sit alongside an analysis of Shakespeare's plays just as the Bear Garden sat alongside the theater at the time he was writing.

This argument about the relevance and significance of animals to a reading of early modern literature emerges out of wider developments currently taking place in the Humanities. No longer regarded as simply the home of humans, the Humanities, paradoxically, are being reinterpreted to include non-humans (see, for example, Kean 1998; Fudge 2000; Rothfels 2002). This inclusion of animals recognizes their centrality in human culture now and in history. As geographers Chris Philo and Chris Wilbert have written, "With the human domestication of animals and plants, the number of non-humans existing alongside people proliferates exponentially, making it impossible to recognize a pure 'human' society" (Philo and Wilbert 2000: 17). From this perspective, to ignore animals is to ignore key aspects of our own culture.

Using the work of the sociologist of science Bruno Latour, scholars such as Philo and Wilbert, Jonathan Burt in history, and Philip Armstrong in literary studies have argued for the inseparability of the human and the animal and for the logical and necessary inclusion of animals in our study of culture. They also argue that we must now regard animals as having an active and not simply a passive role to play in the construction of that culture (Latour 1991; Burt 2002; Armstrong 2004, 2005). For Jonathan Burt, for example, animals were not simply objects for early filmmakers to record, they were central to the development of the medium and thus the history of early cinema is in large part the history of human relationships with animals (Burt 2002: 85). The same can be said in other fields of human life: in 1978, for example, Joan Thirsk presented a compelling case for the significance of the horse to the development of the early modern English economy (Thirsk 1978). But it is not only real animals that are significant to so-called human culture. It is also conceptual animals – that is, animals of the mind – that are important. For the French philosopher Jacques Derrida, for example, animals lie at the heart of philosophy. He writes that "Interpretive decisions (in all their metaphysical, ethical, juridical, and political consequences) . . . depend on what is presupposed by the general singular of this word *Animal*" (Derrida 2002: 409). Western philosophy, he argues, relies upon the concept, not just the being, of this creature called "the animal" in order to establish and construct its own arguments. By implication, without the animal there would be no human, and thus no metaphysics, no ethics, no law, no politics.

But the real and the conceptual are not, of course, wholly separate spheres. In the early modern period they can become enmeshed, as in the image of the dog lying at the feet of the philosopher as he worked in his study, which was popular in sixteenth-century woodcuts of thinkers including St. Jerome and St. Augustine. Such images reflect, Karl Josef Höltgen notes, the perception of the dog that "may most aptly convey the properties of those natural human faculties – reason, imagination, and memory – that search out and 'retrieve' ideas. . . . Dog-like, the mind ranges through its memories and associations to retrieve thought otherwise hidden" (Höltgen 1998: 1). This dog it would seem is purely conceptual: a visual metaphor for a very human thought process. In 1598, then, the Danish astronomer Tycho Brahe followed convention when, in an engraving in his *Astronomiae Instauratae Mechanica,* he pictured himself with a dog at his feet (plate 8.1).

Brahe's explanation of the image, however, reveals this dog to be more than a concept:

> At the number 12, one of my hounds is lying at my feet. This dog was exceptionally faithful and sagacious and is shown in shape and size much as he was in life, a symbol not only of his noble race, but also of his sagacity and fidelity. (Brahe 1602: sig.B1v)[1]

Undercutting the convention in which the animal was not animal but merely symbol, this hound's meaning emerges from both its life and its iconographic context. Brahe has fulfilled humanist convention by placing the dog at his feet, but he has also challenged that convention by reiterating that this dog is *his* dog; that it is not just an image of a human trait. Perhaps it was by living with a real dog that Brahe came to understand what it was to really think?

From different perspectives then, that take in real animals, that look at conceptual ones, and that conflate the two, it is possible to make the case that a study of culture that does not take in animals ignores a central aspect of its object of analysis.

As this new field called animal studies in the humanities continues to develop so it will inform and expand the horizons of more orthodox areas of academic inquiry. Shakespeare studies, for example, is already beginning to reflect the development of these new ideas, and I will discuss a number of recent works that have begun to bridge the gap between the study of early modern literature and the study of animals in the following discussion of Shakespeare's first play.

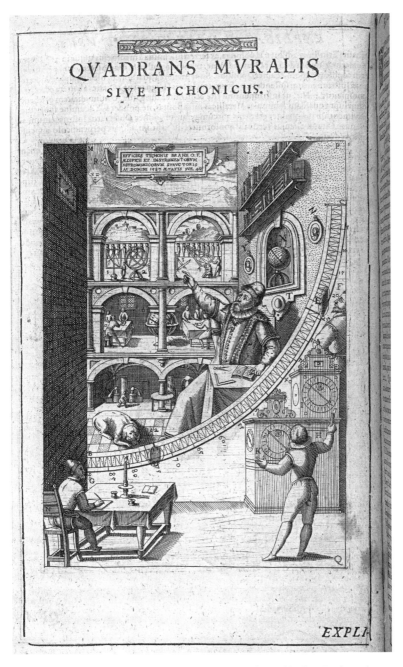

Plate 8.1 "Quadrans Muralis sive Tichonus" from Tycho Brahe, *Astronomiae Instauratae Mechanica* (Noribergae, Levinvn Hvlsivm, 1602), sig. A6v. Reproduced by permission of the British Library, classmark 48e11.

The Critical History of a Dog

The Two Gentlemen of Verona is, for many modern critics, a problematic play. While it contains elements that were to become the staple of later comedies – a cross-dressing female character, changeable masculine desire, the lovers' retreat to the forest – the concluding scene of the play is generally regarded as, to say the least, unsatisfactory. In 5.4 one of the two gentlemen of the title, Proteus, attempts to rape Silvia who is running away from Milan and her father to meet up with her beloved, Valentine, the other gentleman who is also the best friend of Proteus.

> *Proteus* Nay, if the gentle spirit of moving words
> Can no way change you to a milder form,
> I'll woo you like a soldier, at arms' end,
> And love you 'gainst the nature of love – force ye.
> [*Seizes her.*]
> *Silvia* O heaven!
> *Proteus* I'll force thee yield to my desire. (5.4.55–9)[2]

At this point Valentine, who has hidden himself in order to watch his mistress and his friend, steps forward: "Ruffian, let go that rude uncivil touch, / Thou friend of an ill fashion!" (5.4.60–1). It would seem at this point that the amity of the two gentlemen is at an end, but a mere twenty-two lines later Valentine forgives Proteus and states "All that was mine in Silvia I give thee" (5.4.83). This strange offer led Arthur Quiller-Couch to write in 1921 that "there are, by this time, *no* gentlemen in Verona" (cited in Masten 2003: 273). Silvia does not have a response to Valentine's suggestion, but is silent for the remainder of the play. However, Julia, the patient lover of Proteus who has disguised herself as a page in order to follow her beloved to Milan, finally reveals herself and agrees to marry the repentant gentleman. At the end Proteus blames human nature for his falling from the path of good:

> O heaven, were man
> But constant, he were perfect. That one error
> Fills him with faults, makes him run through all th' sins;
> Inconstancy falls off ere it begins. (5.4.109–12)

Stanley Wells termed Proteus' treachery a "loss of moral coherence" in his 1963 essay "The Failure of *The Two Gentlemen of Verona*" (Wells 1963: 167). Such a negative assessment that focuses on the play's lack of consistency has a role in relegating it to the status of an interesting but early and imperfect attempt by a novice writer, and is given impetus by the presence on stage of a dog, Crab. The dog belongs to Proteus' servant Lance and these two characters, so Inga-Stina Ewbank argued, have "probably received more critical attention than all the other scenes of the play put together" (Ewbank 1972: 101). Since 1972 when Ewbank made this statement critical attention may have shifted from the dog to questions of masculinity and male friendship (such has been a key interest in Shakespeare studies in the last quarter century), but Crab remains of critical interest.

It is Lance's first monologue that has received most attention from critics. In 2.3 he enters the stage with Crab and relates the scene of his farewell to his family as he follows his master to Milan: "'twill be this hour ere I have done weeping; all the kind of the Lances have this very fault" (2.3.1–2) he states. He then turns to the one member of the household to challenge this view:

> I think Crab my dog be the sourest-natured dog that lives: my mother weeping, my father wailing, my sister crying, our maid howling, our cat wringing her hands and all our house in a great perplexity, yet did not this cruel-hearted cur shed one tear. He is a stone, a very pebblestone, and has no more pity in him than a dog. (2.3.4–10)

Lance attempts to reenact the scene of his departure, but what follows is a confusion of subjects, objects, and identities:

> I'll show you the manner of it. This shoe is my father. No, this left shoe is my father. No, no, this left shoe is my mother. Nay, that cannot be so neither. Yes, it is so, it is so: it hath the worser sole. This shoe with a hole in it is my mother, and this my father. A vengeance on't – there 'tis. Now, sir, this staff is my sister; for, look you, she is as white as a lily and as small as a wand. This hat is Nan, our maid. I am the dog. No, the dog is himself, and I am the dog. O, the dog is me, and I am myself. Ay, so, so. (2.3.13–22)

Gail Kern Paster has noted that in the humoral psychology of the early modern period there was a "whole analogical network" that linked humans not only with animals but with objects as well. She cites Prince Hal and Falstaff's dialogue in 1.2 *I Henry IV* in which Falstaff's melancholy links him with a cat, a bear, a lion, a lute, a set of bagpipes, a hare, and a sewage ditch (Paster 2004: 137–8).[3] Such a network may also be visible in Lance's monologue, and what is clear is the potential for comic confusion in that network: comparisons can work to deflate as much as to explain human passions. But in *The Two Gentlemen of Verona*, amid all the emotional confusion and status shifting of Lance's monologue, there is one constant: the silence of the canine. "Now the dog all this while sheds not a tear nor speaks a word; but see how I lay the dust with my tears" (2.3.29–30).

The dog's lack of interest in the world around him is visible once again in his next appearance in the play when Lance and Speed, Valentine's servant, discuss Proteus and Julia's relationship: "will't be a match?" asks Speed. Lance replies: "Ask my dog. If he say 'Ay', it will; if he say 'No', it will; if he shake his tail and say nothing, it will" (2.5.30–3). The dog we can assume – there are no stage directions – does nothing. Crab's final appearance is perhaps his most active (although as dogs are not necessarily to be trusted to act on cue, his activity, very sensibly, is given by report). Lance tells how he has been sent by the faithless Proteus to present Silvia (Valentine's mistress) with a lapdog. The lapdog is, however, "stolen from me by the hangman's boys in the market-place," says Lance, and so he selflessly offers Silvia his own dog in its place (4.4.53–5). Crab's behavior, however, is unacceptably currish: he steals a "capon's leg" and then, as Lance narrates it,

> thrusts me himself into the company of three or four gentleman-like dogs under the Duke's table. He had not been there – bless the mark! – a pissing-while but all the chamber smelt him. 'Out with the dog', says one; 'What cur is that?' says another; 'Whip him out', says a third; 'Hang him up', says the Duke. (4.4.16–22)

As if to exemplify true loyalty, Lance bears Crab's beating himself before being dismissed by a furious Proteus never to reappear.

For many critics the dog's relationship with the main plot of the play is non-existent and as such Crab becomes emblematic of the play's overall failure of dramatic coherence. In 1927 Louis B. Wright argued, for example, that Lance and Crab merely "furnish a series of variety show performances" (Wright 1927: 661): they are mere interludes between the real moments of the drama. Likewise, almost seventy years later, Matthew Bliss wrote of their performances filling "the action in the manner of a vaudeville" (Bliss 1994: 55). Kathleen Campbell, while admiring Lance's scenes, argues that they are comic set pieces which "seem to be grafted onto the plot" (Campbell 1996: 180). And Richard Beadle, in a detailed historical analysis of the relationship of the non-weeping Crab to the weeping dog of the medieval theater, still views the dog as only marginally significant to the play as a whole: "Though Lance and Crab are effective in reflecting aspects of the main plot and the principal characters in a parodic or ironic light," he writes, they "were almost certainly not part of the original scheme of the play" (Beadle 1994: 13–14). For these writers, Crab is of interest in terms of theater history, not literary criticism.

But some critics do attempt to situate the dog and his owner within the play's wider thematic structure. Harold F. Brooks, for example, writes of a comparison between Proteus and Crab: "The want of sensibility to old ties and to his friend Launce's feelings which Crab is alleged to show at parting from home, is ominous as a parallel to Proteus' parting from Julia and impending reunion with Valentine" (Brooks 1963: 99). An alternative parallel is offered by John Timpane, who proposes that Lance's constant devotion to his unresponsive dog is not only "a comic corrective to the inconstant Proteus," but is also "a very funny parallel to Valentine and his love for Sylvia" (Timpane 1996: 189). Likewise, Jeffrey Masten states that "Launce's comic monologues (dialogues?) with his dog Crab take up and parodically rewrite both male-female relations in the play *and* the idea of the male friend as an indistinguishable second-self" (Masten 2003: 275). (I return to this latter point.) For these critics the dog is part of the meaning of the play: Crab is not simply grafted onto an existing play in order to provide the clown with his part, or to offer the audience some comic interludes.

In a recent critical analysis Michael Dobson brings theater history and literary analysis of the play together and he interrogates the conception of identity that can be traced when confronting Crab. Dobson traces the history of what he terms "non-performing dogs" on the stage: that is, dogs that do not attempt any tricks. "What is unusual about [Crab]," he states, "is the way in which Shakespeare draws attention to, and thinks through his sheer lack of a performance." Other critics have drawn a parallel between Crab's indifference to Lance and the silence at Proteus' parting from Julia in 2.2. Dobson, however, argues that Crab's lack of performance offers a very different parallel:

> While Proteus, superficially the most important and independent char-
> acter in this play, is too busy generating the main plot to be anyone
> much in his own right, the unwilling mongrel at the end of his servant's
> string is obdurately and supremely himself throughout. . . . Crab is
> visibly irreducible to the roles the play requires of him, serving neither
> as a sympathetic confidant to Lance nor as an acceptable present to
> Silvia, but just wonderfully being "as it were, a dog at all things."
> (Dobson 2000: 118–19)

Such an assessment of the dog can also be traced in Bruce Boehrer's discussion of the play in his study *Shakespeare Among the Animals.* Here Boehrer takes note of Crab's and Lance's lack of performance: the two are, he writes, "deliberately constructed to serve as theatrical anomalies: central failures in a play about the failures of playing." He continues:

> while the dog clearly "is himself" for all commonplace purposes, to
> make the dog be "himself" upon the stage is to ask him to participate
> in patterns of deliberate doubling of which any dog, by virtue of
> being a dog, is incapable. Crab is certainly himself – no one more
> contentedly so – but for that very reason Crab is unable to *act* himself,
> since acting involves an alienation from the persona being adopted,
> and that alienation, in turn, is a function of language. Being wholly
> "himself" and nothing other, Crab cannot perform himself, for
> performance is the province of imitation rather than identity. (Boehrer
> 2002: 160, 165)[4]

Certainly, Boehrer's analysis places an important focus upon Crab that has often been missed by earlier critics – the dog is not simply a parallel to other (human) characters, but is significant in and of himself – but like Dobson before him, Boehrer posits a notion of animal identity that, I want to argue, is not present in the play. In fact, as I will show, Crab is not a representation of nature in its posi-tive glory (Dobson's and Boehrer's conception of the contented and stable identity of the dog); he is a representation of nature as the uncivilized that stands against the rational civility that is understood to be truly human.

Selfless Dogs

"When didst thou see me heave up my leg and make water against a gentlewoman's farthingale? Didst thou ever see me do such a trick?" (4.4.35–8). This is the final question that Lance asks his dog in *The Two Gentlemen of Verona* and it is a question that symbolizes a crucial opposition between human and animal. This is an opposition made most clearly in the image of Crab pissing under the Duke's (Silvia's father's) table. Where in humanist iconography the dog at the philosopher's feet was a metaphor of rigorous contemplation, in Shakespeare's play the dog at the feet of the human signifies the difference of man and canine. But this is not, as Dobson and Boehrer have argued, because the dog has a stable, non-fragmented identity. Reading this moment in Shakespeare's first play within the context of contemporary ideas about urine, about civility, and about conceptions of private and public, we can begin to piece together, I think, another meaning in Crab and another way of thinking about Shakespeare's humans.

In the anonymous text *The Seing of Urynes* (1562) the author takes the reader through the meaning of the various colors of urine (white "betokeneth indigestion," "blacke as a cole . . . betokeneth death"). What can also be told from the urine, so this text proposes, is the species of the being from whence it came: "Beastes water smelleth more then the mans." As well as this difference in degree it would seem there is also a difference in nature of human and animal urine: "medle the vrin of a beaste with a mans vrine, and they shall part a sonder" (Anon. 1562: sigs. Aiv, Avir, Bvir). Like oil and water, human and animal piss can never be mixed. Similarly, in *The Differences, Causes, and Judgements of Urine* (1623), John Fletcher also proposes urine as a means to distinguish humans from beasts, arguing that an animal's water is "thicke." But unlike the earlier text, where the difference between human and animal is in one representation absolute – like the difference between oil and water – Fletcher proposes that it is possible for human urine to come to be just like that of an animal. He writes that "their urines which have crammed themselves with meate and drinke are more easily turned and waxe thicke" (Fletcher 1623: 17–18, 8). This transformation of human into animal urine offers us one place in which vice – here greed – is understood to lead humans physiologically – *not just metaphorically* – to become indistinguishable from the lower animals. The impossibility of telling the urine of one from the urine of the other offers empirical evidence for this transformation.

But writers also reiterate the dangerous slippage from human to animal in another way that plays into ideas that go beyond the body. When, for example, the question of when and where urination should take place is raised we find that the discussion of physiology has become a discussion of civility. For James Hart, writing in 1625, involuntary urination can be due to bodily sickness, but it can also be caused by "some perturbations of the mind, as great and sudden feare and astonishment makes men often void, not the urine onely, but other excrements also against their will" (Hart 1625: 107, 118). In the same vein William Fiston argued in 1595 that "These are wordes of fooles to say: I was like to bepisse my selfe with laughing" (W. F. 1595: sig. B8r). In both of these cases, as in greed, passions have overwhelmed reason; the body overcome the mind.[5]

John Fletcher took the idea of "involuntary pissing" in a slightly different way. While mentioning the possibility of sickness leading to weakness of the bladder, Fletcher also wrote of the "Principall Agent the braine not directing the animal facultie, nor [communicating with] the sinnewes and muscles of the vessels of urine, wherupon they cease from their function, and let the urine passe away by droppes, as they receive it, as in mad men, raving, doting, in sharpe diseases" (Fletcher 1623: 98–9). Here, lack of control over the bladder is not simply the result of organic injury or illness; it is a lack of *reasonable* control over the body. The madman, in his abandonment of accepted reality, has also abandoned his self-control. And as the other side of the coin to this loss of humanity, it might be worth noting in passing that Tycho Brahe, the astronomer with the dog at his feet, died – so myth had it – of a burst bladder when he attempted to hold back his urine out of politeness while at a dinner party in 1601.[6] Brahe, in this story, died because he attempted to assert too much self-control; to be, if you like, too human.

Michael C. Schoenfeldt has outlined the way in which ill-health was linked with immorality in early modern medical writing (Schoenfeldt 1999: 7), and in the discussions of involuntary urination we find a clear comparison being made between a person with a "weakned, or decaied" bladder and a person with a weakened or decayed mind, but it is not absolutely clear which came first. In this discourse, to be mad is to be sick, but by the same token to be sick is to be mad, and madness, whether it precedes or follows sickness, because it is a loss of use of reason, is also a loss of human status.[7] To lose control of one's bladder, then, is to be unreasonable and therefore urinating inappropriately can stand for a lack of humanity. But inappropriate urination is not simply about self-control (or its lack). It is also about being civilized. As Norbert Elias argued in his seminal study *The Civilizing Process*, in the period we are looking at there was a "shift in the frontier of embarrassment," "a notable rise of the shame threshold, compared to the preceding epoch" (Elias 1994: 107, 110). Stephen Greenblatt, following Elias, writes:

> The behavior manuals of the fifteenth through eighteenth centuries return again and again to codes elaborated for the management of the body's products: urine, feces, mucus, saliva, and wind. Proper control of each of these products, along with the acquisition of the prevailing table manners and modes of speech, mark the entrance into civility, an entrance that distinguishes not only the child from the adult, but the members of a privileged group from the vulgar, the upper classes from the lower, the courtly from the rustic, the civilized from the savage. (Greenblatt 1990: 61)

The figure of the speechless Crab pissing under the table of the Duke clearly asks us to add to Greenblatt's list of binaries. The distinction of human from animal (self-controlled man from urinating dog) is also a cornerstone of the civilizing process. The fact that Greenblatt does not include this opposition in his list signals, perhaps, that he assumes that the difference between human and animal does not need to be elaborated upon as it is one that has existed across history and thus can be taken for granted. I would argue instead that the difference between humans and animals as we understand it now is itself a creation of the civilizing process. As such it is anachronistic for Elias and the many critics who follow him to ignore the animals in the Renaissance debates about civility as they do because ignoring them assumes a position that can exist only after the civilizing process has taken place. Early modern writers – as the presence on stage of Crab in *The Two Gentlemen of Verona* argues – did not ignore these animals.

So if we do turn to ruminate upon the animal what can we find?[8] If we take Crab's activities beneath the Duke's table as a marker of absolute incivility we can begin to establish what it is that might demarcate civil behavior in this period. Self-control (of the bladder as of all things) is clearly important, and alongside this is an increasing awareness of the distinction of the private and the public; of the appropriate place for urination: as Paster has written, "the history of the civilizing process is also the history of social space" (Paster 2001: 142). Increasingly, as the period under examination here progressed, controls on where urination should take place came into being. Elias records warnings against relieving oneself in public from the second half of the sixteenth century. In Germany in 1589, for example, gentlemen were advised: "Let no one, whoever he may be, before, at, or after meals, early or late, foul the staircases, corridors, or closets with urine or other filth, but go to suitable, prescribed places for such relief" (Elias 1994: 107). The fact that such a statement seems so odd to us – imagine having to tell an adult where to pee – signals how successful the civilizing process has been. We are so inculcated in the ways of civility that we no longer need to be told not to urinate on staircases, and when we come upon urine-soaked staircases we are likely to regard them as dangerous, as a place of the uncivil, the barbaric.

What the civilizing process reinforces in humans then is a distinction between reasonable and unreasonable, self-controlled and uncontrolled, civil and savage. It also underlines a conception of the difference between the private and the public: in one, urination is allowed, in the other, prohibited. Thus, lacking reason, self-control, and civility, and displaying no concept of the difference between the private and the public, a pissing dog comes to stand for everything that a human is not, and cannot be. I use "cannot" here rather than "should not" because the logic that underpins the civilizing process means that if a person does piss in a prohibited place they cannot any longer be counted as human.

But we can go further than this opposition of the pissing dog and the human: identity, so Burton Hatlen has noted, "is born at the interface between the public and the private realms. But because it is ambiguously both personal and social, identity is inherently flawed, vulnerable, and shame represents the (always reluctant) acknowledgment of the problematic status of individual identity" (Hatlen 1997: 394). But what happens to identity if the individual has no concept of the distinction of public and private, if the individual does not experience shame when that distinction is violated? What happens if one is a being for whom concepts of civil and uncivil are meaningless and yet it is those very concepts that form identity? Such,

I think, are questions that we must have in mind as we think about Crab. In early modern terms Crab's identity is not, as Dobson and Boehrer argue, stable; it is, in fact, non-existent. Indeed, it could be said that if a dog has no self then it can never, like the human fool in William Fiston's text, "bepisse" itself. A dog can only ever simply piss.[9]

Thus the presence of a live dog on stage signals in the most explicit way possible the very real danger of incivility that hangs over the play. In Shakespeare's later plays dogs exist as symbols – the dog Cordelia would have allowed into her house on a stormy night in *King Lear*; the breeds of dogs that suggest the different levels of humanity in *Macbeth*, for example. In this play though the dog is, like Tycho Brahe's hound, real and it is the reality of the animal that is his meaning. But as well as this very important real presence of the pissing canine in *The Two Gentlemen of Verona*, we can also see that Crab plays a role in another crucial aspect of the play; its representation of friendship. What we can also begin to see, in fact, is that the two – the representation of urination and the representation of friendship – are inextricably linked.

Crab's first appearance in the play is in the report of his failure to act as a true friend. He has "no more pity in him than a dog." Such a failure reveals in another way the true doggishness of the dog and, by default, offers an alternative illustration of how the human could be traced in early modern ideas. In fact *The Two Gentlemen of Verona* shows that the distance between the pissing dog and the human friend is a dangerously short one. As such, the current critical interest in male friendship might be enhanced and supported by an understanding not simply of the friend, but of man's best friend, the dog.[10]

The Limits of Friendship

A key conception of early modern friendship can be found in Cicero's *De amicitia*, which was translated into English as *The Booke of freendeship* in 1550 by John Harington, who was also, it should be noted in the context of this discussion, the designer of the first flushing toilet (see Harington 1962). For Cicero, friendship is never "wythout vertue," it is "never unreasonable" (Cicero 1562: sigs. 14v, 16r). Friendship is thus doubly inseparable from human status: only humans can be virtuous and thus friends, and because virtue requires reason, and only humans are reasonable, thus only humans can be friends. As such it is clear from the start of *The Two Gentlemen of Verona* that we are witnessing not simply the separation of two friends, but a challenge to human status. "Cease to persuade, my loving Proteus" is the play's opening line and it signals a breakdown in the rational order that friendship offers. Valentine, the speaker of this line, has chosen to travel, "To see the wonders of the world abroad" (1.1.6), while Proteus has decided to stay at home in Verona and, in Valentine's opinion, be mastered by his love for Julia (1.1.39). This division between the friends is the stimulus for the subsequent action of the play.

But it is, as Jeffrey Masten has shown, a particular aspect of friendship that is particularly important in *The Two Gentlemen of Verona*. In the *Nicomachean Ethics* Aristotle wrote that "his friend is another self" (Aristotle 1952a: IX, 4), and likewise in *De amicitia* Cicero wrote "even as another hym selfe shal his frende bee to hym"; and later in the same text, "For hee surely is a freende, that is an other I" (Cicero 1562: n.p. and sig. 51v). This idea is repeated, as Masten shows, by Michel de Montaigne in the late sixteenth century in his essay "Of friendship" (1572–6, 1578–80):

> In the friendship I speak of, our souls mingle and blend with each other so completely that they efface the seam that joined them, and cannot find it again. If you press me to tell you why I loved him, I feel that this cannot be expressed, except by answering: Because it was he, because it was I.

Montaigne goes on to say of his friend Etienne de la Boétie: "not only did I know his soul as well as mine, but I should certainly have trusted myself to him more readily than to myself." The friend is, for Montaigne, as for Aristotle and Cicero, "not another man: he is myself" (Montaigne 2003: 169, 170–1, 172).[11] Likewise, in *The Two Gentlemen of Verona* Valentine tells the Duke – using, significantly, the past tense – "I knew [Proteus] as myself" (2.4.60).

This sense of friendship in which self dissolves into other might appear to align friend with canine: both, it would seem, lack individual identity. In fact, Lance's statement "I am the dog. No, the dog is himself, and I am the dog. O, the dog is me, and I am myself" seems to offer a comic version of such true friendship. However, the fact that Lance finds himself inseparable from his *dog* signals his failure as a human: because, as Thomas Aquinas wrote, "all friendship is founded on some community of life . . . and irrational creatures have no share in human life, which of its nature is rational, therefore no friendship is possible with them except metaphorically speaking" (Aquinas 1975: 89). Friendship, once again, is human and so a breach of friendship is also a breach of humanity – of civility, rationality, self-control. Thus, when Proteus states "I to myself am dearer than a friend" (2.6.23) as he decides to pursue Valentine's beloved Silvia for himself, he is laying aside the kind of bond outlined in classical theories of friendship, and it is at this point that Proteus' humanity truly comes under threat. It might seem paradoxical to our modern conception of selfhood, but it is as he asserts his individual identity – as he becomes simply one gentleman of Verona – that Proteus' potential to exist as a self collapses. And indeed Proteus' actions reveal his lack of humanity in a particular way two scenes later: he violates what he himself calls the "law of friendship" when he reveals to the Duke Valentine's plot to elope with Silvia to which he has been "made privy" (3.1.12) – and the coincidence of "privy" meaning in confidence, as a friend, and the term privy used to describe a toilet provides yet another link between friendship and urination in the period.

But this is not the end of the destruction of humanity in the play; there are more complex violations to come. In the same scene as Proteus' revelations to the Duke, when his plot is uncovered and he is banished from Milan on pain of death, Valentine bemoans his fate in the following terms:

> And why not death, rather than living torment?
> To die is to be banished from myself,
> And Silvia is myself; banished from her
> Is self from self – a deadly banishment. (3.1.170–3)

Valentine has by this point replaced Proteus in his friendly affection with Silvia; it is she who is now his other self. But this is a problematic substitution: Montaigne writes, "the ordinary capacity of women is inadequate for that communion and fellowship which is the nurse of this sacred bond [friendship]" (Montaigne 2003: 167). As such, Valentine's relationship with Silvia is not reasonable; it is, like Lance's love for his dog, a violation of reason as well as a violation of the rules of friendship. By the beginning of the third act, then, the threat to human status present in the very first line of the play has been made real: neither of the gentlemen can register themselves any longer as a friend, and thus as a human.

At this point it is utterly logical that Valentine should travel to the "wilderness" outside of Milan; that he should leave behind the civility and community of court life to join up with the "wild faction" who live outside the law (4.1.62 and 37). It is also logical that in this same wilderness in the following act Proteus should attempt to rape Silvia; that he should try to violate the lady that he has stolen from his former friend. And what provides a link between these two scenes in which humanity is witnessed only in its destruction is the pissing dog. The lapdog has been stolen away by the hangman's boys and the dog offered as a replacement gives immediate evidence of his inappropriateness. In the first version of this triangular relationship we have two former friends and a stolen lady, in the second a stolen dog and the separation of Lance and Crab, two other inseparable companions. It is not simply that "there are, by this time, *no* gentlemen in Verona," by this time there are no *humans* in Verona. "Did I not bid thee still mark me, and do as I do?" Lance chides Crab after his actions beneath the table of the Duke (4.4.34–5). Ironically, of course, we can now see that the dog has followed his so-called human superiors and that his currish behavior is simply another rendition of their incivilities of which the play is so full.

But, of course, the play does not end on such vulgarities. First of all there is Proteus' repentance. He is accused by Valentine not of being a rapist but of being a "friend of an ill fashion," a "common friend, that's without faith or love" (5.4.61 and 62). It is when Valentine notes that "The *private* wound is deepest" (5.4.71 – my italics) that Proteus sees the error of his ways: his following line is "My shame and guilt confounds me" (5.4.72). Proteus' statement does not only represent his own humanity – shame and guilt are both traits that only humans possess; it also illustrates the humanity of his friend. Aristotle wrote in his *Rhetoric*, "no one feels shame before small children or animals" (Aristotle 1952b: II, 6). It is as a signal of the return of their friendship, and thus their human status, that Valentine can make the – to us – uncomfortable offer to Proteus: "All that was mine in Silvia I give thee." We can turn to Montaigne for an explanation for this strange offer. He writes of the friendship

of Caius Blossius and Tiberius Gracchus: "Having committed themselves absolutely to each other, they held absolutely the reins of each
other's inclination" (Montaigne 2003: 170). Where Valentine loves
and respects Silvia, so will Proteus, but where Valentine is betrothed
to Silvia, so Proteus will respect that betrothal. To make the offer of
Silvia to Proteus, then, is to make no offer at all. Alternatively, as
Jeffrey Masten notes, Valentine's offer can be read rather differently:
it may signal that Valentine has transferred "all his love for Silvia to
Proteus" (Masten 2003: 273); that he has replaced the inappropriate
other self with the appropriate one. It is only Julia – Proteus' abandoned mistress – who misses the true meaning of this offer; but then,
within this discourse, she is a woman with an "inadequate" capacity
for understanding.

The play, of course, ends with two marriages, but most importantly,
it ends with friendship. The final four lines of the play are
Valentine's:

> Come Proteus, 'tis your penance but to hear
> The story of your loves discovered.
> That done, our day of marriage shall be yours,
> One feast, one house, one mutual happiness. (5.4.168–71)

It is tempting – following Alan Bray's (2003) important study of the
rituals of friendship in early modern Europe – to read the mention of
marriage here as not simply referring to the linking of Valentine and
Silvia and Proteus and Julia. Perhaps by the end of *The Two Gentlemen
of Verona* what is being planned is also a "handfast" ceremony whereby
two male friends can be joined in "marriage." If not this, then at
the very least what is witnessed here is a reaffirmation of their
friendship.

By the end of the play, then, the status of humanity has with the
friendship been reasserted and what has been learned is the difficulty
of being human. Proteus blamed his fall on his human nature – "O
heaven, were man / But constant, he were perfect" – and what the
presence of the dog emphasizes is the constant danger of inconstancy.
Humans, this argument goes, cannot rely on the stability of their
humanity, they must struggle to maintain it. In fact, the struggle represented in *The Two Gentlemen of Verona* is, it seems, typical of its age.
Not only is Crab a twist on the established image of the dog at the

feet of the human; as two further examples show, the urinating canine remained a symbol of the fragility of human status in the century after Shakespeare was writing.

Svetlana Alpers has argued that "if the theater was the arena in which the England of Elizabeth most fully represented itself to itself, images played that role for the Dutch" (Alpers 1983: xxv), and we can turn to one genre of Dutch art – the church interior – to see the significance of dogs in the human construction of itself. In this genre artists depict the interiors of the plain, beautiful churches of the period, and in doing so represent the distinction between human life on earth and the life everlasting in their emphasis on the distinction between the light of the roof of the church and the darkness of its base. At the bottom of numerous of these paintings, alongside prosaic human activities, are dogs, brought into the buildings by owners as part of their daily round. But in one painting by Hendrick van Vliet (ca. 1611–75) the dog is not simply loitering by its owner. Van Vliet makes the distinction between the life of the spirit and the life of the body explicit when, alongside a man being watched by a dog as he digs what appears to be a grave, he depicts another dog urinating on one of the church's main columns (plate 8.2).

As the eye travels up the painting away from the dogs, the grave, and the people, it enters the world of light. It seems significant that such a world can only be understood when it is contrasted with the inevitable decay of the human body and the constant threat of incontinence, inconstancy: with death and the pissing dog.

The final version of this trope comes from across the Atlantic. In 1700 Cotton Mather found himself forced to contemplate his nature:

> I was once emptying the cistern of nature, and making water at the wall. At the same time, there came a dog, who did so too, before me. Thought I; 'What mean and vile things are the children of men . . . How much do our natural necessities abase us, and place us . . . on the same level with the very dogs!'

> My thought proceeded. 'Yet I will be a more noble creature; and at the very time when my natural necessities debase me into the condition of the beast, my spirit shall (I say *at that very time!*) rise and soar . . .'

Plate 8.2 Hendrick van Vliet, *The New Church at Delft* (n.d.). Oil on panel, 40 × 35 cm. Reproduced by permission of Koninklijk Museum voor Schone Kunsten, Antwerp.

> Accordingly, I resolved that it should be my ordinary practice, whenever I step to answer the one or other necessity of nature to make it an opportunity of shaping in my mind some holy, noble, divine thought. (*Diary of Cotton Mather*, quoted in Thomas 1983: 38)

From an English comedy, to a Dutch church interior, to the anxious realization of a New England clergyman, the urinating dog persists to remind humans of their fragility; to prompt us that we are who and what we are only because there are animals standing, sitting, urinating at our side. As well as this, the presence on stage of a dog should not be read as a failure of dramatic coherence on Shakespeare's part. It should remind us that even in this first play Shakespeare is already contemplating the difficulty of being human. For Hamlet's "What a piece of work is a man?" (2.2.305) read Lance's "I am the dog. No, the dog is himself, and I am the dog. O, the dog is me, and I am myself."

Notes

1   Translation from the original Latin in Reuterswärd (1991: 216).
2   All in-text references are to Shakespeare (2004).
3   Paster is citing *1 Henry IV*, 1.2.73–81. For an analysis of the copious comparisons in this dialogue, see Julie Maxwell's essay in this volume.
4   Boehrer situates his own work within ecocriticism and makes no mention of debates taking place in animal studies. For a difference between the two compare Garrard (2004: 136–59) with the essays in the special issue "Representing Animals," *Society and Animals* 9:3 (2001), and the essays in the special issue "Viewing Animals," *Worldviews: Environment, Culture, Religion* 9:3 (2005).
5   On laughter, control of the body, and the establishment of human status, see Fudge (2003: 277–94).
6   See, for example, the brief outline of Brahe's death on www.nada.kth.se/~fred/tycho/death.html, accessed on September 12, 2006.
7   On the significance of rationality to the status of the human, see Fudge (2006).
8   Friedrich Nietzsche proposed: "One thing is necessary above all if one is to practice reading as an *art* . . . something for which one has to be a cow and in any case not a 'modern man': *rumination*." Nietzsche, *On the Genealogy of Morals*, cited in Fuss (1996: 1).
9   Indeed, the prefix "be-" not only derives from the Old English "by" – so "bepisse" means to piss all over – it has more meaning. Historian of linguistics Jonathan Hope writes that "be-" "is not just an intensifier, since it also makes the verb transitive – i.e. requires an object. So 'piss' is (almost always) intransitive: I piss, the dog pisses. But 'bepiss' has to be transitive: 'I bepiss myself.'" (Email, 2005.) I am very grateful to Jonathan for his help on the

linguistic meanings possible in this quotation. It is significant in the light of this that Lance refers to Crab as "himself" throughout the play, thus giving the dog a self and compounding Lance's own misunderstanding.

10   The phrase "love me, love my Dogge" appears in Philip Stubbes' *Anatomie of Abuses* (1583), where Stubbes asserts that it is "a common saiyng amongest all men" that has a French origin: "Qui aime Iean, aime son chien" (Stubbes 1583: sig. Qvir).

11   For extended discussion of this topic in Montaigne, see Richard Scholar's essay in this volume.

Works Cited

Alpers, Svetlana 1983: *The Art of Describing: Dutch Art in the Seventeenth Century*. Chicago: University of Chicago Press.

Anon. 1562: *The Seing of Urynes*. London: Wyllyam Powel.

Aquinas, Thomas 1975: *Summa theologiae*. Trans. R. J. Batten. London: Blackfriars.

Aristotle 1952a: *Nicomachean Ethics*. Trans. W. D. Ross. In *The Works of Aristotle*. Chicago: Encyclopaedia Britannica.

Aristotle 1952b: *Rhetoric*. Trans. W. Rhys Roberts. In *The Works of Aristotle*. Chicago: Encyclopaedia Britannica.

Armstrong, Philip 2004: "*Moby-Dick* and Compassion." *Society and Animals* 12, 19–37.

Armstrong, Philip 2005: "What do Animals Mean, in *Moby-Dick*, for example." *Textual Practice* 19, 93–111.

Beadle, Richard 1994: "Crab's Pedigree." In Michael Cordner, Peter Holland, and John Kerrigan (eds.) *English Comedy*. Cambridge: Cambridge University Press, 12–35.

Bliss, Matthew 1994: "Property or Performer? Animals on the Elizabethan Stage." *Theatre Studies* 39, 45–59.

Boehrer, Bruce 2002: *Shakespeare Among the Animals: Nature and Society in the Drama of Early Modern England*. New York: Palgrave.

Brahe, Tycho 1602: *Astronomiæ Instauratæ Mechanica*. Noribergæ, apud Levinum Hulsium. Trans. Patrik Reuterswärd 1991. "The Dog in the Humanist's Study." In *The Visible and Invisible in Art: Essays in the History of Art*. Vienna: IRSA, 206–25.

Bray, Alan 2003: *The Friend*. Chicago: University of Chicago Press.

Brooks, Harold F. 1963: "Two Clowns in a Comedy (to say nothing of the Dog): Speed, Launce (and Crab) in *The Two Gentlemen of Verona*." *Essays and Studies* 16, 91–100.

Burt, Jonathan 2002: *Animals in Film*. London: Reaktion Books.

Campbell, Kathleen 1996: "Shakespeare's Actors as Collaborators: Will Kempe and *The Two Gentlemen of Verona.*" In June Schleuter (ed.) *The Two Gentlemen of Verona: Critical Essays.* New York: Garland, 179–87.

Cicero 1562: *The Booke of freendeship of Marcus Tullie Cicero.* Trans. John Harington. London.

Derrida, Jacques 2002: "The Animal that therefore I am (More to Follow)." Trans. David Willis. *Critical Inquiry* 28, 369–417.

Dobson, Michael 2000: "A Dog at all Things: The Transformation of the Onstage Canine, 1550–1850." *Performance Research* 5, 116–24.

Elias, Norbert 1994: *The Civilizing Process.* Trans. Edmund Jephcott. Oxford: Blackwell.

Ewbank, Inga-Stina 1972: "'Were Man But Constant, He Were Perfect': Constancy and Consistency in *The Two Gentlemen of Verona.*" Reprinted in June Schleuter (ed.) *The Two Gentlemen of Verona: Critical Essays.* 1996. New York: Garland, 91–114.

[Fiston, William] W. F. 1595: *The Schoole of good manners.* London.

Fletcher, J. 1623: *The Differences, Causes, and Judgements of Urine.* London.

Fudge, Erica 2000: *Perceiving Animals: Humans and Beasts in Early Modern English Culture.* Basingstoke: Macmillan.

Fudge, Erica 2003: "Learning to Laugh: Children and Being Human in Early Modern Thought." *Textual Practice* 17, 277–94.

Fudge, Erica 2006: *Brutal Reasoning: Animals, Rationality, and Humanity in Early Modern England.* Ithaca: Cornell University Press.

Fuss, Diana 1996: "Introduction." In Diana Fuss (ed.) *Human All Too Human.* New York: Routledge.

Garrard, Greg 2004: *Ecocriticism.* London: Routledge.

Greenblatt, Stephen 1990: "Filthy Rites." In *Learning to Curse: Essays in Early Modern Culture.* New York: Routledge.

Harington, John 1962: *A New Discourse of a Stale Subject, Called the Metamorphosis of Ajax.* Ed. Elizabeth Story Donno. London: Routledge and Kegan Paul.

Hart, James 1625: *The Anatomie of Urines.* London.

Hatlen, Burton 1997: "The 'Noble Thing' and the 'Boy of Tears': *Coriolanus* and the Embarrassments of Identity." *English Literary Renaissance* 27, 393–420.

Höltgen, Karl Josef 1998: "Clever Dogs and Nimble Spaniels: On the Iconography of Logic, Invention, and Imagination." *Explorations in Renaissance Culture* 24, 1–36.

Kean, Hilda 1998: *Animal Rights: Political and Social Change in Britain since 1800.* London: Reaktion Books.

Latour, Bruno 1991: *We Have Never Been Modern.* Trans. Catherine Porter. Cambridge, MA: Harvard University Press.

Masten, Jeffrey 2003: "The Two Gentlemen of Verona." In Richard Dutton and Jean E. Howard (eds.) *A Companion to Shakespeare's Works*, Vol. 3: *The Comedies*. Oxford: Blackwell, 266–88.

Montaigne, Michel de 2003: "Of friendship." In *The Complete Works*. Trans. Donald M. Frame. London: Everyman.

Paster, Gail Kern 2001: "The Epistemology of the Water Closet: John Harington's *Metamorphosis of Ajax* and Elizabethan Technologies of Shame." In Curtis Perry (ed.) *Material Culture and Cultural Materialisms in the Middle Ages and Renaissance*. Turnhout: Brepols, 139–58.

Paster, Gail Kern 2004: *Humoring the Body: Emotions and the Shakespearean Stage*. Chicago: University of Chicago Press.

Philo, Chris and Wilbert, Chris 2000: "Animal Spaces, Beastly Places: An Introduction." In Chris Philo and Chris Wilbert (eds.) *Animal Spaces, Beastly Places: New Geographies of Human–Animal Relations*. New York: Routledge, 1–34.

Quiller-Couch, A. 1921: "Introduction" to William Shakespeare, *The Two Gentlemen of Verona*. Cambridge: New Cambridge Shakespeare.

Reuterswärd, Patrick 1991: "The Dog in the Humanist's Study." In *The Visible and Invisible in Art: Essays in the History of Art*. Vienna: IRSA, 206–25.

Rothfels, Nigel 2002: *Savages and Beasts: The Birth of the Modern Zoo*. Baltimore: Johns Hopkins University Press.

Schoenfeldt, Michael C. 1999: *Bodies and Selves in Early Modern England: Physiology and Inwardness in Spenser, Shakespeare, Herbert, and Milton*. Cambridge: Cambridge University Press.

Shakespeare, William 1988: *The Complete Works*. Ed. Stanley Wells and Gary Taylor. Oxford: Oxford University Press.

Shakespeare, William 2004: *The Two Gentlemen of Verona*. Ed. William C. Carroll. London: Arden.

Stubbes, Philip 1583: *The Anatomie of Abuses*. London: J. R. Jones.

Thirsk, Joan 1978: *Horses in Early Modern England: For Service, for Pleasure, for Power*. Reading: University of Reading Press.

Thomas, Keith 1983: *Man and the Natural World: Changing Attitudes in England 1500–1800*. London: Penguin.

Timpane, John 1996: "'I Am But a Foole, Looke You': Launce and the Social Functions of Humor." In June Schleuter (ed.) *The Two Gentlemen of Verona: Critical Essays*. New York: Garland, 189–211.

Wells, Stanley 1963: "The Failure of *The Two Gentlemen of Verona*." *Shakespeare Jahrbuch* 99, 161–73.

Wright, Louis B. 1927: "Animal Actors on the English Stage Before 1642." *PMLA* 42, 656–69.

Chapter 9

Sheepishness in *The Winter's Tale*

Paul Yachnin

Rationale

"When I play with my cat," Michel de Montaigne commented, "how do I know that she is not passing time with me rather than I with her?" One of the indications of the new thinking about human personhood that was characteristic of the Renaissance was a burgeoning interest in the nature of "brute beasts." One new and surprisingly illuminating way to think about Shakespeare's plays is through his interest in animals, his often intensely felt animal imagery, and what we can call "animalities" – the qualities of character, mentality, and behavior associated with dogs, bears, asses, falcons, horses, deer, and even monsters. Most important, to understand Shakespeare's animals is to begin to grasp something about his thinking about people. In this essay, I try to understand Shakespeare's great tragicomedy, *The Winter's Tale*, and especially the character King Leontes, by thinking about Renaissance ideas about sheep.

In addition to what they can tell us about his view of personhood, Shakespeare's animals can open to us his complex representations of the social world of early modern England. In an age before plastics, synthetic fibers, electric light, or the internal combustion engine, animals were the main supports of the economic life of society. They performed all sorts of work and provided the very stuff of living. Farming, tanning and glove-making (Shakespeare's father was in the business), cloth-making, transportation, warfare, and forms of entertainment from bear-baiting to hawking to writing with quill pens to reading by the light of tallow or beeswax candles – these and many other human activities depended on the strength, intelligence, courage, and bodies of animals. In fact, the primary industry in Shakespeare's England was sheep-raising and wool production.

The involvement of animals in the material economy of early modern England was, furthermore, inseparable from their place within its symbolic economy. Everywhere one looks in the writing of the period, one discovers that to think about animals is also to think about human relations of domination and subordination, about human life-values, and even about suffering and spiritual destiny. It was a commonplace that woman was to man as horse was to rider, a common idea also that the king governed by right of nature just as the lion ruled by dint of his inherent superiority to the other animals, but it is was also not unusual to measure the cruelty and violence of human power against the native innocence and goodness of the wild creatures. In my essay in this volume, I focus not on relations of power but rather on the relation between creatures (human and animal creatures) and the divine.

I should note that I did not begin this adventure of understanding alone. Not only did I reread and rethink Shakespeare's plays, but I was also guided by the work of several other scholars – Erica Fudge (who also has an essay in this book and whose searching examinations of the cultural negotiations going on in early modern England through human/animal relations provided a model for my thinking), Ed Berry (his book, *Shakespeare and the Hunt*, shines new light on a number of plays), Bruce Boehrer (whose lively and wide-ranging work offers a wealth of ideas and material), Laurie Shannon (her work is not yet published, only so far presented at conferences, but is brilliantly illuminating about early modern animality), and Keith Thomas's important book, *Man and the Natural World: Changing Attitudes in England, 1500–1800*. Not only are these works of great value in themselves, but they can also lead readers to the extraordinary wealth of Renaissance writing about animals. These fascinating old books, by writers such as Edward Topsell, Conrad Heresbach, and Gervase Markham, allow us to read plays like *The Winter's Tale* with new eyes and with a much richer historical understanding of Shakespeare's culture.

Almost everything I know about good manners I learned from my dogs. I don't want to slight my mother or the memory of my father, since they provided me with an unimpeachable upbringing, and I must also acknowledge the civilizing influence of my wife (a benefit that married partners give each other and a benefit that bears on the argument that follows), but I must nevertheless affirm that you can learn crucial lessons about how to behave as a human among other humans from watching the civility of dogs. They are expert at getting along with each other: they know how to defer to their elders, they endure the rambunctiousness of puppies with grace (and an occasional sharp word), they know how to test the limits of other dogs in order to find their social place promptly and without a lot of friction, and they are very good at saving face and at leaving enough distance for their fellows to be able to save face too. To their humans, they are attentive, caring, forgiving, and loving. Like many other dog owners, I marvel at their natural civility and goodness and also at the complexity and general good order of their social relations.

All this started me wondering several years ago about Shakespeare, which is something I do anyway as a university teacher and a professional Shakespeare scholar. Shakespeare's understanding of human life had always seemed to me both capacious and penetrating, but I was troubled because his representation of dogs seemed to me perversely limited, even mean-spirited. The truth is, Shakespeare doesn't seem to like dogs very much. To be sure, some of his characters evidently have an eye, or an ear, for a well-bred hunting dog. Theseus' admirable hounds are "match'd in mouth like bells" (*Midsummer Night's Dream*, 4.1.123);[1] the Lord and his huntsman in the Induction to *The Taming of the Shrew* compete in their praise of Silver (that "made it good . . . in the coldest fault"; Ind. 1.19–20) and Belman (that "twice . . . pick'd out the dullest scent"; line 24); and sometimes characters express sympathy for canine suffering, as Cordelia does when she compares how her sisters drove her father into the storm with how she would treat *even* a dog in similar circumstances (so this is not exactly a declaration of her love for dogs): "Mine enemy's dog, / Though he had bit me, should have stood that night / Against my fire" (*King Lear*, 4.7.35–7). Mostly, however, Shakespeare uses the word "dog" as a term of abuse, and he does so in a very wide range of phrases ("dog-hearted" in *Lear*, 4.3.45, "inexecrable dog" in *Merchant of Venice*, 4.1.128, "inhuman dog" in *Othello*, 5.1. 61) or simply with "you" as in "you dog!"[2] Dogs seem to be natural bottom-feeders who make love to their employment. They are by turns fawning and vicious – self-serving, base, and not to be trusted. Even their loyalty is in reality a kind of masochism (where, importantly, the desire to be hurt is never far from the desire to cause hurt). Richard II says that traitors are like dogs because they are "easily won to fawn on any man" (*Richard II*, 3.2.130). And here, in the wood just outside Athens where Theseus will later praise his hounds, Helena describes her love for Demetrius as a dog-like self-abnegation (and we recall how sharp she will be with her "sister" Hermia when the love of the two young men is at stake):

> I am your spaniel; and, Demetrius,
> The more you beat me, I will fawn on you.
> Use me but as your spaniel; spurn me, strike me,
> Neglect me, lose me; only give me leave,
> Unworthy as I am, to follow you.
> What worser place can I beg in your love
> (And yet a place of high respect with me)
> Than to be used as you use your dog.
> (*Midsummer Night's Dream*, 2.1.203–10)

Why, I asked myself, does Shakespeare hate dogs? To answer that question was to begin an exploration into the extraordinary ways in which Shakespeare maps the human world onto the world of animals. What I discovered is that Shakespeare's dogs embody the obsequiousness and also the fierce contest for status that were near the heart of the early modern system of rank in which he was brought up. No doubt on account of his social training he would have been deferential to his "betters." That he sought a coat of arms and the right to call himself a gentleman suggests how invested he was in the system of rank. When, seven years after his elevation to the status of gentleman, he and his fellows were taken by the new King into the fold of royal patronage, and when the newly constituted King's Servants took part in the royal entry, with what proud humility must Shakespeare have marched, clothed as would have been in the King's livery? A servant to be sure, but a socially imposing one on account of his new royal master.

Shakespeare's feelings must have been ambivalent, to say the least. We can think of the extraordinary range of social climbers who seek to attach themselves to higher-ranking others in his plays – Orlando (who marries a princess), Sebastian in *Twelfth Night* (who marries a countess), Malvolio (who, in the same play, is publicly humiliated for *his* social aspiration), Helena in *All's Well* (who aspires to marry and does marry a worthless aristocrat), Oswald (Goneril's loathsome steward in *King Lear*) and Caliban – that creature of the human-animal threshold – who foolishly tries to carry out his aggression against Prospero by means of an act of submission to the butler Stephano. Shakespeare, we might say, worked through his own mixed feelings of pride and shame by means of telling the stories of these characters (and no doubt part of the appeal of the plays was that they allowed many playgoers also to work through their own aspiration, emulation, and shame).[3]

Not surprisingly, dogs receive a less complex portrayal than an Orlando or a Caliban; in their case, Shakespeare seems mostly to have scapegoated them by projecting onto them the fawning and fierceness of the typical Elizabethan struggle for social success. Shakespeare's representation of dogs is thus keyed to the system of rank and the culture of deference of his time. (Is it any wonder that dogs nowadays, at least those who live in democratic, egalitarian societies, serve as "natural" exemplars of civil public conduct and an ethos of mutual recognition?) Dogs and a host of other animals, the relationships among animals, and the relations between humans and animals provide Shakespeare with a rich language for the critical description of human relations and human personhood in social settings. In the case of dogs, furthermore, their use as symbols in the theatrical representation of social relations was of a piece with their physical, instrumental use in the day-to-day preservation of the actual system of rank. Dogs are creatures that, to a significant degree, are *made by culture*. Dogs in a law-abiding democracy will tend to be mild-tempered and approachable (they are bred and raised to be that way), whereas dogs in a culture like Shakespeare's will tend to be fierce and unfriendly toward strangers. There will be far more hunting hounds and guard dogs (like Theseus' hounds or like dogs that threaten harmless beggars – *King Lear*, 4.6.154–5) and far fewer pets (though there are those too, like Petruchio's spaniel Troilus, a figure of loyalty and relational harmony that is significantly absent, or the wonderfully inarticulate Crab in *The Two Gentlemen of Verona*, 2.3).[4]

In what follows, I want to keep in view the instrumental and often cruel use of animals by humans (after all sheep-raising and the production of meat, skins, tallow, and especially wool amounted to the leading industry in early modern England) (Bowden 1962: 1–40), and also the

way Shakespeare projects human life onto animals, even to the point
of scapegoating them for the injustices of human society. But I want
also to turn my attention in another direction. There is another and
more dominant early modern view where animals exemplify the abundance of Nature and the goodness of the Creator. This view, which
indeed is often articulated in tandem with praise for the usefulness of
animals, is founded in the elemental sense of wonder we feel at the
beauty of the world. The Psalmist cries out in praise: "O Lord, how
manifold are thy works! in wisdom hast thou made them all: the earth
is full of thy riches" (Psalm 104.24, KJV). John Maplet, writing in
1567, lauds the order, plentitude, and perfection of the created world,
which he personifies in the figure of "Dame Nature" (compare "good
goddess Nature" in *The Winter's Tale*, 2.3.103): "For this is the close
and wise working of Dame Nature . . . she laboreth in hers to have them
[i.e., creatures] reach to the chiefest perfection in whom are all things
absolute, full and without any point of lack or imperfection, she giveth
to each of them in their kind a several gift" (67).

In a world conceived of as the second book of God (the first being
the scriptures), the animals often embody a naturally virtuous disposi-
tion that humans would do well to emulate. We find many expressions
of this in Shakespeare – in a back-handed way in Hamlet's castigation
of his widowed mother ("a beast that wants discourse of reason," he
says, would have mourn'd longer"; 1.2.150–1); in the fierce maternal
virtue of the "poor wren, / The most diminutive of birds, [that] will
fight, / Her young ones in her nest, against the owl" (*Macbeth*,
4.2.9–11); or in the maddened beast who, in contrast to the King's
own daughters, acknowledges naturally the graciousness of King Lear
("A father, and a gracious aged man, / Whose reverence even the
head-lugg'd bear would lick" (4.2.41–2).[5] In the face of her brothers'
opposition to her marriage to a man of lower social station, John
Webster's Duchess of Malfi makes a particularly poignant appeal to
the order of animals:

> The birds that live i'th' field
> On the wild benefit of nature, live
> Happier than we; for they may choose their mates
> And carol their sweet pleasures to the spring. (3.5.17–20)

"Infinite are the other endowments of brute beasts," wrote the physi-
cian Ambrose Paré, "and such as can hardly be imagined or described.

For if we diligently search into their nature, we shall observe the impressions and shadows of many virtues, as of magnanimity, prudence, fortitude, clemency, and docility. For they entirely love one another, follow those things that are good, shun those that are hurtful, and gather and lay up in store those things that are necessary for life and food" (Paré 1634: 56). As we will see, and as I have already suggested by my references to Cordelia's and Hamlet's attitude toward animals, Shakespeare's thinking about animals and humans is generally more complex than is Webster's or Paré's. Shakespeare seems never to idealize animals to the point where they become unmixed symbols of a higher order. Nevertheless, I think that *The Winter's Tale* shows us a Shakespeare who, while he continues to use animality as a language of critical social description, also seems disposed to learn something about morality, social ethics, and even religion from the animals and from the interactions of animals with humans in somewhat the same way that I have learned from my dogs about how to live a life worth living and how to treat other people with what we like to call "humanity."

It is often said of *The Winter's Tale* that the pastoralism of the second half of the play (with all those sheep just off-stage) is at the center of the renewal of life and hope after the paranoia and violence of the all-too-human marital and political disasters of the first half.[6] On this account, the arc of the action rises from the fallen world of courtly life into the regenerative world of nature, which is represented by the Bohemian sheepcote and the sheep-shearing feast. In this essay, I would like to suggest that, in the world of *The Winter's Tale*, it is sheep all the way down. That means that the entire dramatic action, the psychology of the characters, and the themes of the play are well explained in terms of the animality of human beings. From "the shepherd's note" in the second line of the second scene of the play, to Polixenes' nostalgic reference to his and Leontes' boyhood ("We were as twinned lambs that did frisk i'th' sun," 1.2.66), to Leontes' imagined horns, which make him baleful to those that love him, to his subsequent sheepish obedience to the Lady Paulina through his long period of mourning, to the two best sheep that the Shepherd abandons when he finds the treasure of gold, to all those sheep that are the instruments of the Shepherd's growth "into an unspeakable estate" (4.2.40), Shakespeare's play interprets human psychology, value, and destiny in the terms of ovine life.[7] The play elaborates the Christian metaphor of the virtuous human community as a flock of sheep along lines derived from animal husbandry and everyday, Christian knowledge about people and animals. The general ethical idea underlying the play's account of human life is well suggested in a 1616 homiletic text, *A Pastoral Charge*, by Richard Carpenter:

> . . . where God loveth most, we should love most also. Now the Lord loves all his creatures in a general manner, approving them as the workmanship of his own hands, and therefore there should be correspondency in our affections, to love and like all the creatures, as they are his creatures. But as for Christians, they are his peculiar, his children, the sheep of his pasture, his treasure, his chosen generation . . . (Carpenter 1616: no sig.)

We owe the creatures our love because God created them; and since he created us also, there is a God-given bond between us and them, which is why Carpenter's commonplace comment that Christians are "the sheep of his pasture" has here a particular appropriateness. "We are sheep that run astray," wrote Thomas Cranmer, "but we cannot of our power come again to the sheepfold, so great is our imperfection and weakness" (Cranmer 1595: B4).

I should note, by the way, that Shakespeare's menagerie includes other animals, such as horses, domestic fowl, and the notorious bear that performs an act of rough justice by consuming the Sicilian courtier Antigonus on the seacoast of Bohemia. Also, I should note that while much of the play can be explained in animal and ovine terms, language remains an exclusively human attribute, so that while Hermione's redemption from death is celebrated in the ordinary creaturely terms of the warmth of living flesh and naturalness of eating, her being a living human must be confirmed by her ability to speak – indeed, by her speaking a benediction on her daughter Perdita's head.[8]

Although the play develops a sheepish ideal of human conduct and community, even an ovine theodicy that explains suffering and sacrifice as of a piece with a providential order, it is by no means unaware of the instrumental use of sheep by people. Sheep in Shakespeare's time were commodities within a complex economy as well as figures in a pastoral or scriptural landscape. Gervase Markham tellingly links "praise" and "profit" at the start of a chapter on the care and feeding of sheep (Markham 1614: 64). His lengthy manual includes advice about breeding, which suggests the degree to which sheep, like dogs, are made by culture:

> . . . in the choice of sheep for your breed, have a principal respect to
> your rams, for they ever mar or make a flock: let them then, as near as
> you can, have these properties or shapes. First, large of body in every
> general part, with a long body, and a large belly; his forehead would be
> broad, round, and well rising, a cheerful large eye, straight short nostrils,
> and a very small muzzle, by no means any horns, for the dodded [i.e.,
> polled, hornless] sheep is the best breeder, and his issue never dangereth
> the dame in yeaning [i.e., in the process of giving birth], as the horned
> sheep do. (Markham 1614: 67)

Of course, given the broad social consequences of a burgeoning
wool industry, sheep also became instruments of the economic
domination of the poor by their richer fellow humans. The production of wool claimed much arable land and put many tenant farmers
out of work. According to the character Raphael in Thomas More's
Utopia, the trade in wool transformed sheep themselves into monsters
bent on the destruction of traditional rural ways of life: "These
placid creatures, which used to require so little food, have now
apparently developed a raging appetite, and turned into man-eaters.
Fields, houses, towns, everything goes down their throats" (More
1965: 46).

The books of husbandry discuss animals in terms of economic prac-
ticality, but the broader tendency is nevertheless to think about beasts
as characters within God's second book, interpreting their natures and
conditions of living in Christian terms. Erica Fudge draws our attention to a number of writers who blame the savagery of beasts on
human sin. "[I]f there be any defect or untowardness in their nature,"
Thomas Draxe wrote in 1613, "or any want of duty and observance
in them towards us, our sin hath been and is the cause and occasion
of it" (quoted in Fudge 2000: 38). For John Rawlinson, preaching in
London in 1612 on Proverbs 12.10 ("A righteous man regardeth the
life of his beast," KJV), the humane treatment of animals is a Christian
duty. Sheep and lambs have a particular prominence in this argument
about our connections with animals and our duty of care to them,
especially because of the scriptural authority of the metaphor of the
human flock and the sacrificial and redemptive figure of the Lamb of
God. So strong is this tendency to read animals, and our relationship
with animals, within a Christian context that the practical uses of sheep
can be assimilated to the idea of a loving God. Here Edward Topsell
offers an anatomy of the serviceable parts (that is, all the parts) of
the sheep:

> Now in the next place we are to discourse of the utilities that cometh
> by sheep, for as it is the meekest of all other beasts, so as the reward
> for meekness, there is no part on him but is profitable to man: his flesh,
> blood, and milk is profitable for meat, his skin and wool both together
> and asunder for garments, his guts and entrails for music, his horns and
> hooves for perfuming and driving away of serpents, and the excrements
> of his belly and egestion [i.e., defecation] or dung for the amending
> and enriching of plowed lands . . . (Topsell 1607: 621)

Topsell is not being ironic when he speaks about the sheep's reward
for meekness as its exhaustive usefulness to human beings. The human
use of sheep bodies is not automatically opposed to their place as
animals created and loved by the same creator that created us. What
Topsell decries is the cruelty that comes from treating animals as
things. That, in his view, is a desecration, as is clear when he describes
the practice of beating living rams in order to tenderize their flesh and
to make it resemble venison: "for if it be not sufficient to kill and eat
the beast, but first of all put it to tyrannical torments, I cannot tell
what will suffice, except we will deal with beasts as Pilate did with
Christ, who was first of all whipped and crowned with thorns, and yet
afterward [Pilate] did crucify him" (Topsell 1607: 622). That there is
a threshold between legitimate and sacrilegious uses of animals simply
reinforces the point that animals and humans occupy a common space
within a divinely supervised moral order. Shakespeare plays along this
threshold when he has the naturally good Shepherd abandon his two
"best sheep" on the carnivore-infested Bohemian shore after he has
found the infant Perdita and especially the treasure of gold, which is
in his view worth far more than sheep, even excellent ones. His abdica-
tion of pastoral responsibility mirrors in a comic mode Leontes' ill
(and impious) treatment of his own children, his violent objectification
of them in terms of adult sexual and marital relations.

Particularly important for our understanding of *The Winter's Tale*
is how the instrumentalization of animals and the causing of pain and
suffering to animals (and to other people as if they were animals) can
be understood within a Christian sacrificial and soteriological economy
– a dynamic system that works to save humans from sin by revealing
to them their own animality and also by subjecting them to the kind
of suffering to which animals are routinely subjected. In the play, the
overall effect of this painful confrontation with animality is, ironically
enough, the restoration of humanity and the institutions of marriage

and family. Hermione plays an important part in the soteriological economy of the play as an animalized sacrifice, a restorer of her husband, and herself a work of restoration, but the central character in the story of animality, suffering, and salvation is, as we will see, the rammish King Leontes.

This way of thinking about *The Winter's Tale* requires not a philosophical determination about the essentially animal nature of human beings (or about their essentially non-animal nature), but rather the recovery of early modern common knowledge about animals and early modern vernacular wisdom about the shared conditions of human and animal living. This play's insight is ordinary, traditional, and Christian. When he touches the newly living hand of his resurrected Queen, Leontes cries, "O, she's warm! / If this be magic, let it be an art / Lawful as eating" (5.3.110–12), an exclamation that imbues creaturely sentience and sustenance with Eucharistic resonance. The moment is the culmination of the whole action and also a visible reminder of how the play uses the word "grace" to suggest repeatedly the presence of the theological virtue of grace ("the free and unmerited favour of God as manifested in the salvation of sinners and the bestowing of blessings"; OED "grace," 11) in the comeliness and gracefulness of Hermione's person. We remember her hopeful response when Leontes orders her to prison: "this action I now go on / Is for my better grace" (2.1.121–2).

Hermione begins her story of animality and sacrifice with a playful remark to her husband. She has persuaded Polixenes to extend his sojourn in Sicilia and is anticipating Leontes' commendations: "cram's with praise, and make's / As fat as tame things – one good deed dying tongueless / Slaughters a thousand waiting upon that" (1.2.90–2). The image of overfed domestic animals connects her with the agricultural practice of force-feeding poultry for quicker, more profitable slaughter. In *The Whole Art of Husbandry*, Conrad Heresbach instructs the farmer on the best means of raising birds for market: "As you cram and feed capons, so you may fat, cram or feed hens also and in a shorter space. Also you may cram chickens [i.e., chicks] sooner than either of them both" (Heresbach 1631: 309–10). Although she does not grasp their full implications, the lines look ahead to the sacrifice of her life on the altar of her husband's jealousy – an apparent sacrifice only, of course, but one that will lead to Leontes' reformation.[9] This knowledge of farming practice and its relationship to providential practices relies on an everyday recognition of the commonality of animals and people and the linkages of the divine and natural; and it promotes the understanding of human states of mind, social institutions and activities, and spiritual matters as continuous with animal minds, communities, and behaviors.

This recognition of commonality is different in kind from the Renaissance project of philosophical skepticism, which, as Laurie Shannon has remarked, was leveraged to a large degree on the issue of species relatedness (private communication). What is at stake in philosophical skepticism are claims about the essential nature of humanity. Hamlet, himself a philosophical rather than a practical thinker, articulates the traditional anthropocentric position when he says, "What is a man, / If the chief good and market of his time / Be but to sleep and feed? a beast, no more" (4.6.33–5). As we have noted, Hamlet thinks his mother is worse than a beast since a beast "that wants discourse of reason" (1.2.150) would have mourned longer for its mate than she mourned for his father. Michel de Montaigne's attack on human pride and his skeptical investigation of the foundations of human self-knowledge are carried out by putting in question these putative differences between humans and beasts:

> Man [he tells us in *The Apology for Raymond Sebond*] . . . knows and sees that he is lodged down here, among the mire and shit of the world, bound and nailed to the deadest, most stagnant part of the universe . . . yet, in thought, he sets himself above the circle of the moon, bringing the very heavens under his feet. The vanity of this same thought makes him equal himself to God; attribute to himself God's mode of being; pick himself out and set himself apart from the mass of other creatures; and (although they are his fellows and his brothers) carve out for them such helpings of force or faculties as he thinks fit. How can he, from the power of his own understanding, know the hidden, inward motivations of animate creatures? What comparison between us and them leads him to conclude that they have the attributes of senseless brutes? (Montaigne 1991: 505)

Later in the essay, Montaigne discusses several cases of animals in mourning for the loss of their human masters. Of course, he also enumerates many instances of animal rationality and of their capacities for learning, introspection, and articulate expression; and he even reports on the evident natural religiosity of some elephants, who "after ablutions and purifications . . . can be seen waving their trunks like arms upraised, while gazing intently at the rising sun" (Montaigne

1991: 522). Shakespeare has Lear make a similar but different case for the near-identity of human and animal: "Is man no more than this? Consider him well. Thou ow'st the worm no silk, the beast no hide, the sheep no wool, the cat no perfume. . . . Thou art the thing itself: unaccommodated man is no more but such a poor, bare, fork'd animal as thou art" (3.4.102–8). Indeed, Lear suggests that men are worse off and more brutish than the animals since they cover up their essential animality beneath the products of animal bodies.

In *The Winter's Tale*, the question of the animality of human beings tends not to rise to this pitch of philosophical generalization. I can note, by the way, that Montaigne and Lear both tend to reformulate as philosophy what people have anyway always known about themselves – simply that we are more like than unlike animals. In *The Winter's Tale*, the category of animality operates in more particular terms, and it is therefore more illuminating about human states of mind and action than is Lear's or Montaigne's meditation on unaccommodated man. It is true that Leontes uses the language of animality in order to degrade women, especially his wife, who, he says, "holds up the neb, the bill" to Polixenes (1.2.181). The first effect of this is to call strongly to mind Hermione's humanity, as opposed to her imputed bestiality; that is, the first effect is anthropocentric (she does not, after all, have a "neb" or "bill"), but that in turn is framed by a larger pattern in which she is to be understood as a kind of animal whose larger fate within the action of the play requires her sacrifice. This embeddedness of humanity in animality applies to Leontes too, who, in spite of his repeated descriptions of himself as horned, fails to glimpse the resemblance between himself, his fears, and his rage on the one side and the violent instincts of horned beasts on the other.

In her study of masculinity and fantasies of maternal origin in Shakespeare, Janet Adelman argues that Leontes exemplifies "the anguish of a masculinity that conceives of itself as betrayed at its point of origin, a masculinity that can read in the full maternal body only the signs of its own loss" (Adelman 1992: 222). The psychological dynamic that grows out of this anguish is founded, according to Adelman's analysis, in the vexed struggle to maintain a sovereign male personhood of self-knowledge and self-mastery: "If the possibility of Hermione's betrayal first plunges him into the nothingness of maternal abandonment, it becomes his stay against nothingness as it hardens into delusion: the world is nothing, he tells Camillo, *if Hermione is not unfaithful*. Threatened by absolute loss, he seizes on the fantasy of Hermione's adultery as though it in itself could give him something to hold onto: better the 'something' of cuckoldry than the nothing-ness into which he would otherwise dissolve" (Adelman 1992: 224). Topsell's description of the relationship among lambs, ewes, and rams provides an alternative model to Adelman by suggesting that Leontes is a man whose underlying motivation is the desire to kill his own children, whose motive, that is, has more to do with a violent, rammish instinct than with the maintenance of masculine identity against the constitutive threat of the maternal body:

> The lamb is a most simple beast and erreth many times from his moth-er's sides, having no other means to provoke his mother to seek him out but by bleating, for in the middest of a thousand sheep it discerneth the voice of his parent, and so hasteneth to her when it heareth her; for such is the nature of this poor beast, that although there be many other ewes which give suck, yet they pass by all their udders to taste of their mother's fountains, and the ewe knoweth her young one by smelling to the backer part – the lamb all the while it sucketh, waggeth and playeth with the tail. When the lamb is newly fallen, for a day or two in some countries they put them up close into a stable for a day or two or three, till they grow strong, and are well filled with milk and know their dams, and so long as the rams feed with the females they / keep in the lambs, that so they may be clear day and night from all violence of the rams, for at night they lodge single and alone by their dams' sides. (Topsell 1607: 640–1)

Leontes' instinctual harmfulness toward his own children does not result in a flattening of his psychological complexity. What it does suggest is that his delusion about his wife's adultery is not designed to shore up his masculine identity so much as it is seized upon as a culturally specific occasion and excuse for infanticide. Consider the harshness of his language and the underlying sense of danger that characterize his first scene with his son, where, in the face of his espoused belief in his son's legitimacy, he nevertheless characterizes Mamillius as the embodiment of female falseness: "yet they say we are / Almost as like as eggs – women say so, / That will say anything" (1.2.128–30). When he confronts his wife with explicit charges of adultery and then removes his son from closeness with her, the sense of threat is even more palpable.

The scene begins with Hermione's impatience toward Mamillius, signaled by her telling her women to take the boy off her hands and by her use of the third person: "Take the boy to you; he so troubles me / 'Tis past enduring" (2.1.1–2). This brilliant real-life touch of maternal ill-temper gives way to the return of physical closeness, the playful use of deferential language, and second-person address: "Come, sir, now / I am for you again. Pray sit you by us, / And tell's a tale" (21–3). Leontes interrupts the scene of playful intimacy between mother and son. He enters already in conversation with his lords, ignores his family's presence through the conversation with the men as well as through his weird quasi-soliloquy about drinking poison and seeing spiders, and then rounds on his wife and son. His use of the imperative voice as well as the third person vis-à-vis his son picks up and hardens the grammar of Hermione's opening speech (note that he continues to address his wife in the second person). He says, "Give me the boy" (56), but what he means is "give up the boy to my authority": "Bear the boy hence; he shall not come about her. / Away with him" (59–60). The violent separation of Mamillius from his mother leads, in the end, to the boy's death. That just such an outcome is in Leontes' mind is suggested by the command, "Away with him."

An infanticidal motive is more strongly intimated by the odd swerve that Leontes' language takes in his nighttime contemplation of revenge. He is thinking about killing Hermione and Polixenes (2.3.1–8) when a servant enters with good news about Mamillius:

> *Servant* He took good rest tonight; 'tis hoped
> His sickness is discharged.
> *Leontes* To see his nobleness
> Conceiving the dishonour of his mother!
> He straight declined, drooped, took it deeply,
> Fastened and fixed the shame on't in himself,
> Threw off his spirit, his appetite, his sleep,
> And downright languished. Leave me solely; go,
> See how he fares. *Exit Servant*
> Fie, fie, no thought of him;
> The very thought of my revenges that way
> Recoil upon me – in himself too mighty,
> And in his parties, his alliance; let him be
> Until a time may serve. (2.3.11–22)

Stephen Orgel tells us that the "him" in "Fie, fie, no thought of him" is Polixenes (2.3.18n.), and that is certainly correct from the point of view of line 20, "in himself too mighty"; but the natural reading, especially if we are listening to the words as they are spoken, is that "him" is Mamillius. Leontes is thus scolding himself for thinking about killing his son. That impression is reinforced by "Fie, fie." The word is an "exclamation expressing . . . disgust or indignant reproach" (OED); Hamlet, we remember, says, "Fie on't, ah fie! 'tis an unweeded garden / That grows to seed, things rank and gross in nature / Possess it merely" (1.2.135–7). The word is thus not an appropriate response to the thought of killing Polixenes, but it does express a justly disgusted self-reproach for thoughts of infanticide. Notice also that the servant is bringing Leontes good news about Mamillius, yet all the King can think about is his son's sickness, which, ironically, serves to confirm the justice of the charge of adultery against Hermione.

Even more striking is Leontes' rage in the face of the presence of his infant daughter. He says that he wants it killed because it is Polixenes' child, but his murderous determination is strengthened rather than alleviated by Paulina's persuasive anatomical demonstration of his fatherhood. At first he prevaricates between ordering the baby removed from his sight and ordering its death (2.3.73–5, 92–5, 111). Paulina's demonstration of resemblance between father and daughter hardens his resolve to do the baby harm. She says, "Although the print be little, the whole matter / And copy of the father – eye, nose, lip, / The trick of's frown . . ." (98–100). His response is to shift his indecision from a choice between burning and removal from the room to a choice among burning, dashing its brains out (139–40), and exposure in "some remote and desert place" (175). Fortunately, he decides on the third course, and, by miracle, the child survives.

That Leontes is bent on infanticide is, I suggest, confirmed not only by his violent language and his injurious treatment of his son, and not only by the exposure of his infant daughter, but also by the striking fact that he recovers his reason the instant the double killing seems to have been accomplished. With his son dead and his daughter presumed dead, he is suddenly keen to take up just where he left off – to beg Apollo's pardon, reconcile with Polixenes, new woo his queen, recall the good Camillo:

> Take her hence.
> Her heart is but o'ercharged; she will recover.
> I have too much believed mine own suspicion.
> Beseech you tenderly apply to her

> Some remedies of life.   *Exeunt Paulina and Ladies,*
> *carrying Hermione*
>
> Apollo, pardon
> My great profaneness 'gainst thy oracle.
> I'll reconcile me to Polixenes,
> New woo my Queen, recall the good Camillo,
> Whom I proclaim a man of truth, of mercy;
> . . . I chose
> Camillo for the minister, to poison
> My friend Polixenes; which had been done,
> But that the good mind of Camillo tardied
> My swift command . . . (3.2.147–61)

The only injured parties that he fails to mention in this remarkably high-spirited speech are the children whose deaths, I suggest, are the underlying goal of his delusional jealousy. In this view, Hermione's sacrificial death and her resurrection once Perdita has been found, which makes the mother's life dependent on the daughter's, are intended to persuade Leontes that he cannot have his wife at all unless he also has the offspring of their marriage. Hermione and Paulina, we might say, practice a kind of moral husbandry in order to domesticate the rammish king. That Leontes is being tamed helps us understand the curious sheepishness of his attitude to Paulina in the latter half of the play (5.1.1–84). He puts aside the fulfillment of his own desire, his manhood, the deference owed his rank, and his duty to the well-being of the state in exaggerated deference to a woman whose sixteen-year reign over him is founded on his passion for his dead wife. His own sexual instinct is thus used by Paulina as a disciplinary instrument:

> Good Paulina,
> Who hast the memory of Hermione,
> I know, in honour, O that ever I
> Had squared me to thy counsel! Then, even now,
> I might have looked upon my Queen's full eyes,
> Have taken the treasure from her lips – (5.1.49–54)

This account of the animality of Leontes' rage and recreation suggests, finally, that Shakespearean psychology is focused not on the dynamics of identity formation within the transhistorical field of gender, but rather on a historically situated ideological system of relations among animality, humanity, and divinity. Shakespeare's Leontes has a psychology whose shaping narratives derive from Christian ideas about sin and sacrifice, suffering and redemption within a moral space shared by people and animals. What I am suggesting is that playgoers who brought with them to the playhouse a common knowledge about animal husbandry and a vernacular, Christian wisdom about people and animals would have appreciated that the Bohemian sheep-shearing feast represented a change of genre but not of topic and that the Bohemian sheepcote represents a culmination of the play's interest in the ovinity of human life, where strong lines of continuity run from Leontes' violence and domestication, to the sacrificial deaths of Mamillius, Hermione, and Perdita (the latter two only apparent), to the profitability and community that issue from the raising, shepherding, and use of sheep.

Notes

I am grateful to audiences at GEMCS in Newport Beach CA and at McGill. I am particularly indebted to my research assistant Yael Margalit for a wealth of material and a sharp and generous critique of an early version of the argument.

1   All quotations from Shakespeare, except for those from *The Winter's Tale*, are from *The Riverside Shakespeare* (1974).
2   For arguments that offer a more positive account of Shakespeare's view of dogs, see Empson (1977) and Garber (1997: 230).
3   I have discussed how the plays allowed early modern playgoers to work through their own contradictory attitudes toward the system of rank in Dawson and Yachnin (2001: 38–65).
4   The insight about the meaning of Troilus' absence was suggested to me by my graduate student Amy Britton.
5   Two lines before his allusion to the bear's instinctual recognition of Lear's graciousness, Albany calls Goneril and Regan "Tigers, not daughters." In the space of a breath, animals can stand for and stand against human savagery.
6   For a particularly intelligent version of this reading, see Frye (1995).
7   All quotations and citations from *The Winter's Tale* are from the edition by Orgel (Shakespeare 1996).
8   For language as a defining characteristic of humanity, see Boehrer (2002: 6–17).
9   For an extended discussion of Hermione's repletion and sacrifice in very different terms, see Yachnin (1997: 129–45).

Works Cited

Adelman, Janet 1992: *Suffocating Mothers: Fantasies of Maternal Origin in Shakespeare's Late Plays, Hamlet to The Tempest.* New York: Routledge.

Berry, Edward 2001: *Shakespeare and the Hunt: A Cultural and Social Study.* Cambridge: Cambridge University Press.

Boehrer, Bruce 2002: *Shakespeare Among the Animals: Nature and Society in the Drama in Early Modern England.* New York: Palgrave.

Bowden, Peter J. 1962: *The Wool Trade in Tudor and Stuart England.* London: Macmillan.

Carpenter, Richard 1616: *A Pastoral Charge, Faithfully Given and Discharged, at the Trienniall Visitation of the Lord Bishop of Exon.* London.

Cranmer, Thomas 1595: *Certain Sermons.* London.

Dawson, Anthony B. and Yachnin, Paul 2001: *The Culture of Playgoing in Shakespeare's England: A Collaborative Debate.* Cambridge: Cambridge University Press.

Empson, William 1977: "Timon's Dog." In *The Structure of Complex Words.* London: Chatto and Windus, 175–84.

Frye, Northrop 1995: "Recognition in *The Winter's Tale.*" In Maurice Hunt (ed.) *The Winter's Tale: Critical Essays.* New York: Garland, 106–18.

Fudge, Erica 2000: *Perceiving Animals: Humans and Beasts in Early Modern English Culture.* New York: Macmillan.

Garber, Marjorie 1997: *Dog Love.* New York: Touchstone.

Harraway, Donna 2003: *The Companion Species Manifesto: Dogs, People, and Significant Otherness.* Chicago: Prickly Paradigm Press.

Heresbach, Conrad 1631: *The Whole Art of Husbandry Contained in Four Books.* Trans. Barnabe Googe. London.

Jackson, William 1616: *The Celestiall Husbandrie: Or, The Tillage of the Soul.* London.

Maplet, John 1567: *A Greene Forest, or a Naturall Historie.* London.

Markham, Gervase 1614: *Cheape and Good Husbandry.* London.

Montaigne, Michel de 1991: *The Complete Essays.* Trans. M. A. Screech. London: Penguin.

More, Thomas 1965: *Utopia.* Trans. Paul Turner. London: Penguin.

Paré, Ambroise 1634: *The Works of that Famous Chirurgion Ambrose Parey.* Trans. T. Johnson. London.

Shakespeare, William 1974: *The Riverside Shakespeare.* Textual ed. G. Blakemore Evans. Boston: Houghton Mifflin.

Shakespeare, William 1996: *The Winter's Tale.* Ed. Stephen Orgel. Oxford: Oxford University Press.

Thomas, Keith 1984: *Man and the Natural World: Changing Attitudes in England, 1500–1800.* London: Penguin.

Topsell, Edward 1607: *The Historie of Four-Footed Beastes*. London.

Webster, John 2001: *The Duchess of Malfi*, 4th edn. Ed. Brian Gibbons. New Mermaids. London: A&C Black; New York: W. W. Norton.

Yachnin, Paul 1997: *Stage-Wrights: Shakespeare, Jonson, Middleton, and the Making of Theatrical Value*. Philadelphia: University of Pennsylvania Press.

Part V

How To Do Things with Posterity

Editor's Introduction

The three contributors whose essays conclude this volume have very different research interests. Georgia Brown is a poetry specialist; Emma Smith publishes on (*inter alia*) Shakespeare in performance; and Anne Coldiron positions herself at the interface of English and French literature. Despite such different starting points, the three essays are linked by the subject of time and place.

I asked Georgia Brown to write on the sonnets because her recent work on the epyllion had reconceived the relationship of these poems to the 1590s; I wanted her to help me think about the sonnets in a similarly innovative, connected way. The 1590s fashion for epyllia – self-consciously erotic Ovidian mini-epics – is often dismissed as a trivial, aesthetic indulgence, all *dulce* no *utile*. But Brown found in this apparent triviality a deliberate poetic politics. She showed epyllia to be defiant inaugural gestures in a young man's poetic career: they were literary gauntlets which challenged the Spenserian, Virgilian pastoral paradigm, replaced it with an Ovidian career model, and redefined aestheticism as a literary virtue. I had long had difficulty in knowing how to read Shakespeare's sonnets (or any sonnet sequence); as a drama specialist I am more at ease with narrative than with lyric poetry. What, then, to make of 14-line units, multiplied 154 times? How to approach their repetition-with-variants? How to strike the balance between analyzing the well-wrought urn and reading historical context? So I asked Georgia Brown to show me (and us) how to do things with sonnets.

The critical literature on Shakespeare's sonnets is full of analyses of time (because the sonnets themselves are full of references to time and explorations of human and literary immortality). In her essay Brown considers the difficulties of representing time – that is, sequence – in life (sundials, clocks) and in poetry. Her essay provides a fascinating account of Renaissance methods of measuring time and relates this search for a "reliable referent" to the amorous difficulties of the poet when faced with his partner's instability. Equally fascinating is the way Brown's account of time has analogous applications to poetry. Each moment is the last until it is superseded, she says (just like the lines of a sonnet); repetition encourages us to see similarity where there is in fact difference (a statement also true of rhyme); and the repetitions of the sonnet sequence are paradoxically a development (as Julie Maxwell demonstrates so ably in chapter 3 in her discussion of rhetorical *copia*).

Most significant is the way in which Brown shows how the sonnets' debate about offspring is also a literary debate about "poetic forebears" and "literary succession." The key word here – one used in the sonnets – is "preposterous": what is "pre" is "post," what is before is behind (hence its dictionary meaning of absurd). Brown's achievement is to show via her historical account of early modern time measurement that Shakespeare's sonnets are literally preposterous: that tradition (what is past) may produce innovation (something new).

Time and space are also the subject of Anne Coldiron's essay, but in a completely different context: eighteenth-century France. Before we get there Coldiron offers a stimulating interrogative rumination on how authors stand the test of time and place, how canons are formed, and literary values decided and defined. She points out the ways in which Shakespeare's writing is both suited and, in certain respects, surprisingly unsuited to transhistorical appreciation or durability. She then illustrates her argument with a specific historical case study: Shakespeare in the criticism of Voltaire and his contemporary, Jean François de la Harpe.

Emma Smith's essay looks to the future by first taking stock of a newcomer to academic respectability: performance criticism. Theater history has a long pedigree because this is a properly archival and material topic (or can be made so): it focuses on stages, theaters, contracts, buildings, legal disputes, company personnel, and repertoire. But its sibling, performance criticism, was long eschewed or sidelined to theater departments; few academics concentrated on what contemporary productions of Shakespeare and conversations with theater practitioners could teach us. For decades the only place which took performance criticism seriously as an academic topic was the Shakespeare Institute in Stratford-upon-Avon, whose students followed courses in it, whose Fellows wrote about it, and whose institution had links to the Royal Shakespeare Company.

The critical climate changed sometime in the 1980s. Cambridge University Press published interviews with RSC actors – *Players of Shakespeare* – in 1985; journals began to devote considerable space to reviews of contemporary productions; series of Shakespeare in Performance and Renaissance Drama in Performance were published by Manchester University Press and Macmillan, followed later by Cambridge University Press's innovative series of performance editions; university theses were devoted to production histories of plays.

What are the rules of this new academic discipline, the qualifications for practicing it? These are the questions which Emma Smith poses, questions which lead her to an examination of unwritten rules, ideological assumptions, tacitly agreed geographical restrictions, the adoption of specific kinds of authoritative voice. Given that we are two or more decades into this new academic territory, Smith's reflective retrospective analysis is timely; given the theme of this volume on *how* we practice criticism, it is most apt; and given this last section's focus on time, it is highly appropriate that Emma Smith conclude her essay, and this book, with a fantasy vision of how performance criticism might proceed in the future.

Chapter 10

Time and the Nature of Sequence in Shakespeare's *Sonnets*: "In sequent toil all forwards do contend"

Georgia Brown

Rationale

The seed for this essay came with a visit to the Landesmuseum in Zurich. Among the wealth of exhibits in the Renaissance section are some beautifully labeled clocks. I found the darkened, cathedral-like interior of this part of the museum very conducive to reflection, and the exhibit started me thinking about the implications of moving time indoors, of domesticating it and making it personal, once technology had advanced far enough to enable craftsmen to make smaller clocks. My essay tries to do two things: firstly, it focuses on, and pursues a detailed analysis of, individual sonnets, to try to do justice to the density of these poems; and then it sits back, and tries to do bigger things with these small poems, by considering what it means to write a sequence, and how the sequence fashions, and is fashioned, by a sustained interest in time. I've tried to consider these lyrics both as highly literary verses, and as texts that grow out of a specific historical period, and I've tried to relate the poems to Renaissance objects – in this case, to timepieces. The issue of time is, in some ways, a neglected issue for literary critics, probably because as a subject it does not respect academic boundaries and strays into the history of art, mathematics, and the history of science and technology. Its mathematical roots are off-putting and the principles of time-measurement are not always easy to follow, but the *Sonnets* do show Shakespeare thinking about the mechanisms of time. I came to this essay from a wide reading in other sonnet sequences, and behind it lies the question of why sonnet sequences, as opposed to individual sonnets, should have become such a resonant and popular form in the 1590s.

> Like as the waves make towards the pebbled shore,
> So do our minutes hasten to their end,
> Each changing place with that which goes before,
> In sequent toil all forwards do contend.
> Nativity, once in the main of light,
> Crawls to maturity, wherewith being crowned,
> Crooked eclipses 'gainst his glory fight,
> And time that gave doth now his gift confound.
> Time doth transfix the flourish set on youth,
> And delves the parallels in beauty's brow,
> Feeds on the rarities of nature's truth,
> And nothing stands but for his scythe to mow.
> And yet to times in hope my verse shall stand,
> Praising thy worth, despite his cruel hand.
>
> (Sonnet 60)[1]

Shakespeare's *Sonnets* are love poems, but when read in the context of the Fall, and the story of Adam and Eve, love and sex have a very particular relationship to time. Milton describes the nature of this relationship in *Paradise Lost*. Before the Fall, love-making is leisured and unhurried. It works in conjunction with time, and incorporates the delights of postponement. It is specifically opposed to the kind of love Shakespeare's poet-lover endures, as pre-lapsarian love is not like the "serenade, which the starved lover sings / To his proud fair, best quitted with disdain."[2] The kind of love Shakespeare's poet-lover experiences is a consequence, and a repetition, of the Fall, Moreover, it is precisely the changes in the way love is experienced that mediate, or relay, the post-lapsarian experience of time (in both Milton and Shakespeare), as both the pressure to hurry, and as relentless change.

Post-lapsarian love is hurried, desperate, passionate, and impelled by restlessness. The apprehension of time's relentless pressure introduces the mode of *carpe diem*, with its injunction to seize any opportunity in the face of time wasted and pleasures lost: "Carnal desire inflaming, he on Eve / Began to cast lascivious eyes, she him / As wantonly repaid; in lust they burn: / Till Adam thus gan Eve to dalliance move" (Milton 1998: Book IX, 1013–16). Before the Fall, the ecliptic (the course of the sun through the sky) coincides with the equator, the earth's axis is perfectly aligned perpendicularly to the direction of the sun, and the solstices and equinoxes simply do not exist. The Fall dislocates time, and humanity's relationship to time. Passion, macrocosmic disorder, and moral disorder are all conceived in terms of the misuse and misapprehension of time, as change floods the universe, pushing things off kilter.

It is no surprise, therefore, that Shakespeare's sequence of love lyrics is obsessed with time, with the ways the passage of time produces loss, and the ways it may produce gain, even if, in the case of the poet-lover, what is gained is undesirably bitter wisdom based on the cumulative discovery of shared defectiveness. The *Sonnets* open with the argument that the beloved can, and indeed should, overcome time by producing offspring, and then explore the possibility that the poems themselves will conquer time and allow the beloved to live for ever, but they also return obsessively to the depredations of time and the inevitability of passing and fading. They explore different ways of being in time, and examine endurance, reiteration, recapitulation, degeneration, growth, persistence, contingency, succession, and productivity, as well as the different ways we gauge time, use time, relate to time, and indeed relate time, in the sense of telling time, imposing a pattern on it, and finding a means to represent it. In sonnet 60, for example, time has several material manifestations which offer different ways of telling and identifying it. Time is expressed through the relentless movement of the waves on the shore, and by the movement of celestial bodies. "Nativity" (l.5) invokes both a new-born baby, and a new-born sun, which climbs up to its zenith, but then is obscured by eclipses and the interference of other celestial bodies. The idea of solar "maturity" (l.6) is paradoxical because the moment of the sun's greatest glory, the noontime when it is at its height, is precisely the time, according to medieval Christian tradition, when the Fall, the Expulsion from Eden, and the death of Christ occurred, and, in any case, the only way to leave the topmost point is to go down. Time is also materialized on people's faces, as it tarnishes youthfulness, and digs wrinkles, "parallels" (l.10), on people's foreheads. Faces become ways of telling time, and in Shakespeare's sequence, the beloved does indeed become a temporal gauge, as he is compared to the sun, whose passage across the sky registers the passage of time (sonnet 21, for example), and as he loses the first blush of beauty (sonnet 22, for example), with the result that his human face assumes the attribute of the face of a clock, which is to indicate time. Gradually, the sequence reveals the different ways in which both the beloved and the poet-lover become "watchm[e]n" (sonnet 61).

In addition to these natural or biological ways of gauging or registering the passage of time – wave movement, the movement of celestial bodies in the sky, the changes in our physical appearance – sonnet 60 also alludes to artificial, or mechanical, ways of telling time. The allusion to the sun in the context of time suggests the sundial, and the choice of "parallel" for wrinkle suggests the parallels projected by geometry onto charts of the earth and the sky, as aids to navigation and the specification of time, which depends on coordinating the exact position of the sun with the exact position of the observer, in order to measure how much the sun has actually moved. In addition, the sonnet invokes different ways of patterning time. Waves and the passage of the sun suggest recurrence, eternal recurrence as the sun moves in a line across the sky, but also always returns to its beginning, as dawn will inevitably follow night. On the other hand, the second and third lines suggest something different, with the idea that time is an endless continuum stretching out into the endless future where nothing is repeated and no limit, or end point, is ever reached: "So do our minutes hasten to their end, / Each changing place with that which goes before." Each minute of time is the last minute, or ultimate point, until time passes and that minute is replaced by another minute, so that what was last, is no longer the last, but is superseded by the next minute in endless, neutral succession. The force of these two lines may be attenuated for us because minutes are not as rare in our experience, nor as elusive a phenomenon, as they were for Shakespeare. Many clocks in use in the sixteenth century did not have minute hands, as timepieces were so inaccurate that it was just not worth measuring minutes, while clocks that could measure minutes were received as remarkable technical achievements and remained luxury items.[3] Moreover, sundial time was not divided into one-minute intervals until 1671.

Sonnet 60 raises the question of succession in a particularly literary way, as well, because it is a reworking of part of Pythagoras' famous speech in Book XV of Ovid's *Metamorphoses* which explores time and the paradox that endless change becomes a kind of constancy, and that, by its own logic, change must itself change, and cannot last for ever. The first quatrain introduces the play of parataxis against hypotaxis, a game that is characteristic of Shakespeare's *Sonnets*, both on the micro level of individual sonnets, and on the macro level of the sequence as a whole. Parataxis is the simple accumulation of elements connected by the conjunction "and," without any indication of the relation between them, and is exemplified in the first quatrain by the sequence of minutes simply added to minutes. Hypotactic relationships are more complicated, as they set up hierarchies and temporal relationships that are indicated by such conjunctions as "therefore" and "consequently." As the reader grapples with the ways things can be joined together, both on grammatical and ideational levels, she/he is simultaneously invited to consider the relationship between poetic forebearers and their offspring, the question of literary succession, and the ways in which tradition may produce innovation. The struggle to find a proper means of following on is not just an issue for the young man, who is exhorted to procreate, but also for the poet who has to negotiate his place in a poetic line of succession. Syntax is the term we apply to the grammatical ordering of words in a sentence or phrase, which, put another way, is the ordering of words in time to give meaning. In typical Shakespearean fashion, the complicated syntax of sonnet 60 forces readers to go back over what they have read, only to find that the phrases now work in different ways, and some of the words serve different functions. To further complicate the issue of registering and articulating time, the word "nativity" (1.5) also invokes the zodiac, as a nativity referred to the particular configuration of celestial bodies that prevailed at birth which would determine the character and future of that child. The zodiac is yet another scheme for measuring time. In the Ptolemaic system, the earth is conceived as occupying a point in the middle of concentric spheres. The outer-most sphere is fixed and contains the fixed stars whose constellations make up the signs of the zodiac. As seen from the earth, the sun and moon seem to rotate through the circle of fixed stars, so their movement, and hence time, can be calculated by their relation to the zodiacal signs.

In fact, the sonnet sequence itself is the most obvious way that Shakespeare establishes of gauging time, and of registering its passage.

Although details of time are most usually absent from the sequence, and it does present problems of temporality, which will be explored in the next section, it still registers the passage of time, as the sequence becomes more jaded, and the traces of change and of the Fall become increasingly apparent on faces, in types of behavior, in language, in syntax, and in style, as the play of anachronism and invention offers another way of recording the flow of past into present. Writing is subject to time, as sonnets 15 to 17 make clear, and "perfection" only lasts "but a little moment" (sonnet 15). The analogy between text and timepiece is also based on the fact that writing and time-measurement share certain instruments. The rod-like element of a sundial that casts the shadow on the dial is made from metal or string, and is called a gnomon (from the Greek for "one who shows"), or a style, which comes from the Latin, *stilus*, meaning a stake or pole, a pointed instrument for writing, or a style of speaking or writing. (All these senses of *stilus* are alluded to in sonnet 78, which also mixes the feathers (quills) with which we write, with intimations of the wings that enabled Icarus' tragic flight upwards to the sun.) The sun writes with a style on the face of the sundial, just as time marks lines or wrinkles on the face of the beloved (sonnet 16), and just as the poet marks the page with a pen in ways that also mark time and are marked by time (sonnets 15, 16, 59).

The Problems of Sequence

All our editions of Shakespeare's *Sonnets* are based on the version published by Thomas Thorpe in 1609, but this 1609 Quarto was probably not authorized by Shakespeare. As a consequence, there is no compelling reason to believe that the order of the sonnets in Thorpe's edition (and hence in our own editions) is either the order in which they were written, or the order in which Shakespeare intended them to be read, even if he intended them to be read as a single text. The *Sonnets* themselves sometimes cluster into groups that are related by common themes or echoed terms, but in the majority of cases there is no over-arching narrative that structures the disparate components into a whole and makes it inevitable that a particular sonnet must necessarily follow sonnet "x" and precede sonnet "y." The *Sonnets* issue from a present, and there is a developing sense of time before and time after, but beyond this, the temporality of the sonnets, their precise location in time, as well as their precise relation to each other, is often unclear. "Text" derives from the Latin verb *texere*, meaning to weave. Shakespeare's *Sonnets* unravel our understanding of text, separating text into disparate elements, and then experimenting with methods of juncture, at the same time as they probe the psychological and philosophical implications of the drive to couple and unite. By the 1590s, when Shakespeare probably produced most of the *Sonnets*, the sonnet had become established as the most literary of literary forms.[4] Shakespeare's sequence confronts its own literariness, probing the ways in which a text might be woven together, toying with integration and disintegration, and mounting an assault on the philosophical, literary, and ontological understanding of integrity. It undermines the assumption, implicit in most discussions of the *Sonnets*, that in order to be classified as a great work of literature, a text must present the reader with a unified whole.

The *Sonnets* are urgent utterances and clearly record a profound need to put feelings and ideas into words, and they are held together by subject matter, meter, and rhyme, but when they arrange themselves into patterns, those patterns are fragile and provisional. Given both their fluidity, and the tantalizing suggestion, and then retraction, of a story, offered by the *Sonnets* themselves, it is no surprise that there have been many attempts to reorganize the *Sonnets* into a "proper" story, one that is usually based on the assumption that the *Sonnets* directly relate to incidents in Shakespeare's own life.[5] The *Sonnets* do form a continuous meditation on love, and most readers accept that the first 126 sonnets are addressed to a young man, while numbers 127 to 152 are addressed to a dark lady. Nevertheless, even these two groups are interrupted, and not all the poems in the first group are necessarily addressed to the young man, nor all those in the second group to the dark lady. The relationship between the individual sonnets, and the precise nature of the sequence, both remain enigmatic. What is surprising, given the problems readers have always had with the idea of a sequence, is that the question of sequence has received very little consideration, and that attempts to deal with the issue have either provoked fanciful reconstructions of Shakespeare's biography, or the critical equivalent of throwing up one's hands in despair, with the result that the problem of sequentiality is noted, but not engaged. Those critics who have attempted to go further include Robert Montgomery, who gives the question of sequence careful consideration, noting that while there are "hints of a narrative" in, for example, sonnets 34 and 35, which discuss the young man's sin, "The continuation of connected circumstance that one would expect to lend substance to a story is absent, here and elsewhere" (Montgomery 2006: 2). Montgomery explains the "apparent randomness of the *Sonnets*" both in terms of their source in Petrarch's sonnet sequence, whose title, *Rime sparse*, or scattered rhymes, foregrounds the fragmentariness of the sequence, and in terms of characterization:

> The tentativeness, that use of occasional grouping to hint at coherence only to shy away towards some different, disparate interest enables the turbulence and inconsistency of mood, of desire and resentment, of anxiety and relief, of metapoetic rumination and rhetorical fireworks with which the sequence impresses and often frustrates us. (Montgomery 2006: 3)

The "randomness" certainly does contribute to the characterization of the poet-speaker and to the mood of the sequence, as Montgomery goes on to demonstrate, but what critics miss in Shakespeare's *Sonnets*, and what they so desperately desire, is a linear narrative, what Montgomery calls "progress." However, linearity is not the only way of organizing a narrative, nor the only model for organizing the representation of time. To cite one example, out of the many ways of organizing a sequence which are mentioned in the *Sonnets*, the seasons of the year combine circularity with linearity in their progression, because the progression from spring, to summer, to autumn, to winter, repeats itself from year to year. To many readers, Shakespeare's sequence may seem to stagnate or stall in repetitiousness, a danger the sequence itself acknowledges: "Since all alike my songs and praises be / To one, of one, still such, and ever so" (sonnet 105). Nonetheless, proliferation invites comparison, and repetition, juxtaposition, and comparison bring about their own kinds of development, and their own modifications of thought and feeling, as sonnet 105 demonstrates:

> Therefore my verse to constancy confined,
> One thing expressing, leaves out difference.
> Fair, kind, and true, is all my argument,
> Fair, kind, and true, varying to other words;

And in this change is my invention spent –
Three themes in one, which wondrous scope affords.
Fair, kind, and true, have often lived alone,
Which three, till now, never kept seat in one. (ll.7–14)

The repetitiousness of the *Sonnets* is both condemned as being in "constancy confined," while, at the same time, repetition is revealed to be an accurate means of representing constancy in love. Then the possibility is raised (line 8) that repetition is a form of distortion, that it imposes similarity where there is, in fact, difference. The poet perhaps does not see difference, and in any case leaves it out, but the reader is left with the consciousness of differences that could have been noted, even as the sonnet emphasizes and reemphasizes its sameness. In fact, difference and sameness interact, with the result that what might appear to be simple repetition becomes much more complicated, and acknowledges both sameness and difference simultaneously. Punning is one example of how sameness and difference can coexist. The line, "One thing expressing, leaves out difference," actually expresses more than one thing because of the bawdy pun in "thing," which means pudenda or penis. So the line also means that because the poet's verse, and his love, bring out, or express, the penis, and because both the poet and the beloved are men, there is only one kind of sexual organ involved in this relationship. The statement that there is no difference may thus also imply that there is no woman involved, as a woman would bring another kind of "thing" to the relationship. As well as being an affirmation that poet and young man are perfect images of each other, these lines allude to narcissism and to willful ignorance. Yet there is another pun in this line, in the word "difference," which means a distinctive mark, a mark of distinction, and a quarrel, so perhaps the only way to avoid a quarrel is to ignore differences and confine oneself to writing verse that lacks distinction. What once seemed to be an affirmation of constant love, through the acknowledgment of repetition as a way of representing what is unchangeable, now begins to sound like a complaint on the part of the poet-lover who has been driven to mediocrity.

These are only some of the ways in which sonnet 105 engages with the issue of repetition, and its disadvantages and advantages, as a scheme of sequence. Moreover, like all Shakespearean sonnets, which end with a rhyming couplet and crown the interwoven lines of the body of the sonnet with a concluding epigram, sonnet 105 confronts the problems of sequence, in miniature, as the last two lines do not flow clearly out of the rest of the poem. Indeed, the last line is rhythmically ungainly, while the couplet does not offer a clear logical culmination to the argument. It asserts that the beloved unites fairness, kindness, and truth, with epigrammatic force, when the rest of the poem has intimated that there are lurking differences in the lover, in the beloved, and in the relationship between the two, as well as blindspots in the poet's vision. The conclusion raises more questions than it settles, because it may be asserting that the three virtues of fairness, kindness, and truth have never come together "till now," until this verse, in other words, they do not exist in the beloved young man, only in the fictionalized account of the young man. The very last line also seems to acknowledge a logic of repetition, in that the three virtues up until now have never been confined in one statement, they have "never kept seat in one," or perhaps never been comprehended by one statement, the implication being that we need to multiply, repeat and go beyond one, to comprehend them fully.

On a micro level, as well as on a macro level, thematically as well as formally, Shakespeare's *Sonnets* explore the problems of sequence and its related issues, including joining, whether sexual or formal, repetition, inheritance, succession, interconnection, and separation. To put it another way, the sonnet sequence returns to the relationship between triviality and seriousness, small trifles and larger, more important units, parts and wholes, consequence and inconsequentiality. In sonnet 105, not only does the final couplet threaten inconsequentiality, in that it does not offer a clear conclusion, summation, or culmination to the preceding argument, the possibility that the beloved, and hence the love the poet has for the beloved, and the verse in which that love is expressed, are nothing but trifles, and therefore inconsequential, is raised by the pun on "idol show," which could just as easily be an "idle show:" "Let not my love be called idolatry, / Nor my beloved as an idol show"(ll.1–2).

The problems of sequentiality are compounded by the method in which sonnet sequences were written and transmitted. Sonnets were often occasional verses – verses written for a specific occasion, and written from time to time, that is occasionally. This became particularly the case once Petrarchism developed into one of the preferred modes of social and political communication after the accession of Elizabeth I. Sonnets tended to be transmitted through manuscript circulation, rather than through print, because manuscript circulation was generally thought to be a more controllable, exclusive, and therefore gentle form of publication (the potential for whoredom in both print, but also manuscript circulation, is one of the subjects of sonnets 110 and 111). Sonnet sequences were often culled together by editors from manuscript sources, with the result that unrelated lyrics, destined for different occasions and different readers, could find themselves neighbors in a publication that masqueraded as a unitary text.

The sonnet sequence experiments with ways of adapting the sonnet into larger structural designs and it is this impulse towards extending the sonnet which is specifically characteristic of the 1590s. The sonnet had traditionally been associated with the expression of personal feeling, and in the 1590s authors started to explore the ways in which the impression of subjectivity could be sustained by juxtaposing lyric instants. While there had been earlier attempts to join sonnets into an expanded design, for example, by Thomas Watson in *Hekatompathia* (1582), and by George Gascoigne in *A Hundreth Sundrie Flowres* (1573), which uses tag-lines to unify groups of three sonnets into what Gascoigne calls "sequences," it was the publication of Sidney's *Astrophel and Stella*, in Thomas Newman's pirated edition of 1591, that sparked off the sonnet sequence vogue. The sonnet sequence quickly developed into a miscellaneous structure which mixes a variety of genres with the sonnet. For example, Barnabe Barnes' sequence, *Parthenophil and Parthenophe* (1593), comprises 105 sonnets, 26 madrigals, 5 sestine, 21 elegies, 3 canzoni, a translation of *The First Eidillion of Moschus*, and 20 odes. Thomas Lodge's *Phillis* (1593) comprises 20 sonnets, an eclogue in defense of love poetry, an elegy, another eclogue, a final sonnet, a satirical ode, and concludes with a complaint. In fact, sequences are often complemented by complaints, which function as a counter-genre to the sequence, disrupting the reader's identification with the poet-lover and usually establishing a contrast between the male perspective of the sonnet sequence and the female perspective of the complaint. Shakespeare not only adds a complaint to his sequence with *A Lover's Complaint*, but, as Rosalie Colie argues (Colie 1973: 69–75), he renovates the sonnet by adding epigram to sonnet.[6] The generic mixtures and accretions of the sonnet sequence are evidence not only of the sonnet's aspirations, of its formal tendency to be what it is not, and to break out into a more spacious form, they are also attempts to represent the multiform nature of love which is varied and inconstant. Although the sonnet sequence has an established repertoire of conventional imagery and diction drawn from Petrarchism, it is also very open to change and structural variation. Its syncretic structure resembles that of other forms popular in the 1590s and turns it into a place of experiment, a place where new thoughts and mixtures can find expression. By incorporating other elements which counterpoint and/or develop the discourse of the sonnets, the sequence expands its subjective and cultural potential. The miscellaneous structure of the sonnet sequence not only defines the author, but it also defines culture, as the sequence becomes an anthology of cultural forms which perpetuates culture. Through its prolix, miscellaneous, and apparently endless structure, the sonnet sequence acquires generic fragments, digressions, and ornaments which contribute to the cultural increase which is one of its themes.

Dials, Clocks, and Sequences

The randomness and inconsequentiality of the *Sonnets*, and their complicated intermingling of progression and regression, is a reflection of, and a reflection on, the nature of time. John Kerrigan has noted that the sequence's focus on time is not the expression of some abstract philosophical or literary obsession, but a response to the real intrusion of time into people's private lives in the sixteenth century (Shakespeare 1999: 33–46). In fact, sundials had long been available for private use, but what was new in the sixteenth century was the appearance of clocks indoors, as mechanical clocks became smaller. Our word "stanza" comes from the Italian for room, and each sonnet in Shakespeare's sequence is like a stanza of a longer work. Indeed, when the poet-lover claims that praise of the young man "shall still find room" in sonnet 55, he is playing on the etymological root of the word "stanza." The sequence explores the consequences of bringing time inside, inside a sonnet, inside a room, and inside the self. A fashion for the luxury objects that were clocks swept Europe in the sixteenth century, particularly a fashion for wearing watches, which were usually worn on a cord or chain around the neck, although Francis I of France bought two watches to place in the hilt of a dagger in 1518, and Elizabeth I had a watch set in a ring, complete with an alarm mechanism, that consisted of a small piece of metal that would spring out at the appointed time and scratch her hand. The earliest recorded English watch dates to 1580. By the 1620s, Cipolla (1967: 53) estimates that there were sixty master clockmakers in London, and by 1631 they had established their own guild.

Mechanical clocks had existed in Europe since the beginning of the fourteenth century, but eventually the use of brass to make clocks, in preference to iron, and the discovery that clocks could be driven by a coiled spring, rather than a falling weight, led to their miniaturization and a new-found portability. Sundials need the sun to work, and convert the movement of the sun into a register of time (sonnet 7 produces the same conversion), although night-time dials, called nocturnals, which used the position of ursa major or ursa minor to pinpoint time, had been developed. They also need to be adjusted to the coordinates of the location in which they will be used, and they depend on the visibility of the sun, so are less useful in northern regions in winter.[7] A portable clock, on the other hand, is self-contained in its operation, and binds those activities and places, which had been beyond the reach of sundials, into the framework of time. (The spread of time's dictatorship into the night, which is no longer sequestered from the concerns of the day and of clockwatching, is one of the subjects of sonnets 27 and 28.)

The great innovation in the development of mechanical clocks was the discovery that the flow of time could be tracked by oscillation, by a back and forth motion. The sonnet sequence, itself, is a time indicator which uses oscillation, and backwards and forwards motion, to register the passage of time. Like the linear narratives which critics so desperately want to find in Shakespeare's *Sonnets*, time is a continuous and unidirectional phenomenon, so one might have expected it to be measured by other continuous and unidirectional phenomena, such as water-clocks, sundials, or sonnet sequences with a clear narrative. In a mechanical clock, the oscillating device (or regulator) tracks the passing moments and beats time. The escapement counts the beats by blocking and then releasing the cogs and wheels of the clock so that they move an equal distance, in equal intervals, and turn the hands of the clock. A continuous, onward movement can be gauged by stops and starts, and can be translated into other codes by the ceaseless interchange of advancement and retraction.

When we consider clocks we tend to view them as instruments for settling the question of time, but in the early modern period clocks and sundials, which were more common than clocks, actually unsettled the question of time. We do not see our timepieces as unreliable, but, by the sixteenth century, the complexities of time-measurement by sundial had been known for centuries. A sundial relies on the sun's changing direction in the sky and traces that path by means of a shadow that moves across the dial with the sun. The gnomon needs to be aligned with the earth's polar axis, so a compass is necessary to set up a dial. The sun's altitude and path, observed from a specific place, also vary according to the time of the day and the season, with the result that all kinds of adjustments have to be made to the operation of the dial. The meridian is an imaginary line which runs in a north-south direction through a locale and the poles. All places on a meridian will have the same time and the gnomon must be aligned with the meridian of the place where it is being used. However, there is a difference between magnetic north and true north, as the sixteenth century was aware, and during the sixteenth and early seventeenth centuries magnetic north in Europe lay to the east of true north, and gradually drifted to zero by about 1650. Ostensible points of reference, and points of stability, like clocks and sundials, are, in fact, anything but stable and reliable, and sonnets 123 and 124 explore the different ways in which time "doth lie" (sonnet 123). Clocks were even more inaccurate than sundials and had to be constantly readjusted in relation to the most stable referent available – the sun – so that sundials, for all the problems they themselves posed, were used to set clock time. Renaissance time-measurement is still in search of a reliable referent and the problems of finding a dependable temporal standard are echoed in, and exacerbate, the problems of finding a reliable linguistic referent. Indeed, Shakespeare's sequence is constantly in search of a reliable referent, whether that is a beloved who can remain loyal, or a language which is both adequate to the task and stable, or a statement of belief, or an item of knowledge, that does not collapse into paradox or spiraling complication.

Timepieces translate time into other codes. With a sundial, time is translated into the movement of the sun, which is then translated into the movement of a shadow across a dial, and that dial then translates position into a number by way of calibrations based on particular time-systems. Shakespeare's sequence is woven out of paradoxes, or statements which link opposites in ways that at first seem to be nonsensical, but on closer inspection turn out to be meaningful. The sundial slips perfectly into this fabric of paradox as it uses a shadow (the shadow of the gnomon on the dial) to tell the time. It uses a shadow to reveal meaning and, in a sense, enlightens through the use of darkness and shade. A very similar paradoxical process is at work in the sonnets that meditate on shadows and shades, such as sonnet 43. In this poem, the

poet-lover argues that he sees things best in sleep. His desire for clarity
and truth actually turns him away from brightness, which in fact blinds,
and turns him towards shadows, which reveal, as well as conceal.
Obscurity, both in the sense of complication and of darkness, is
explored as a way of conveying meaning.

Renaissance subjects are embedded within multiple time schemes
and the provisional, unpredictable quality of the sequence derives
partly from the superposition of different temporal systems, none of
which is allowed to dominate. So the *Sonnets* register nature's time,
the time of the seasons and biological recurrence (sonnet 12, for
example). They also register the hours indicated by a clock or sundial
(sonnet 12). They refer to cycles of history and introduce the idea of
chronological recurrence (sonnet 59), while they also invoke the
process of degeneration implicit in the myth of the world's collapse
from the golden age, into the brazen and iron ages (sonnet 68). Other
sonnets, like 30, 98, and 109, set the personal apprehension of time
against shared ways of apprehending time. So in sonnet 30, for example,
the poet-lover feels that the past is very present and so lives out a time
that differs from clock time. Although the clock, and history, may say
otherwise, the individual experience confuses past, present, and future,
even dislocating their order and producing what the clock tells us are
preposterous temporalities (sonnet 109). Added to these different
patterns, to complicate the computation of time still further, there
were several systems for reckoning time and numbering the hours in
the Renaissance. Until the fourteenth century, the most common
system divided daylight into twelve equal parts and night time into
twelve equal parts. As a result, the length of a daylight hour differed
from a night time hour, except at the equinoxes, and both varied
according to the season. These changing hours were known as unequal,
temporal, canonical, or planetary hours. From the middle of the fourteenth century, a new system spread through Europe, encouraged by
the development of the mechanical clock, which could not easily
measure unequal hours. This divided the day and night into twenty-
four equal hours, but complications remained as there were several
ways of numbering those hours. So-called german, common, or french
hours (in Latin *horae communes*) divided time into two groups of
twelve. So-called italian, bohemian or welsh hours started counting
the hours from sunset. So-called babylonian or greek hours started
counting with sunrise. The systems based on twelve-hour tranches
were called small hours, and the systems based on twenty-four hour

tranches were called large hours. Then there was the zodiac, the phases of the moon, the Julian and Gregorian calendars, all of which computed time differently. Different places in Europe were on different times and a traveler had to take conversion tables, as well as timepieces, in order to tell the time, although the dials of sundials were often engraved with a system that enabled the observer to convert from one kind of time to another.

With clocks we learn obedience to time and responsiveness to its silent cues. The private use of clocks lays the basis for time discipline and internalizes that discipline as punctuality. A clock also makes productivity an issue and produces individuals who are hypersensitive to the passage of time, as they are confronted with a constant reminder of the passing hours. The renewed desire that time should be filled, conserved, and not wasted inevitably became interwoven with financial and economic concerns, as productivity is the place where time, labor, and money meet. Sonnet 30, to take just one example, is obsessed with wasting time, with opportunity, useless expenditure, consumption, and the idea that time lays waste. In sonnet 58, wasting time is specifically associated with the private experience of love, as if the domestic clock and portable sundial have extended the tyranny of clockwatching into the most private of spaces, and demand that we give an account of time spent, and fill the hours of the day, so that inactivity must be explained. The poet-lover gives an account of his own time, but excuses the beloved from making such a reckoning, because the beloved is lord, and lord of time, and can dispose of it as he wishes: "That god forbid, that made me first your slave, / I should in thought control your times of pleasure, / Or at your hand th'account of hours to crave, / Being your vassal bound to stay your leisure." In some ways, Shakespeare's sequence resists the imposition of time and its dictatorship, and certainly, at the start of the sequence, the intensity of the positive experience of love is indulged for its own pleasures with little thought that the poet-lover, as opposed to the beloved, is wasting time. Time measured by clocks is, broadly speaking, a symptom of, and an enabler of, urbanization. Rural dwellers measure time by natural events, and the tasks that these events require, such as ploughing, or harvesting, or haymaking. Nature is the time-giver, as night follows day, and the seasons follow each other, but it functions as a general cue to timing and to activity, and is not as narrowly constraining as the clock, which assigns activities an allotted, numbered hour. On the other hand, urban living requires city dwellers to learn a different

common language of time-measurement, to regulate the round of
business. Clocks dissociate time from human events and human events
from nature. The clock is a means of keeping track of the hours, but
also of synchronizing the actions of people in greater detail, and is an
essential tool for standardization. It introduces a new kind of morality,
as punctuality becomes not just possible, but also morally desirable.

The word "clock" derives from the French word *cloche*, meaning a
bell, and before the proliferation of mechanical clocks in houses, bells
told (tolled) the time and divided up the day for the community. These
bells were not only church bells which called people to services and
rang out on Holy Days, they were also secular bells that were set up
by royal and civic authorities. Town councils invested in public clocks
as symbols of municipal prestige and these clocks sounded bells for
the start of work, for the ending of work, for the closing of the town
gates, for the opening and closing of fairs, to warn of invasion, to celebrate a coronation, and so on. Time belonged to the group, and one
time was heard by all. The bells were drivers to particular forms of
behavior, sending out temporal messages that were received by all.
They were also a reminder of a higher authority that, in a sense, owned
time and then shared it out with the community.

Sundials, and to a lesser extent clocks, apply astronomical phenomena to everyday purposes. They combine revelation and enigma, and
translate the abstract into material form, as time is registered by a
sundial, a clock, or the wrinkles on a face. Time links movement with
meaning. Shakespeare's *Sonnets* also link movement with meaning, in
that conclusions and conclusiveness are either provisional, or viewed
skeptically. It is as if readers are never allowed to rest, and when they
reach what they think is a conclusion, further reflection reveals its
contingency. In the *Sonnets*, apparently simple statements, and sometimes simple words, become unexpectedly complicated. Puns are
thrown in the way of straightforward understanding, repetition gives
a word or phrase unforeseen associations, ambiguous syntax, poetic
meter and the verbal and aural patterns that are a feature of the highly
literary, highly regulated form that is a sonnet, establish unexpected
connections and disconnections between words and ideas. The process
of understanding in Shakespeare's sequence is often based on a process
of misunderstanding. Things get darker, more obscure, and more
difficult to comprehend as we move through a sonnet and between
sonnets, but, in doing so, they move closer to a meaning that is more
accurate and filled with greater significance. Time and movement are

interconnected and produce meaning in Shakespeare's sequence in ways that are illuminated by the mechanisms of Renaissance timepieces.

Notes

1 All quotations from *Shakespeare's Sonnets* are from Booth (1977).
2 Milton (1998: Book IV, 769–70).
3 On the problem of minutes, see Landes (1983: 104–5).
4 For the dating of the *Sonnets*, see Kerrigan's "Account of the text" in his edition of *The Sonnets and A Lover's Complaint* (Kerrigan 1999: 429).
5 The most exhaustive source of information about the *Sonnets*, including the attempts to rearrange them, is Rollins (1944). Dubrow (1995: 119–34) explores the issue of narrative in relation to the *Sonnets*.
6 On the relationship of *A Lover's Complaint* to the *Sonnets*, see Kerrigan (1999: 7–18). I discuss some of the characteristic trends of the 1590s in Brown (2004).
7 Sundials and their operation are discussed by Gouk (1988) and by Chandler and Vincent (1967). My discussion of timepieces and their effects is indebted to Cipolla (1967), Baillie et al. (1982), Landes (1983), and Turner (1987).

Works Cited

Baillie, G. H., Ilbert, Courtenay, and Clutton, Cecil (eds.) 1982: *Britten's Old Clocks and Watches and Their Makers*, 9th edn. London: Methuen and E. & F. N. Spon.

Booth, Stephen (ed.) 1977: *Shakespeare's Sonnets*. New Haven: Yale University Press.

Brown, Georgia 2004: *Redefining Elizabethan Literature*. Cambridge: Cambridge University Press.

Chandler, Bruce and Vincent, Clare 1967: "A Sure Reckoning: Sundials of the 17th and 18th Centuries." *Metropolitan Museum of Art Bulletin* 26, 154–69.

Cipolla, Carlo M. 1967: *Clocks and Culture 1300–1700*. London: Collins.

Colie, Rosalie 1973: *The Resources of Kind: Genre-Theory in the Renaissance*. Ed. B. K. Lewalski. Berkeley: University of California Press.

Dubrow, Heather 1995: *Echoes of Desire: English Petrarchism and Its Counterdiscourses*. Ithaca: Cornell University Press.

Fowler, Alastair (ed.) 1998: *Paradise Lost*. London: Longman.

Gouk, Penelope 1988: *The Ivory Sundials of Nuremberg 1500–1700*. Cambridge: Whipple Museum of the History of Science.

Kerrigan, John (ed.) 1999: *The Sonnets and A Lover's Complaint*. London: Penguin.

Landes, David S. 1983: *Revolution in Time: Clocks and the Making of the Modern World*. Cambridge, MA: Belknap Press of Harvard University Press.

Milton, John 1998: *Paradise Lost*. Ed. Alastair Fowler. London: Longman.

Montgomery, Robert L. 2006: *The Perfect Ceremony of Love's Rite: Shakespeare's Sonnets and A Lover's Complaint*. Medieval and Renaissance Texts and Studies 30. Tempe: Arizona Center for Medieval and Renaissance Studies.

Rollins, Hyder Edward (ed.) 1944: *A New Variorum Edition of Shakespeare: The Sonnets*, 2 vols. Philadelphia: Lippincott.

Shakespeare, William. See Kerrigan.

Turner, Anthony 1987: *Early Scientific Instruments: Europe 1400–1800*. London: Sotheby's Publications.

Chapter 11

Canons and Cultures: Is Shakespeare Universal?

A. E. B. Coldiron

Rationale

This essay began as a musing on how national treasures are understood and valued – or not – by outsiders. Is participation in the national sensibility, in the spirit of the *patria*, necessary for full appreciation of those works of art that have achieved national symbolic status? Is "Englishness," or at very least a feel for that elusive and ever-changing set of qualities, a prerequisite for understanding Shakespeare? More generally, one wonders how non-native speakers and/or those reading in translation can apprehend at all those literary works that draw greatest power from the textured polyvalence of words. If literary works are embedded in language and culture – and especially if they have become iconic, identified strongly with one language, one culture or nation – then how are they to travel well? Finally, how portable can such literary works be across the rather different, inevitable cultural distances created by the erosions of time about which Shakespeare himself was so concerned?

These questions invited attention to Shakespeare as a test case, at once a seemingly permanent icon of Englishness and also a seemingly ultraportable poet, one of those called "universal" by those who can entertain such a possibility. Shakespeare seems so portable perhaps because of certain qualities in the work that I had thought of as "Rorschach Shakespeare": he contains enough malleable irregularities to allow the processes of identificatory projection to take place in the audience. The resulting "Shakespeare is us" phenomenon can indeed seem to transcend historical distance and linguistic disjunction. But now we've got to wonder if literary and cultural embeddedness can be overcome by such a powerful "Rorschach" effect without other processes of canon and reception at work. When I saw another critic use the term "Rorschach Shakespeare" to discuss this mirroring effect, I abandoned that part of the essay, which was already too psychoanalytic in direction, and took up these questions of canon, history, and aesthetics. This essay, then, looks at Shakespeare as an extreme and rather paradoxical test case of a seemingly "universal" and yet iconic poet identified strongly with one nation – one whose work looks portable and yet nevertheless is inextricably embedded in one specific culture, historical moment, and language.

Where, and when, might we best test this curious problem of reception – that of national and temporal distances so steadily spanned? I thought first of France, a nation that, during the near-millennium since 1066, has variously been England's colonizer, colony, cousin, twin, doppelganger, alter ego, nemesis, invader, and ally. Certainly, one ought to find some interesting issues in reception where relations have been so vexed for so long. Temporally, I sought a moment that might be least sympathetic to certain qualities I find essential in Shakespeare: the eighteenth century might serve. When else would a rage for order, clarity, balance, symmetry, "unities" (as troublesome as that concept has been), hierarchy, harmony, formality, and topical decorum be as likely to eschew Shakespearean variety, characterization, colloquialism, ornament, antitheses, ambiguities, suggestive contrasts, untied ends, and unresolved complexities? So I had my questions: if Shakespeare's the quintessential English poet, what did France make of him; and if he's also "universal," portable across time, culture, and language, how was he appreciated in the eighteenth century? Au *dix-huitième*, then, for an inquiry into Shakespeare and transnational, transhistorical literary reception.

Our virtues lie i'th'interpretation of the time . . .
Shakespeare, *Coriolanus* 4.7.50

. . . les pièces de Shakespeare ne peuvent raisonnablement soutenir le
parallèle avec les chefs-d'oeuvres des tragiques français . . .
Jean François de La Harpe, *Lycée*, XIV.128

What's Shakespeare, what are the works of Shakespeare, or "What's
aught," as Troilus says in *Troilus and Cressida*, "but as 'tis valued?"
(2.2.52). Canonically central and culturally magnetized, Shakespeare by any measure enjoys extremely high valuation in Anglophone
cultures – so persistently high that it can appear universal. With
Shakespeare, it's easy to forget that literary reputation, like Coriolanus's or Cressida's virtue, is contingent, a function of "th'interpretation
of the time." We have in Shakespeare a rather extreme case of
what is generally true of literary reputation and canonization: the
valuation of authors and works begins in the aesthetic – in the
appreciations of initial audiences – and immediately begins to participate in complicated historical processes.[1] The works of Shakespeare
were popular from the start, and they, and the idea of "Shakespeare,"
soon became important aesthetic territory that came to stand for
England and Englishness. It may not therefore be too surprising
that one of the few times and places Shakespeare did not enjoy universal acclaim was in late-eighteenth-century France. Shakespeare's
uneasy, fluctuating fortunes in that time and place, however, can show
us a lot about literary (re)valuation and the workings of canons across
cultures. First, the essay considers what features tend in general to
make literary works easier to receive and canonize, and what features
of Shakespeare's works in particular have aided their apparently
universal high valuations. Second, the essay uses certain specific
eighteenth-century French responses to Shakespeare to illuminate
the curious workings of transnational and transhistorical literary
reception.

Universals, Contingencies, Canons

For four centuries, systems of literal and cultural capital have con-
verged to elevate the reception of Shakespeare. Critics before the
twentieth century devoted energy to describing the inherent qualities

that made Shakespeare and his works universally great, "for all time" as his friends and first editors, John Heminge and Henry Condell, phrased it. Critics of the past several decades, on the other hand, have spent their energy demystifying the material processes or "contingencies of value" (Smith 1988) that have gone into creating Shakespeare's reputation. Among political conservatives this demystifying turn in critical attention is read as a sign of the fall of civilization or as an implicit denigration of Shakespeare's works – as if acknowledging complex constructions of literary values means denying value itself; or as if the only values possible were transhistorical, transnational, transcendent; or as if "value" had no plural form.[2] However, we need not fear knowledge: to discover an elaborately constructed Bardolatry is in no way to devalue Shakespeare's works. In fact, to attend to the economics of theatrical production or systems of financial support to artists or to the power of editors and publishers is to be quite "Shakespearean" (that is, to be practical and aware of the motions of history). Few serious thinkers now doubt the contingency of aesthetic values and the cultural embeddedness of literary meaning.[3] Perhaps in literary reception, as in translation studies, the only universal is contingency itself.

But the long-term, cross-cultural phenomenon of high Shakespearean valuation does keep the question of universals in play. If we think that literary meaning is embedded in context, as evidence from cognitive science, linguistics, and common sense indicates – and especially if one thinks, as I usually do, that literary meaning is made in the radically changeable, individualized and specific interactions *between* text and context – then it is indeed remarkable for the same set of literary works to have been so well appreciated over four centuries, in countless languages, and in widely varying contexts. In light of contingency and embeddedness, it seems untenable to claim transcultural, transhistorical literary value; nevertheless, the apparent "universality" of the appreciation of Shakespeare's works – even if only an illusion of consensus – invites further consideration of such claims.

Might we identify elements in Shakespeare's works and principles of reception relevant to the long-term valuations of those works that, if not "universal," contribute to his transhistorical, transnational success? Practically speaking, some works are simply easier to canonize than others and more likely to gain reputation over the long term. A large corpus is easier to canonize; an author who writes in several genres is easier to canonize. On the latter count Shakespeare is actually at some relative risk: no epic poetry, no romance narratives, no high pastoral, no treatises or essays. An author whose works are initially cheap to reproduce and later take on some cachet and the promise of profits is easier to canonize. Works are easier to canonize if their authors connect easily with the means of production – if they have their own press, for instance, or are widely printed or reissued (in our own times, in paperback or in world distribution). Shakespeare gains here as a sharer in the theater company for which he wrote that large, profitable, and fairly easy-to-produce corpus. Having print-savvy friends to create a posthumous First Folio, complete with commendatory verse, certainly helps. Over time, having a Dr. Johnson, a Coleridge, a Bevington on one's production staff helps even more. Works tend to be canonized more easily if they are convenient to the means of production, if they adapt easily to alternative media, and if they adapt easily to changes in media or the means of production (try to find movies that were only made on Beta videotape, or the machines to play them). Again, Shakespeare's works readily adapt to different kinds of stage, to different textual formats and media, and to film and internet production.

An author is easier to canonize if he or she is in an "in-club" of some kind, at least at the start (but that is a highly contingent and fluid social category as well).[4] Writers with high patronage and writers near a throne do well over the long term, even if they suffer exile or execution in their own lifetimes; Shakespeare kept an appropriate near-distance from his monarchs and stayed rather closer to certain aristocrats. Becoming a member of a national in-club – that is, becoming identified as a National Poet – assures a long-term presence in the canon, for at least as long as the nation stands and is studied by historians. When, as in Shakespeare's case, the nation is also an Empire, works may find widespread uptake and adaptation in colonial contexts. There they attract the productive resistance and generative hybridity that take place in contact zones. However, the strong identification of an author with a nation may also interfere with international reception: a work's "translatability," its capacity to be understood successfully when translated or adapted into other cultures, can be reduced, depending on the relative positions of and the relations beween the two nations in question. In such a case, a work may come into a receiving culture as an alien oddity, too easily categorized as Other and not fully assimilated, too easily shelved as a curiosity.[5] Shakespeare's worldwide longevity, however, hardly seems to have been harmed by his iconic status as English Poet. This status may even have countered a negative factor in his translatability: works like Shakespeare's that rely for their power on effects of language and verbal nuance pose problems in translation.[6] As we shall see below, if a poet's connection to the national image is great enough, it can create literary reputation even when actual texts and translations are not available. It is perhaps a measure of the power of iconic national reputation that a poet like Shakespeare, whose use of language is essential to his works' achievement, is nevertheless (usually) esteemed in translation.

Writers with scandalous, mysterious, or intriguing biographies tend to enjoy canonical longevity. Donne's romantic and religious stories, for instance, were posed as a biographical split as early as Isaak Walton. The Jack Donne-Dean Donne split kept us talking about parallel dualities in the poems until relatively recently, when more nuanced accounts began to gain ground. But the exciting biography probably helped fuel interest in the poetry. Biography can influence reception negatively too, as in the cases of Oscar Wilde or Ezra Pound. Continuing to talk about the writer's life, however, is one way of keeping the works in view. If a poet's life records don't provide enough factual detail, we'll invent the excitement: for Shakespeare, this has meant extended controversies over the Oxford authorship question, or the endless biographical readings of dark ladies and young men in the sonnets.

In addition to works' relations to production contexts, sociopolitical connections, and biography, certain literary features seem to affect long-term reception, and here Shakespeare's distinctiveness emerges. Didactic works, thank goodness, die as soon as their moral imperative expires. Likewise topical works and satires have all too short a date: they rely on knowledge of current events for their impact, and future audiences cannot be trusted to recall the details of the dusty past. Shakespeare does fairly well on both these counts, for he is no tedious moralizer, and he generally masks his topicality with imaginary or historically distant settings, connecting it to broader, perennial human problems such as the right use of power. In a similar way, intertextuality of various sorts is dangerous to a work's longevity. Parodies, imitations, and allusions risk a work's long-term appeal by relying for their effectiveness on specific subtexts and intertexts in the audience's mind. Literary self-referentiality and metatextuality, on the other hand, do not risk such future losses. The one text we know future readers will have in mind is the one they're reading or hearing. Anyone who has taught, made speeches, or been misunderstood in print knows never to count on an audience's inner equipment; no wonder T. S. Eliot supplied future readers of his poetry with the right footnotes. The faster the pace of cultural change, the less stable are the intertexts any given readership can be counted on to have in its head; lost allusions may consign a great work to oblivion, or to Compact Shelving. While Shakespeare adds no footnotes, he frequently secures his future against readers' failing memories by using appositives, verbal settings, contextual cues, internal self-references of various sorts, and plot expositions and recapitulations. He usually tells us most of what we need to know, glossing places, names, and back-story right in the dialogue or in soliloquy, and sometimes tells us twice in case we missed a plot point or two, as in the dénouement(s) of *The Winter's Tale*. Thus his material works both for audiences bringing heavy intertexts to bear and for those traveling quite lightly. (We usually think of such techniques as playing to groundlings, but this kind of self-containment insures against future losses, as well. In other words, what may have been a strategy aimed at class actually serves reception.) Of course, Shakespeare's interpreters have helped guarantee his longevity. Armies of scholars and teachers supply vanishing contexts, propping up and restabilizing the works' meanings wherever necessary audience knowledge sags or is missing. Although Shakespeare's works are more self-explanatory than those of, say, Ben Jonson or John Heywood, we vigorously gloss what time has only somewhat dulled.

Furthermore, works seem to live longer if they treat sympathetically the concerns of more than one kind of audience. Shakespeare gives sympathetic voice to the viewpoints of rich and poor, old and young, female and male, rogue and princess, allowing many kinds of audience members and readers the pleasure of identifying with his characters. An author is easier to canonize when his or her work ranges enough to contain something for nearly every imaginable sensibility. From high eloquence to broad comedy, Shakespearean works are in a sense repositories of aesthetic potentiality, different parts of which may be adapted into alien cultures and languages, or into the alien future. It's not that any particular feature in the works – any character, any theme, any technique – will be "universal" over time or across cultures, but rather that there is enough variety, sympathetically depicted, in a large enough oeuvre so that subsequent audiences and critics can find something of identificatory interest or of value.[7] When the times turn, when fashions and politics change, new aspects can be taken up, fore-grounded in staging, discussed in criticism, and (since the nineteenth century) taught in classrooms. This factor in reception, this aesthetic amplitude and thematic plenitude, is, like Shakespeare's non-didactic open-mindedness, the mark of a writer's (or a person's) inner spacious-ness and abundance. The qualities of amplitude and plenitude are not only extremely attractive but are practical helps in assuring a work's future. They are connected to what Keats long ago identified as "nega-tive capability": "when a man is capable of being in uncertainties, mysteries, doubts, without any irritable reaching after fact and reason" (letter to George and Thomas Keats, December 21, 1817). To dwell in uncertainty in this way means to allow contradictions, to allow several points of view a hearing, to grant each character what each audience member, regardless of contingencies of culture and language, also needs: an honest sympathy.

So, at the level of plot, theme, and character, Shakespeare's negative capability yields a plurivocality and a richly textured, complex world presented in a non-didactic way. At the critical level, it yields a malle-ability or elasticity that encourages widely varying interpretations. I include as "interpretations" all sorts of transformations that make new meaning of Shakespeare or some part of the work: translations, stag-ings, adaptations, modernized texts, critical editions, films, artistic appreciations, curated exhibitions, and other Shakespeareana. As the object of reshaping – whether from one medium to another, or from one culture and language to another, or across historical distances – the Shakespearean text permits nearly infinite transformations (and reveals the nature of the transformer). Like an indeterminate, ambigu-ously shaped Rorschach inkblot, the works of Shakespeare have enough amplitude, plenitude, and irregularity to mean very different things to different interpreters over the long term. Contradictory, unresolved, and ambiguous elements in a work allow adaptations and critical appreciations that can continue to engage audiences over time as tastes and contexts change. More rigid works may not be as transformable, so not as often adapted, translated, reimagined, and thus not as long-lived in canons. Bunyan, on this score, may not last as long as Jane Austen; Marlowe perhaps not as long as Shakespeare and morality plays less long still. Like poetic *indirection*, the elusive, malleable shape of Shakespeare facilitates changing responses and thus enduring pres-ence in changing canons.

France: Transnational Reception as Synecdoche

In eighteenth-century France, Shakespearean texts were translated, abridged, embellished, staged, and discussed by influential writers with widely varying views.[8] But neoclassical aesthetics may be fundamentally at odds with Shakespeare's plays, and an *esprit gaulois* with the English temper.[9] This section considers one of the negative responses to Shakespeare at the end of the century, that of Jean François de La Harpe (1739–1803), a writer almost unread now but very influential then, whose name "evokes . . . all the polemics that characterize the literary world of the end of the ancien régime."[10]

In the age of Voltaire, French neo-classicism ruled European tastes,[11] and the island attached at least some of its opinions to the main. R. A. Foakes explains that for most of the century,

> editors and critics felt obliged to consider Shakespeare in relation to what were called the "Rules of Art," rules derived from the French and from Horace, though often ascribed to Aristotle, especially the three unities of time, place, and action. Shakespeare was regarded as a prodigy, whose "wild and extravagant" works possessed genius but lacked refinement, the "Turn and Polishing of what the French call a *Bel Esprit*."
> (Foakes 2002: 224; quoting *The Spectator* 161, September 3, 1711)

French-led preferences for clean-lined symmetries, as for balanced couplets and high protagonists and topics, seem to have informed English opinions about – and adaptations of – Shakespeare (Branam 1956; Vickers 1974–81; Dobson 1992; Foakes 2002; George 2004). Some of the more galling French aesthetic attacks were spiritedly rebuffed as a matter of national pride and in the context of changing French–English relations, as Dobson shows. Yet even the national Bard on his native turf was subjected to the powerful, cosmopolitan imperatives of French neo-classicism – and was devalued by its standards.

Few would doubt the importance of France as the eighteenth century's worldwide cultural and aesthetic arbiter. But against that general background, Shakespeare's "international currency," as John Russell Brown calls it, fluctuated considerably over the course of the century.[12] Before Le Tourneur's major translation in 1776 (*Shakespeare Traduit de l'Anglois, Dédié au roi*), relatively little of Shakespeare's work was available at all on the continent (Larson 1989; Miller 1989). La Place's translation of 1746 was just a partial selection of scenes with plot descriptions. Jusserand (1898) digs up numerous mentions and partial imports,[13] but the relative scarcity of Shakespeare in France, which persisted until 1776, seems to have given added weight to "a few frequently discussed passages of particular plays that were taken to stand for Shakespeare as a whole" (Larson 1989: 107). This was especially true of the "to be or not to be" soliloquy from *Hamlet*, Voltaire's translation of which was first published in 1733 in the English version of his *Lettres philosophiques*. As Larson puts it, "the soliloquy took on a life of its own, reappearing in several other works by Voltaire [and numerous other works]" (Larson 1989: 107; cf. Miller 1989). However, "the reliance of most of continental Europe for most of the century upon Voltaire's translation of the soliloquy to understand what Shakespeare was like" (Larson 1989: 108) suggests to me a process of reception-by-synecdoche. France could respond to only a portion of "Shakespeare" and mainly to that portion filtered through Voltaire's words and views. To put it another way, the relatively limited number of French readers who encountered Shakespeare were most likely to meet him in Voltaire's description of very restricted parts of the works.[14]

Most transnational reception does, I think, work by means of such processes of translation-filtered synecdoche. As fewer people read works in their languages of composition and fewer still read source-language "complete works," reception-by-synecdoche (that is, by translation and in part) is increasingly common. In a less pragmatic, more theoretical sense, transnational reception is inevitably synecdochal, because translation always involves selection and filtering, and it results in necessarily partial reproduction of a work's elements. Additions to the source-language work and the inevitable changes of context render "the work," if we can still call it that in translation, always already unreadable. Such theoretical issues in transnational reception aside, the practical point is still that Voltaire's severely selected readings and opinions carried more than their share of the weight of Shakespeare criticism in that century. Synecdochal as French opinions were, they had sufficient force to return and circulate in England, where, with plenty of texts available, neither translation nor synecdoche needed to intervene in the reception of Shakespeare.[15] Given an active, uneven cross-Channel traffic in aesthetics, it is hard to tease out precisely who influences whom, but both sides of the Channel register Gallic opinion.

Le Tourneur's *Shakespeare Traduit de l'Anglois, Dédié au roi* of 1776 marks a major turn in reception in France, insuring a better future for Shakespeare on the Continent by bringing complete French texts to an influential set of subscribers (including many English nobles, royals, and literati). This single edition may have done more to enhance Shakespeare's worldwide reputation than anything since the First Folio. If it hadn't been for Le Tourneur's proto-Romantic intimations of Shakespeare's immortality, Shakespeare's reception, certainly in France and probably elsewhere on the Continent, might have languished in the doldrums of neo-classical litotes. "Shakespeare, tout grossier qu'il était, n'était pas sans lecture et sans connaissances" is a typically reluctant concession that despite the works' unpalatable roughness, ungainliness, and unseemliness, they are not utterly without value (La Harpe 1777: I.5). Yes, we Bardophiles should say with relief *Enfin Le Tourneur vint* – but we should also understand that Le Tourneur's power to redirect the canons of taste is clearer from hindsight than it could have been at the time.

La Harpe and His Opinions of Shakespeare

Le Tourneur made his surprising, pro-Shakespearean mark against prevailing opinions that followed Voltaire's negative judgements of 1733–4. One important French tastemaker, Jean François de La Harpe, nourished richly what Voltaire had hatched. Sometimes called a disciple of Voltaire, La Harpe disagreed often enough with his respected elder correspondent (sometimes, in fact, about Shakespeare). La Harpe was a prolific critic, playwright, and poet. From the publication of his *Héroïdes* in 1759 until his death in 1803, La Harpe was writing and lecturing in Paris. His essays in (among other periodicals) *Le Mercure de France* and *Le Journal de politique et de littérature* were widely influential. He was a member of the Académie française, but was most famous for his extremely popular public lectures on literature and society called the "Lycée." These were later printed and expanded as the 18-volume *Lycée, ou Cours de littérature ancienne et moderne* (1797–1803). Long after his death, La Harpe's literary opinions held sway in France and across Europe. The *Lycée* was steadily reprinted in at least 38 complete and at least 25 partial or abridged editions between 1799 and 1842.[16] His *Oeuvres*, a separate publication reprinted in at least ten editions after 1777, contains in 16 volumes his own original plays, poems, and other compositions (Todd 1979: items 1–12, pp. 31–6). Despite La Harpe's influence, then, he is now relatively little known. But as Joan De Jean points out, La Harpe's literary history and criticism shaped the tastes and canon of his generation and those of the subsequent century. De Jean calls *Lycée* the "compilation that may best represent the view of the canon that the nineteenth century inherited from the eighteenth" (De Jean 1991: 33).

In addition to La Harpe's authoritative critical work, he also practiced an anti-Shakespearean method in his own playwriting. One of La Harpe's compositions is a version of *Coriolanus* (1784; his play had appeared in at least 17 editions by 1822).[17] When printing the play in his *Oeuvres*, La Harpe included a detailed preface and a long epilogue. The latter partially reproduces a debate about the play that had appeared in *Le Mercure de France*, along with a witty commendatory poem styling La Harpe the Coriolanus of letters. La Harpe's *Coriolan* and the paratexts attached to it show us Shakespeare disputed and give us a good if indirect look at La Harpe's view of Shakespeare's dramatic technique. Here La Harpe's exciting, unusual life is relevant: always in some controversy or other, he was imprisoned during 1792; released, he helped his Revolutionary former-captors found the École Normale (perhaps ensuring a permanent place for anti-Shakespearean sentiment in French public education). Late in life he reconverted to a renounced Catholicism; he had ties with the ancien régime, but he has also been called "La Harpe Robespierriste" (Anon. 1912). His is no Jacobin *Coriolan*, however.[18]

La Harpe's main grounds of objection to Our Bard were typical: Shakespeare is rough, unlearned, and while he has some natural talent, his plays do not follow the Rules of Art. In discussing the related matter of the value of learnedness in literature, La Harpe argues that while some poets may seem to have written well without rules or classical learning, such a thing cannot be. Whatever is good in their monstrous works can be attributed to some exposure to the rules of art through reading classical authors:

> On a cité des écrivains qui ont réussi, dit-on, sans connaître ou sans observer les règles de l'art, tels que le Dante, Shakespeare, Milton, et autres. C'est s'exprimer d'une manière très-fausse. Le Dante et Milton connaissent les anciens, et s'ils se sont fait un nom avec des ouvrages monstrueux, c'est parce qu'il y a dans ces monstres quelques belles parties executées selon les principes. (I.5)

Reading the ancients, it seems, can make up for a monstrous lack of artistic knowledge, apparently just by osmosis. But this is in no way to diminish the importance of classical learning and rules of art in literature: monstrous, exceptional Shakespeare proves the rule(s).

However, La Harpe does admit that rules are not everything, and that exposure to classical authors can call forth in a writer an instinct or feeling for beauty. Good literature may result without conscious adherence to the rules of art. In speaking of Shakespeare, Milton, and Dante, La Harpe grants further that "leur génie leur a fourni des details où règne le sentiment du beau, et les règles ne sont autre chose que ce sentiment réduit en methode" (I.5). This idea – that there can be a natural genius based on a feeling for beauty, that it may generate valuable details in a work, and that rules are simply that feeling for beauty "reduced to a method" – well, it's a big concession for a neo-classicist, and one that anticipates Romantic ideas of natural expression and talent. He nearly posits here an aesthetic Unconscious at work. This concession to the existence of some writerly quality antecedent to "the rules" allows La Harpe that grudging praise: "Shakespeare lui-même, tout grossier qu'il était, n'était pas sans lecture et sans connaissances: ses oeuvres en fournissent la preuve" (I.5). Even vulgar, monstrous Shakespeare, judging from his works, had at least enough learning to have absorbed somehow this natural feeling for beauty that ended up creating good artistic effects. But in the litotes La Harpe distinguishes Shakespeare from the more learned, and thus more highly valued, Dante and Milton: *even* Shakespeare, apparently the most extreme case of literary monstrosity, was "*not without* reading and knowledge."

The limp praise, if it's praise at all, continues. When La Harpe pursues the importance of the rules of art, he treats the issue of genius and discusses the need to connect the parts and wholes of a work. These three monstrous poets, he says, "ont manqué de la conception d'un ensemble" (I.5). Theirs is a problem of too much uncoordinated detail, which he elsewhere criticizes in Shakespeare. "Qui peut douter," he says, in a discussion of the principle of unity of action, "que les pièces de Lopez de Vega et de Shakespeare qui contiennent tant d'événements que la meilleure mémoire pourrait à peine s'en rendre compte après la représentation, qui peut douter que de pareilles pièces ne soient hors de la mesure convenable, et qu'en violant le précepte d'Aristote on n'ait blessé le bon sens?" (I.62). It's not so much that Shakespeare's event-rich plays violate the rules or Aristotelian principles, but that they exceed the bounds of good sense and "appropriate measure." La Harpe continues, however, with a more thoughtful, audience-based line of reasoning against multiple plot details. "Nous ne sommes susceptibles que d'un certain degré d'attention, d'une certaine durée d'amusement, d'instruction, de plaisir" (I.62), so the principle of unity is really about not overtaxing the audience's attentive capacity. We might not now think of the *dix-huitième* as an era of short attention spans, but La Harpe sees fixed limits to what an audience can absorb. (Funny how he relaxes those limits for the long speeches in Racine or Corneille.) The same textured and multiple plots that allow, I think, for Shakespeare's transhistorical and transnational adaptability, are precisely what exceed the limits for La Harpe. Aristotle understood, La Harpe says in explaining the essence of the beautiful, that one must only offer the spirit what it can take in (I.62). In this view, Shakespeare offers the spirit an overwhelming experience that exceeds audience capacities and thereby becomes unbeautiful.

An excess of detail is not the only problem with Shakespeare, it seems. The question of parts and wholes in drama was usually treated in terms of Aristotelian unity of action. La Harpe treats it in those terms, too (I.63). But he also brings up the related issue of manner of composition (I.63–4). La Harpe, like Voltaire and most of his contemporaries, valued smoothness, coherence, and balanced composition of detail, in which the parts' relation to the whole is tighter. "Harmonious" is a key word in this discussion, and La Harpe brings up Aristotelian *melopoeia* several times as a feature of good composition. Here La Harpe's facility with English, a matter of some minor critical disagreement, becomes a factor in his reception of Shakespeare.[19] Native English speakers generally find Shakespeare melopoetic. Critics such as Helen Vendler or Stephen Booth have anatomized the power of Shakespeare's language to move, which is an aim of Aristotelian melopoesis. (That so many Shakespearean phrases have taken on the status of proverbs or singsong catchphrases perhaps testifies to the works' aurally pleasing and memorable dimension, yet it's hard to separate such things from their cultural prominence and canonical centrality.) Anglophone or not, La Harpe does not directly chastise a lack of *melopoeia* in Shakespeare, and he does not use Shakespearean texts directly to discuss literary "harmony." However, in his own playwriting, he does eliminate some of the best dissonant energies in Shakespeare's noisiest play, *Coriolanus*. La Harpe's *Coriolan* is a much statelier, less cacophonous (if I can't quite say harmonious) version of the story. Granted, Shakespeare's *Coriolanus* would stretch anyone's definition of "harmony" to a Schoenbergian limit; it's not really a fair basis for judging Shakespeare's *melopoeia*. And in any case, reading Shakespeare only in translation or with unskilled English may have left La Harpe unable to appreciate Shakespeare's better harmonies, melopoetic or compositional; or was his era simply deaf to this kind of polyphonous music?

Shakespeare, Milton, Dante, Lope de Vega: monstrous, and – tiens! – all foreigners. But La Harpe curiously does not link their literary and etymological barbarities. Like most French writers, La Harpe assumes the superiority of French letters and a transnational (French-based) standard of taste against which all writers everywhere and for all time are to be judged. On the other hand, he does acknowledge the distorting powers of nationalist prejudices in literary criticism and reception – at least, the distorting powers of *English* nationalist prejudice. English patriotism, explains La Harpe, must surely account for pro-Shakespeare literary opinions, which otherwise are hardly comprehensible. Part of the reason Shakespeare's works are so bad is historical, says La Harpe, to be attributed to the rough, primitive age in which he lived. But more enlightened moderns have somehow still seen Shakespeare as their chief playwright, and this oddity must surely result from nationalism:

> Quoique les Anglais du temps de Charles II fussent déjà loin de la grossièreté [*sic*] et du pédantisme qui régnaient au siècle de Shakespeare; quoique ceux d'aujourd'hui en soient encore bien plus éloignés, il n'en est pas moins demeuré le premier des poètes dramatiques pour les Anglais en général, si l'on excepte un petit nombre de juges impartiaux. (XIV.128)

These few impartial judges, says La Harpe, "s'élevant au-dessus des préjugés de l'amour-propre national, conviennent que les pièces de Shakespeare ne peuvent raisonnablement soutenir le parallèle avec les chefs d'oeuvre des tragiques français" (XIV.128). Many educated French people still agree, and some lack La Harpe's awareness of national self-regard as a factor.

La Harpe goes on to question what, if anything, beyond this English "amour-propre national," might have created such an inexplicably high opinion of Shakespeare. He proposes that the local and national history of staging popular spectacles may well have shaped English preferences. "C'est qu'à Londres les spectacles sont essentiellement populaires, et que partout le goût du peuple est grossier."[20] Here Shakespeare is used to underscore the division between popular and high culture, and La Harpe explains the political context of the aesthetic problem (in an opinion that also bears on La Harpe's *Coriolan*). "Ce goût [i.e., the vulgar popular taste] devient dominant, et entraîne plus ou moins les classes même supérieures, quand le peuple est riche, et même une puissance politique, comme il l'est en Angleterre, le seul grand état de l'Europe moderne oú il a pu l'être" (XIV.128). At this point he names names: Shakespeare, Pope, and Montagu. The combined effect of vulgar public taste, a history of popular theater, and patriotism can spoil the critical judgement of even a learned writer trained in the classics. "Il ne faut donc pas s'étonner si l'on vit Pope lui-même, formé à l'école des anciens, et plein de goût dans ses écrits, s'aveugler, dans sa critique, au point de transformer en beautés les plus grands défauts de Shakespeare" (XIV.128–9). Tasteful Pope has succumbed in his otherwise learned criticism to the political power of a popular aesthetic favoring the monstrous Shakespeare. And it's not just Pope whose judgement is blinded.

> Une Anglaise de beaucoup d'esprit, Madame de Montaigu, a essayé de nous faire goûter ce qu'il y a de plus vicieux dans le poète des Anglais. Ce titre sera toujours celui de Shakespeare, parce qu'au théâtre de Londres il est éminemment le poète du peuple, dont il sut flatter tous les goûts, d'autant plus aisément que c'étaient les siens propres. (XIV.129)

National self-love of the kind that makes such writers turn Shakespeare's faults into beauties is rooted in the culture, the politics, the stage history, the popular taste of England. (After the Revolution, this democratic quality in Shakespeare would be better appreciated in France, and in this the proto-Romanticism of Le Tourneur anticipates post-Revolutionary political-aesthetics by more than a decade.) However, Shakespeare's inclusion of all classes and kinds of characters, another quality that favors his long-term global adaptability, polarizes opinion in La Harpe's era. (This opinion breaks on unexpected lines: consider the high-culture subscription list of Le Tourneur's pro-populist Shakespeare, versus the public, multi-class audiences for La Harpe's anti-populist, anti-"grossier" views.)

Holding the prevailing pre-Revolutionary view, however, La Harpe seems to accept, as Voltaire did, that national stereotypes had at least some basis, validity, and influence. In a long chorographic section about the respective vices and virtues of nations and how this matters to literature, he says this about England:

> L'Angleterre, destinée à devenir bientôt la legislatrice du monde dans les sciences exactes et dans la saine métaphysique, pouvait dès-lors opposer à tous les grands hommes que j'ai nommés le chancelier Bacon, l'un de ces esprits hardis et indépendants qui doivent tout à l'étude approfondie de leurs propres idées, et à l'habitude de considérer les objets comme si personne ne les avait considérés auparavant. (VI.37–8)

By citing Bacon and by understanding the experimental method as a manifestation of a national habit of mind – English independence – La Harpe can understand the idiosyncrasy of Shakespeare, as well as the pro-Shakespearean views of Pope and Montagu who counter what he sees as all Europe's opinion.

La Harpe does thus grant the English a certain right to their own literary spirit apart from the worldwide (i.e., French) standard of taste. He even comments that Voltaire's opinion of Shakespeare and *Julius Caesar* was shaped by his exposure to such independent, Baconian English ideas:

> cet ouvrage [Voltaire's *Le Mort de César*] était . . . un des fruits de l'étude qu'il avait fait du théâtre anglais dans son séjour à Londres, et du goût qu'il y avait pris pour les beautés fortes et les idées républicaines. . . . Frappé de plusieurs traits sublimes qui étincellent dans le drame de Shakespeare, il essaya d'abord de traduire quelques morceaux du *Jules César*; mais bientôt rebuté d'un travail contredit à tout moment par la raison et le bon goût, il aima mieux refaire la pièce suivant ses principes, et ne prenant de celle du poète anglais . . . que la conspiration de Brutus et de Cassius, qui ne forme qu'une seule action, il reserra dans trois actes ce sujet, qu'il voulait traiter avec toute la sévérité de l'histoire . . . (XI.266–7)

Voltaire and La Harpe discount anything that later writers will come to appreciate as the "Romantic sublime." Shakespeare's play may have some sublime sparkling moments, but it violates taste and reason (or at least, the work [of translating it] is countered by reason and good taste). Voltaire sets *Julius Caesar* right by concentrating the action, taking only the conspiracy from Shakespeare. One wonders which "strong beauties" were lost in that concentration, but the aesthetic principle is clear.

On the other hand, one of the English "strong beauties" – and for La Harpe, one of the only praiseworthy elements in all of Shakespeare – is the handling of the ghost in *Hamlet*. The ghost in Voltaire's *Sémiramis* did not live up to it. Although Shakespeare, says La Harpe, is obviously inferior to Voltaire, and *Hamlet* to *Sémiramis*, the way Shakespeare manages the ghost is unquestionably superior. The English poet gets an important dramatic principle right:

> Je suis fort loin de comparer à *Sémiramis* un monstre de tragédie tel que *Hamlet*, de Shakespeare; mais j'avoue que, dans l'auteur anglais, le spectre est beaucoup mieux motivé, et produit plus de terreur que celui de Ninus [the ghost in *Sémiramis*]. Pourquoi? C'est qu'il vient dévoiler ce que tout le monde ignore, et, de plus, qu'il ne parle qu'au seul prince de Danemarck. Cette dernière circonstance n'est pas indifférente: je ne crois pas qu'un spectre doive paraître sur la scène à la vue d'une grande assemblée; au milieu de tant de monde, la terreur s'affaiblit en se part-ageant. (XII.91–2)

La Harpe goes on to say (very respectfully) that Voltaire seems to have wanted to make the ghost scarier but that the result was, unfortu-nately, mediocre. La Harpe does a bit of post-hoc rewriting of Voltaire's play, following Shakespeare's method: "si Ninus fût apparu devant Ninias, seul et dans le silence de la nuit, et que, sans avoir avec lui une longue conversation, comme le spectre anglais avec Hamlet, il eût, en quelques mots, révélé le crime et demandé la vengeance, il eût pu inspirer beaucoup plus de terreur" (XII.92). He continues in sub-sequent pages to explain the dynamics of *Sémiramis* and the drama-tist's evocation of fear; his main point is that Shakespeare knew how to handle not only the plotting of dramatic irony (not La Harpe's term), but also how to create in the text the possibility of staging that evokes suspense and fear in an audience. For La Harpe to have used Shakespeare as a model of how to improve Voltaire's technique is a remarkable compliment in the contexts – a compliment to Shake-speare, I mean.

Other than this moment of clear excellence, English nationalism, republican ideas, and popular theater seldom carried good aesthetic consequences, according to La Harpe. La Harpe's 40-page section on Voltaire's *Mort de César* and its style provides a kind of anti-Shake-spearean theory of drama that aligns well with what La Harpe himself actually does in 1784 in writing his own *Coriolan*. That play and La Harpe's other opinions on the power of the people in the polis are beyond the scope of this brief essay.[21] But even a brief look at La Harpe's views reveals Shakespeare as a site of controversy in "th'interpretation of the time."

To conclude, it would seem that some of the very factors that favor Shakespeare's longevity and apparently "universal" transnational appeal were not appreciated in this particular cultural moment. Shakespeare may provide a clear marker of how different English and French sensibilities were at that particular moment in that particular context. There may also be something more general at work; one thinks of the commonplace, "la litterature française, c'est l'absence de Shakespeare"; French literature has nearly everything else, so this telling absence may be a defining feature of the difference in these two literary polysystems over time. The case surely illustrates some general facts about literary reception and canons: transnational reception necessarily works by a kind of synecdoche, and cross-cultural study can nearly always illuminate aspects of reception that would be unavailable from a monolingual or monocultural perspective. Literary "virtues" also "lie i'th'interpretation" of the places.

Notes

1 Since the nineteenth century, university and secondary curricula have kept Shakespeare alive in the minds of generations of students. The practices of editors and printers have resulted in multiple textual versions from the start, not just quartos and folios but composite facsimiles, controversial modernizations, variora, and a succession of "definitive" and "authoritative" texts. Critics and scholars have exercised their acumen on Shakespeare, and major movements like the New Criticism, the New Historicism, Marxism, and feminism have proven their mettle and gained credibility through their applications to Shakespeare. Beyond the Academy, films, theatrical productions, and reviews have shaped and extended Shakespeare's reputation. And the high valuation of the Shakespearean has never been innocent of economics, from Renaissance patronage systems and payments to the Lord

Chamberlain's Men, all the way to the modern-day NEH and British Academy. For a lucid and witty historical survey, see Taylor (1989).

2 This is politically charged territory in the Academy today: conservative proponents of universalism tend to fight liberal proponents of contingency. But a criticism of contingency could come from poststructuralists as well as from cultural-conservative universalists: since the signified, "literary value," is easily detached from the signifiers of critical praise that mark it, the whole critical enterprise dissolves into self-referential tautologies of opinion. *Rezeptiongeschichte* and canon formation are then just a hollow, self-fueling, juggernaut, in which any literary reputation gains momentum over time as more readers are indoctrinated by particular editorial choices, critical opinions, and curricular dicta: Bardolatry reproducing itself.

3 Anthropologist Laura Bohannon's (1998) witty, now-classic essay pleasantly debunks universalist interpretations of *Hamlet* and demonstrates in detail the influence of cultural assumptions on literary interpretation. For a theoretical review and proposal on the value of taking embeddedness seriously in interpretation, see Kastan (1999).

4 The WASP aristocrats' club helped writers beginning in the nineteenth century stay in print by private subscription. The Roxburghe Club, or Spenser Society editions, and university curricula and the Early English Text Society and the Scottish Text Society helped preserve many writers in print whose work would not have been available outside archives. In our own times certain university degrees make a kind of club, as do connections to periodicals and presses; but Outsiders' Clubs have also been very helpful to literary reception (as with the beat poets, for example, or French *pied-noir* intellectuals after 1959, or African-American women writers after Angelou). Was Shakespeare in an in-club?

5 Adaptability into other media is another kind of translatability (as, for example, Jane Austen's dialogue making her easily translatable into film).

6 Or if they do well, they do it not by achieving the same aesthetic ends in translation – theoretically and pragmatically impossible – but rather by recreating a new set of effects. Aesthetic effects are especially embedded in language, cultural context, and literary history; for summary discussion, see Even-Zohar (1980) on literary polysystems.

7 Post-World War II Brechtian theater appreciated the ironic distancing of *Troilus and Cressida*, an appreciation registered by an

increase in productions. *Love's Labour's Lost*'s fortunes on stage increased with the advent of feminism. R. A. Foakes analyzes the alternating ascendancy of *King Lear* and *Hamlet* in the twentieth century as the tragedy that defines an age.

8 See Jusserand (1898), Haines (1925), Green (1935), Vickers (1974–81), Dobson (1992), and Pemble (2005). Jusserand details the history of a long early phase in which Shakespeare was nearly unknown in France, followed by a phase, beginning roughly with Voltaire, during which he was thought of as a rough, savage writer, followed by a post-Le Tourneur phase, during which he was well appreciated in France, in my opinion because he was adapted to French proto-Romantic tastes.

9 We might expect that Shakespeare, the icon and embodiment of Englishness – English temper, English national identity, English cultural greatness, and what Jonathan Bate has identified as the "Deep English" quality in him – would not translate well or be appreciated properly in France. After all, French–English literary-cultural relations had been complex and highly charged since 1066, usually involving a conflicted English appropriation of French texts and tastes. And in any nation, neo-classical critics would seem unlikely to favor Shakespeare unreservedly: even beyond truisms about the three unities, neo-classical aesthetics do involve such notions as balanced proportion, symmetrical simplicity, decorum of subject and style, appropriate restraint in what is depicted onstage, clean-lined singleness of purpose, clarity, reduced detail, and congruence of each part to the whole. Shakespeare instead presents, for instance, multiple plots, multiple purposes, high and low subjects and mixed styles, slippery ambiguities, rich detail, deaths on stage, characters of different classes entering at the same time, and so on. "Th'interpretation of the time" in the eighteenth century differed radically from the earliest interpretations of Shakespeare, as has been well explained in criticism and well demonstrated in the strongly revised adaptations of Shakespeare on the eighteenth-century stage. French and English literary aesthetics have always revealed points of friction. But "neo-classical aesthetics" and "eighteenth-century France," like the changes called "Revolution" and "Romanticism," are anything but monolithic notions; the century saw vibrant aesthetic and political debates.

10 Todd (1972: 9): "[évoque] . . . toute la polémique qui caracterise le monde littéraire vers la fin de l'ancien régime"; all translations are mine unless otherwise noted.

11 Kenneth Larson points out "the centrality of the French translation of *The Spectator* in mediating Shakespeare to Germany" and

"the centrality of Voltaire to German as well as French Shake-speare reception" (Larson 1989: 105, 107). French literary criticism also shaped English opinion.

12 Brown (1998) considers some elements in Shakespeare's works that, if not permanently valuable or "for all time," seem to enjoy an "international currency." Brown's metaphor of exchange, one that translators in Shakespeare's day often used to describe their practice, does not imply that what is valuable in Shakespeare evades or transcends the contingencies of historical and cultural contexts – on the contrary, the punning idea of "currency" means that Shakespeare's works participate in systems of negotiable and negotiated value, and they do this between cultures.

13 Including Ducis and Mercier; see also Miller (1989).

14 Voltaire's opinions of Shakespeare, of course, changed from initial partial approbation to more thorough disapproval as his own changing contexts removed him from his "English phase." Voltaire's changing opinions of Shakespeare thus diagnose his own changes; they are noted in Jusserand (1898), Haines (1925), Green (1935), Todd (1972), and Miller (1989).

15 He was already the iconic national poet, steadily in print and on the stage (although often and severely revised there). Complete works of Shakespeare were profusely available in English, so there was no need at home to take the word of (nor to restrict oneself to the selections of) Voltaire or any French critic. And yet, as Michael Dobson (1992) demonstrates, French opinion is read and taken seriously in England, and opinions against Shakespeare provoked strong reactions.

16 Todd (1979: items 13–111, pp. 37–74). Some partial editions remained in print as late as 1894, and parts of his works were frequently translated into Russian, for he had personal connections there, but also into Italian, Dutch, and English; I have not found his opinions on Shakespeare translated into English yet.

17 In fact the pattern of publication of La Harpe's *Coriolan* is quite revealing: six editions in 1784, one in 1788, one in 1791, two editions in 1792, then none at all until a Dutch edition in 1814, a French edition in 1815, four in 1818, and one in 1822 (Todd 1979: items 269–87, pp. 122–8). Clearly, the play spoke to the concerns of the French public in the years leading up to 1792, but spoke far too loudly to be reissued between 1793 and 1814.

18 I haven't yet assembled everything La Harpe said about Shakespeare, but even the first pass at it helps us relocate Shakespeare in a rapidly changing political and aesthetic climate.

19 Todd (1972) implies he had English; Haines (1925), Sproull (1939), and Green (1935) imply not. I frankly can't tell.

20 La Harpe's note: "S'il faut excepter le peuple d'Athènes, et à quelques égards celui de Rome, quand les lettres grecques y furent connues, on a vu ailleurs les raisons qui séparent ces deux peuples de tous les autres." La Harpe's classicism is such that he equates the vernacular and the vulgar – a common equation.

21 A detailed study of the French translations and versions of *Coriolanus* made around the time of the Revolution would be, I think, most revealing of how the languages of liberty, equality, and fraternity both do and do not find their literary and theatrical analogues. Shakespearean expressions of the problem of shared power in the polis – the (too?) strong beauties and republican ideas Voltaire and La Harpe identify with Shakespeare and English theater – are only unevenly accepted in late-eighteenth-century France, and then violently asserted after 1792. I'm uneasy with the idea that aesthetics and politics here are seamlessly equivalent or even mutually dependent, because I think this case points to a more vexed relation between the two.

Works Cited

Alexander, Catherine M. S. 1998: "Shakespeare and the Eighteenth Century: Criticism and Research." *Shakespeare Survey* 51, 1–16.

Anon. 1912: "La Harpe Robespierriste." *La Révolution Française* 62, 546–9.

Barton, Anne 1985: "Livy, Machiavelli, and Shakespeare's *Coriolanus.*" *Shakespeare Survey* 38, 115–29.

Bohannon, Laura 1998: "Shakespeare in the Bush." In Virginia P. Clark, Paul A. Escholz, and Alfred F. Rosa (eds.) *Language: Readings in Language and Culture*. New York: St. Martin's Press, 27–36.

Branam, George C. 1956: *Eighteenth-Century Adaptations of Shakespearean Tragedy*. Berkeley: University of California Press.

Brewer, Daniel 1997: "Political Culture and Literary History: La Harpe's *Lycée.*" *Modern Language Quarterly* 57, 163–84.

Brown, John Russell 1998: "Shakespeare's International Currency." *Shakespeare Survey* 51, 193–204.

De Jean, Joan 1991: "Classical Reeducation: Decanonizing the Feminine." In Joan De Jean and Nancy K. Miller (eds.) *Displacements: Women, Tradition, Literatures in French*. Baltimore: Johns Hopkins University Press, 22–36.

Dobson, Michael 1992: *The Making of the National Poet: Shakespeare, Adaptation, and Authorship 1660–1769*. Oxford: Clarendon Press.

Even-Zohar, Itamar 1980: "Interference in Dependent Literary Polysystems." In Béla Köpeczi and György M. Vajda (eds.) *Actes du VIIIe Congrès de l'Association Internationale de Littérature Comparée / Proceedings of the 8th Congress of the International Comparative Literature Association, II: Littératures de diverses cultures au vingtième siècle / Twentieth Century Literatures Originating in Different Cultures*. Stuttgart: Bieber, 617–62.

Foakes, R. A. 2002: "The Critical Reception of Shakespeare's Tragedies." In Claire McEachern (ed.) *The Cambridge Companion to Shakespearean Tragedy*. Cambridge: Cambridge University Press, 224–40.

George, David (ed.) 2004: *Coriolanus, 1687–1940*. London: Thoemmes Continuum.

Green, Frederick C. 1935 & 1966: *Minuet*. New York: Dutton; London: J. M. Dent and Sons. Reprinted as *Literary Ideas in Eighteenth-Century France*. New York: Frederick Ungar Publishing, 1966.

Haines, C. M. 1925: *Shakespeare in France: Criticism from Voltaire to Victor Hugo*. Oxford: Oxford University Press.

Hardy, Alexandre 1978: *Coriolan*. Ed. Terence Allott. Exeter: Exeter University Printing Unit.

Hogsett, Charlotte 1988: "The Causality of Reform and Counter-Reform." *French Review* 61, 429–32.

Jusserand, J. J. 1898: *Shakespeare sous l'ancien régime*. Paris: Armand Colin.

Kastan, David Scott 1999: "Shakespeare After Theory." In Peter C. Herman (ed.) *Opening the Borders: Inclusivity in Early Modern Studies*. Newark: University of Delaware Press; London: Associated University Presses, pp. 206–24.

Keats, John 1817: *Poems*. London.

La Harpe, Jean François de 1777: *Coriolan*. In *Oeuvres*, II.456–540.

La Harpe, Jean François de 1826: *Lycée, ou Cours de Littérature ancienne et moderne*, 18 vols. Paris: Chez LeDentu et Chez P. Du Pont.

La Harpe, Jean François de 1968: *Oeuvres de La Harpe, de l'Académie Française*, 16 vols. Geneva: Slatkine Reprints.

Larson, Kenneth E. 1989: "Introduction: Traditions and New Directions in the Study of French and German Shakespeare Reception." *The Reception of Shakespeare in Eighteenth Century France and Germany: Special Issue of Michigan Germanic Studies* 15, 103–13.

Le Coat, Nanette C. 1988: "Philosophy vs. Eloquence: Laharpe [*sic*] and the Literary Debate at the École Normale." *French Review* 61, 421–8.

Leggatt, Alexander and Norem, Lois 1989: *Coriolanus: An Annotated Bibliography*. New York: Garland.

Le Tourneur, Pierre 1776: *Shakespeare Traduit de l'anglois, dédié au roi*. Paris: la Veuve Duchesne et al.

Le Tourneur, Pierre 1990: *Préface du Shakespeare traduit de l'anglois.* Ed. Jacques Gury. Geneva: Droz.

Miller, Arnold 1989: "Voltaire's Treason: The Translation of Hamlet's Soliloquy." *Michigan Germanic Studies* 15, 136–59.

Pemble, John 2005: *Shakespeare Goes to Paris: How the Bard Conquered France.* London: Hambledon and London.

Smith, Barbara Herrnstein 1988: *Contingencies of Value: Alternative Perspectives for Critical Theory.* Cambridge, MA: Harvard University Press.

Sproull, G. M. 1939: "The Critical Doctrine of J. F. de la Harpe." PhD dissertation, University of Chicago.

Taylor, Gary 1989: *Reinventing Shakespeare: A Cultural History from the Restoration to the Present Day.* New York: Weidenfeld and Nicolson.

Todd, Christopher 1972: *Voltaire's Disciple: Jean-François de La Harpe.* London: MHRA.

Todd, Christopher 1979: *Bibliographie des oeuvres de Jean François de la Harpe.* Studies on Voltaire and the Eighteenth Century, vol. 181. Oxford: Voltaire Foundation at the Taylor Institution.

Vickers, Brian (ed.) 1974–81: *Shakespeare: The Critical Heritage,* 6 vols. London: Routledge and Kegan Paul.

Wells, Byron 1989: "Translating in Eighteenth-Century France: The Case of Shakespeare's Theatre." *Michigan Germanic Studies* 15, 160–70.

Chapter 12

"Freezing the Snowman": (How) Can We Do Performance Criticism?

Emma Smith

Rationale

I began with the image that director Richard Eyre uses for the theater: that lost, beautiful snowman created by Michelangelo in an unusually severe Florentine winter. Perhaps this was crossed in my mind with Raymond Briggs' graphic fairytale *The Snowman*, which ends, wistfully, with the thought that the whole wonderful adventure never happened at all (the film of the book, directed by Dianne Jackson in 1982, is more sentimental, and less theatrical, in providing a snowman's scarf as material evidence that it did indeed happen). The wonderful, ineffable point is that theater, like the snowmen of Michelangelo and Briggs, is gone. Over. Finished. Irretrievable. Perhaps it never really was; and even if it once was, it now exists only and variously in the transformative memory of its participants and witnesses. "The earth hath bubbles as the water hath," Banquo recognizes, as the witches disappear before his eyes, and Macbeth acknowledges that "what seemed corporal / Melted as breath into the wind" (1.3.77–9).

Performance criticism has become a prominent and exciting aspect of Shakespeare studies in recent years. Accounts of different productions and their interpretation of the plays have placed new emphasis on their particular forms of contingency, destabilized any vestigial belief that they have singular or authorial meanings, and brought the plays into stimulating collision with different theatrical traditions and historical moments. But I think that this deference to the theater has also some critical blindspots, practical problems, and ideological biases which are not often acknowledged. In this essay I concentrate on one particular area: the ways in which performance criticism is always secondary, and sometimes secondarily secondary – removed from the experience of live theater and transformed into writing, as reviews, promptbooks and other records. In this ontological shift from event to text, performance criticism tries to fix the evanescence it purports to value about theater. Play is turned into work, as Barthes might have it.

My sense that the traces of performance intervene between us and the lost theatrical event, or that they substitute for it in ways performance criticism does not always acknowledge, derives from my work on historical performances of *Henry V*. Reading different newspaper reviews of the same production, it quickly became clear that neutral or agreed records of performance do not exist. Our records purport to give us access to the event, but they are in fact always and already critical, interpretive, interpellated in and by critical discourses that are not always immediately visible. Because these documents are all we have, as performance critics we have been unwilling to challenge their evidential content. Relatively little performance studies seems to be theoretically or methodologically reflexive; and, in fact, performance criticism has enabled the return of some otherwise discredited interpretive maneuvers, most notably, unreconstructed Bradleian character criticism in, for example, the *Players of Shakespeare* volumes.

So, what to do? I don't advocate a retreat from the theater. Nor is my contribution to this volume intended as a jeremiad against reviewers, or as a barely disguised exercise in superior understanding – how *not* to do things with Shakespeare. Instead, I propose that we should make up, conjure, imagine, fantasize the productions we want to have seen. I'm arguing that that's essentially what we do anyway, using the props of unknowable historical productions to pursue our own interpretive agendas. So my essay ends with a call to production as fantasy, rather than archeology. I hope this will be a liberating call to armchair directors everywhere, and that we will thus renew our attachment to theater as imagination rather than documentation, to crystalline snow rather than damp woolen scarf.

The kind of things we can do with Shakespeare change over time. When A. C. Sprague wrote in his groundbreaking *Shakespeare and the Actors* that "Shakespeare's plays were written for performance, and surely, through performance, light has been shed on many dark places in them" (Sprague 1944: xxv), he inaugurated a genre of criticism which located interpretive authority in the theater rather than the study. Or, to put it another way, in the theater via the study: Sprague's interest was in historical, rather than contemporary, performance, in that past theatrical history which was, by definition, irretrievable in a manner analogous with that of the Elizabethan theater itself. "To have passed beyond the year of Irving's death [1905]," wrote Sprague in justifying his terminal date, "would have been to intrude upon a time well within living memory, and to court repeated correction at the hands of those who had seen (and even taken part in) English productions which I had not attended": that the productions he discusses are out of reach is an important constituent of his academic authority (Sprague 1944: vii). Like those other more prominently ideological critical interventions of the wartime year 1944 discussed by Graham Holderness in his *Shakespeare Recycled*, therefore, Sprague's work is marked by nostalgia, or by a turn to a Shakespearean past as a comforting supplement to a politically uncertain present.[1] Implicit in Sprague's introduction to his book is the knowledge that because that theatrical past is ultimately unverifiable, it is available to be co-opted for contemporary critical service. And his choice of words – that the lighted, organized space of the stage can cast an interpretive "light" on the sometimes obscure or darkened places in the Shakespearean text – is one to which this chapter will return.

Since Sprague, performance criticism has extended its material range and its institutional hold. Encompassing academic writing about performance, the semiotics of theater and film, performance practitioners describing particular roles or productions, and theatrical history, the reminder that Shakespeare originally wrote for the stage has made its presence felt in university syllabi, in critical editions, and in all aspects of Shakespearean commentary. Gary Taylor's warning that "we mislead ourselves if we imagine a play moving *from* text *to* stage, as though textuality and theatricality were separate entities, or as though one evolved into the other. For Shakespeare, a play began life in the theater" is a reminder much of the academy has already internalized (Taylor 2002: 1). But that abiding sense of nostalgia – that to be written about, performance is already over – intrinsic to performance criticism from the outset is the aspect I want to interrogate in this essay. I discuss the ways in which performance criticism is conducted through substitutes for the performance itself – the textual traces of the evanescent theatrical event – and the ways in which the materiality of these forms prevents them from bearing transparent witness to the lost performance. I use Freud's idea of the fetish as a focus for this discussion, and investigate how the institutional rise of studies of Shakespeare on film seeks to sidestep the problem of the absent text of live performance, despite the fact that film can be conceptualized as itself an aesthetic of absence.

In the end I suggest that performance criticism should embrace, rather than efface, its own radical contingency, by replacing theater archeology with fantasy. Instead of trying to unearth the details of past performances we persist in thinking of as actual, perhaps performance criticism can project forwards, out of the never-was into the never-will-be. Since the lost productions of the past already occupy a space of fantasy which we fill with our own interpretive priorities, we might as well decouple this imaginative process from the semblance of his-torical fact. The real space for doing things with Shakespeare is a ludic theater of the mind, and here I want to encourage readers of Shake-speare to direct their own mental productions, cast their own plays, and fantasize their own staged meanings. Rather than privileging the lost theater of the past, therefore, performance criticism can stand as an individually creative and enabling interpretive strategy, remaking multiple imaginary Shakespeares which enact those fleeting and con-tingent practices of the theater that our critical attempts at perfor-mance analysis threaten to clot.

I want to identify the difficulties of performance criticism under two related headings: the problem of authority – "who" – and the problem of evidence – "how." Performance criticism is one of the most undem-ocratic of recent developments in Shakespearean criticism, since few critics or students of Shakespeare in performance have direct access to the productions they want to consider, not least because the canon of significant productions is constructed of necessity post hoc. There are historical, geographical, cultural, and not least financial reasons why access to live theater is severely limited, and why it thus retains the elitist connotations which until recently attached themselves to higher education itself. These factors mean that the majority of productions discussed as part of the critical discourse on the plays will be accessed via secondary accounts. These secondary accounts themselves derive largely from secondary preserved traces of the performance such as reviews in newspapers or academic journals, promptbooks and other archival material such as costumes, props, set designs, etc. connected with the production, and the still photographs commissioned to memorialize and publicize the production. When Ric Knowles decides to limit the productions in his *Reading the Material Theatre* to those he has himself seen, he is unusual in that most performance criticism is, like Sprague's, concerned with that history of productions unwitnessed by the author (Knowles 2004: 21).

Of course, each of these recoverable categories registers its own generic trace: its own material form discredits its self-appointed role of testimony, making it an imperfect witness to the performance it attests. Reviews, photographic stills, and promptbooks aren't, severally or compositely, the performance, but material proxies for it. This is to say something more than that theater history has had, institutionally, a literary bias. We tend to want to look through the transparent forms of the evidence as if to the performance behind them: rather, the very forms are themselves the opaque texts that in other circumstances should arrest our critical attention.

Take reviews, for example. For the mainstream Shakespearean theater productions with which performance criticism has been traditionally concerned – with the subsidised theaters of the Royal Shakespeare Company and the National Theatre in the UK, and with metropolitan theater or high status festivals in the US – two prominent forms of testimony are journalistic and academic reviews. The fact that theaters and newspapers and journals or the universities which sponsor them coexist in metropolitan centers means that they are mutually reinforcing: so-called "provincial" theater is unlikely to be foregrounded by reviewers, and thus the larger metropolitan theaters perpetuate the sense of their own permanent cultural importance. (This in turn makes it difficult for individual students or readers of Shakespeare to interpolate their own theatrical experiences into the narrative of theater history: non-mainstream or non-professional productions, often those available to people outside large cities, do not seem to have a role in the dramatic canon.) If we consider reviews we can see how, firstly, they establish the categories of performance which they discuss, and secondly, they *make* meanings from these performances rather than recording them: they are acts of criticism which in the necessary absence of the theatrical event substitute for it.

Reviews can show us less what a production was actually *like* and more what meanings were available to a particular professional audience member, attending a particular performance and, crucially, writing for a particular context. All of these factors are important. Firstly, the reviewer is a professional theatergoer and thus, even more than any other single member of an audience, *a priori* unrepresentative of that audience. Secondly, the review is usually based on a single performance, often at the start of a run, and thus it retrospectively homogenizes productions that haven't yet happened at the time of its writing. A review from the press night of a production and one from the thirtieth or three hundredth performance clearly aren't writing about the same thing, and it is not clear whether the general preference in performance criticism for the singular "production" over the plural "performances" is merely academic pragmatism or a real attempt to fix the fluctuating space of performance into a singular text. We sentimentalize theater as a unique event, uniquely susceptible to the vagaries of live audience/ actor interaction, at the same time as we seek to minimize its problematic and empirically undocumented multiplicity. Perhaps the analogy of the now-largely discredited idea of the New Bibliography – the idea of the perfect or ideal text of Shakespeare, which is not any of the texts we actually have but an ideal projection of what the text ought to be like and which used to function as the holy grail of textual criticism and editing – is useful here. More recent bibliographical theory has rubbished this idea of the ideal text, and replaced it with those multiple, heterogeneous, fragmented texts we *do* have and which represent the text in its material relationship to the world – to printers, to readers or audiences at different historical moments. While performance criticism seems to be constitutionally connected to this more contingent textual understanding, it also partakes of the idealizing tendencies of older bibliography.[2] The third factor is that reviews are written for a particular context and readership. This context is important: press books of newspaper reviews such as the invaluable collections kept as part of the Royal Shakespeare Company Archive at the Shakespeare Centre Library in Stratford, tend, for practical reasons, to remove the review from its original context. What this practice tells us is that we are immediately interested in what the reviewer thought of the particular production, not what the front page headline was or what was preoccupying the day's leader writers. But this habitual excision works to disconnect the review from its own discourse within the newspaper and to present it instead as "evidence" of the performance.

Ric Knowles has recently suggested that theater history should proceed from "contextualizing and locating the reviewers themselves within their cultural and journalistic settings, and considering them neither as consumer reporters nor aesthetic judges, but as providers of evidence of receptions and interpretations" (Knowles 2004: 21): we could follow his advice by considering, for example, national press reviews of a contentious production of *Henry V* directed by Nicholas Hytner as part of his opening season as artistic director of London's National Theatre in 2003, against the background of the US/UK war in Iraq. I have elsewhere discussed the intimate relation between *Henry V*'s stage history and war ever since its first performances in 1599: publicity for the National Theatre production made every attempt to draw parallels between Henry's war in France and the campaign by premiers Bush and Blair against Saddam Hussein, particularly focused around questions of the legitimacy of going to war (Smith 2002). *Henry V* had already been explicitly implicated in the Iraq conflict, with an address to British troops on the eve of the attack on Basra by Lieutenant Colonel Tim Collins – "Henry V in aviator sunglasses" – widely seen as a modern version of Henry's St. Crispin's Day before the battle of Agincourt (*Observer*, January 23, 2005).

Reviewers were not slow to pick up the cues from this widely touted topical production and to compare it to the war which elsewhere dominated their newspapers. What is striking about this process, however, is how closely the reviews of the Shakespearean performance echo the host papers' editorial line on the war. Theater reviewers comment on *Henry V* along the lines established by their newsroom colleagues' commentary on Iraq. Thus Charles Spencer's review for the *Daily Telegraph* felt that "when Henry galvanizes his troops on the eve of Agincourt, it is impossible not to recall the wise and beautiful words of Lt. Col. Tim Collins at Basra," and argued that "between them, Hytner and [Adrian] Lester have made Henry neither patriotic hero, nor warmongering villain, but a man caught in the moral no-man's land of war that lies between" (*Daily Telegraph*, May 15, 2003). In this sympathetic interpretation of Lester's performance of Henry, Spencer echoes the broadly sympathetic coverage of the Iraq war in his newspaper. One example will have to stand for many. A few days before Spencer's review, a *Daily Telegraph* editorial strongly supported government plans for a thanksgiving and (premature, as subsequent events have revealed) victory parade: "as the debate about the appropriate form of celebration continues, the grounds for gratitude should not be forgotten. A hideous tyranny that threatened the stability of the Middle East and beyond has been overthrown. Thanks to huge advances in weapons technology since the first Gulf war, the casualties were remarkably low. Under allied tutelage, Iraq now has the chance of becoming a model of democracy and prosperity in a region chronically short of both" (*Daily Telegraph*, May 9, 2003).

So the *Daily Telegraph* broadly supported the war in Iraq, and its reviewer interprets Hytner's production as broadly supportive of Henry's own campaign in France. As the caption to one of the production photographs reproduced in the newspaper suggests, "[Lester's] Henry V invites comparisons with Tony Blair": and Spencer's review works simultaneously as commentary on the prime minister and the Shakespearean character. Ultimately, in both cases, "his genuine anguish and courage" outweigh the negative aspects of his characterization and the situation in which he finds himself. Hytner's production allows the *Telegraph* reader to deplore the war and praise Blair's leadership qualities. If we compare this to Michael Billington's review in the *Guardian*, a paper with a more ambivalent editorial line on the war in Iraq, we can see something of how the political context of the newspaper impacts on the theatrical review.

For Billington, Hytner's approach is consistently "satiric . . . and at no point does he let Henry off the hook." He sees the production as having "pacifist leanings," but wishes "it had a bit more emotional ambivalence." Billington's review stresses the negative aspects of Henry's characterization which hardly feature in the *Daily Telegraph* review – his execution of Bardolph, his threats to the citizens of Harfleur, his order for the French prisoners to be killed – but expresses a wish that the production had allowed Lester "to give us a hint of the king's residual humanity" (*Guardian*, May 14, 2003). Parallel to the newspaper's attitude to the prime minister, that is, Billington *wants* to be allowed to sympathize with Henry. This chimes with the tone of the paper's ambivalent coverage of the Iraq war, in, for example, these two leader articles: "This war is wrong. It did not need to happen; it is unnecessary and was avoidable"; "Tony Blair's televised address to the nation last night was rightly sombre. There was not a word in it of false optimism, facile nationalism or glib tabloid militarism" (*Guardian*, March 20, 2003; March 21, 2003).

What is striking about these reviews, therefore, is how difficult it is to use them to arrive at any view of the production itself. Was it essentially pro- or contra- Henry? Was it "satiric" (Billington) or "a genuine National epic" (Spencer)? Taken together, the two reviews identify something of the conflict between these positions that many critics have seen in the play itself, memorably captured in Norman Rabkin's abiding image of the gestalt "rabbit duck" drawing (Rabkin 1981). They can give us only a very shifting and contradictory sense of where the production stood, and, as we have seen, the different reviewers report on the play in a way which is shaped by the political context in which they are writing. Hytner's *Henry V* has vanished, replaced by the newspaper coverage of the Iraq war of which these reviews form a part. The reviews can tell us only about the context of the production rather than about the production itself: performed Shakespeare is here a pretext for continuing the debate about the war which is pursued elsewhere in the same edition of the papers.

Part of this context for theatrical reviews in newspapers is their different audience, purpose, and context from reviews in academic journals. The newspaper, like the theater production, is itself an essentially ephemeral form: the review has an immediate, rather than archival, purpose. When, on the other hand, Robert Smallwood writes in *Shakespeare Survey* about the previous year's significant Shakespeare productions, the function is more about memorializing and recording in a form which will continue to be available for consultation and report. We might expect – want – a newspaper review to be opinionated, but feel that academic reviewing should be more descriptive, neutral, transparent. Here, too, we need to attend to the dense materiality of the genre.

Academic accounts of Shakespeare productions seen by the reviewer tend to eschew, like much academic writing on other subjects, the first person, whereas for theater critics in newspapers, their own persona is crucial to their critical authority. In his *Shakespeare Survey* pieces, Smallwood almost never uses the first person, preferring the "we" of an unspecified, shared response, despite the fact that his observations are, necessarily, his own. Did all viewers of the RSC's 1999 *Antony and Cleopatra*, for instance, find that "there was something rawly embarrassing about the needy, desperate, manipulative woman that Frances de la Tour presented and about her slightly absurd, slightly grotesque, passion for Antony," or should this comment be taken as a personal response, disguised by the apparently objective academic register "there was . . ."? When Smallwood writes in the same piece, after a disappointing visit north to see Sir Ian McKellen performing

Prospero, "One had travelled to Leeds to hear a star actor speak Shakespeare and the surprises were worth the journey. Nothing else in the production was," who is the "one" – why not I? – and who are the implicit auditors of this remark? Clearly not citizens of Leeds (Smallwood 2000: 248, 267).[3] Smallwood, like many other academic reviewers, at once takes on the mantle of authoritative interpretation even in the act of memorializing the productions for those who will never see them, but the curious syntactic absence of the first person attempts to evade the necessary subjectivity of this process. The double singularity of "one" performance and "one" individual combine in a partial account which cannot bear witness to the multiplicity of actual performances.

The point here is that reviews cannot give us access to the lost performance. They are at once the evidence of, or substitute for, the performance (the substitute "primary" text) and the already critical interpretation of that text (the parasitic "secondary" text). Or they demand that we acknowledge the theoretical and practical impossibility of maintaining that distinction. Instead, reviews are marked by their own material form as they present themselves as imperfect substitutes for the event to which they profess to attest. Even the term "review," with its impossible promise of "seeing again," establishes expectations it cannot fulfill.

We could argue something similar about all the other sources of apparent evidence about past performance. Promptbooks replace the flow of scenes and individuals with the static hieroglyphics denoting stage blocking and directorial cuts. Iconic photographic images from productions freeze dynamic moments of interaction into two-dimensional form, often cropping areas of "empty" theatrical space to focus on a tightly framed central character. Often, the medium or close-up shot presents a view of the theatrical action which no spectator in the theater could ever have seen: instead of the standard view of the stage framed with intervening rows of spectators, areas of spotlit and darker space, distant figures blocked into patterns on the stage, we get an idealized, cinematically framed fantasy of proximity to the key actors. Production images tend to represent theater as film, replacing the scopic freedom of live performance which must perforce allow spectators to look wherever they please at any given moment, with the restrictive *mise-en-scène* of the directorially controlled cinematic point of view, and as such, they are profoundly unrepresentative of the experience of the play.

Practical difficulties about reproducing images also mean that the ratio of words to pictures in published performance criticism is heavily skewed. In influential publications such as the valuable *Players of Shakespeare* series from Cambridge University Press, ensemble productions are viewed through the perspective of one of the lead actors, with illustrations corroborating this star centrality. A picture accompanying Nigel Hawthorne's discussion of his performance of King Lear, for example, in which Lear, crowned with a sunburst coronet, rants and a pigtailed Cordelia looks quizzically from the left-hand edge of the frame illustrates a moment from act 1 scene 1: the photograph gives no sense that the scene also includes, at least, Lear's other two daughters, their husbands, Kent, and what the stage direction calls "attendants." The idea that this is a moment between Lear and Cordelia is a post-hoc photographic construction. When in the same volume Philip Voss discusses his performance of Prospero, it is striking that the racial implications of the accompanying illustration, in which he cradles the black actor Nikki Amuki-Bird who plays Miranda, are never mentioned: the volume refocuses *The Tempest* as *Prospero*, with both pictures and words reducing the challenge of live performances to a version of old-fashioned character study (Smallwood 2003).

Reading the material traces of performance as practiced in performance criticism involves, then, a series of unsatisfactory substitutions: archival research reifies the absent performance event into a series of metonymic texts. As a discipline which has emerged from that of literary studies, performance criticism has been insistently textual. The textual substitutes for performance carry their own markers, which means that they serve less as lenses through which to perceive the performance and more as obstacles to its recovery, supplementary textual artifacts which simultaneously promise and refuse transparency. That words on pages stand in for bodies on stages is less a convenience of memorial storage and more, perhaps, the desire of Shakespeareans that this newer critical arena conform to those kinds of verbal analysis with which it has long felt comfortable. Shannon Jackson has called this institutional process of assimilation "a narcissism of minor samenesses": an obverse of damaging institutional splits over the so-called "culture wars" in which disparate disciplinary inquiries can be bunched together to give an illusory sense of belonging (Jackson 2004). In making performance studies more like the textual analysis dominant elsewhere in literary studies, therefore, we have effectively neutralized the radical challenge posed by this contingent form to our critical praxis.

It is in this light that we might consider the rise of film in Shake-spearean pedagogy and criticism. Aided by technological developments which have privatized the ownership and consumption of film, first via video and now DVD, Shakespeare on film has become a dominant disciplinary constituent. And it is easy to think that this resolves the problem of the absent critical text of performance. While we can none of us see Hytner's *Henry V* – that impossibility of "re-viewing" – we *can* see Kenneth Branagh's (1989) or Olivier's (1944) film version of that play. We replay, rewind, freeze-frame. We can watch it together or separately, and discuss what we have seen, and then watch it again. We can juxtapose scenes – the different depictions of Agincourt, for example, or the interpretations of the episcopal conspiracy of 1.1. – or review the whole text. In place of the vanished performance on the stage we have the apparently durable textual artifact of film. But this is where the study of Shakespeare on film, particularly as it is deployed within teaching and criticism, offers itself, too, as a kind of absence.

This is in part an ontological point. Since Walter Benjamin's "The Work of Art in the Age of Mechanical Reproduction," the absent simultaneity of actor and audience in cinema has been asserted as its crucial point of departure from its theatrical origins. Benjamin sees it as the forfeiting of the actor's aura: "for aura is tied to his presence; there can be no replica of it" (Benjamin 1992: 223). Christian Metz puts it from a different perspective: at the cinema, "not only am I at a distance from the object, as in the theater, but what remains in that distance is now no longer the object itself, but is a delegate it has sent me while itself withdrawing" (Metz 1975: 62). We know that films are composed in the editing studio from a number of discontinuous shots, a collage of moments stitched into a fictionally diachronic narrative, and we also know that where we have apparent evidence for that narrative, such as a published screenplay, these documents are avowedly fictive. When, as Laurie E. Osborne observes, "Ian McKellen reveals that he finished the manuscript for the screenplay edition [of *Richard III*] on the same day that Loncraine completed editing of the film, this coincidence effectively insures that the text cannot be a fully accurate representation of the actual film production": the screenplay is a rival product, not a testimony (Osborne 2005: 174). Cinema thus dramatizes the absence of its subject: it is a medium of that absence. Rather than casting light, it *is* light.

This has practical consequences, too. If it is true that cinema circles around the same absence – is crucially dependent on that absence – as performance criticism itself, it follows that to take filmed Shakespeare as the focus of our critical energies is to distance ourselves from our ostensible object in ways which may by now seem familiar. It is as if the object of critical desire, the theatrical performance, continues to be in infinite regress. But even without this sense of inevitable belatedness, we can see that the availability of filmed Shakespeare, long after its original "theatrical" release, means that certain historically constituted meanings are lost. The film lives in a suspended state, contrary to its own contingent placing in the cultural moment in which it participated. In encouraging us into a false syntax of the present tense, unlike the past tense used to discuss past theatrical performances, that is to say, the reviewable film attempts to deny the historicity which is performance criticism's most valuable insight, offering itself in an illusory continuous present. For instance, we might think that Laurence Olivier's *Hamlet* (1948) has been done few favors by its deracination from the mannered Shakespearean verse delivery and matinee-idol posing of mid-century theatrical and cinematic conventions. Few modern viewers can access the excitement of contemporary spectators; watching the film now is more likely to prompt laughter than tragic awe. Similarly, when viewing the Russian film of *Hamlet* directed by Grigori Kozintsev in 1964 now, the specific connotations of the casting of the dissident Innokenti Smoktunovsky in the central role are entirely lost. These limited examples indicate that changes over time in acting style and expectations on the one hand, and historically and culturally specific meanings on the other, each challenge the apparent fixity of the film text in performance criticism.

That the magical illusion of theater becomes instead the self-deluding illusion of disciplinary sameness and of the recoverability of the fugitive dramatic event, indicates how far the practices of performance criticism have moved from its ostensible object. Perhaps, though, this process of critical substitution is axiomatic rather than extraordinary. As Douglas Lanier acknowledges, "the question of how to conduct Shakespearean criticism in the absence of a determinant critical object has preoccupied many in our critical generation" (Lanier 1996: 188): performance criticism's "determinant critical object" is the shadow of the theatrical event, as attested by its substitutive material traces, rather analogous to bibliography's lost determinant of the authorial manuscript, and historicism's lost determinant of those "dead" voices with whom Greenblatt famously desired to speak (Greenblatt 1988: 1). Contemporary literary criticism might be seen as an art of writing about something it simultaneously constructs and anatomizes: perfor-mance criticism's central absence is thus a figure, a substitutive meta-phor, for the unknowable critical object itself.

A number of different metaphors can clarify the precise contours of the aporia at the heart of performance criticism. Robert Shaughnessy has written of performance criticism as "a fundamentally elegiac critical form": "in its attempts to reconstruct an authoritative record through the sifting of the fragmentary and contradictory textual traces of dead productions, the stage history frequently reaches towards the imagined felt life of a vanished performance," a formulation which suggestively links performance criticism with the art of biography. W. B. Worthen approaches the same theme when he states that "performance signifies an absence, the precise fashioning of the material text's absence, at the same time that it appears to summon the work into being, to produce it as performance"; Peggy Phelan warns against responding to the loss of performance by memorializing it, "for what one otherwise preserves is an illustrated corpse" (Shaughnessy 1994: 31; Worthen 1997: 17; Phelan 1997: 3).[4] The director Richard Eyre made a lyrical analogy with another art form, beginning – appropriately – a television series on the British theater in the twentieth century. The theatrical perfor-mance, Eyre argued, is the equivalent of Michelangelo's most perfect creation – a snowman built for Piero di Medici in the courtyard of the Medici palace in Florence. Michelangelo's snowman was perfect despite, or rather because of, its ephemerality. After the unprecedent-edly cold winter days of January 1494 the sculpture melted, leaving no trace behind. There's little documentary evidence to support this anecdote and thus it's a doubly wonderful image of a dissolving and transient aesthetic beauty, perfectly suited to the art of the theater.

If performance criticism is elegy, its function is to bear witness to a death it is powerless to prevent. If it is a kind of critical cold-storage, it attempts to arrest the melting of the illusion of the theater. But there is another kind of paradigm that is useful here in its stress on the material surrogates for a traumatic visual experience: Freud's concept of fetishism. What would it mean to say that performance criticism has fetishized the material traces of the theater?

For Freud, the fetish object – fetishism is always material – is a sub-stitute for the maternal phallus in which the young child believed prior to the abiding castration anxiety brought on the discovery of its loss.

In Freud's 1927 essay "Fetishism," fetishism is clearly connected to the visual. The only case in his essay is of that of a young man who "had exalted a certain kind of 'shine on the nose' into a fetishistic precondition." The "shine on the nose" needed to be understood in English as a "glance at the nose." While Freud argues that the nose is the fetish object, the substitute for the maternal phallus, the "glance," the act of looking, becomes itself significant. Fear of castration is itself "fright at the *sight* of the female genital" (my italics); the inquisitive boy "peered at the woman's genitals from below" and preferred fetish objects, such as feet, shoes, fur, velvet and pieces of underclothing, all related to the process of visual perception, concealment, and display (Freud 1991: 351, 355, 354).[5] Fetish objects either mask the discovery of the truth of female castration or halt the process of that discovery, but they attempt both to preserve the belief in the mother's penis from extinction even as their existence necessarily attests to its loss. They form a visual replacement for something the subject never wanted to see; they substitute for the belief in the mother's penis that the boy does not want to relinquish. The idea, therefore, that the fetish stands in place of, or even precludes, that sight which is both desired and feared, is interesting in relation to the protocols of performance criticism. That the fetish substitutes for something – the maternal phallus – that never was in the first place is doubly significant in thinking of the textual traces of theatrical performance as Shakespearean critical fetish.

Most interesting – and here we can return to Sprague's original claim for the relevance of Shakespeare in performance to an understanding of the plays – is Freud's engagement in the essay "Fetishism" with the suitability of the word "scotomization." Scotomize comes from the Greek, "to darken" or make obscure, and it refers to the psychic processes by which the subject refuses to see clearly. While Freud suggests that this "new technical term," derived from the French psychoanalyst Rene Laforgue, is unnecessary, since the familiar *Verleugnung*, translated as "disavowal," will serve, he goes on to use "scotomization" to describe fetishistic substitution. The fetishist's experience is a kind of visual disturbance, a darkening, a scotomization. Like the fetishist, then, we as performance critics are in the kind of self-imposed darkness – the unlit house rather than the spotlit stage – sitting in the dark after the performance is over. Far from casting light on the darkened texts *pace* Sprague therefore, performance criticism represents a fetishistic scotomizing: the willed darkening of the memory of the past.

So far, then, I have been arguing for the fictiveness of those processes by which performance criticism attempts to reconstitute the lost
productions which are its ostensible object. The point about live
theater – its ontological nature, that which makes it theatrical – is its
evanescence. The fetishistic substitution of textual substitutes to arrest
or mask this transience merely mystifies the inescapable conclusion that
we are inventing, rather than recovering, these past events. So how
does that help us do things with Shakespeare?

While thinking about my contribution to this book, I have been
attempting to suppress the vaguely suggestive connotations of its title
– and as with all recognitions of innuendo, particularly in formal contexts, I confess this rather awkwardly lest it seem puerile. But if "How
to do things with Shakespeare" does have a hint of the user's guide to
experimentation at once critical and sexual, it does so within a very
particular context. Most of us are with Shakespeare for the long term,
perhaps not exclusively, but nevertheless, committedly. This is a continuing critical partnership rather than a single night of hermeneutic
rapture. So we are looking to keep the magic alive, to combine familiar
intimacy with excitement. Fantasy – imagining how things might be –
hurts no one, as the sexologists tell us: perhaps this could be true for
performance studies, too. And since all we can ever do when we try to
cite and interpret the theater of the past is to reconstruct it for our own
purposes, we might unfetter this imaginative process into something
like, on the model of fantasy football, fantasy performance.

Fantasy football managers can pick any player for their squad;
fantasy Shakespearean directors can take any actors, settings, concepts,
or blocking for their production. Fantasy Shakespeare is almost end-
lessly permissive. As Dennis Kennedy observes,

> though normally based upon an idea or a vision engendered by the
> words of a play, stage, costume, and lighting design can easily disregard
> or transcend both the words and the notional setting, reminding us that
> though performance may seek as its goal the faithful transmittal of the
> dramatist's writing, it need not do so. We are also reminded that ideas
> about what constitutes fidelity are shifting; they may encompass a fidel-
> ity to the spirit of the play as understood at a given moment as well as
> a literal fidelity to the details of its fable. (Kennedy 2001: 9)

Fidelity in fantasy is not required; that's why it's fantasy. If a reader
wants to cast Heath Ledger as Coriolanus or Sharon Stone as Gertrude, why not? If she or he wants to set *Two Gentlemen of Verona* in

a locker room or *The Tempest* in purple silk, why not? Often, we use past performances to authenticate or make possible our own imaginative responses: fantasy performance frees us from that deference to the past. By refocusing the energies of performance criticism towards dramatic fantasy rather than dramatic recovery, we can do something really creative with Shakespeare.

Notes

1   Holderness (1992: ch. 7) discusses G. Wilson Knight's "The Olive and the Sword," E. M. W. Tillyard's *Shakespeare's History Plays*, and Laurence Olivier's film of *Henry V*.
2   For an elaboration of what is here a rather truncated argument, see de Grazia and Stallybrass (1993) and Berger and Lander (1999).
3   Smallwood's analysis here might be compared with those examples collected in Fitz's (1977) provocative essay.
4   Phelan quoted in Hodgdon (2005: 8).
5   Marjorie Garber (1990) has written engagingly with adjacent themes in her "Shakespeare as Fetish."

Works Cited

Barthes, Roland 1979: "From Work to Text." In Josué V. Harari (ed.) *Textual Strategies: Perspectives in Post-Structuralist Criticism*. Ithaca: Cornell University Press, 73–81.
Benjamin, Walter 1992: "The Work of Art in the Age of Mechanical Reproduction." In *Illuminations*. London: Fontana Press.
Berger, Thomas L. and Lander, Jesse M. 1999: "Shakespeare in Print, 1593–1640." In David Scott Kastan (ed.) *A Companion to Shakespeare*. Oxford: Blackwell.
Fitz, L. 1977: "Egyptian Queens and Male Reviewers: Sexist Attitudes in *Antony and Cleopatra* Criticism." *Shakespeare Quarterly* 28, 297–316.
Freud, Sigmund 1991: "Fetishism." In *The Penguin Freud Library 7: On Sexuality*. London: Penguin.
Garber, Marjorie 1990: "Shakespeare as Fetish." *Shakespeare Quarterly* 41, 242–50.
de Grazia, Margreta and Stallybrass, Peter 1993: "The Materiality of the Shakespearean Text." *Shakespeare Quarterly* 44, 255–83.
Greenblatt, Stephen 1988: *Shakespearean Negotiations: The Circulation of Social Energy in Renaissance England*. Oxford: Clarendon Press.

Hodgdon, Barbara 2005: "Introduction: A Kind of History." In Barbara Hodgdon and W. B. Worthen (eds.) *A Companion to Shakespeare and Performance*. Oxford: Blackwell.

Holderness, Graham 1992: *Shakespeare Recycled: The Making of Historical Drama*. Hemel Hempstead: Harvester Wheatsheaf.

Jackson, Shannon 2004: *Professing Performance: Theater in the Academy from Philology to Performativity*. Cambridge: Cambridge University Press.

Kennedy, Dennis 2001: *Looking At Shakespeare: A Visual History of Twentieth-Century Performance*, 2nd edn. Cambridge: Cambridge University Press.

Knowles, Ric 2004: *Reading the Material Theatre*. Cambridge: Cambridge University Press.

Lanier, Douglas 1996: "Drowning the Book: *Prospero's Books* and the Textual Shakespeare." In James C. Bulman (ed.) *Shakespeare, Theory and Performance*. London: Routledge.

Metz, Christian 1975: "The Imaginary Signifier." *Screen* 16, 14–76.

Osborne, Laurie E. 2005: "Shakespearean Screen/Play." In Barbara Hodgdon and W. B. Worthen (eds.) *A Companion to Shakespeare and Performance*. Oxford: Blackwell.

Phelan, Peggy 1997: *Mourning Sex: Performing Public Memories*. London: Routledge.

Rabkin, Norman 1981: *Shakespeare and the Problem of Meaning*. Chicago: University of Chicago Press.

Shaughnessy, Robert 1994: *Representing Shakespeare: England, History and the RSC*. Hemel Hempstead: Harvester Wheatsheaf.

Smallwood, Robert 2000: "Shakespeare Performances in England, 1999." *Shakespeare Survey* 53, 244–73.

Smallwood, Robert (ed.) 2003: *Players of Shakespeare 5*. Cambridge: Cambridge University Press.

Smith, Emma (ed.) 2002: *Shakespeare in Production: King Henry V*. Cambridge: Cambridge University Press.

Sprague, A. C. 1944: *Shakespeare and the Actors: The Stage Business in his Plays (1660–1905)*. Cambridge, MA: Harvard University Press.

Taylor, Gary 2002: "Shakespeare Plays on Renaissance Stages." In Stanley Wells and Sarah Stanton (eds.) *The Cambridge Companion to Shakespeare on Stage*. Cambridge: Cambridge University Press.

Worthen, W. B. 1997: *Shakespeare and the Authority of Performance*. Cambridge: Cambridge University Press.

Index

Abbott, George, Archbishop of
    Canterbury   89
Act for the Restraint of Abuses   73
Adelman, Janet   222–3
aesthetics   274n.
    in film   283
    neoclassical   263
    relation to politics   277n.
Aethiopica   35–43, 45, 48–51
affinity   *see* antipathy
All is True   see Shakespeare, *Henry
    VIII*
Allott, Robert   143
Alpers, Svetlana   204
amplitude and plenitude   262
animals   185–206, 210–27
    animal studies   186–8
    dogs   185–206
    and the economy   187, 210–11,
        214, 217–18
    in film   187
    and identity   199
    and loyalty   213
    horses   187
    in hunting   212
    mistreatment of animals   219
    in performance   192–4
    in philosophy   187–8

poultry   220
and reason   188, 194
references to dogs in
    Shakespeare   212–13, 214,
    215
sheep   216–19
versus humans   195
welfare organizations   186
see also urination
antipathy   8, 12–32
Apollonius of Tyre   37–8
apostasy   112
Aquinas, Thomas   201
Aristotle   37, 45, 47, 200, 202,
    267–8
Armstrong, Philip   187
Ascham, Roger   61
Asquith, Clare   103
Aubrey, John   72
Auden, W. H.   27, 30

Baker, Richard   154
Baldwin, T. W.   60, 61, 64
Barnes, Barnabe   246
Barroll, Leeds   46
Barton, Anne   119
Basse, William   142
Bate, Jonathan   275n.

Beadle, Richard   193
Beaumont, Francis   143, 145
  see also Fletcher, John
beauty   267, 270
Belvedere   107
Benjamin, Walter   291
Bentley, G. E.   46
Bérenger, Jean   89
Berger, Thomas L.   296n.
Berry, Edward   211
Bible   9, 54, 59
  Acts   67
  1 Corinthians   60, 64, 66, 67
  Ecclesiastes   59
  Ezekiel   67
  Genesis   63, 65
  Isaiah   68, 69
  Luke   71
  Mark   68
  Matthew   60, 61, 63, 64, 65,
    67, 68, 74
  1 Peter   71
  Proverbs   59, 60, 64, 69, 218
  Psalms   59, 65, 215
  Revelations   63
  see also St. Paul
Bible translations
  Bishops' Bible   63–4, 66, 69, 71
  Coverdale   69
  Geneva Bible   60, 64–5, 66, 69
  King James   64, 65, 215, 218
  Tyndale   125n.
  Vulgate   62, 125n.
Biblical plays   70
Billington, Michael   287–8
Bilton, Peter   7
Blayney, Peter   141
Bliss, Lee   47, 88
Bliss, Matthew   193
Blount, Thomas   147
Bluett, Henry   87
Boccaccio, Giovanni   97n.
Boehrer, Bruce   194, 199, 211

Bohannon, Laura   274n.
Boleyn, Anne   86
Booth, Stephen   268
Bouhours, Dominique   20
Boutcher, Warren   14
Bowden, Peter   214
Brabant   112
Brahe, Tycho   188, 189, 196
Branam, George   277
Bray, Alan   203
Britain, Roman   36, 47–9
Brockbank, Philip   7
Brockliss, L. W. B.   89
Brome, Richard   148
Brooks, Harold   193
Brown, John Russell   263, 276n.
Bullen, A. H.   125n.
Bullough, Geoffrey   95
Bunyan, John   68
Burke, Kenneth   106
Burt, Jonathan   187
Bush, Douglas   37
Butterfield, Herbert   86

Campbell, Kathleen   193
Candido, Joseph   95
canon
  and adaptation   262
  and ambiguity   262
  and biography   260
  and canon formation   257–63
  and class   261–2
  and didactic literature   260
  and genre   258–9
  and interpretation   262
  and intertextuality   260
  and means of production   259,
    273n.
  and medium   259, 274n.
  and patronage   259, 273–4n.
Capell, Edward   13
Cardano, Girolamo   31n.
Cardinal Wolsey   88

1 Cardinal Wolsey 88
Carpenter, Richard   217
Carr, Robert, earl of Somerset   90
Cartwright, William   140, 148
Catholic League   103, 116, 126n.
Catholicism   102–29
Cave, Terence   15
Cawdry, Robert   112
Caxton, William   58
Cecil, Robert, earl of Salisbury   89, 91
censorship   55, 72–3
Cervantes, Miguel de   56
Chambers, E. K.   70, 73, 125n.
Chapman, George   75, 126n.
Charles de Bourbon, Cardinal   116
Charles, prince (son of James I)   94
Chaucer, Geoffrey   61, 89, 167
Cheney, Patrick   137
children   223–5
   illegitimate   223
   infanticide   223, 225
Children of the Queen's Revels   46, 47
Cicero   61, 62, 199
Cipolla, Carlo   253
civility   195, 196, 198, 201, 202, 203
Clark, A. M.   125n.
classics   8–9, 11
   classical tags   62
   Greek drama   16
   Greek romance   36–8, 45, 47–50
   influence of   37, 45, 46, 51
Clayton, F. W.   124n.
Cogswell, Tom   93
Coleridge, Hartley   72–3
Colie, Rosalie   246
collaboration   163, 170–2, 177
Collier, Jeremy   72
commonplace books   55, 58–9, 137, 142, 144, 155n.

commonplaces   14, 18
Condell, Henry   88, 258
Coote, Edmund   112
copytext   162–3, 178
Corum, Richard   126n.
Cowley, Abraham   154
Cranmer, Thomas   217
criticism
   comparative   11–32
   feminist   1
   lexical studies   12, 14
   methodologies   2, 55, 80, 102, 185, 273n., 282, 290–1
   New Bibliography   162, 285
   New Criticism   7, 79
   New Historicism   34, 79–80
   performance criticism   234–5, 280–96
   Renaissance literary criticism   45
Cross, Henry   70
cues, actors'   135
cultural capital   257–8

Daniel, Samuel   126n.
Dante   12, 266, 267, 269
Davenant, William   149, 152
death, fake   39, 41
De Grazia, Margreta   296n.
De Jean, Joan   266
Dekker, Thomas   138, 142, 148, 150
De La Boétie, Étienne   21, 29
Della Porta, Giovanni Battista   31n.
Demosthenes   61, 62
dénouement   42
Derrida, Jacques   187
Desan, Philippe   14
Dessen, Alan   151
Devereux, Robert, earl of Essex   90
Dobson, Michael   193–4, 199, 263, 275n., 276n.
Doleman, R. *see* Persons, Robert
Donne, John   56, 260

Draxe, Thomas 218
Drayton, Michael 126n.
Du Bartas, Guillaume de
  Salluste 106, 111
Duffy, Eamon 105
education 55, 57–67, 70
eighteenth century 63–73, 256,
  257

Elias, Norbert 197, 198
Eliot, George 55, 71
Eliot, T. S. 12, 79, 261
Elizabeth, princess (daughter of
  James I) 95
Elizabeth I 113
  succession crisis 117–21
Elliot, J. H. 89
Ellrodt, Robert 14–15
Elze, Karl 95
England, relations with France
  103
England's Helicon 107
England's Parnassus 107
English sensibility 263, 275n.
epic 37, 48
epyllion 233
Erasmus, Desiderius 56, 58, 62,
  66
Erne, Lukas 13, 133, 136, 137,
  141, 166, 168
Ewbank, Inga-Stina 191

Feil, J. P. 73
Felperin, Howard 89
Field, Richard 125n.
film 289, 291–2
  Branagh *Henry V* 125n., 291
  Kozintsev *Hamlet* 292
  Olivier *Henry V* 291
  Olivier *Hamlet* 292
Fiston, William 196
Fitz, Linda 296n.
Fitzgeffrey, Henry 141

Fleay, F. G. 125n.
Fletcher, John 45, 88
  Beaumont and Fletcher 46, 166
Fletcher, John (not the dramatist)
  195–6
  see also Shakespeare, *Henry VIII*
    and *Two Noble Kinsmen*
Florio, John 13
  see also Montaigne
Foakes, R. A. 86–7, 88, 95, 263,
  275n.
Forcione, Alban 37
Ford, John 149
Fowler, Elizabeth 183
Foxe, John 83
France 103, 256–79
French religious wars 102, 107,
  117–18, 122, 126n.
Frederick, Elector Palatine 95
Freeman, Arthur 124n.
Freud, Sigmund 283, 293–4
friendship 21–5, 199–203
Frye, Northrop 89
Fulbecke, W. 126n.

Gallagher, Lowell 104
Garber, Marjorie 296n.
Garrett, M. 73
Gascoigne, George 246
Gayton, Edmund 158
Gell, Robert 93–4
George, David 263
genre 8–9, 15, 34–50, 101–30,
  147, 227, 246
Gesner, Carol 36
Gilbert, Sandra 1
Goffe, Thomas 149
Gold, Field of the Cloth of 91,
  96
Goldberg, Jonathan 7
Gosson, Stephen 38
Gower, John 37–8
Grafton, Anthony 10

Green, Frederick   275n., 276n.,
    277n.
Greenblatt, Stephen   7, 29, 197,
    292–3
Greene, Robert   37
Greenhalgh, Darlene   7
Greg, W. W.   125n., 162
Gregory, T.   104, 115
Grey, Catherine   118
grief   40–2
Grinke, Paul   124n.
Guarini, Giambattista   45, 46, 47
Gubar, Susan   1
Gurr, Andrew   125n., 147

Hackel, Heidi   10
Haines, C. M.   275n., 276n., 277n.
Halio, Jay   89
Hall, Edward   83
Hall, Joseph   37, 143
Harington, John   199
harmony   268
Harris, Jonathan Gil   7
Hart, James   196
Harvey, Gabriel   103, 111
Hatlen, Burton   198
Heliodorus   see Aethiopica
Heminge(s), John   88, 258
Henke, Robert   45, 47
Henri III   115
Henry, prince of Wales (son of
    James I)   94, 95
Henslowe, Philip   70
Herbert, Philip, earl of
    Pembroke   89
Heresbach, Conrad   211, 220
Heywood, Thomas   143
Hibbard, G. R.   162, 168
Holderness, Graham   282
Holinshed, Raphael   7, 83
Holmes, P.   118
Höltgen, Karl   188
Homer   36, 48, 61, 167

Hope, Jonathan   46
Howard, Frances   90
humanism   see education
Hurstfield, Joel   79, 118

identity   21, 23–4, 198–9, 201,
    210
Infanta Isabella of Spain   118
intertext   13

Jackson, Shannon   290
James I (and VI)   86, 118
James, Heather   48
Jardine, Lisa   10
Je-Ne-Sais-Quoi   12–32
Johnson, Samuel   35
Jones, Zachary   31–2n.
Jonson, Ben   58, 69, 72, 73, 74–5,
    89, 126n., 143, 145–6, 147,
    151
Jowett, John   175
Jusserand, J. J.   264, 275n., 276n.

Kastan, David Scott   120, 274n.
Kean, Hilda   187
Kennedy, Dennis   295
Kermode, Frank   89
Kerrigan, John   247
Kipling, Rudyard   69
Knight, Charles   170–1
knowledge   12
Knowles, Ric   284, 285
Kyd, Thomas   149–50

La Harpe, Jean-François de   263–73
    see also Lycée
Lake, Peter   89–90, 93
Lamb, Mary Ellen   103
Lander, Jesse   296n.
Lanier, Douglas   292
La Place   263–4
Larson, Kenneth   263, 264,
    275–6n.

Latour, Bruno 187
law 25
   see also trial
Lawrence, W. J. 155
Le Loyer, Pierre 31–2n.
Lesser, Zachary 46
Le Tourneur 265, 270
Lever, J. W. 79
literary versus performative
   see reading versus performance
Lodge, Thomas 126n., 150, 246
Longus, *Daphne and Chloe* 37
Lope de Vega 267, 269
Lord Have Mercy Upon Us 151
Lycée, ou Cours de littérature
   ancienne et moderne 265–73

McDonald, Russ 13
Maclean, Ian 13
McLeod, Randall 162
McMillin, Scott 165
McMullan, Gordan 46, 88
madness 28–9, 196–7, 201, 225
   see also reason
Magna Carta 75
Maplet, John 215
Marcus, Leah 162
Margeson, John 96
Markham, Gervase 211, 217–18
Marlowe, Christopher 89, 115–16,
   117, 126n., 141, 167
Marston, John 75, 142, 154–5,
   155n., 156n.
Martindale, Charles and Michelle
   50
Massinger, Philip 72–3
Masten, Jeffrey 193, 200, 203
Mather, Cotton 204
Maus, Katherine 120
Mayne, Jasper 150
Mazzola, Elizabeth 123
Melanchthon, Philip 58
melodrama 40, 42–3, 49

melopoeia 268–9
Mentz, Steven 37
Meres, Francis 59, 138
metatheatricality 15, 42–3
Metz, Christian 291
Middleton, Thomas 105, 139,
   170–1
Miller, Arnold 263, 264, 276n.
Miller, Stephen 8
Milton, John 237–8, 266–7, 269
Miola, Robert S. 50
Mirror for Magistrates 89
misquotation 54–76
Montaigne, Michel de 8, 11–32,
   200, 201, 202–3, 210,
   221–2
   Apology for Raymond Sebond
     17
   Cannibals 11, 13
   essai 15, 23
   Florio's translation of 13, 14,
     16, 22
   manuscript circulation 14
Montgomery, Robert 242
More, Thomas 218
Moss, Ann 59
Mucedorus 47, 49
Munday, Anthony 148
Munro, Lucy 46

Nabbes, Thomas 149, 151
Nashe, Thomas 143
national literature 259–60
Navarre, Henri IV 101–16
   character in *Faerie Queene*
     112–13, 126n.
   character in *Love's Labour's*
     Lost 102–12, 119, 121,
     123–4, 126n.
   character in *Massacre at*
     Paris 115–16
   character in *Trial of Chivalry*
     122

neo-classical period   257–79
Norbrook, David   80
Norton, D.   58, 62
nostalgia   49, 282–3
Nuttall, A. D.   11, 13, 16, 51

oaths   106, 110
  see also apostasy
Olivares, Count-Duke   89
onomastics   101–30
  see also Navarre
Orgel, Stephen   224
Osborne, Laurie   291
Ovid   167, 240

pamphlets, news   106, 108–9, 111,
  113
paradox   13
Paré, Ambrose   215–16
Parker, Patricia   112
Parmelee, Lisa   126n.
parody   35
Parrot, Henry   138
Partial Law   149
Passionate Pilgrim   107
Paster, Gail Kern   183, 191–2
Pemble, John   275n.
Percy, William   152, 153
performance criticism   234–5,
  280–96
  as derivative   283–4
  as fantasy   283
  as nostalgia   282–3
  personal voice in   288–9
  and reviews   284–9
  as substitute   284, 289
Persons, Robert   118
Phelan, Peggy   293
Philo, Chris   187
philosophy   8, 11–32
phobia   17, 18
playbills   154

playhouses
  Blackfriars   46, 149
  Globe   46, 47, 87
  Red Bull   143–4
  Rose   148
  Salisbury Court   149
playhouses, trading in   139–40,
  155
  pamphlets on sale in   139
  notebooks in   142, 143–4
Plutarch   48, 167, 176
politics   48, 88–9
Pollard, A. F.   86
Poole, William   13
Pope, Alexander   73–4
popular culture versus high
  culture   270
Prescott, Anne Lake   104, 111
private versus public   195, 198
promptbooks   289
Pudsey, Edward   155n.
Purkiss, Diane   80

Questier, Michael   108
Quiller-Couch, Arthur   190
quintessence   17, 22

race   28
Rawlinson, John   218
reading versus performance   164–7,
  168–9, 178–9
reason   188, 194, 196–7, 200
  see also madness
reception   255–79
  cross-cultural   255–79
  by synecdoche   264
  transnational   255–79
Reformation   105, 123
religion   28, 30
Relle, Eleanor   112
revision   23
Reynolds, Simon   36

rhetoric   45, 61
  copia   67
  imitation   61–3
  proverbs   61, 67
  quotations   54–76
  repetition   62, 75
  sententiae   57–9
  similes   59–60
  synonyms   57–62
  see also commonplace books
rhetorical exercises   13
Rhodes, R. Crompton   147
rhyme   234
Rich, Barnaby   142
Richelieu, Cardinal   89
Richmond, Hugh   103
Ricks, Christopher   68
Robertson, J. M.   14, 15
"Rohrschach" effect   256, 262
Rothfels, Nigel   187
Rowe, Nicholas   50
Rowley, Samuel   87, 88, 94, 95
Rules of Art   266–8
Rumbold, Kate   57

St. Augustine   70
St. Paul   66
St. Paul's School   59
Sanford, James   37
Sawday, Jonathan   183
Scaliger, Julius Caesar   37, 48
scene-boards   156n.
Schoenfeldt, Michael   183, 196
Scot, Reginald   31n.
Selden, John   58
Shaheen, Naseeb   57, 64, 65, 70, 72
Shakespeare, William
  First Folio   8, 72, 133, 161–80
  translations of   262
Shakespeare, William, individual
    works
  A Lover's Complaint   246

All's Well that Ends Well   15, 39, 46, 214
Antony and Cleopatra   39, 176, 288
As You Like It   213
Comedy of Errors   63, 65, 67, 117
Coriolanus   64, 257, 266, 268–9
Cymbeline   34–53, 125n., 147
Edward III   71–2
Hamlet   24, 59, 63, 64, 65, 142, 162–3, 164–5, 166, 167, 179n., 206, 215, 221, 264, 272, 274n., 275n.
1 Henry IV   59–60, 89, 144, 192
2 Henry IV   64, 65, 72, 89
Henry V   48, 97–8, 120, 286–8
1 Henry VI   83, 120
2 Henry VI   65, 83, 120
3 Henry VI   83, 120, 151
Henry VIII   177
  All is True   87–8
  Duke of Buckingham in   90–1
  pageantry in   95, 96
  plot of   84–5
Julius Caesar   83, 89, 170, 271–2
King John   85, 120
King Lear   15, 64, 176, 179n., 275n., 290, 212, 214, 215, 222
  dogs in   199
Love's Labour's Lost   56, 102–29, 275n.
  title page of   124n.
  topical names in   102, 104–5, 124n.
Macbeth   15, 215, 280
  animals in   199

Shakespeare, William, individual
    works (*cont'd.*)
  Measure for Measure   15, 39, 46,
    67
  Merchant of Venice   15, 18–19,
    24, 58, 67, 72, 212
  Midsummer Night's Dream   15,
    16, 24–7, 65–6, 212, 213, 214
  Much Ado About Nothing   24,
    39, 67
  Othello   24, 64, 144, 147, 155n.,
    165–6, 179n., 212
  Pericles   38, 39, 46
  Richard II   63–4, 67–8, 72, 89,
    145, 176, 213
  Richard III   69–71, 83, 143
  Romeo and Juliet   39, 142, 144,
    154–5, 155n., 164, 170
  Sir Thomas More   88
  Sonnets   *see Sonnets*
  Taming of the Shrew   8, 212
  Tempest   11, 13, 147, 152,
    290
  Timon of Athens   68–9, 169–77
    epitaphs in   172–7
  Troilus and Cressida   48, 64,
    65, 164, 168, 170, 257,
    274–5n.
  Twelfth Night   38, 145, 146,
    213–14
  Two Gentlemen of Verona
    190–206, 214
    Crab in   192–4
    Lance in   191–4
  Two Noble Kinsmen   46, 61, 67,
    177
  Venus and Adonis   39
  Winter's Tale   39, 46, 65, 122,
    139–40, 210–27
  see also Passionate Pilgrim
Shannon, Laurie   211, 221
Shaugnessy, Robert   293
Shelling, F. E.   125n.

Sherman, William   10
Shirley, James   146–7, 148, 149,
    151, 152
Sidney, Philip   37, 38, 39, 46, 62,
    80, 116, 143, 148
Silk, Michael   51
Sir John Oldcastle   148
Slater, Ann Pasternak   69
Smallwood, Robert   288–9, 290,
    296n.
Smith, Barbara   258
Smith, Logan P.   87
Sonnets   236–54
  manuscript circulation of   245–6
  narrative arrangement in   242–3
  procreation in   238
  1609 Q   241
  sonnet 7   248
  sonnet 12   250
  sonnet 27   248
  sonnet 28   248
  sonnet 30   250, 251
  sonnet 43   249–50
  sonnet 58   251
  sonnet 59   250
  sonnet 68   250
  sonnet 98   250
  sonnet 105   243–5
  sonnet 109   250
  sonnet 110   246
  sonnet 111   243–5, 246
  sonnet 123   249
  sonnet 124   249
sources
  classical influence   8–9, 51
  quotations from sources   54–76
  source-study   7, 8, 9
  sources of ideas   14
Spencer, Charles   286, 288
Spenser, Edmund   104, 112–13,
    115, 143
Sprague, A. C.   282, 294
Sproull, G. M.   277n.

stage-boards 137
    see also scene-boards; title-boards
Stafford, Edward, duke of
    Buckingham (in *Henry VIII*)
    90–1
    see also Villiers, George
Stallybrass, Peter 296n.
Steiner, George 57, 59
Sterling, John 13
Stuart, Arabella 118
succession crisis 117–21
Summers, Will 94
sympathy *see* antipathy

Tacitus, Publius (Gaius) 89
Taming of a Shrew 8
Tanselle, Thomas 169
taste, literary 255–6
Tatius, Achilles 37
Taylor, Gary 274n., 282
Taylor, George Coffin 14, 15, 19
text 160–80
    and authorial intention 161–2,
    171–2
    copytext 162–3, 178
    cuts in 165–6
    and manuscripts 177
    and performance 165, 168
theater companies
    Admiral's Men 125n., 148
    Beeston's Boys 149
    Derby's Men 125n.
    King's Men 149, 152
    King's Revels 148, 149
    Ogilby's Men 147
    Paul's Boys 152, 153
    Pembroke's Men 125n.
    Queen Henrietta's 148, 149
    Strange's 149
Theobald, Lewis 73–4
Thomas, Keith 211
Thomas, Lord Cromwell 88
Thomas of Woodstock 89

Thomson, Leslie 151
Thornberry, Richard 47
time 233–4
    after the Fall 237–8
    and church bells 252
    clocks 239, 247–8, 252
    nightdial 248
    punctuality 251–2
    sundials 239, 241, 248–9
    unreliability of measuring 249
    watches 247–8
    ways of measuring 238–9,
    250–1
    and writing 241
    zodiac 249
title-boards 144–3
    see also scene-boards;
    stage-boards
title pages 124n., 147
Todd, Christopher 275n., 276n.,
    277n.
topicality 101–30
Topsell, Edward 211, 218–19,
    223
tragicomedy 36, 45, 46, 47, 49
translatability 256–8
translation 56
Trescot, Thomas 142
trial 12–32
    definition of 15, 23, 24, 27, 30
    of Duke of Buckingham 86
Trial of Chivalry 116–17, 119,
    122–3, 125–6n.
Tricomi, Albert H. 103, 105
Tudeau-Clayton, Margaret 124n.
Twine, Laurence 37

unities 256, 268
universality 255–79
urination 195–7

values, literary 255–7, 263–73
Van Vliet, Hendrick 204, 205

Vendler, Helen   268
Venice   30
Vickers, Brian   62, 275n., 279
Vignolle   117
Villiers, George, Duke of
    Buckingham   89, 92, 93
Virgil   61
Voltaire   263, 264, 272, 276n.
Voss, Paul   101, 102, 103–5

Watson, Thomas   246
Webster, John   155n., 215
Wells, Stanley   36, 88, 191
Wentworth, Peter   118
Whitmarsh, Tim   48

Wilbert, Chris   187
Wilkins, George   38
Wilson, Arthur   149
Wily Beguiled   145
Wolfe, Michael   126n.
Wolsey, Cardinal   84–5, 86, 90–2
Worden, Blair   80, 89, 97n.
Worthen, W. B.   293
Woudhuysen, Henry   104, 105,
    126n.
Wright, Louis B.   192–3
Wriothsley, Henry, earl of
    Southampton   89

Zouch(e), Edward de la, Baron   89